Handbook of Pragmatics
27th Annual Installment

Handbook of Pragmatics
ISSN 1877-9611

Founding Editors
Jan-Ola Östman and Jef Verschueren (University of Antwerp)

Prepared under the scientific auspices of the **International Pragmatics Association (IPrA;** https://pragmatics.international).

IPrA Presidents
1987–1990: John Gumperz (Berkeley)
1991–1994: Sandra Thompson (Santa Barbara)
1995–1999: Ferenc Kiefer (Budapest)
2000–2005: Susan Ervin-Tripp (Berkeley)
2006–2011: Sachiko Ide (Tokyo)
2012–2017: Jan-Ola Östman (Helsinki)
2018–2023: Stephen Levinson (Nijmegen)
2024-present: Marina Sbisà (Trieste, Italy)

IPrA Secretary General
Jef Verschueren (Antwerp)

IPrA Adjunct Secretary General
Mieke Vandenbroucke (Antwerp, Belgium)

IPrA Consultation Board (acting as Editorial Board for the Handbook 2018–2025)

Nana Aba Appiah Amfo (Accra, Ghana)
Rukmini Bhaya Nair (New Delhi, India)
Charles Briggs (Berkeley, USA)
Frank Brisard (Antwerp, Belgium)
Lucien Brown (Melbourne, Australia)
Xinren Chen (Nanjing, China)
Rebecca Clift (Colchester, UK)
Jonathan Culpeper (Lancaster, UK)
Mark Dingemanse (Nijmegen, Netherlands)
César Félix-Brasdefer (Bloomington, USA)
Yoko Fujii (Tokyo, Japan)
Pilar Garces-Conejos Blitvich (Charlotte, USA)
Helmut Gruber (Vienna, Austria)
Yueguo Gu (Beijing, China)
Hartmut Haberland (Roskilde, Denmark)
Michael Haugh (Brisbane, Australia)
Sachiko Ide (Tokyo, Japan)
Cornelia Ilie (Strömstad, Sweden)
Shoichi Iwasaki (Los Angeles, USA)
Helga Kotthoff (Freiburg, Germany)
Dennis Kurzon (Haifa, Israel)
Stephen Levinson (Nijmegen, Netherlands)
Miriam Locher (Basel, Switzerland)
Sophia Marmaridou (Athens, Greece)
Rosina Marquez Reiter (Surrey, UK)
Yael Maschler (Haifa, Israel)
Yoshiko Matsumoto (Stanford, USA)
Michael Meeuwis (Ghent, Belgium)
Maj-Britt Mosegaard Hansen (Manchester, UK)
Melissa Moyer (Barcelona, Spain)
Neal Norrick (Saarbrücken, Germany)
Akin Odebunmi (Ibadan, Nigeria)
Tsuyoshi Ono (Edmonton, Canada)
Jan-Ola Östman (Helsinki, Finland)
Salvador Pons Bordería (Valencia, Spain)
Yongping Ran (Guangzhou, China)
Marina Sbisà (Trieste, Italy)
Gunter Senft (Nijmegen, Netherlands)
Daniel Silva (Florianopolis, Brazil)
Marina Terkourafi (Leiden, Netherlands)

Handbook of Pragmatics

27th Annual Installment

Edited by

Mieke Vandenbroucke
IPrA & University of Antwerp

Jana Declercq
IPrA & University of Antwerp

Frank Brisard
IPrA & University of Antwerp

Sigurd D'hondt
IPrA & University of Jyväskylä

John Benjamins Publishing Company
Amsterdam / Philadelphia

The paper used in this publication meets the minimum requirements of the American National Standard for Information Sciences – Permanence of Paper for Printed Library Materials, ANSI z39.48-1984.

DOI 10.1075/hop.27

Cataloging-in-Publication Data available from Library of Congress.

ISBN 978 90 272 1819 3 (HB)
ISBN 978 90 272 4632 5 (E-BOOK)

© 2024 – John Benjamins B.V.
No part of this book may be reproduced in any form, by print, photoprint, microfilm, or any other means, without written permission from the publisher.

John Benjamins Publishing Co. · www.benjamins.com

Table of contents

Editors' note	VII
User's guide	XI

Handbook A–Z

Autism   3
 Agustin Vicente, Zuriñe Abalos, Isabel Martin-Gonzalez, Sara Ramos-Cabo & Elena Castroviejo

Elite multilingualism   43
 Elisabeth Barakos

Formulaic language   69
 Natalia Filatkina

Nils Erik Enkvist   87
 Jan-Ola Östman & Tuija Virtanen

Indirectness   101
 Nicolas Ruytenbeek

Indexicality   129
 Tomi Visakko & Heini Lehtonen

Intervision   155
 Marie Jacobs

Posthumanism and pragmatics   169
 Leonie Cornips, Ana Deumert & Alastair Pennycook

Poststructuralist discourse theory   187
 Jan Zienkowski

Revisiting talk in space: The inescapable mobility of social interaction   215
 Elwys De Stefani & Lorenza Mondada

Cumulative index   243

Editors' note

This year's Annual Installment of the *Handbook of Pragmatics*, the 27th edition, contains one article about a scholar who has made an important impact on the field: Nils Erik Enkvist (Jan-Ola Östman and Tuija Virtanen). In the other articles, a variety of pragmatic topics is dealt with. Two articles cover a wide overview of pragmatics research from a particular perspective: Agustin Vicente, Zuriñe Abalos, Isabel Martin-Gonzalez, Sara Ramos-Cabo and Elena Castroviejo examine the topic of autism, while Elwys De Stefani and Lorenza Mondada revisit talk and discuss the inescapable mobility of social interaction. An equally broad overview is presented by Leonie Cornips, Ana Deumert and Alastair Pennycook in their chapter on posthumanism and pragmatics. Two chapters focus on linguistic phenomena: formulaic language is extensively discussed by Natalia Filatkina and Nicolas Ruytenbeek presents a thorough introduction to indirectness. Turning our attention to multilingualism, Elisabeth Barakos dedicates a chapter to elite settings and how elite multilingualism surfaces there. The Handbook also includes two chapters on more theoretical topics: Jan Zienkowski outlines the contours of poststructuralist discourse theory and Tomi Visakko and Heini Lehtonen delve into indexicality. Finally, a chapter on intervision as an emerging methodological approach in the study of language is authored by Marie Jacobs.

This installment of the *Handbook of Pragmatics* is the third one prepared by the new editorial team, which took over after Jan-Ola Östman and Jef Verschueren handed over this task in 2022. For those less familiar with the Handbook, a few words about its history and development may be useful here.

When Jan-Ola Östman and Jef Verschueren launched the idea of a **Handbook of Pragmatics** under the auspices of the **International Pragmatics Association** (IPrA; https://pragmatics.international) in the early 1990s, they wanted to create a format that would be endlessly moldable for and by the readership. The very essence of scientific research is that scientific insights are dynamic, guided by uncertainty. In a field like pragmatics, with the functioning and use of constantly changing styles and registers of language as its focus of research, they did not want to produce a single book as the ultimate 'handbook of pragmatics'. Since they saw this venture as a task that would take decades, if they wanted to do it properly, what they did not want either was to start with categories and traditions beginning with "A" and after a couple of decades finally reaching "Z".

At that time, Jan-Ola and Jef settled for a loose-leaf publication format, relatively unorthodox in the humanities and social sciences. The idea was that this would enable the editors to gradually build up a changeable and expandable knowledge base for the users of the Handbook. Moreover, each individual reader would be able to group and re-group the entries according to their own preferences and particular interests, which no doubt would themselves be changing over time. So, with every three or four annual installments of the Handbook, the subscriber received a new ring binder in which to collect and order the new entries. The series of loose-leaf installments was preceded in 1995 by a hardback bound **Manual**, which provided background information on a wide range of traditions and research methods underlying much of the pragmatic research described in the more topical entries of the annual installments. Needless to say, this background information has evolved as well and has necessitated numerous new entries on traditions and methods in the loose-leaf installments. So far, 23 installments of the Handbook of some 300 pages each have been published, in addition to the 658-page Manual. Subscribers to the printed version of the *Handbook of Pragmatics* should have a bookshelf filled with the Manual plus 7 ring binders.

Meanwhile, the world has gradually become more and more digital. In the early 1990s hardly anyone could have foreseen the radical changes that have come to take place on the publishing scene. The *Handbook of Pragmatics* quickly followed suit, went online, and is available for readers as, precisely, the *Handbook of Pragmatics Online* (https://benjamins.com/online/hop/). The online version has been continuously updated with new materials whenever and as soon as a new installment of the Handbook was published; and in cases where an entry has been totally rewritten, the older version has been retained in the Archive — all in the interest of giving readers a feeling of how the discipline itself has changed and evolved over the decades.

Meanwhile, the online version has become the most often used version of the Handbook, both by individual scholars (especially by members of the International Pragmatics Association) and by many of the institutions and universities they are affiliated with. The loose-leaf version on paper was seldom subscribed to by individuals, but we are happy to say that it did attract the interest of university libraries and research groups. It is, however, challenging for libraries to make loose-leaf versions of books available for the general readership in a shape where all leaves/pages are physically "a-loose".

Faced with this situation, Jan-Ola and Jef decided in close concertation with John Benjamins Publishing Company to produce further installments of the *Handbook of Pragmatics*, from the 21st onwards, in the form of bound volumes, of which the one you are now holding in your hands is the sixth. We are convinced that this makes the Handbook easier to handle and more attractive not only for libraries, but also for individual scholars who cherish the sensation and satisfaction of perusing a physical book. Meanwhile, the online version continues to integrate all additions and changes.

The gist of the User's Guide for the *Handbook of Pragmatics* and its online version largely remains the same as before — see below. As in the loose-leaf version, we have a cumulative index (at the end of each volume), covering not only the present installment, but linking it to the entire *Handbook of Pragmatics*.

Acknowledgments

A project of this type cannot be successfully started, let alone completed, without the help of dozens, or even hundreds, of scholars. First of all, there are the authors themselves, who have sometimes had to work under harsh conditions of time pressure. Further, members of the IPrA Consultation Board have occasionally, and some repeatedly, been called upon to review contributions. Countless other colleagues, too many to list, have provided essential input as well by reviewing manuscripts.

The former editors (as well as the present ones) want to make sure that the contribution made by the co-editors of the Manual and the first eight annual installments of the Handbook is not forgotten: Jan Blommaert[†] and Chris Bulcaen were central to the realization of this project. Similarly, Eline Versluys acted as editorial assistant for a five-year period ending in 2009. Our sincerest thanks to all of them.

In this installment, the editorial team also wishes to thank Pedro Gras for his coeditorship of the 25th and 26th installments and welcome Jana Declercq warmly as the new fourth editor in the HoP team taking over from Pedro.

Last but not least, the new editorial team wants to express its deepest appreciation for the people who started it all and who are responsible for carrying on the Handbook project for almost 30 years: Jan-Ola Östman and Jef Verschueren. They are an inspiration for all of us to remain honest and rigorous in our academic work.

Meanwhile, we hope the 27th installment of the Handbook will continue to serve your needs and inspire your future work.

Antwerp & Jyväskylä, September 2024.
Mieke Vandenbroucke, Jana Declercq, Frank Brisard and Sigurd D'hondt, editors

User's guide

Introduction

For the purpose of this publication, *pragmatics* can be briefly defined as *the cognitive, social, and cultural study of language and communication*. What this means exactly, and what it entails for the scientific status of linguistic pragmatics, was explained in detail in the introductory chapter, 'The pragmatic perspective' by Jef Verschueren, of the **Manual** (*Handbook of Pragmatics: Manual*, edited by Jef Verschueren, Jan-Ola Östman & Jan Blommaert, 1995).

The overall purpose of the **Handbook of Pragmatics** is that it should function as a tool in the search for *coherence*, in the sense of cross-disciplinary intelligibility, in this necessarily interdisciplinary field of scholarship. The background of the Handbook and its historical link with the International Pragmatics Association (IPrA), as well as its basic options, were described in the preface to the Manual. The Handbook format, although described in the same preface, will here be presented anew in this **User's Guide** for the sake of clarity.

The **Handbook of Pragmatics** will continue to be available *online* (see https://benjamins.com/online/hop). The printed version will continue to be expanded with *new articles* and will also incorporate *revised versions* of older entries. *Updates* that require minimal changes will be published only in the annual online releases. In addition, ***Highlights*** from the Handbook have been published in ten thematically organized paperbacks (in 2009, 2010, and 2011; cf. https://benjamins.com/catalog/hoph), making the contents accessible in an affordable way for use as practical teaching tools and reading materials for a wide range of pragmatics-related linguistics courses focusing specifically on general pragmatic, philosophical, cognitive, grammatical, social, cultural, variational, interactive, applied, or discursive aspects, respectively.

The handbook format

In addition to the main body of the Handbook (including the topics listed under ***Handbook A-Z*** in this volume), the **Handbook of Pragmatics** contains three distinct types of articles:

i. *Traditions*: Major traditions or approaches in, relevant to, or underlying pragmatics, either as a specific linguistic enterprise or as a scientific endeavor in general. Collectively, the articles in this section give an overview of the traditions and approaches in question, with historical background information and a description of present and potential interactions with other traditions or approaches and the field of pragmatics as a whole.
ii. *Methods*: Major methods of research used or usable in pragmatics or pragmatics-related traditions.
iii. *Notational systems*: Different kinds of notational systems, including the most widespread transcription systems.

The main body of the *Handbook* (represented in this volume by the section *Handbook A-Z*) consists of articles of various sizes, organized around entry-like keywords, alphabetically organized. They range in generality: some provide a general overview of a particular field (which cannot be captured under the label of a 'tradition'; see above), others discuss a specific topic in quite some detail. They present a state-of-the-art overview of what has been done on the topic. Where necessary, they also mention what has not been dealt with extensively (e.g. acquisitional and diachronic aspects), thus suggesting topics for further research. Important research in progress is mentioned where appropriate. In addition, some references to major works are given.

A different type of article in the body of the Handbook (listed separately as 'Linguistic scholars' in the online version) is devoted to the contributions made by an individual influential scholar and may contain interesting biographical information as well.

The Handbook attempts to document pragmatics dynamically. Consequently, a *loose-leaf* publication format was initially chosen for maximum flexibility and expandability (see the Editors' Note above) — properties that are even more characteristic of the **Handbook of Pragmatics Online**, which has therefore taken over that specific functionality to the point of rendering the loose-leaf printed format superfluous and replaceable by bound annual installments. By definition, there is no point in time when it is possible to say that the Handbook will be complete, though a reasonably comprehensive overview could be said to have been obtained after the eighth annual installment published in 2002, so that from then onwards, in addition to further *expansion*, there have been regular *revisions* and (in the online version) *updates* of older contributions. In the case of articles that are being replaced completely, the older versions are kept in the Archive section of the online version.

Even though we have given up paper publication in loose-leaf format, the very idea of continuous flexibility and expandability is retained. Being a vibrant field, pragmatics sees new openings and coherent subfields emerging constantly. Thus, most annual installment of the **Handbook of Pragmatics** will naturally also contain entries on such new directions of research.

About the cumulative index

At the end of each printed annual installment of the *Handbook of Pragmatics*, you will find a complete index, with all necessary cross-references to ensure easy access to the available information (which continuously accumulates over the years). The index thus does not only contain references to concepts and matters to be found in the annual installment at hand, but cross-references to all Handbook entries that have appeared in the *Handbook of Pragmatics*. Needless to say, this cumulative index is also continuously updated in the online version of the Handbook, under the heading 'Subjects,' where it also contains direct links to relevant articles.

In addition to references to specific Handbook entries, the index also contains lists of terms which are not used as entry headings but which do occur as alternative labels in the literature, with an indication of where exactly the topics in question are treated in the Handbook.

Handbook A–Z

Autism

Agustin Vicente,[1,2] Zuriñe Abalos,[2] Isabel Martin-Gonzalez,[2]
Sara Ramos-Cabo[2] & Elena Castroviejo[2]
[1] Ikerbasque Foundation for Science | [2] University of the Basque Country

1. Introduction

Autism is a neurodevelopmental condition characterized by difficulties in social communication and social interaction, and the presence of restricted and repetitive behaviors (American Psychiatric Association [APA] 2013). The global prevalence of autism is 1% approximately (Zeidan et al. 2022), although there is vast variability in the capacity to detect and diagnose autism across different cultural and socioeconomic contexts (see, e.g., Maenner et al's (2023) prevalence study among 8-year-olds in the United States).

To this day, autism diagnosis remains behavioral. That is, because there are no sensitive and specific enough biomarkers of the condition, no medical test (e.g., blood samples, MRI scans, etc.) can yet be used for its diagnosis. In fact, some experts remain skeptical about the possibility of finding a biomarker for autism (see Parellada et al. 2023). Autism is diagnosed (ideally, by multidisciplinary teams) through a combination of screeners, clinical observation and standardized tests based on the clinical description of autism, such as the one by the International Classification of Diseases, ICD-11 (World Health Organization 2022) or more commonly, the diagnostic criteria in the Diagnostic and Statistical Manual of Mental Disorders, DSM-5 (APA 2013).

The DSM-5 describes two main diagnostic criteria for autism: (1) Persistent difficulties in social communication and social interaction, including difficulties in socioemotional reciprocity, non-verbal communication and the development, maintenance and understanding of relationships, (2) Restrictive and repetitive behaviors, including stereotyped or repetitive movements, behavioral inflexibility, restricted and fixated interests, and hyper- or hypo-reactivity to sensory input. Besides these two criteria, an autism diagnosis also requires symptoms to be present early in development, to have an impact on the individual's everyday functioning, and to not be better explained by intellectual disability or global developmental delay.

The DSM-5 characterization of autism has been contested on two main grounds. On the one hand, many researchers and clinicians call for different approaches towards stratification or sub-typing within the broad autistic spectrum (e.g., Lombardo et al.

2019; Petrolini and Vicente 2022). On the other hand, critics of the so-called "medical model" exemplified by the DSM-5, argue that such a model falls very short of capturing the relevance of social factors that contribute to turn a neurodivergence into a disability (Bervoets and Hens 2020; Chapman 2020).

Concerning language, the DSM-5, in contrast with the DSM-IV, does not mention any aspect of language in the characterization of autism, which has been a matter of contention (Eigsti and Schuh 2016). Language difficulties and idiosyncrasies are in fact frequent across the autism spectrum (Schaeffer et al. 2023 for an overview). However, ever since Tager-Flusberg's (2006) classification proposal, it is also common to distinguish three subgroups within the spectrum according to purely linguistic abilities: autistic individuals who remain non-verbal or minimally verbal; autistic individuals with concomitant language impairments; and autistic individuals whose language is within the typical range (see e.g. Tek et al. 2014). Researchers often note that this distinction relates to structural language (grammar and vocabulary) and not to pragmatics or to language use in general, since difficulties with pragmatics are common to all subgroups (Baron-Cohen 1988; Tager-Flusberg 1981; 1988; Tager-Flusberg et al. 2005). Indeed, difficulties with pragmatics across the spectrum are all but expected, given that one of the diagnostic criteria of autism spectrum disorders according to the DSM-5 is difficulties in social communication and social interaction, which are *prima facie* both cause and effect of pragmatic difficulties, that is, the ability to use language in context.

In this chapter, we will cover different aspects of pragmatic abilities in autism. In Section 2.1., we provide an overview of precursors of linguistic communication in autism, focusing on abilities such as eye contact, pointing, or joint attention, which are widely acknowledged to be important in pragmatic development as well as in language acquisition more generally (§Pragmatic acquisition; Bohn and Frank 2019; Falkum 2019; Matthews 2014). However, as we explain in Section 2.2., while there plausibly is a connection between prelinguistic communicative abilities and linguistic communication, often explained in terms of Theory of Mind (ToM) deficits, there are complementary proposals highlighting the role of executive functions, local processing, and general linguistic abilities, and the relative weight of each factor is disputed, also depending on which kind of pragmatic abilities are considered. Thus, in Section 2.2., we propose a characterization of pragmatic abilities involved in linguistic communication, and outline the main theories proposed to explain autistics' difficulties with these.

In Sections 3 and 4 we present and discuss the evidence concerning pragmatics in autism. We have grouped two types of pragmatic difficulties in autism: those which typically concern utterance interpretation, with an emphasis on non-literal uses of language, and those which involve narratives and longer fragments of discourse, with an emphasis on how autistic individuals produce them. We have also opted for this distribution, because non-literal language and discourse make two broad research lines that have developed somewhat independently. While both research lines study communication in autistic individuals, they have done it following different paradigms. In the area of non-literal communication, researchers have mainly focused on comprehension studies in controlled settings, while in the area of discourse structure the main paradigm has been the analysis of (semi-)spontaneous speech.

Section 3 is thus concerned with non-literal uses of language in autism. Non-literal uses of language, and especially figurative language, have been the focus of much research in the broad area of autism and language (see Kalandadze et al. 2018 for review). Autistic individuals have been assumed to have a stronger tendency than neurotypicals to understand non-literal language literally since the first descriptions of autism (Kanner 1943), and their difficulties with non-literal language have attracted much attention in research as well as in public imagination.

In Section 4, we present and discuss research done in the area of discourse structure, and in particular in narratives and in conversation. Narratives offer a window into the difficulties autistic individuals encounter when using language for the purpose of communicating with an audience. These challenges go from establishing complex rhetorical relations between the sequences of events to efficiently using the referential apparatus of the language (especially, pronouns). On the other hand, mastering conversation can be especially demanding to those who find it difficult to interact with other interlocutors and to dynamically keep track of the topics that have already been addressed and resolved.

Finally, Section 5 wraps up by going back to the pragmatic phenomena that have been studied in autism research and summarizing the explanatory theories that have attempted to account for them.

2. Cognitive and linguistic skills that influence pragmatics in autism

2.1 Precursors of pragmatic development

Autistic individuals often have difficulties ascertaining and/or correctly interpreting cues related to communicative intentions, such as facial expressions, gestures, intonation, etc. (Tager-Flusberg et al. 2005). These difficulties relate in good part to challenges in foundational cognitive skills that are presumed to underpin pragmatic abilities, which are acquired, typically, early in development. This section will delve into the cognitive underpinnings of such pragmatic abilities from a developmental standpoint and will offer a review of the specific challenges that these skills pose to autistic individuals.

2.1.1 Eye contact

An efficient way to register social clues in interaction and to interpret them in sighted individuals is eye contact. Eye contact and eye gaze provide important information about who the interlocutor is engaging with, what their intentions are (Baron-Cohen 1995) and serve to regulate social interactions (Kleinke 1986).

Typically developing (TD) individuals pay attention to eyes and faces establishing eye contact with them very early on (Farroni et al. 2002, 2006), which enables them to pay attention to relevant social and communicative input in the environment. In this sense, towards the 4th month of life, TD infants can better identify objects that have been eye-gazed (Reid et al. 2004). This indicates that, even at this young age, infants leverage eye-gaze cues to acquire information about the socio-communicative context.

In contrast with neurotypical individuals, autistic individuals show significant difficulties in face recognition (Klin et al. 1999) and eye contact (Tanaka & Sung 2016). Autistic children exhibit a reduced preference for looking at people (Pierce et al. 2016), and particularly, for looking at faces (Chawarska et al. 2013; Wang et al. 2018). This has a negative impact on social and communication skill development, as it hinders these children's opportunities to learn the social norms around communicative interactions (Klin et al. 2015). Moreover, limited eye contact has cascading effects that can affect the other pragmatic foundational skills described below.

2.1.2 Joint attention

Joint Attention (JA) is directly associated with eye contact in sighted children. JA is the child's and a partner's ability to focus the attention on the same external referent, while being aware of the shared engagement (Tomasello 1995). In typical development, JA is therefore scaffolded by the abilities to establish eye contact and to follow the interlocutor's eye gaze. Early in development, interactions are simply dyadic, that is, communicative exchanges are bidirectional and only involve the infant and the partner (most commonly a parent or caregiver). Later on, when JA is acquired, interactions progress into triadic exchanges, and both the infant and the partner can refer to an object in the environment (Brooks and Meltzoff 2005; Franco 2005; Scaife and Bruner 1975). This way, the complexity of infants' socio-communicative interactions rapidly advances, allowing for reference-making to entities in the immediate environment. This is taken to be a building block of pragmatics as it enables gathering key contextual communicative information.

The developmental course of JA is, however, altered from the outset in autism. Difficulties in JA in autism have been extensively described (Charman 2004; Mundy et al. 1994; Mundy and Sigman 1989a, 1989b) and are so salient that they are considered a defining feature of the condition. Because JA is associated with other socio-communicative behaviors early in development, difficulties with this ability permeate the acquisition of those other skills. This is the case of the pointing gesture, which is regarded as the main JA tool.

2.1.3 Pointing gesture

Once infants have mastered eye contact and eye gaze following, gesture provides the next stepping-stone in communication development by providing the infant with a tool to establish JA (Kita 2003). When an interlocutor points at an object, the child can respond by looking at it and engage in interaction. When the child spontaneously points at an object, they initiate an interaction and may be able to modify the focus of attention of the adult they are communicating with.

To be able to either respond or initiate a communicative interaction via pointing, the child needs to have a minimal grasp of the notion of *common ground* (Clark and Brennan 1991). In particular, they need to recognize that they are in a shared communicative context (see §Pragmatic acquisition). This is especially important for pointing gesture comprehension, as contrary to many other gesture types (iconic, representational, etc.) pointing is not symbolic and does not have a specific meaning prescribed to it. Thus, the child must infer the meaning of pointing gestures utilizing the contextual information at hand. Some evidence suggests that, by the first year of life, TD infants can make such inferences (Behne et al. 2005; Liszkowski et al. 2012). This is a crucial stage in communication development, as it prepares the child to be able to make higher-order inferences based on verbal information later in development.

Similar to inference-making in pointing comprehension, pointing production calls for an emerging precursor of ToM (Liszkowski 2013). When they point, infants understand that by doing so, they have the ability to influence adults' behavior (Diessel 2006; Tomasello et al. 2007). They can point to make the adult look into something they find interesting, like a dog (declarative expressive pointing), they can point to help or let the adult know about something they need (declarative informative pointing), or they can point to ask for help or make a request, such as to get a toy that is out of reach (imperative pointing). Declarative pointing is more closely associated with the emerging ToM (Camaioni et al. 2004).

Pointing production revolutionizes the early human communicative repertoire as for the first time, the infant can initiate intentional communicative interactions (Tomasello 2003). With pointing, infants can refer to objects, locations and needs (Liszkowski et al. 2007, 2009). In other words, pointing opens a window of opportunity for the infant to connect with the world and go beyond the previously constrained parent-infant interactions. Thanks to reference-making, infants are able to incorporate an advanced form of turn-taking that include external referents in their initiating-responding communicative sequences.

Autistic children, however, have marked difficulties with pointing and they produce significantly less pointing gestures than their neurotypical peers (Attwood et al., 1988; LeBarton and Iverson 2016; Mundy et al. 1987; Özçalışkan et al. 2016). Crucially, it is declarative pointing but not imperative pointing that appears more limited in autism (Baron-Cohen 1989; Goodhart and Baron-Cohen 1993). In addition, while neurotypical children tend to produce pointing with an extended index finger and without touching the referent when engaging in social interaction with their parents, such morphological pattern is not observed in autistic children (Ramos-Cabo et al. 2021). This is an important difference as it is no-contact index finger pointing which shows the highest complexity from a social, communicative and cognitive standpoint (Butterworth 2003; Cochet and Vauclair 2010; Drew et al. 2007; Liszkowski et al. 2012).

Eye contact, joint attention, and pointing form part of the communicative repertoire that TD infants develop very early on and tend to be delayed in autistic children. Difficulties in these three elements of communication are characteristic of autism as a condition (Lord et al. 2012; Rutter et al. 2003). While such difficulties impact the development of communication in autistic individuals, they are not the only factors that account for the general difficulties experienced by autistic individuals with communication, and in particular, with linguistic communication. Different researchers have proposed that, besides these precursors of communication that enable children to display and be attuned to communicative intentions, other cognitive and linguistic factors plausibly affect the pragmatics of linguistic communication in autism. In that sense, research on pragmatics in autism has provided support to the idea that (neurotypical) pragmatics involves more abilities than expressing and being attuned to communicative intentions (see Matthews et al. 2018 on the different abilities required for pragmatics in TDs).

2.2 Beyond communicative intentions: On other factors that impact pragmatics

The main general cognitive theories of autism proposed in the 80s-90s had important and immediate corollaries for pragmatics. In the 80s-90s three global theories of autism were advanced: the ToM deficit account (Baron-Cohen et al. 1985; Frith 1989; Baron-Cohen 1993), the executive dysfunction theory (Demetriou et al. 2018, 2019; Hill 2004; Joseph et al. 2005), and the Weak Central Coherence (also known as Local Processing) account (Frith and Happé 1994; Happé and Frith 2006). The ToM deficit account of autism has it that the main factor that explains socio-communicative difficulties in autism is the challenge autistic individuals face when ascribing mental states to other people. The executive dysfunction theory, in turn, explains such difficulties in terms of issues concerning inhibition, working memory, and cognitive flexibility, which also impact the ability to adopt the perspective of other individuals. Finally, the local processing account holds that autistic individuals have a different way of processing information, which makes them be more attentive to details than to global features of situations; this impacts social cognition, among other things (see e.g. Hassall 2016 for a summary of strengths and shortcomings of these "three big" accounts, and Happé et al. 2006 for the claim that one of the three hypotheses on its own cannot be explanatory of all the traits defining autism).

These three theories had resources to explain pragmatic difficulties observed in autistic individuals. According to the ToM deficit account of autism, ToM difficulties can already be observed in JA and pointing scenarios. According to the early proponents of the theory, such difficulties accompany autistic individuals throughout development. The ToM account predicts difficulties in pragmatics under the assumption that pragmatics involves the mind-reading abilities that Grice (1975, 1989) and followers (e.g., Sperber and Wilson [1986] 1995) postulated. This was precisely Baron-Cohen's (1988) and Baron-Cohen et al.'s (1985, 1986) approach to the "pragmatic deficits" observed in autistic children: pragmatic deficits are the results of an "impaired theory of mind." Struggling with attributing mental states to others has an impact on the pragmatic skills of autistic individuals. Specifically, in order to communicate in a socially appropriate way, the speaker must be aware of the mental state of the listener (see on this §Speech act theory). When this does not happen, we may expect that Grice's Cooperative Principle is not observed (Ball 1978) or (some of) its maxims, violated. Another consequence would be that language is used instrumentally — i.e., as a means to fulfill goals — rather than communicatively. Phenomena such as the difficulties understanding the speaker-listener role would presumably follow from this cognitive approach. These difficulties include not getting a full grasp of turn-taking dynamics (Baltaxe 1977; Fay and Schuler 1980), performing a limited range of speech acts (Wetherby and Prutting 1984), or struggling producing utterances that are relevant in context (Tager-Flusberg and Anderson 1991; Colle et al. 2008). The early works on the struggle with communicative intent were based on the in-depth study of few participants, and were taken by the ToM proponents as the basis for a cognitive explanation of both social and pragmatic issues in autistic individuals. But it was not until Happé's (1993) seminal study when the results on ToM (false belief) tasks were compared with pragmatic tasks to yield evidence in favor of this predicted relationship. In this work, she showed that difficulties with metaphor understanding related to difficulties with first-order ToM (ascribing beliefs to a third person), while difficulties in grasping ironic utterances related to second order ToM (ascribing beliefs to a third person about a yet fourth person's beliefs).

However, as said, the ToM hypothesis was not the only one of the "big three" cognitive theories that could explain pragmatic difficulties of autistic individuals. The executive dysfunction account has it that autistic traits relate to difficulties with keeping information in working memory, inhibiting preponderant responses, being cognitively flexible, and planning (Hill 2004; Demetriou, et al. 2018; Geurts et al. 2009). Such difficulties impact understanding non-literal uses of language (where the literal meaning is difficult to inhibit: Mashal and Kasirer 2011; Chouinard and Coummine 2016). Also, executive dysfunction can affect updating information and keeping track of the common ground (see Horton 2005; Horton and Gerrig 2016; McKinley et al. 2017 for a cognitive approach to the common ground and the role played by memory in its development). Relatedly — and although it is far from being fully understood (see Greco et al. 2023, and Scionti et al. 2023 for a recent meta-analysis) — there also seems to be a relationship between the development of executive functions and the ability to structure a narrative in early childhood, especially in the case of atypical development.

General pragmatic difficulties in autism were also related to local processing, i.e., not seeing the "big picture" but focusing on details (Happé and Frith 2006; López and Leekam 2003). Local processing is a well-attested characteristic across the spectrum (Frith 2008). It accounts well for the difficulties that many autistic individuals exhibit in narratives and stories, where they may focus on details and not grasp the global coherence of the story (e.g., Barnes and Baron-Cohen 2011). In principle, local processing can also account for pragmatic phenomena that require integrating contextual information. Thus, López and Leekam (2003) suggested that homophone resolution (assigning a meaning to words that share pronunciation) was more difficult for autistic than for non-autistic individuals, and that this was due to non-autistic individuals' being able to take into account contextual information in a more efficient way (see Vicente and Martín-González 2021 for a critique).

Until the first decade of 2000, the "big three" cognitive theories of autism (ToM, executive dysfunction, and local processing) were considered the most promising and plausible rival accounts of pragmatic atypicalities in autism, and in particular of difficulties with understanding non-literal or non-explicit communication. Norbury (2005) constituted a turning point. In her paper, Norbury compared the performance on a metaphor task in three groups: autistic children, children with DLD (developmental language disorder; formerly, SLI), and neurotypical children. Contra Happé (1993), she found no relation between ToM measures and accuracy in her metaphor task. Instead, she found that the best predictor of success in metaphor comprehension was verbal mental age (VMA). That is, according to her results, the eventual difficulties that autistic individuals exhibit in metaphor comprehension relate to general structural language difficulties. Since then, evidence obtained by different research teams has supported Norbury's initial findings concerning metaphor (see Kalandadze et al. 2018 and 2019 for reviews), and some authors have been led into proposing that there can be two kinds of pragmatic phenomena in language: one sort of phenomena that does not involve mind-reading and relates to general linguistic abilities, and another that recruits mind-reading abilities, or at least, adopting the perspective of another person. Such views are grounded on evidence concerning non-literal uses of language that we review in the next section.

Probably the two more influential views inspired by Norbury's observations are Kissine's (2016) and Andrés-Roqueta and Katsos' (2017) views (see also Andrés-Roqueta and Katsos 2020; Katsos and Andrés-Roqueta 2021). According to Kissine, pragmatic phenomena can be divided in two domains: some pragmatic phenomena require adopting the perspective of the interlocutor, but many other phenomena that pragmatics as a discipline studies can be computed from an *egocentric* perspective. Therefore, Kissine's distinction is between *egocentric* and *allocentric* pragmatics. Egocentric pragmatics includes phenomena such as scalar implicatures, material implicatures (Jary 2013, 2022), as well as figures of speech such as metonymy and metaphor. Allocentric pragmatics includes irony and sarcasm and some other pragmatic phenomena, as for instance, ignorance implicatures (e.g., *A: Do you know if all swans are white? B: Some swans are white*: see Kissine 2016).

Andrés-Roqueta and Katsos (2017) draw an extensionally similar distinction, although their distinction is based on the notions of *linguistic* and *social* pragmatics. Linguistic pragmatics applies to pragmatic phenomena that relate to general linguistic abilities. Following Norbury's idea, such phenomena plausibly include metaphor comprehension, but evidence also suggests that the ability to compute scalar implicatures and other quantity implicatures also relates to structural language level, at least in cases where individuals are not required to adopt the perspective of the speaker (see Section 3 for discussion). In general, when speaker and hearer are "mentally aligned," grasping the speaker's meaning should not be more difficult for an autistic individual than for a neurotypical one, provided their intellectual and linguistic abilities are within the typical range. According to Andrés-Roqueta and Katsos (2017), autistic individuals exhibit specific difficulties with pragmatic processes that involve adopting the perspective of another person, which is typically the case of ironic utterances. Such processes are called "social" because they are assumed to involve mind-reading. Some results within the domain of narrative production appear to lend further support to this perspective. For instance, in a recent study, Zane and Grossman (2023) found that autistic individuals in their sample produced more ambiguous references stemming from a lack of recognition of the listener's background knowledge, whereas they were as able as their TD peers to produce referential expressions that did not necessitate consideration of the listener's perspective (see Section 4.1. for more details on this study).

Now, while many studies support the structural language hypothesis concerning linguistic pragmatics, some other results question it (e.g., Mazzaggio et al. 2021 on scalar implicatures; Chahboun et al. 2017 on metaphors: see Section 3 for discussion). In the area of narratives, some studies also suggest that even autistic individuals whose structural language falls within the typical range appear to exhibit challenges in pragmatic skills that do not rely on perspective-taking abilities (see, for instance, Kenan et al. 2019). However, the main reason for skepticism concerning proposals such as Kissine's (2016) and Andrés-Roqueta and Katsos' (2017, 2020) comes from first person accounts (e.g., Mol 2020; Morra 2016), where many autistic people and their caregivers report a literalist bias, i.e., a stronger tendency in the autistic population to interpret many non-literal uses of language literally. Intervention programs also target specifically non-literal uses of language, independently of eventual structural language difficulties (e.g., McMahon et al. 2013; Melogno et al. 2017; Melogno and Pinto 2022). The literalist bias has not been explored in depth, but it questions the idea that non-literal uses of language that do not require perspective shifting only relate to structural language. The literalist bias has been recently proposed to relate to rigidity or inflexibility, a characteristic trait of many autistic individuals (Vicente and Falkum 2023). *Prima facie*, assigning the same meaning to the same words may be an expression of rigidity features such as insistence on sameness (Kanner 1943), and strict rule following (Vicente and Falkum 2023), or to relate to the higher levels of uncertainty experienced by autistic individuals compared to neurotypicals, which may make autistic individuals go for literal interpretations in general as the safer bet (Vicente et al. 2023).

A way to summarize this section until now can be that while the observed difficulties in communicative development in autism suggest a relation between ToM and pragmatic difficulties throughout development, it is unclear that all pragmatic difficulties are actually caused by ToM issues. A commendable attitude can be to be ecumenical with respect to the big three accounts, as well as to incorporate more recent approaches to pragmatic difficulties. To begin with, not all pragmatic phenomena seem to involve mindreading abilities to similar extents. Difficulties in the area of executive functions may preclude optimal pragmatic functioning, irrespective of ToM capacities, especially in those processes where working memory and cognitive flexibility are involved, like keeping track of and updating the common ground (or even keeping track of the perspective of the interlocutor). Local processing, in turn, can explain several features of narratives and conversations of autistic individuals, which may diverge from neurotypicals' narratives and conversations in appearing less coherent. Also, some pragmatic phenomena can be more affected by vocabulary breadth and depth and by general linguistic abilities than by ToM abilities. Rigidity traits (see Petrolini et al. 2023 for an analysis of rigidity in autism) can also play a role in explaining why autistic individuals show a stronger preference for literal interpretations of non-literal uses of language, making non-explicit communication more costly for them than for neurotypicals. Finally, given the heterogeneity characteristic of autism, it is also possible that there will be no single explanation for difficulties exhibited in a particular area of pragmatics. Difficulties understanding metaphors, for instance, may relate in some individuals to an "excess" of local processing (e.g., getting a too vivid depiction of the metaphorical vehicle), and in some other individuals to being inflexible about what words can mean.[1] As Vulchanova et al. (2015) point out with respect to figurative language comprehension, a wide range of cognitive and linguistic abilities can play important roles in that particular area of pragmatics, including syntactic and semantic knowledge, vocabulary size, conceptual knowledge base, the ability to make inferences and perform the integration of information, mentalizing and understanding intentions, and the ability to suppress irrelevant information: difficulties with figurative language processing may relate to any of those components.

---

1. E.g., https://undercoverautism.org/2022/01/24/taking-things-literally-theres-more-to-it-than-meets-the-eye/

Finally, the neurodiversity paradigm, compatible with the Double Empathy problem hypothesis (Milton 2012; Fletcher-Watson and Bird 2020), would have it that breakdowns in autistic-non-autistic conversations can be an effect of the different ways in which autistic and non-autistic people think and communicate.[2] In the Morra (2016) study mentioned above, several autistic people complain that their metaphors are not understood by non-autistic people: Speaker A: "I understand metaphors just fine and use them quite often [...]"; Speaker B: "Same here, but sometimes they aren't caught by others"; Speaker C: "I try to use metaphors to help them understand. Unfortunately, using motorcycle metaphors is lost on most people". In this respect, it remains to be explored whether the difficulties that autistic people experience in the terrain of, e.g., figurative language, are due to difficulties with figurative language *per se* or only with the neurotypical figurative language. Likewise, general issues with non-literal uses of language may be due to different approaches to communication, where, for instance, informativeness, truthfulness, and moving the conversation forward are more valued in the autistic than in the neurotypical population. The view that autistic priorities in conversation may be different to that of neurotypicals has not only been suggested as an explanation for differences in conversation style, as reported by Ball (1978), but may also be found in online forums and blogs featuring entries such as: "Why do so many neurotypicals refuse to say what they mean?"; "Why do neurotypicals like subtlety?" (Quora).

In a similar vein, recent research by Crompton et al. (2020) has suggested that conversational difficulties of autistic individuals may relate to the kind of interlocutor they engage with. Crompton et al. explored whether non-mixed dyads, and more specifically, pairs of autistic-autistic speakers, would encounter difficulties in the same fashion as they had been found in autistic-TD pairs. By comparing mixed (autistic and neurotypical) and non-mixed (autistic-autistic, neurotypical-neurotypical) dyads in their ability to transfer information, they concluded that autistic interlocutors know how to efficiently transfer information, contra previous observations based on designs where the type of conversational partner had not been considered. In an 8-person diffusion chain whereby each interlocutor was supposed to recall and tell the story which they have heard, the results showed that non-mixed chains were equally successful, while mixed chains performed significantly poorly. The authors claimed that these results challenge previous findings according to which "autistic people lack the skills to interact successfully".

After this review of accounts of the difficulties and differences exhibited by autistic individuals in pragmatics, we now turn to describe the evidence amassed in the last decades concerning non-literal uses of language and the pragmatics of discourse in

---

2. The Double Empathy problem has it that many of the difficulties autistic individuals face when socializing with non-autistic individuals stem from a lack of mutual understanding between the two groups, rather than from inherent difficulties or impairments of autistic individuals in the socio-communicative area.

autism. These are the two areas that have received more attention by researchers working on pragmatics in autism. We describe the main results in both areas, focusing mostly on the results suggesting differences or lack of differences between autistic and non-autistic groups.

3. Non-literal language

Comprehension of non-literal and figurative uses of language has been one of the main areas of research in autism and pragmatics. Different types of difficulties with non-literal uses of language are frequently experienced by autistic individuals of different profiles and, as such, they have attracted the attention of researchers since Kanner's (1943) pioneering investigations, where he observed that autistic individuals exhibited an unusual tendency to interpret non-literal language literally. Asperger ([1944]1991) also noticed that the children he studied exhibited characteristic difficulties understanding jokes. The topic of comprehension of non-literal meaning became the focus of research about autism and language in the 1980s, when Gricean pragmatics (Grice 1975, 1989) met the ToM account of autism (Baron-Cohen 1995; Frith 2003). While Gricean pragmatics postulated that understanding non-literal language required reasoning about the speaker's intentions, the ToM hypothesis had it that autism was characterized by a deficit in understanding the intentions behind the behavior of other people. Thus, since autistic individuals are challenged by attributing mental states to others, they will also fail to grasp uses of language that depart from what is literally or explicitly communicated.

Many years of research have proven that the picture is more complicated. Results concerning non-literal uses of language in the autistic population are typically mixed. The evidence is diverse according to the methodologies and cognitive-linguistic profiles examined and according to the specific kind of non-literal use studied (see, e.g., Kalandadze et al. 2018, 2019; Lampri et al. 2023 for a review on figurative language comprehension, and Morsanyi et al. 2020 for a review focused on metaphor). It is now widely accepted that not all uses of language that depart from literal communication pose the same interpretative demands. For instance, according to the now influential view proposed by Andrés-Roqueta and Katsos (2017, 2020) presented in the previous section, pragmatic phenomena can be divided into "linguistic" and "social." As explained above, linguistic pragmatics includes all non-literal uses of language whose comprehension does not involve a perspective shift (i.e., adopting the perspective of the speaker). It is called "linguistic," because comprehension of such uses is supposed to be predicted by general linguistic abilities, such that individuals with an average level of structural language should not exhibit difficulties understanding uses of language that do not involve perspective shifts (though see Section 2.2. for reasons for caution concerning attempts at identifying one single factor in pragmatic competence). In turn, social pragmatics refers to phenomena that require perspective taking, and also some ToM skills. Contrary to the received ToM/Gricean view, only in such cases would mentalizing be necessary. Accordingly, several authors argue that in autism, social pragmatics is generally more difficult than linguistic pragmatics (Andrés-Roqueta and Katsos 2020; Schaeffer et al. 2023). While difficulties with linguistic pragmatics will be common in autistic people with concurrent linguistic difficulties, social pragmatics is expected to be generally difficult across the spectrum. Yet, as we show, some results also question this general idea, especially those obtained by online measures in metaphor processing, which supposedly belongs in the linguistic pragmatics camp.

In what follows in this section, we review and discuss some of the most relevant results, dividing non-literal language comprehension into comprehension of implicatures and indirect speech acts, and comprehension of figurative language. We close with a summary and some recommendations for future research.

3.1 Implicatures and indirect speech

Probably the most researched area in implicatures in autism is 'scalar implicatures' (see §Conversational implicature and §Experimental pragmatics for a definition; Geurts 2010; Grice 1975; Horn 1989), which, according to Andrés-Roqueta and Katsos (2020) fall in the area of linguistic pragmatics. Independently of whether scalar implicatures are taken to be grammatical phenomena or not (Chierchia et al. 2012), they depend on highly conventionalized aspects of meaning (e.g., the "ranking" relationship between *some* and *all*), and less on reflecting on the speaker's intention or the general context of the conversation. In line with this view, most recent literature on scalar implicatures working with autistic individuals with average language skills has not found differences between autistic and non-autistic groups of children and adults (Chevallier et al. 2010; Pijnacker et al. 2009; Su and Su 2015; Van Tiel and Kissine 2018; Andrés-Roqueta and Katsos 2020). Nonetheless, other studies have found such differences (e.g., Pastor-Cerezuela et al. 2018; Schaeken et al. 2018; Mazzaggio et al. 2021). Interestingly, Mazzaggio et al.'s (2021) study with young children (mean age: 7 years old) not only found differences between groups (autistic and non-autistic), but also a relation between performance in scalar implicatures and ToM measures in both groups (see also Foppolo et al. 2021). They also found that *ad hoc* quantity implicatures were slightly more difficult than scalar implicatures for autistic children, finding the reverse pattern in the case of non-autistic children (Foppolo et al. 2021), who are reported to find scalar implicatures easier than *ad hoc* quantity implicatures (an example of an *ad hoc* quantity implicature is: *(A and B have two cars) A: Have you taken the cars to the garage? B: I have taken the BMW*).

Concerning 'indirect speech acts', studies from the 1980s and '90s report difficulties grasping indirect ways of speaking (Paul and Cohen 1985), for example requests such as *I'll be happy if you color this circle blue*. More recent results, however, suggest that there are no special difficulties in this area: for instance, autistic children perform the action that is appropriate in the game if the experimenter requests Mr. Potato's hat by saying *Oh! Mr. Potato has no hat on!* (Kissine et al. 2015, and see also Marocchini et al. 2022 for similar results). According to Kissine et al. (2015) the difference between their results and Paul and Cohen's are being more natural due to Kissine et al.'s stimuli. However, autistic individuals may be more surprised with indirect, more impolite and unconventional, speech acts such as *Who do you think you are?* (extracted from A. Stout's blog, "The Autism Site").[3]

The study of 'particularized conversational implicatures' (Grice 1975, 1989; also see §Conversational implicature) in autism is more recent. As mentioned, Mazzaggio et al. (2021) found group differences in *ad hoc quantity implicatures* in their sample of TD and autistic children. Katsos and Ostashchenko (2021), however, did not find such differences between autistic and non-autistic adults with linguistic and cognitive abilities within the typical range. Yet, they observed differences when the task made participants take into account the perspective of the interlocutor. In this variant of the *ad hoc* implicature task, autistic participants exhibited more difficulties than neurotypical participants, thus supporting the linguistic vs social pragmatics account.

In a series of papers, Wilson and Bishop (2020, 2021, 2022) have compared autistic and non-autistic reactions to *relevance conversational implicatures* that *prima facie* do not require mentalizing (e.g., Q: Can the two of us sit here? R: The children just went to find the toilet. Impl: No, you cannot sit here). This is the kind of implicatures that Jary (2013, 2022) calls "material implicatures", where hearers can derive the implicature just by accessing world knowledge, and without having to consider why the speaker said what they said. Controlling for core language abilities, Wilson and Bishop found that, compared to neurotypicals, autistic participants were over twice as likely to endorse a non-normative interpretation of an implied meaning and over five times as likely to select an "I do not know" answer if given the opportunity. Still, in general terms, autistic participants performed way above chance in retrieving the implied meaning, since the number of errors was very low in both groups. The fact that autistic participants were much more likely than non-autistic participants to choose the "I do not know" option when available is hypothesized to relate to a higher level of intolerance to uncertainty in the autistic population (on intolerance to uncertainty, see South and Rodgers 2017; see Vicente et al. 2023 for discussion).

---

3. https://blog.theautismsite.greatergood.com/author/323566/

3.2 Figurative language

Regarding figurative language, most of the research on alleged difficulties in the autistic population concerns 'metaphors' (but see Rundblad and Annaz 2010 on metonymy). According to a growing number of authors (Andrés-Roqueta and Katsos 2017; Gernsbacher and Pripas-Kapit 2012; Kalandadze et al. 2018, 2019), metaphor processing falls within the linguistic pragmatics side of the linguistic/social pragmatics distinction (i.e., it does not require mind-reading). Consequently, in the absence of linguistic difficulties, autistic people are not expected to exhibit difficulties in metaphor comprehension. Results by, *inter alia*, Whyte and Nelson (2015), Kasirer and Mashal (2016) and Norbury (2005), and meta-reviews such as Kalandadze et al. (2018, 2019), indeed suggest that one of the main predictors of difficulties in metaphor interpretation is linguistic delay. However, some other studies have found that even autistic adults with typical structural language skills exhibit atypical metaphor processing profiles (Chahboun et al. 2017; Chouinard and Cummine 2016; Gold and Faust 2010; see Lampri et al. 2023 for a recent review).

In this respect, Vulchanova et al. (2019) report that 10 to 12-year-old autistic children, matched on structural language to TD children, performed similarly to the latter in a picture selection task, even though their gaze pattern differed from TD's, especially in their preference for literal competitors. Such results suggest potentially atypical strategies in metaphor processing. Lexical priming studies have found similar differences between autistic and non-autistic groups. For instance, Chahboun et al.'s (2017) study on metaphor comprehension examined reaction times in a cross-modal lexical decision task within a priming paradigm. The task used both conventional and novel metaphors as primes, and their facilitation effect was compared to that of a literal prime. Performance was compared across four groups: autistic children, TD children, autistic adults with average linguistic abilities, and neurotypical adults. The authors concluded that autistic individuals who exhibit within average linguistic abilities "nonetheless show a delay in metaphorical processing, supporting the hypothesis that metaphorical reasoning requires skills beyond general structural language skills." Similar results were obtained by Walenski and Love (2017) on idiom processing in a priming task.

Some results also suggest that autistic individuals may experience a developmental delay in metaphor processing (Vulchanova and Vulchanov 2022; Whyte and Nelson 2015). A longitudinal study by Van Herwegen and Rundblad (2018) found that the development of the capacity to interpret novel metaphors appeared to be delayed in autistic children, even if their performance improved with age. It is also important to note that, notwithstanding several lab results that do not observe discrepancies between autistic and non-autistic populations matched on structural language, many fully verbal autistic individuals report experiencing issues with metaphor interpretation in daily life. In her study of the exchange dedicated to metaphors in the Wrong Planet Forum, Morra (2016) found that 63% of participants reported struggling with metaphor interpretation. Interestingly, only 37% reported similar difficulties producing them (for studies on metaphor production, see Kasirer et al. 2020; Kasirer and Mashal 2016). It is suggestive to think that autistic individuals may find highly structured tasks such as multiple-choice tasks unproblematic, while struggling with the open-ended character of daily life metaphors produced in a noisy environment. That is, even though metaphor interpretation may not require perspective shifting or mind-reading, it seems to be more difficult for autistic individuals than for neurotypicals to integrate metaphorical meanings in the flow of conversation.

Finally, another widely explored area of figurative language in autism is 'irony'. In principle, irony falls under the notion of social pragmatics, for, in irony, hearers need to reflect on the speakers' attitudes and perspectives in order to understand that the speakers' intention is not to deceive hearers, but to convey a message that speakers believe, by saying something they obviously do not believe (Geurts et al. 2019). Irony has actually been found to be particularly difficult for autistic individuals in many studies (e.g., Baron-Cohen 1995 Happé 1993; Martin and McDonald 2004; Saban-Bezalel et al. 2019). In her seminal paper, Happé (1993) reported that irony comprehension was only predicted by success in second-order ToM tasks. Recently, Deliens et al. (2018) also found that when ironical utterances are not systematically associated with cues like prosody, autistic people with good language skills perform below the typical range, a finding that has been replicated by other groups (Andrés-Roqueta and Katsos 2020; Panzeri et al. 2022). However, while there is widespread agreement that irony comprehension is generally difficult for autistic individuals, some studies show that difficulties can be mitigated. In this regard, studies that include marked prosody (Chevallier et al. 2011), or evident contextual incongruence (Colich et al. 2012), found that autistic adults' performance lies within the typical range. Interestingly, the Panzeri et al. (2022) study found that a minority of autistic participants did not exhibit difficulties in irony comprehension. It has been suggested that, in general, autistic people may process ironic utterances in an atypical way based on compensatory strategies that make them more dependent than neurotypicals on some external clues (Schaeffer et al. 2023; but see Marrochini 2023 for different views).

3.3 Summary and future lines of research

Several studies suggest that autistic individuals do not exhibit difficulties in understanding indirect speech acts, material implicatures, and metaphors and idioms, at least when autistic participants and neurotypical participants are matched on structural language. Yet, other studies, especially those including online measures, find differences between both groups, and first-person accounts suggest that many autistic individuals struggle with non-explicit language as well as with figurative language even in adulthood. In general, behavioral studies that employ a multiple-choice paradigm tend not to find differences between the autistic and non-autistic population when matched on language level, while sometimes differences arise when on-line measures are employed. Future research should explore the possibility that there is indeed an effect of methodology, and it should aim at explaining the reason for this eventual effect.

Concerning theories, it seems that the most promising explanation of many of the experimental results is the account that makes a distinction between phenomena that involve perspective shifting and phenomena that do not. Yet, results in the lab are not neat. In particular, as explained, differences between groups emerge when designs tap onto processing. On the other hand, lab results do not coincide with the experiences that autistic people report. It is recommendable that future research incorporates first person accounts and qualitative and phenomenological studies to the pool of data, as well as studying production of non-literal language, not focusing exclusively on the interpretation side. To have a complete picture of difficulties in the area of non-literal language, it is important to listen to autistic people's experiences and pay attention to how they employ non-literal language in communication and how they react to the uses of other (autistic or non-autistic) people.

4. Monologic and dialogic discourse

The development of skills in monologic and dialogic discourse (i.e., narratives and conversation) is a primary concern in clinical and educational environments.[4] In fact, difficulties in narratives and conversations have been identified as key to diagnose autism (Lord et al. 2012), and reciprocity and social communication have been associated with a core deficit in the DSM-5 (APA 2013). As developed in some depth in Section 2, both the Theory of Mind approach and the Local Processing hypothesis based their claims on the basis of texts and speech produced by autistic children. In the early works from the 1980s, differences were identified between autistic and non-autistic individuals that concerned the way they described events or participated in conversations. While the Local Processing approach focused on how autistic children may concentrate on details and lose track of the general context (e.g., the main topic of conversation, or the story plot in the case of narratives), the Theory of Mind hypothesis appealed to the difficulties understanding the interlocutor's perspective and intentions, to explain the children's non-neurotypical behavior in conversation or in storytelling tasks.

The early works that pointed at a differential use of language in autistic children (recall from Section 2.1., where an instrumental rather than a communicative use was observed) analyzed the speech of a small sample of autistic individuals. Later on, comparisons were

---

[4] By establishing this distinction, we do not mean to suggest that narrating a story can be carried out without taking into account the listener's perspective and knowledge, as will become clear shortly.

carried out through a larger number of individuals and with stricter criteria for the matching of groups (experimental and control). On the other hand, as we will shortly show, narratives and conversations, which are generally analyzed through production studies in experimental settings, are prone to contradictory outcomes. While they are ecologically more valid than controlled comprehension experiments, as we have seen in previous sections, they sometimes suffer from lack of systematicity or even replicability, due to divergences in variable definition or in the characteristics of the studied sample of participants. Let us present the research on each discourse type in turn, starting with monologic discourse.

4.1 Narratives

The production of a proficient narrative is a complex endeavor that demands a diverse set of linguistic, cognitive, and social skills.[5] While lexical and morphosyntactic skills (structural language) are indeed crucial, the development of a coherent and cohesive narrative involves a careful consideration of the listener's knowledge and perspective, to ensure clear reference to the participants in the events described in the story and to select story elements that are relevant. Moreover, a skilled storyteller must also establish temporal and causal connections between the events of the story, as well as identify the characters' motivations and reactions (Capps et al. 2000; Diehl et al. 2006; Hudson and Shapiro 1991; Kenan et al. 2019). Thus, not surprisingly, evaluating monologic discourse, particularly in the context of narrative production, has been regarded as a valuable approach to exploring the pragmatic challenges experienced by individuals on the autism spectrum.

Previous research has underscored the significance of assessing children's oral narrative abilities by examining narratives at both microstructural and macrostructural levels, which refer to specific linguistic features (e.g., syntactic complexity) and global narrative features (e.g., coherence), respectively. However, it should be noted that the distinction between these two dimensions of a narrative is not as clear-cut as it might appear, given that certain microstructural elements have also been recognized as contributing to the overall organization of the narrative. For instance, while cohesion (involving the use of connectives and referential expressions) is often considered part of the microstructural level, studies such as Heilmann et al. (2010); Mäkinen (2014) treat it as a macrostructural measure, since those cohesive elements are said to be fundamental in the construction of coherent narratives.[6] In line with the chapter's central theme, our attention will be directed toward narrative skills which are closely intertwined with

---

5. See §Narrative for a more in-depth account of the properties of narratives.
6. See §Cohesion and coherence for a broad insight into the different perspectives on these concepts within linguistic analysis.

pragmatic abilities, that is, those that go beyond grasping the compositional meaning of sentence-long sequences.

The acquisition of pragmatic skills associated with narrative production covers an extended time period in typical development, ranging from early childhood to adolescence (see, for instance, Aksu-Koç and Aktan-Erciyes 2018; Berman and Slobin 1994). Specifically, a notable improvement is shown when transitioning from early childhood to elementary school years, as demonstrated by numerous studies (Berman and Slobin 1994; Caballero et al. 2020; Crais and Lorch 1994; Hudson and Shapiro 1991; Mäkinen 2014; McCabe and Peterson 1984; Roch et al. 2016; Sah 2015; Schneider et al. 2006; Zanchi and Zampini 2021). As these studies show, around the ages of 3–4, children's storybook narratives lack temporal connections and constitute merely a description of the different pictures (thus, lacking story grammar elements such as plot onset or resolution). However, as they reach approximately 9–10 years of age, they start producing more complex, detailed and structurally coherent narratives. This improvement encompasses a better use of referential expressions, an increase in the quantity of relevant information, establishment of logical connections between events and the conception of an overall plot with most of the story grammar elements.

Turning our attention to autistic individuals, it is worth noting that, as mentioned in Section 2.2., skills closely tied to pragmatic abilities have been reported to be challenging (see Baixauli et al. 2016 for a meta-analysis), regardless of the structural language skills these individuals exhibit (Kenan et al. 2019). Specifically, although the body of evidence is not yet definitive, both autistic children and autistic adults appear to encounter challenges when constructing coherent narratives. But what exactly do these challenges with narrative coherence entail? We will focus our attention to the following key aspects: the expression of causal relations, the identification of relevant story components, the command of the referential system in the language, and the use of mental and affective states vocabulary to describe the behavior of the characters in the narrative.

As mentioned in previous lines, in order to construct a coherent narrative, the narrator must structure the story 'causally' (and temporally), so that all the events are connected in a meaningful manner (Hudson and Shapiro 1991; Trabasso and Sperry 1985). Existing evidence appears to indicate that autistic individuals often face difficulties establishing these causal links between the different events in the story. In a story-retelling task, Diehl et al. (2006) examined the presence of causal connections in narratives produced by autistic children, who were matched in age, gender, language, and cognitive abilities with their typically developing (TD) counterparts. Following the framework by Trabasso and Sperry (1985), they characterized a causal connection as "the direct causal relationship between two story events" (1985: 89), which increases an event's relative importance to a story. The findings from this study revealed that autistic children produced narratives with a significantly lower number of causal connections. Similarly, Losh and Capps (2003) reported that autistic children exhibited a reduced use of causal explanations in both personal and storybook narratives, when compared to those narratives produced by TD children matched in age and verbal IQ. In this case, causality was assessed by examining the presence of causal language (e.g., statements such as "the jar broke *because the dog fell*"). It is worth noting that these apparent challenges seem to persist into adolescence and adulthood (Geelhand et al. 2020), and involve not only production but also comprehension. In fact, difficulties are also reported when it comes to comprehending inferences, including causal inferences (Westerveld et al. 2021; Westerveld and Roberts 2017). That said, conflicting results have also been reported, which could be attributed to methodological issues. Tager-Flusberg and Sullivan (1994) did not identify differences in the use of connectives (including causal connectives) when comparing narratives of autistic individuals with those produced by language-matched children with intellectual disability and TD children. Similar results were shown by Capps et al. (2000), who reported that autistic children demonstrated a comparable ability to employ causal statements when compared to both language-matched TD children and children with developmental delays. Finally, Sah and Torng (2015) did not observe any significant group differences in the use of causal connectives, although they did find differences in the number of causal connections between events, in line with Diehl et al. (2006).

Crafting a coherent narrative is not merely about establishing connections between events; the narrator must also ensure that the events being mentioned are relevant (e.g., in the storybook *Frog, where are you?* by Mayer (1969), a relevant event related to the central plot would involve the boy and the dog looking for the frog, whereas excessive focus on details such as the dog breed would be irrelevant). Some evidence shows that autistic children and adolescents omit crucial events when constructing narratives (Suh et al. 2014; Westerveld and Roberts 2017), although contradictory evidence is also present in this respect (Norbury et al. 2014; Norbury and Bishop 2003; Young et al. 2005). Interestingly, Norbury et al. (2014) identified a negative correlation between receptive and expressive language competence, and the presence of relevant propositions in narratives within the autistic group; that is, higher structural language skills correlated with fewer relevant propositions. This finding supports the claim that good structural language skills do not necessarily equate to good pragmatic abilities.

Effective referencing constitutes another prerequisite for a coherent story, which requires a thoughtful consideration of the listener's knowledge and perspective to distinguish between the referents belonging to either new or shared information (i.e., Common Ground).[7] Failure to employ the adequate referential expressions can result in ambiguity. There are several studies showing that narratives of both autistic children

---

7. See §Common ground for a technical definition in the domain of linguistic pragmatics. See also Section 2 for possible connections between Joint Attention, Theory of Mind or executive functions, and the notion of common ground from a cognitive perspective.

and adults contain more ambiguous references than the ones of their TD counterparts (Colle et al. 2008; Norbury and Bishop 2003; Suh et al. 2014). Notably, the study by Novogrodsky and Edelson (2016) revealed that autistic participants produced more ambiguous 3rd-person subject pronouns than TD controls only in their story-generation task but not in the retelling task. This was attributed to higher mentalizing skills, linguistic demands, and narrative planning required in the former. In a recent study, Zane and Grossman (2023) delved deeper into the type of referential ambiguity present in autistic and non-autistic narratives. They investigated not only whether autistic narratives displayed more ambiguous references, but also whether the ambiguity stemmed from the referent not being introduced before (as in "Once upon a time, *the boy* lost his frog") or from the presence of two or more potential referents competing for the referential expression (as in "The two boys went out. *He* found the frog"). Contrary to previous findings, they found no significant group differences in the overall number of ambiguous references (see also Mäkinen et al. 2014). However, the autistic group did produce proportionally significantly more terms (mainly pronouns) that were ambiguous because the referent had not been introduced. Conversely, no differences were observed when it came to the type of ambiguity shown in the latter example above, where the referential expression lacks a clear antecedent. The authors argue that this distinction may arise from the fact that only the former example requires taking the listener's knowledge into account (i.e., ToM) to ensure familiarity with the specific referent mentioned.

Lastly, and also strongly linked to ToM abilities, inferring characters' mental and emotional states is essential in order to predict and explain their behavior, which, in turn, contributes to the development of a more coherent narrative. Again, findings in the realm of storytelling are mixed. Some studies have revealed that autistic children and adolescents exhibit fewer internal state expressions, which encompass mental and emotional terms (e.g., verbs like "think" or "know," and adjectives like "happy" or "sad," respectively) in comparison to their non-autistic counterparts (Boorse et al. 2019; Rumpf et al. 2012). Moreover, this trend has also been observed in the adult population (Geelhand et al. 2020). However, other investigations have yielded contrary results, reporting no significant differences in the number of internal state terms in autistic and non-autistic narratives (e.g., Mäkinen et al. 2014; Norbury and Bishop 2003; Suh et al. 2014). As suggested by studies such as the one by Losh and Capps (2003), the nature of the task might be influencing their performance. Indeed, they identified fewer evaluative devices (including mental state terms) in personal, but not in storybook narratives.

To sum up, although autistic individuals seem to present certain pragmatic difficulties concerning the production of monologic narrative discourse (particularly in relation to the construction of a coherent narrative), the evidence is far from conclusive. This lack of definitive conclusions can be attributed to several factors, as discussed in more detail in the reviews by Harvey et al. (2023) and Stirling et al. (2014). These include narrative elicitation methods and the nature of the narratives themselves. The different methodologies employed to elicit narratives (retelling vs. story generation tasks, having or lacking picture support, etc.) may involve different linguistic and cognitive demands, potentially resulting in varying performance outcomes (e.g., Novogrodsky and Edelson 2016). Importantly, concerning narrative types, research has shown that autistic children tend to face more difficulties when constructing personal narratives as compared to fictional ones (e.g., Losh and Capps 2003). Another factor to consider is the audience. Given that narrative production requires a careful consideration of the addressee's knowledge and perspective, the addressee's familiarity with the story might also be playing a role. Furthermore, a wide range of methodologies have been used to measure narrative macrostructure/coherence, which hampers the achievement of comparable results. As an example, causality has been approached through various means, including the analysis of causal networks (Diehl et al. 2006), the use of connectives (Geelhand et al. 2020), and the nature of causal explanations (Losh and Capps 2003). In addition, participants in the different studies encompass wide age ranges, which, as mentioned by Diehl et al. (2006), increases the heterogeneity of the groups, given that these ages typically coincide with significant developmental changes in narrative skills. Lastly, the differences in the matching criteria make it difficult to draw direct comparisons between the results.

4.2 Conversation

Let us move now from monologic to dialogic discourse and address the properties of conversational behavior in autistic speakers (see §Conversation analysis and §Conversation types for a more in-depth characterization of conversation in and by itself). Conversation is a highly intricate social act. While conversation can be analyzed in various ways, following the lead of the Question Under Discussion framework (Onea 2016; Riester 2019; Roberts 2012), it could be depicted as an abstract hierarchic structure representing what questions are dynamically raised and (partially) addressed by its interlocutors, and how these questions relate to one another in a coherent way (for instance, one can easily go from *What did you do last summer?* to *Did you climb the highest mountain in the Pyrenees?*, but not so easily to *Is this food poisonous?* unless the in-between sequences in the exchange serve as a reasonable bridge from one topic to the other). Conversing is thus a complex exercise that requires paying attention to linguistic and non-linguistic cues to determine when an interlocutor has started a new topic (by means of an explicit or implicit question), how much information needs to be provided, when the question is resolved, when the speakers are ready to move on to a related or unrelated question, or when it is a good time to take the floor.

From the point of view of development, there is little research on the conversational milestones that have to be met at certain stages in typical language acquisition. Yet, the ability to communicate with peers has a vast impact in critical domains throughout our lifespan, such as making friends, finding a partner or being successful at work. A recent study by Pagmar et al. (2022) has collected data by coding spontaneous conversation in typically developing children on the basis of parameters inspired by Hale and Tager-Flusberg (2005) on autistic children and adolescents, specifically the notion of *non-contingent answers*, that is, the assertions that do not elaborate on the questions that have been raised by a previous interlocutor. While the main goal was to find associations with various cognitive, linguistic and socio-economic measures, results are still modest, pending further research. As reported by Pagmar et al. (2022), in research on autism and pragmatic development more generally, the measures of receptive vocabulary had generally been found to positively correlate with the ability of providing relevant responses, and to negatively correlate with missing speech turns; however, the authors did not find these associations in the said study with TD children.

As pointed out earlier in this chapter, deficits in social communication and interaction are key in the current diagnosis of ASD (DSM-5, APA 2013). The DSM-5 specifically mentions "failure of normal back-and-forth conversation". This clinical observation received support from early research on the characterization of the communicative behaviors in autistic speakers as compared to neurotypicals, based on data collection from production studies. Specifically, difficulties in engaging in conversation was related to problems with taking into account the other person's perspective (i.e., ToM). This relation was explicitly tackled in Hale and Tager-Flusberg (2005); Tager-Flusberg (1996). In these works, the difficulties experienced by autistic people were taken to revolve around comprehension and adhesion to — neurotypical — conversational rules (especially, initiations and reciprocal conversation) (Ball 1978; Baltaxe 1977; Fine et al. 1994) and topic maintenance (especially failure to extend conversation by contributing relevant information) (Capps et al. 1998; Tager-Flusberg and Anderson 1991). In the Hale and Tager-Flusberg study with verbal children and autistic teens, 30-minute-long natural language samples during parent-child interactions were taken at two time slots (T1 and T2, one year apart). These samples were transcribed and segmented, and each segment was coded as contingent, noncontingent, or imitation. These measurements were then used to address two types of questions, namely whether a relationship could be established between the number of contingent answers and the participants' cognitive and linguistic measures, and whether there were any developmental changes in discourse skills and ToM between the two time-windows, T1 and T2. The study concluded that ToM, more than linguistic abilities and IQ, was significantly related to discourse skills, contrary to the previous study by Capps et al. 1998. Moreover, Hale and Tager-Flusberg found that both ToM and discourse abilities improved over time.

Since the seminal papers by Tager-Flusberg and colleagues, several works have analyzed conversation in autistic people in comparison to matched TD peers, each one coding conversation skills differently — hence the difficulty extracting generalizations on how to characterize autistic conversation (more on the limitations of these studies below). In a recent meta-analysis, Ying Sng et al. (2018) gathered the following parameters from 31 published studies, encompassing a wide range of pragmatic features to measure conversational skills (in bold, those variables that most papers studied, even if with a different label): presupposition (this term is used pre-theoretically to measure the provision of background information required to understand the context of a certain statement), repairing (the extent to which the speaker requests or provides clarification for unclear messages), *turn-taking* (the extent to which it is appropriately taken or given), conversational balance (a quantitative measurement that calculates the contribution of the two conversation partners given certain variables, such as number of turns, percentage of responses, etc.), *topic preservation* (this includes topic maintenance — the degree to which interlocutors stay on the same topic — and elaborations — extending the topic with the contribution of new relevant information), *topic shift* (the extent to which the speaker moves to a different topic, including insistence on topics of their interest), initiations or greetings, interrupting, terminations or closings, or *paralinguistic* features (eye-gaze, volume, intonation, gesture, etc.).[8]

Focusing on the bold-faced parameters, concerning turn-taking, Ying Sng et al. found some agreement on the observation that individuals in the autistic group were more likely to avoid responding to their partner than individuals in the TD group. Regarding topic preservation, it was generally found that the autistic group offered more irrelevant answers to questions than the TD group and had more difficulties extending a topic that had been previously opened. As far as topic shift, data are more precarious, because topic shift was oftentimes conflated with other measures and those studies that isolated it presented contradictory results. Finally, in the same vein, results from eye-gaze turned out to be contradictory, too, possibly because of differences in the experimental settings and the different type of conversational partner, to which we turn shortly. Globally, the clinical observation that autistic individuals exhibited difficulties participating in (neurotypical) conversations was not always confirmed in controlled settings where an autistic group and a TD group were compared. Ying Sng et al. attribute the lack of consensus to several causes; for one, the pragmatic variables were operationalized differently — sometimes conflated —, because studies do not draw on definitions in previous papers (or definitions in the formal pragmatics literature). Secondly, the contexts in which the conversational data are collected vary greatly from one study to another, especially with respect to the type of conversational partner. Let us further discuss this major issue.

Recall from Section 2.2. Crompton et al.'s (2020) information transfer research, whereby the dyad variable (whether pairs of interlocutors were both autistic or neurotypical, or mixed) was being examined. The results seemed to point to an effect of type of dyad, and the authors concluded that autistic dyads were as efficient as neurotypical dyads communicating messages. While we should bear in mind that diffusion chains do

---

8. See §Presupposition for a technical definition as conceived of in pragmatics.

not represent the challenges of spontaneous conversation as we have analyzed thus far, it is true that prior conversation studies involved interactions between an autistic person and a clinician (Capps et al. 1998) or between an autistic person and a parent (Hale and Tager-Flusberg 2005). Bauminger-Zviely et al. (2014, 2017) sought to overcome this limitation. They studied in depth the type of partner variable to determine the weights of the mixed/-non-mixed dyad factor and of the friend vs. non-friend factor in a task that involved two children in a free-play scenario (10 minutes of spontaneous speech). The results they collected for preschoolers spoke in favor of the important role played by the friendship variable rather than the mixed/non-mixed dyad, for which no significant difference was found. Rather, interactions with friends in the autistic group involved longer reciprocal conversations, less stereotypic discourse, and more eye contact. This is a question that is far from being resolved, but which highlights the need to take this variable into consideration when drawing any conclusions about the conversation skills of the autistic population.

Following up on the limitation of previous studies, we should mention the diversity of methods for data collection. Some have used naturalistic strategies to obtain conversational excerpts (Bauminger-Zviely et al. 2014; Jones and Schwartz 2009; Tager-Flusberg and Anderson 1991), but most have coded speech taken from semi-structured and structured conversations, starting with the spoken fragments elicited from the ADOS-2. This, again, is a source of potential confound when trying to extract generalizations from published research on conversation in autism. As also mentioned in Section 3 concerning the differences between lab settings and everyday life, we should bear in mind that the pragmatic difficulties or idiosyncrasies that have been attested in clinical settings or in self-descriptions are likely to appear only in the less controlled contexts.

Last, but not least, most studies on conversation have focused on a specific segment of the autism spectrum, namely those within the typical intelligence range (before, High Functioning autism or Asperger's syndrome). This insistence on the same autism profile is not providing a truthful characterization of the wide autism spectrum. Those individuals with more severe autism and with lower Non-verbal IQ who are verbal and who have social interactions deserve to be taken into consideration.

4.3   Summary and future lines of research

In this section we have provided an outlook into the literature on monologic and dialogic discourse in autism. On one hand, the focus on details at the expense of the general plot in the production of narratives or the insistence on one specific topic of conversation were arguments in favor of the Local Processing Account. On the other hand, the ToM hypothesis was resorted to in an attempt to explain difficulties evoking the listener's mind both in narratives (for instance, in the correct use of the referential apparatus) and in conversation (for instance, in the ability to identify the question under discussion and, hence, whether a particular assertion is relevant). Furthermore, executive functions may also play a role in the development of narratives, although the extent to which this association holds is far from clear at the moment, as suggested by Greco et al. (2023) and Scionti et al. (2023).

Several differences between the autistic and the neurotypical groups seem to emerge from production studies, thus mirroring observations in clinical settings. For instance, narratives generated by autistic individuals typically feature fewer causal connections between the different events, or the autistic group tends to produce a fewer number of assertions that bear on a previously raised question (contingent answers). Nevertheless, research in the discourse abilities of autistic individuals could yield more solid results if the following considerations were taken into account in future studies. First, extracting critical data from discourse should go hand in hand with having solid definitions for the studied variables. This is not always the case in theoretical linguistic pragmatics, but coding protocols could certainly benefit from the latest findings in the linguistics community. Alternatively, to overcome this limitation, one could use the variables used in previous studies and with the same definitions. Second, studies should control for the elicitation method and environment. Sometimes researchers are after an ecologically valid elicitation system, but the type of partner is not always taken into consideration (it is not the same if two children are speaking or whether it is a child with a clinician). Likewise, we may want to have more solid grounds for statistical analysis, for which the analysis of a story from a book or a conversation led by a structured interview is more convenient; however, these situations are to be told apart from the not-so-comparable self-created stories or spontaneous conversations. Finally, given the heterogeneity within the autism spectrum, the characterization of the sample (in terms of verbal mental age, non-verbal IQ, autism severity, or chronological age ranges) and the matching criteria with the TD group turn out to be critical if we want to extract relevant information on the conversational abilities of the autistic groups and in the way they differ from the conversational abilities of their TD counterparts.

5. Conclusions

Ever since Kanner and Asperger's pioneering works, pragmatics has been held to be the more challenging linguistic domain to autistic individuals across the spectrum. Difficulties in the area of pragmatics range from pre-linguistic precursors of communication, to understanding figurative language and implied meanings, elaborating narratives tailored to listeners' knowledge, and managing conversations following certain communicative principles. The better-known difficulties exhibited in precursors of pragmatic skills (eye contact, joint attention, pointing…) seem to relate to the development of ToM in particular. However, while ToM used to be considered the main, or even the unique, factor that would explain why pragmatics in general was challenging for autistic individuals, recent research has shown that we should be cautious concerning the involvement of ToM in developing and mastering pragmatics. Thus, new approaches to pragmatic difficulties in autism have highlighted the role of executive functions, local processing, vocabulary and grammar, and autistic traits such as uncertainty and rigidity. Contemporary theorizing about autism has apparently abandoned the goal of providing a unified cognitive account of autistic traits. It is possible that such an attitude is also the most commendable attitude with respect to pragmatics. On the one hand, because pragmatic phenomena are varied; on the other hand, because autistic population is profoundly heterogeneous. That pragmatic phenomena are varied implies that some phenomena may require e.g., more ToM than others. That the population is heterogeneous in turn implies that some individuals may struggle with some pragmatic phenomenon for one reason, while some other group of individuals may struggle with the same phenomenon for some other reason.

The study of pragmatics in autism has already had some impact on pragmatic theorizing in general. It has shown that pragmatics involves the cooperation of several abilities of different nature as well as having an important influence in questioning some prevailing accounts of pragmatics in neurotypical populations. However, it is likely that such an impact, as well as the impact from studies in other atypical developments of language such as DLD, will grow in the near future, as more is known about neurodiverse individuals and their experiences with pragmatics.

In this entry we have tried to reflect the status of investigations on two main camps: non-literal uses of language, and discourse. To date, these two camps constitute research traditions that have developed quite autonomously, both methodologically and theoretically. Research on non-literal uses of language has been more controlled. Research on discourse has focused on production, working with ecologically more valid designs, but in a context of more methodological dispersion, and less theory-driven research. Although we have tried to suggest points of coincidence and mutual relevance of both research traditions, it is necessary to advance towards a better integration of them if we aspire to construct theories about the sources of the difficulties encountered by autistic individuals.

Finally, research on autism in general is changing quickly. The appearance of the neurodiversity paradigm and the incorporation of autistic researchers to the investigation has already changed the landscape of research concerning attitudes and priorities. Until now, research on pragmatics has focused on the difficulties that autistic individuals exhibit with certain pragmatic phenomena characteristic of the neurotypical population (e.g., irony). There is little research concerning how autistic individuals conceive communication and what pragmatic principles guide their linguistic interactions.

Funding

Research for this chapter was funded by the following grants: (1) BBVA Foundation Grant for Scientific Research Projects 2021 (RILITEA) (The Foundation takes no responsibility for the opinions, statements and contents of this project, which are entirely the responsibility of its authors). (2) MICIU/AEI/10.13039/501100011033 and "ERDF/EU", grant number PID2021-122233OB-I00. (3) The Basque Government, grant number IT1537-22.

Acknowledgements

We want to express our gratitude to Mark Jary, Valentina Petrolini, and Antonio Scarafone, who read preliminary versions of this entry and gave us very valuable feedback. We are also indebted to comments and recommendations provided by two anonymous reviewers and by the editors of the Handbook.

References

Aksu-Koç, Ayhan, and Ayça Aktan-Erciyes. 2018. "Narrative discourse: Developmental perspectives." In *Handbook of Communication Disorders*, ed. by Elad Dattner and Dorit Ravid, 329–356. Berlin: De Gruyter.

American Psychiatric Association. 2013. *Diagnostic and Statistical Manual of Mental Disorders*. 5th ed. Washington, DC: American Psychiatric Publishing.

Andrés-Roqueta, Clara, and Napoleon Katsos. 2017. "The contribution of grammar, vocabulary and Theory of Mind in pragmatic language competence in children with autistic spectrum disorders." *Frontiers in Psychology* 8: 996.

Andrés-Roqueta, Clara, and Napoleon Katsos. 2020. "A distinction between linguistic and social pragmatics helps the precise characterization of pragmatic challenges in children with autism spectrum disorders and developmental language disorder." *Journal of Speech, Language, and Hearing Research* 63(5): 1494–1508.

Asperger, Hans. (1944) 1991. "'Autistic psychopathy' in childhood." Translated by Uta Frith. In *Autism and Asperger Syndrome*, ed. by Uta Frith, 37–92. Cambridge: Cambridge University Press. (Originally published in *Archiv für Psychiatrie und Nervenkrankheiten* 117 (1944): 76–136 and *Heilpädagogik* (1952).)

Attwood, Tony, Uta Frith, and Beate Hermelin. 1988. "The understanding and use of interpersonal gestures by autistic and Down's syndrome children." *Journal of Autism and Developmental Disorders* 18(2): 241–257.

Baixauli, Inmaculada, Concepción Colomer, Belén Roselló, and Ana Miranda. 2016. "Narratives of children with high-functioning autism spectrum disorder: A meta-analysis." *Research in Developmental Disabilities* 59: 234–254.

Ball, John. 1978. "A pragmatic analysis of autistic children's language with respect to aphasic and normal language development." PhD diss. Melbourne University.

Baltaxe, Christy A. M. 1977. "Pragmatic deficits in the language of autistic adolescents." *Journal of Pediatric Psychology* 2(4): 176–180.

Barnes, Julia, and Simon Baron-Cohen. 2011. " Language in autism: Pragmatics and theory of mind." In *The Handbook of Psycholinguistic and Cognitive Processes*, 731–745. London: Psychology Press.

Baron-Cohen, Simon, Alan M. Leslie, and Uta Frith. 1985. "Does the autistic child have a 'Theory of Mind'?" *Cognition* 21(1): 37–46.

Baron-Cohen, Simon, Alan M. Leslie, and Uta Frith. 1986. "Mechanical, behavioural and intentional understanding of picture stories in autistic children." *British Journal of Developmental Psychology* 4(2): 113–125.

Baron-Cohen, Simon. 1988. "Social and pragmatic deficits in autism: Cognitive or affective?" *Journal of Autism and Developmental Disorders* 18(3): 379–402.

Baron-Cohen, Simon. 1989. "Perceptual role taking and protodeclarative pointing in autism." *British Journal of Developmental Psychology* 7(2): 113–127.

Baron-Cohen, Simon. 1993. "From attention-goal psychology to belief-desire psychology: The development of a Theory of Mind, and its dysfunction." In *Understanding Other Minds: Perspectives from Autism*, ed. by Simon Baron-Cohen, Helen Tager-Flusberg, and Donald Cohen, 59–82. Oxford: Oxford University Press.

Baron-Cohen, Simon. 1995. *Mindblindness: An Essay on Autism and Theory of Mind*. Cambridge, MA: MIT Press.

Bauminger-Zviely, Nirit, Anna Golan-Itshaky, and Gali Tubul-Lavy. 2017. "Speech acts during friends' and non-friends' spontaneous conversations in preschool dyads with high-functioning autism spectrum disorder versus typical development." *Journal of Autism and Developmental Disorders* 47(5): 1380–1390.

Bauminger-Zviely, Nirit, Edna Karin, Dorit Kimhi, and Gali Agam-Ben-Artzi. 2014. "Spontaneous peer conversation in preschoolers with high-functioning autism spectrum disorder versus typical development." *Journal of Child Psychology and Psychiatry* 55(4): 363–373.

Behne, Tanya, Malinda Carpenter, and Michael Tomasello. 2005. "One-year-olds comprehend the communicative intentions behind gestures in a hiding game." *Developmental Science* 8(6): 492–499.

Berman, Ruth A., and Dan I. Slobin. 1994. *Relating Events in Narrative: A Crosslinguistic Developmental Study*. Hillsdale, NJ: Lawrence Erlbaum.

Bervoets, Jo, and Kristien Hens. 2020. "Going beyond the catch-22 of autism diagnosis and research: The moral implications of (not) asking 'what is autism?'" *Frontiers in Psychology* 11: 529193.

Bohn, Manuel, and Michael C. Frank. 2019. "The pervasive role of pragmatics in early language." *Annual Review of Developmental Psychology* 1: 223–249.

Boorse, Jessica, Miriam Cola, Susan Plate, Lea Yankowitz, Jyoti Pandey, Robert T. Schultz, and Julia Parish-Morris. 2019. "Linguistic markers of autism in girls: Evidence of a 'blended phenotype' during storytelling." *Molecular Autism* 10(1): 14.

Brooks, Rechele, and Andrew N. Meltzoff. 2005. "The development of gaze following and its relation to language." *Developmental Science* 8(6): 535–543.

Butterworth, George. 2003. "Pointing is the royal road to language for babies." In *Pointing: Where Language, Culture, and Cognition Meet*, ed. by Sotaro Kita, 9–33. Mahwah, NJ: Lawrence Erlbaum Associates.

Caballero, María, Mercedes Aparici, Mercè Sanz-Torrent, Rosalind Herman, Annalu W. Jones, and Gary Morgan. 2020. "'El nen s'ha menjat una aranya': The development of narratives in Catalan speaking children." *Journal of Child Language* 47(5): 1030–1051.

Camaioni, Luigia, Paola Perucchini, Francesca Bellagamba, and Cinzia Colonnesi. 2004. "The role of declarative pointing in developing a Theory of Mind." *Infancy* 5(3): 291–308.

Capps, Lisa, Jennifer Kehres, and Marian Sigman. 1998. "Conversational abilities among children with autism and children with developmental delays." *Autism* 2 (4): 325–344.

Capps, Lisa, Mimi Losh, and Christie Thurber. 2000. "'The frog ate the bug and made his mouth sad': Narrative competence in children with autism." *Journal of Abnormal Child Psychology* 12.

Chahboun, Safa, Valentin Vulchanov, David Saldana, Hanna Eshuis, and Mila Vulchanova. 2017. "Can you tell it by the prime? A study of metaphorical priming in high-functioning autism in comparison with matched controls." *International Journal of Language & Communication Disorders* 52 (6): 766–785.

Chapman, Robert. 2020. "The reality of autism: On the metaphysics of disorder and diversity." *Philosophical Psychology* 33 (6): 799–819.

Charman, Tony. 2004. "Why is joint attention a pivotal skill in autism?" In *Autism: Mind and Brain*, ed. by Uta Frith and Elisabeth L. Hill, 315–324. Oxford: Oxford University Press.

Chawarska, Katarzyna, Suzannah Macari, and Frederick Shic. 2013. "Decreased spontaneous attention to social scenes in 6-month-old infants later diagnosed with autism spectrum disorders." *Biological Psychiatry* 74 (3): 195–203.

Chevallier, Coralie, Deirdre Wilson, Francesca Happé, and Ira Noveck. 2010. "Scalar inferences in autism spectrum disorders." *Journal of Autism and Developmental Disorders* 40 (9): 1104–1117.

Chevallier, Coralie, Ira Noveck, Francesca Happé, and Deirdre Wilson. 2011. "What's in a voice? Prosody as a test case for the Theory of Mind account of autism." *Neuropsychologia* 49 (3): 507–517.

Chierchia, Gennaro, Danny Fox, and Benjamin Spector. 2012. "The grammatical view of scalar implicatures and the relationship between semantics and pragmatics." In *Semantics: An International Handbook of Natural Language Meaning*, e. by Klaus Von Heusinger, Claudia Maienborn, and Paul Portner. Berlin: Mouton de Gruyter.

Chouinard, Brianna, and Jaclyn Cummine. 2016. "All the world's a stage: Evaluation of two stages of metaphor comprehension in people with autism spectrum disorder." *Research in Autism Spectrum Disorders* 23: 107–121.

Clark, Herbert H., and Susan E. Brennan. 1991. "Grounding in communication." In *Perspectives on Socially Shared Cognition*, 127–149. American Psychological Association.

Cochet, Hélène, and Jacques Vauclair. 2010. "Pointing gestures produced by toddlers from 15 to 30 months: Different functions, hand shapes and laterality patterns." *Infant Behavior and Development* 33 (4): 431–441.

Colich, Natalie L., An-Tao Wang, Jordan D. Rudie, Lea M. Hernandez, Susan Y. Bookheimer, and Mirella Dapretto. 2012. "Atypical neural processing of ironic and sincere remarks in children and adolescents with autism spectrum disorders." *Metaphor and Symbol* 27 (1): 70–92.

Colle, Livia, Simon Baron-Cohen, Sally Wheelwright, and Heather K. J. van der Lely. 2008. "Narrative discourse in adults with high-functioning autism or Asperger syndrome." *Journal of Autism and Developmental Disorders* 38 (1): 28–40.

Crais, Elizabeth R., and Naomi Lorch. 1994. "Oral narratives in school-age children." *Topics in Language Disorders* 14 (3): 13.

Crompton, Catherine J., Danielle Ropar, Catherine V. Evans-Williams, Emma G. Flynn, and Sue Fletcher-Watson. 2020. "Autistic peer-to-peer information transfer is highly effective." *Autism*, 24(7), 1704–1712.

Deliens, Gaëtane, Fleur Papastamou, Nicolas Ruytenbeek, Peggy Geelhand, and Mark Kissine. 2018. "Selective pragmatic impairment in autism spectrum disorder: Indirect requests versus irony." *Journal of Autism and Developmental Disorders* 48 (9): 2938–2952.

Demetriou, Evdokia A., Andrew Lampit, Daniel S. Quintana, Sharon L. Naismith, Yeonsil J.C. Song, Jessica E. Pye, et al. 2018. "Autism spectrum disorders: A meta-analysis of executive function." *Molecular Psychiatry* 23: 1198–1204.

Demetriou, Evdokia A., Maria M. DeMayo, and Adam J. Guastella. 2019. "Executive function in autism spectrum disorder: History, theoretical models, empirical findings, and potential as an endophenotype." *Frontiers in Psychiatry* 10: 753.

Diehl, Joshua J., Loisa Bennetto, and Emma C. Young. 2006. "Story recall and narrative coherence of high-functioning children with autism spectrum disorders." *Journal of Abnormal Child Psychology* 34 (1): 83–98.

Diessel, Holger. 2006. "Demonstratives, joint attention, and the emergence of grammar." *Cognitive Linguistics* 17 (4): 463–489.

Drew, Alysia, Gillian Baird, Eric Taylor, Emma Milne, and Tony Charman. 2007. "The Social Communication Assessment for Toddlers with Autism (SCATA): An instrument to measure the frequency, form and function of communication in toddlers with autism spectrum disorder." *Journal of Autism and Developmental Disorders* 37: 648–666.

Eigsti, Inge-Marie, and Jessica M. Schuh. 2016. "Language acquisition in autism spectrum disorders: Beyond standardized language measures." In *Innovative Investigations of Language in Autism Spectrum Disorder*, ed. by Letitia Naigles. Berlin: APA/Walter de Gruyter.

Falkum, Ingrid Lossius. 2019. "Pragmatic development. Learning to use language to communicate." In *International Handbook of Language Acquisition*. Routledge Handbooks Online.

Farroni, Teresa, Elena Menon, and Mark H. Johnson. 2006. "Factors influencing newborns' preference for faces with eye contact." *Journal of Experimental Child Psychology* 95 (4): 298–308.

Farroni, Teresa, Gergely Csibra, Francesca Simion, and Mark H. Johnson. 2002. "Eye contact detection in humans from birth." *Proceedings of the National Academy of Sciences* 99 (14): 9602–9605.

Fay, Warren H., and Angela L. Schuler. 1980. *Emerging Language in Autistic Children*. London: Edward Arnold.

Fine, Jonathan, Gina Bartolucci, Peter Szatmari, and Gabrielle Ginsberg. 1994. "Cohesive discourse in pervasive developmental disorders." *Journal of Autism and Developmental Disorders* 24 (3): 315–329.

Fletcher-Watson, Sue, and Geoffrey Bird. 2020. "Autism and empathy: What are the real links?" *Autism* 24 (1): 3–6.

Foppolo, Francesca, Giulia Mazzaggio, Francesco Panzeri, and Luca Surian. 2021. "Scalar and ad-hoc pragmatic inferences in children: Guess which one is easier." *Journal of Child Language* 48 (2): 350–372.

Franco, Francesca. 2005. "Infant pointing: Harlequin, servant of two masters." In *Joint Attention: Communication and Other Minds: Issues in Philosophy and Psychology*, ed. by Naomi Eilan, Christoph Hoerl, Teresa McCormack, and Johannes Roessler. Oxford: Oxford University Press.

Frith, Uta, and Francesca Happé. 1994. "Autism: Beyond 'Theory of Mind.'" *Cognition* 50: 115–132.

Frith, Uta. 1989. *Autism: Explaining the Enigma*. Oxford: Blackwell Publishing.

Frith, Uta. 2008. *Autism: A Very Short Introduction*. Oxford: Oxford University Press.

Geelhand, Pierre, Fleur Papastamou, Gaëtane Deliens, and Mark Kissine. 2020. "Narrative production in autistic adults: A systematic analysis of the microstructure, macrostructure and internal state language." *Journal of Pragmatics* 164: 57–81.

Gernsbacher, Morton Ann, and Shayne R. Pripas-Kapit. 2012. "Who's missing the point? A commentary on claims that autistic persons have a specific deficit in figurative language comprehension." *Metaphor and Symbol* 27 (1): 93–105.

Geurts, Bart, Mark Kissine, and Bart van Tiel. 2019. "Pragmatic reasoning in autism." In *Thinking, Reasoning, and Decision Making in Autism*, ed. by Kinga Morsanyi and Ruth M. J. Byrne, 113–134. 1st ed. Routledge.

Geurts, Bart. 2010. *Quantity Implicatures*. Cambridge: Cambridge University Press.

Geurts, Hilde M., Blythe Corbett, and Marjorie Solomon. 2009. "The paradox of cognitive flexibility in autism." *Trends in Cognitive Sciences* 13: 74–82.

Gold, Ronit, and Miriam Faust. 2010. "Right hemisphere dysfunction and metaphor comprehension in young adults with Asperger syndrome." *Journal of Autism and Developmental Disorders* 40: 800–811.

Goodhart, Frank, and Simon Baron-Cohen. 1993. "How many ways can the point be made? Evidence from children with and without autism." *First Language* 13 (38): 225–233.

Greco, Giulia, Benjamin Choi, Kimberly Michel, and Susan Faja. 2023. "Here's the story: Narrative ability and executive function in autism spectrum disorder." *Research in Autism Spectrum Disorders* 101: 102092.

Grice, H. Paul. 1975. "Logic and conversation." In *Syntax and Semantics 3: Speech Acts*, ed. by Peter Cole and Jerry Morgan, 41–58. New York: Academic Press.

Grice, Paul. 1989. *Studies in the Way of Words*. Harvard University Press.

Hale, Courtney M., and Helen Tager-Flusberg. 2005. "Social communication in children with autism: The relationship between Theory of Mind and discourse development." *Autism* 9 (2): 157–178.

Happé, Francesca, and Uta Frith. 2006. "The weak coherence account: Detail-focused cognitive style in autism spectrum disorders." *Journal of Autism and Developmental Disorders* 36 (1): 5–25.

Happé, Francesca, Angelica Ronald, and Robert Plomin. 2006. "Time to give up on a single explanation for autism." *Nature Neuroscience* 9: 1218–1220.

Happé, Francesca. 1993. "Communicative competence and Theory of Mind in autism: A test of relevance theory." *Cognition* 48 (2): 101–119.

Harvey, Alice, Heather Spicer-Cain, Nicola Botting, Gail Ryan, and Lucy Henry. 2023. "Assessing 'coherence' in the spoken narrative accounts of autistic people: A systematic scoping review." *Research in Autism Spectrum Disorders* 102: 102108.

Hassall, Robert. 2016. "Does everybody with an autism diagnosis have the same underlying condition?" In *Re-Thinking Autism: Diagnosis, Identity, and Equality*, ed. by Katherine Runswick-Cole, Rebecca Mallett, and Sami Timimi. London: Jessica Kingsley Publishers.

Heilmann, John, Jon F. Miller, Ann Nockerts, and Cathy Dunaway. 2010. "Properties of the narrative scoring scheme using narrative retells in young school-age children." *American Journal of Speech-Language Pathology* 19 (2): 154–166.

Hill, Elisabeth L. 2004. "Executive dysfunction in autism." *Trends in Cognitive Sciences* 8 (1): 26–32.

Horn, Laurence. 1989. *A Natural History of Negation*. Chicago: University of Chicago Press.

Horton, William S. 2005. "Conversational common ground and memory processes in language production." *Discourse Processes* 40 (1): 1–35.

Horton, William S., and Richard J. Gerrig. 2016. "Revisiting the memory-based processing approach to common ground." *Topics in Cognitive Science* 8 (4): 780–795.

Hudson, Judith A., and Lauren R. Shapiro. 1991. "From knowing to telling: The development of children's scripts, stories, and personal narratives." In *Developing Narrative Structure*, ed. by Carlota McCabe and Carole Peterson, 89–113. Mahwah, NJ: Lawrence Erlbaum Associates, Inc.

Jary, Mark. 2013. "Two types of implicature: Material and behavioural." *Mind & Language* 28 (5): 638–660.

Jary, Mark. 2022. *Nothing Is Said: Utterance and Interpretation*. Oxford: Oxford University Press. https://academic.oup.com/book/44125.

Jones, Christopher. D., & Schwartz, Ilene. S. 2009. When Asking Questions Is Not Enough: An Observational Study of Social Communication Differences in High Functioning Children with Autism. *Journal of Autism and Developmental Disorders*, 39, 432–443.

Joseph, Robert M., Laura M. McGrath, and Helen Tager-Flusberg. 2005. "Executive dysfunction and its relation to language ability in verbal school-age children with autism." *Developmental Neuropsychology* 27 (3): 361–378. https://doi-org.ehu.idm.oclc.org/10.1207/s15326942dn2703_4

Kalandadze, Tamara, Courtenay Norbury, Tormod Nærland, and Kari-Anne B. Næss. 2018. "Figurative language comprehension in individuals with autism spectrum disorder: A meta-analytic review." *Autism* 22 (2): 99–117.

Kalandadze, Tamara, Valentina Bambini, and Kari-Anne B. Næss. 2019. "A systematic review and meta-analysis of studies on metaphor comprehension in individuals with autism spectrum disorder: Do task properties matter?" *Applied Psycholinguistics* 40 (6): 1421–1454.

Kanner, Leo. 1943. "Autistic disturbances of affective contact." *Nervous Child* 2 (3): 217–250.

Kasirer, Anat, and Nira Mashal. 2016. "Comprehension and generation of metaphors by children with autism spectrum disorder." *Research in Autism Spectrum Disorders* 32: 53–63.

Kasirer, Anat, Einat Adi-Japha, and Nira Mashal. 2020. "Verbal and figural creativity in children with autism spectrum disorder and typical development." *Frontiers in Psychology* 11.

Katsos, Napoleon, and Clara Andrés-Roqueta. 2021. "Where next for pragmatics and mind reading? A situation-based view (response to Kissine)." *Language* 97 (3): e184–e197.

Katsos, Napoleon and Ostashchenko, Ekaterina. 2021. The role of visual perspective-taking in pragmatic inferencing. Lightening talk presented at *MK40: Common Knowledge, Common Ground, and Context in Communication*, University College London (25–26 June 25–26, 2021).

Kenan, Noa, Dov A. Zachor, Lisa R. Watson, and Elinor Ben-Itzchak. 2019. "Semantic-pragmatic impairment in the narratives of children with autism spectrum disorders." *Frontiers in Psychology* 10: 2756.

Kissine, Mikhail, Julie Cano Chervel, Ségolène Carlier, Philippe De Brabanter, Laurent Ducenne, Marie-Christine Pairon, Nicole Deconinck, Vincent Delvenne, and Jacqueline Leybaert. 2015. "Children with autism understand indirect speech acts: Evidence from a semi-structured act-out task." *PloS One* 10: e0142191.

Kissine, Mikhail. 2016. "Pragmatics as metacognitive control." *Frontiers in Psychology* 6.

Kita, Sotaro (ed). 2003. *Pointing: Where Language, Culture, and Cognition Meet*. Mahwah, NJ: Erlbaum.

Kleinke, Chris L. 1986. "Gaze and eye contact: A research review." *Psychological Bulletin* 100 (1): 78–100.

Klin, Ami, Sara S. Sparrow, Anke de Bildt, Domenic V. Cicchetti, Donald J. Cohen, and Fred R. Volkmar. 1999. "A normed study of face recognition in autism and related disorders." *Journal of Autism and Developmental Disorders* 29 (6): 499–508.

Klin, Ami, Sarah Shultz, and Warren Jones. 2015. "Social visual engagement in infants and toddlers with autism: Early developmental transitions and a model of pathogenesis." *Neuroscience & Biobehavioral Reviews* 50: 189–203.

Lampri, Sophia, Eleni Peristeri, Theodoros Marinis, and Maria Andreou. 2023. "Figurative language processing in autism spectrum disorders: A review." *Autism Research* 1–16.

LeBarton, Eve S., and Jana M. Iverson. 2016. "Gesture development in toddlers with an older sibling with autism." *International Journal of Language & Communication Disorders* 51 (1): 18–30.

Liszkowski, Ulf, Malinda Carpenter, and Michael Tomasello. 2007. "Pointing out new news, old news, and absent referents at 12 months of age." *Developmental Science* 10 (2): F1–F7.

Liszkowski, Ulf, Malinda Carpenter, and Michael Tomasello. 2009. "Prelinguistic infants, but not chimpanzees, communicate about absent entities." *Psychological Science* 20 (5): 654–660.

Liszkowski, Ulf, Penelope Brown, Tim Callaghan, Akira Takada, and Connie De Vos. 2012. "A prelinguistic gestural universal of human communication." *Cognitive Science* 36 (4): 698–713.

Liszkowski, Ulf. 2013. "Using Theory of Mind." *Child Development Perspectives* 7 (2): 104–109.

Lombardo, Michael V., Meng-Chuan Lai, and Simon Baron-Cohen. 2019. "Big data approaches to decomposing heterogeneity across the autism spectrum." *Molecular Psychiatry* 24 (10): 1435–1450.

López, Beatriz, and Susan R. Leekam. 2003. "Do children with autism fail to process information in context?" *Journal of Child Psychology and Psychiatry* 44 (2): 285–300.

Lord, Catherine, Michael Rutter, Pamela S. DiLavore, Susan Risi, Katherine Gotham, and Somer Bishop. 2012. *(ADOS®-2) Autism Diagnostic Observation ScheduleTM, Second Edition*. Torrance, CA: Western Psychological Services. https://www.wpspublish.com/ados-2-autism-diagnostic-observation-schedule-second-edition

Losh, Molly, and Lisa Capps. 2003. "Narrative ability in high-functioning children with autism or Asperger's syndrome." *Journal of Autism and Developmental Disorders* 33 (3): 239–251.

Maenner, Matthew J., Zachary Warren, Amy R. Williams, et al. 2023. "Prevalence and characteristics of autism spectrum disorder among children aged 8 years — Autism and developmental disabilities monitoring network, 11 sites, United States, 2020." *MMWR Surveillance Summaries* 72 (SS-2): 1–14.

Mäkinen, Leena, Soile Loukusa, Eeva Leinonen, Irma Moilanen, Hanna Ebeling, and Sari Kunnari. 2014. "Characteristics of narrative language in autism spectrum disorder: Evidence from the Finnish." *Research in Autism Spectrum Disorders* 8: 987–996.

Mäkinen, Leena. 2014. *Narrative Language in Typically Developing Children, Children With Specific Language Impairment and Children With Autism Spectrum Disorder*. Väitöskirja: University of Oulu. https://oulurepo.oulu.fi/handle/10024/35583

Marocchini, Elisa, Sara Di Paola, Guido Mazzaggio, and Filippo Domaneschi. 2022. "Understanding indirect requests for information in high-functioning autism." *Cognitive Processing* 23 (1): 129–153.

Marocchini, Elisa. 2023. "Impairment or difference? The case of Theory of Mind abilities and pragmatic competence in the autism spectrum." *Applied Psycholinguistics* 44 (3): 365–383.

Martin, Ines, and Skye McDonald. 2004. "An exploration of causes of non-literal language problems in individuals with Asperger syndrome." *Journal of Autism and Developmental Disorders* 34: 311–328.

Mashal, Nira, and Adi Kasirer. 2011. "Thinking maps enhance metaphoric competence in children with autism and learning disabilities." *Research in Developmental Disabilities* 32 (6): 2045–2054.

Matthews, Danielle (ed). 2014. *Pragmatic Development in First Language Acquisition*. Amsterdam: John Benjamins.

Matthews, Danielle, Hannah Biney, and Kirsten Abbot-Smith. 2018. "Individual differences in children's pragmatic ability: A review of associations with formal language, social cognition, and executive functions." *Language Learning and Development* 14 (3): 186–223.

Mayer, Mercer. (1969) 2003. *Frog Where Are You?* New York: Dial Books for Young Readers.

Mazzaggio, Guido, Francesca Foppolo, Remo Job, and Luca Surian. 2021. "Ad-hoc and scalar implicatures in children with autism spectrum disorder." *Journal of Communication Disorders* 90: 106089.

McCabe, Allyssa, and Carole Peterson. 1984. "What makes a good story." *Journal of Psycholinguistic Research* 13 (6): 457–480.

McKinley, Gail L., Sarah Brown-Schmidt, and Aaron S. Benjamin. 2017. "Memory for conversation and the development of common ground." *Memory & Cognition* 45: 1281–1294.

McMahon, Catherine M., Laurie A. Vismara, and Marjorie Solomon. 2013. "Measuring changes in social behavior during a social skills intervention for higher-functioning children and adolescents with autism spectrum disorder." *Journal of Autism and Developmental Disorders* 43 (8): 1843–56.

Melogno, Sergio, and Maria Antonietta Pinto. 2022. "Devising trainings to enhance the capabilities of children with autism spectrum disorder to cope with metaphor: A review of the literature." *Frontiers in Communication* 7: 915873.

Melogno, Sergio, Maria Antonietta Pinto, and Margherita Orsolini. 2017. "Novel metaphors comprehension in a child with high-functioning autism spectrum disorder: A study on assessment and treatment." *Frontiers in Psychology* 7.

Milton, Damian E. 2012. "On the ontological status of autism: The 'double empathy problem.'" *Disability & Society* 27 (6): 883–887.

Mol, Jorik. 2020. "Autistic in times of Covid-19." https://www.jorikmol.com/autistic-in-times-of-covid-19-saturday-25th-april-2020/

Morra, Linda. 2016. "Raising awareness of how Asperger persons perceive their capacity to use metaphors." *Med. Stor* 11: 129–146.

Morsanyi, Kinga, Darko Stamenković, and Keith J. Holyoak. 2020. "Metaphor processing in autism: A systematic review and meta-analysis." *Developmental Review* 57: 100925.

Mundy, Peter, and Marian Sigman. 1989a. "Specifying the nature of the social impairment in autism." In *Autism: New Perspectives on Diagnosis, Nature, and Treatment*, ed. by Geraldine Dawson, 3–12. Guilford.

Mundy, Peter, and Marian Sigman. 1989b. "The theoretical implications of joint-attention deficits in autism." *Development and Psychopathology* 1 (3): 173–183.

Mundy, Peter, Marian Sigman, and Connie Kasari. 1994. "Joint attention, developmental level, and symptom presentation in autism." *Development and Psychopathology* 6 (3): 389–401.

Mundy, Peter, Marian Sigman, Judith Ungerer, and Tyler Sherman. 1987. "Nonverbal communication and play correlates of language development in autistic children." *Journal of Autism and Developmental Disorders* 17 (3): 349–364.

Norbury, Courtenay F., and Dorothy V. M. Bishop. 2003. "Narrative skills of children with communication impairments." *International Journal of Language & Communication Disorders* 38 (3): 287–313.

Norbury, Courtenay F., Tanya Gemmell, and Rhea Paul. 2014. "Pragmatics abilities in narrative production: A cross-disorder comparison." *Journal of Child Language* 41 (3): 485–510.

Norbury, Courtenay Frazier. 2005. "The relationship between Theory of Mind and metaphor: evidence from children with language impairment and autistic spectrum disorder." *British Journal of Developmental Psychology* 23 (3): 383–399.

Novogrodsky, Rama, and Lisa R. Edelson. 2016. "Ambiguous pronoun use in narratives of children with autism spectrum disorders." *First Language* 32 (2): 241–252.

Onea, Edgar. 2016. *Potential Questions at the Semantics-Pragmatics Interface*. BRILL.

Özçalışkan, Şeyda, Lauren B. Adamson, and Nevena Dimitrova. 2016. "Early deictic but not other gestures predict later vocabulary in both typical development and autism." *Autism* 20 (6): 754–763.

Pagmar, Daniel, Kirsten Abbot-Smith, and Danielle Matthews. 2022. "Predictors of children's conversational contingency." *Language Development Research* 2 (1): 139–179.

Panzeri, Francesca, Gaia Mazzaggio, Beatrice Giustolisi, Silvia Silleresi, and Luca Surian. 2022. "The atypical pattern of irony comprehension in autistic children." *Applied Psycholinguistics* 43 (4): 757–784.

Parellada, Mara, Álvaro Andreu-Bernabeu, María Burdeus, Ana San José Cáceres, Esther Urbiola, Lisa C. Carpenter, Nina V. Kraguljac et al. 2023. "In search of biomarkers to guide interventions in autism spectrum disorder: A systematic review." *American Journal of Psychiatry* 180 (1): 23–40.

Pastor-Cerezuela, Gemma, Juan Carlos Tordera Yllescas, Francisca González-Sala, Mariángeles Montagut-Asunción, and María-Isabel Fernández-Andrés. 2018. "Comprehension of generalized conversational implicatures by children with and without autism spectrum disorder." *Frontiers in Psychology* 9 (272).

Petrolini, Valentina, and Agustín Vicente. 2022. "The challenges raised by comorbidity in psychiatric research: The case of autism." *Philosophical Psychology* 35 (8): 1234–1263.

Petrolini, Valentina, Marta Jorba, and Agustín Vicente. 2023. "What does it take to be rigid? Reflections on the notion of rigidity in autism." *Frontiers in Psychiatry* 14.

Pierce, Karen, Shanna Marinero, Rachel Hazin, Brooke McKenna, Cassandra C. Barnes, and Amita Malige. 2016. "Eye tracking reveals abnormal visual preference for geometric images as an early biomarker of an autism spectrum disorder subtype associated with increased symptom severity." *Biological Psychiatry* 79 (8): 657–666.

Pijnacker, Janneke, Peter Hagoort, Jan Buitelaar, Jan-Paul Teunisse, and Bart Geurts. 2009. "Pragmatic inferences in high-functioning adults with autism and Asperger syndrome." *Journal of Autism and Developmental Disorders* 39 (4): 607–618.

Quora: https://www.quora.com/Why-do-so-many-neurotypicals-refuse-to-say-what-they-mean

Quora: https://www.quora.com/Why-do-neurotypicals-like-subtlety

Ramos-Cabo, Sofia, Valentin Vulchanov, and Mila Vulchanova. 2021. "Different ways of making a point: A study of gestural communication in typical and atypical early development." *Autism Research* 14 (5): 984–996.

Reid, Vincent M., Tricia Striano, Jennifer Kaufman, and Mark H. Johnson. 2004. "Eye gaze cueing facilitates neural processing of objects in 4-month-old infants." *NeuroReport* 15 (16): 2553–2555.

Riester, Arndt. 2019. "Constructing QUD trees." In *Questions in Discourse*, Vol. 2, 164–193. BRILL.

Roberts, Craige. 2012. "Information structure in discourse: Towards an integrated formal theory of pragmatics." *Semantics and Pragmatics* 5: 1–69.

Roch, Maja, Elena Florit, and Chiara Levorato. 2016. "Narrative competence of Italian–English bilingual children between 5 and 7 years." *Applied Psycholinguistics* 37 (1): 49–67.

Rumpf, Anne-Lise, Inge Kamp-Becker, Katja Becker, and Christina Kauschke. 2012. "Narrative competence and internal state language of children with Asperger syndrome and ADHD." *Research in Developmental Disabilities* 33 (5): 1395–1407.

Rundblad, Gabriella, and Dominique Annaz. 2010. "The atypical development of metaphor and metonymy comprehension in children with autism." *Autism* 14 (1): 29–46.

Rutter, Michael, Ann Le Couteur, and Catherine Lord. 2003. *Autism Diagnostic Interview-Revised*. Los Angeles, CA: Western Psychological Services.

Saban-Bezalel, Revital, Daniel Dolfin, Nathan Laor, and Nira Mashal. 2019. "Irony comprehension and mentalizing ability in children with and without autism spectrum disorder." *Research in Autism Spectrum Disorders* 58: 30–38.

Sah, Wan-hsiang, and Ping Torng. 2015. "Narrative coherence of Mandarin-speaking children with high-functioning autism spectrum disorder: An investigation into causal relations." *First Language* 35 (3): 189–212.

Sah, Wan-hsiang. 2015. "The development of coherence in narratives: Causal relations." *Taiwan Journal of Linguistics* 13 (1).

Scaife, Margaret, and Jerome S. Bruner. 1975. "The capacity for joint visual attention in the infant." *Nature* 253 (5489).

Schaeffer, Jeanette, Maisa Abd El-Raziq, Elena Castroviejo, Stéphanie Durrleman, Sandrine Ferré, Irina Grama, Petra Hendriks et al. 2023. "Language in autism: Domains, profiles and co-occurring conditions." *Journal of Neural Transmission*.

Schaeken, Walter, Maarten Van Haeren, and Valentina Bambini. 2018. "The understanding of scalar implicatures in children with autism spectrum disorder: Dichotomized responses to violations of informativeness." *Frontiers in Psychology* 9.

Schneider, Phyllis, Denyse Hayward, and Rachel V. Dubé. 2006. "Storytelling from pictures using the Edmonton narrative norms instrument" *Canadian Journal of Speech-Language Pathology and Audiology* 30 (4): 224–238.

Scionti, Nicola, Leonardo Zampini, and Gian Marco Marzocchi. 2023. "The relationship between narrative skills and executive functions across childhood: A systematic review and meta-analysis." *Children* 10 (8): 1391.

South, Mikle, and Jackie Rodgers. 2017. "Sensory, emotional and cognitive contributions to anxiety in autism spectrum disorders." *Frontiers in Human Neuroscience* 11.

Sperber, Dan, and Deirdre Wilson. (1986) 1995. *Relevance: Communication and Cognition*. 2nd edition. Oxford: Blackwell.

Stirling, Lesley, Sharynne Douglas, Susan R. Leekam, and Lee Carey. 2014. "The use of narrative in studying communication in autism spectrum disorders." In *Communication in Autism*, ed. by Joanne Arciuli and Jon Brock, 171–215. Amsterdam: John Benjamins.

Su, Yi-Chen, and Li-Yu Su. 2015. "Interpretation of logical words in Mandarin-speaking children with autism spectrum disorders: Uncovering knowledge of semantics and pragmatics." *Journal of Autism and Developmental Disorders* 45: 1938–1950.

Suh, Jinah, Inge-Marie Eigsti, Letitia Naigles, Megan Barton, Elizabeth Kelley, and Deborah Fein. 2014. "Narrative performance of optimal outcome children and adolescents with a history of an autism spectrum disorder (ASD)." *Journal of Autism and Developmental Disorders* 44 (7): 1681–1694.

Tager-Flusberg, Helen, and Kate Sullivan. 1994. "A second look at second-order belief attribution in autism." *Journal of Autism and Developmental Disorders* 24 (5): 577–586.

Tager-Flusberg, Helen, and Marilyn Anderson. 1991. "The development of contingent discourse ability in autistic children." *Journal of Child Psychology and Psychiatry* 32 (7): 1123–1134.

Tager-Flusberg, Helen, Rhea Paul, and Catherine Lord. 2005. "Language and communication in autism." *Handbook of Autism and Pervasive Developmental Disorders* 1: 335–364.

Tager-Flusberg, Helen. 1981. "On the nature of linguistic functioning in early infantile autism." *Journal of Autism and Developmental Disorders* 11: 45–56.

Tager-Flusberg, Helen. 1988. "On the nature of a language acquisition disorder: The example of autism". In F. Kessel (Ed.), *The development of language and language researchers*. Hillsdale, NJ: Erlbaum.

Tager-Flusberg, Helen. 1996. "Brief report: Current theory and research on language and communication in autism." *Journal of Autism and Developmental Disorders* 26 (2): 169–172.

Tager-Flusberg, Helen. 2006. "Defining language phenotypes in autism." *Clinical Neuroscience Research* 6 (3–4): 219–224.

Tanaka, James W., and Alison Sung. 2016. "The 'eye avoidance' hypothesis of autism face processing." *Journal of Autism and Developmental Disorders* 46 (5): 1538–1552.

Tek, Saime, Lindsey Mesite, Deborah Fein, and Letitia Naigles. 2014. "Longitudinal analyses of expressive language development reveal two distinct language profiles among young children with autism spectrum disorders." *Journal of Autism and Developmental Disorders* 44: 75–89.

Tomasello, Michael, Malinda Carpenter, and Ulf Liszkowski. 2007. "A new look at infant pointing." *Child Development* 78 (3): 705–722.

Tomasello, Michael. 1995. "Joint attention as social cognition." In *Joint Attention: Its Origins and Role in Development*, ed. by Chris Moore and Philip J. Dunham, 103–130. Mahwah, NJ: Lawrence Erlbaum Associates, Inc. / Psychology Press.

Tomasello, Michael. 2003. *Constructing a Language: A Usage-Based Theory of Language Acquisition*. Cambridge, MA: Harvard University Press.

Trabasso, Tom, and Linda L. Sperry. 1985. "Causal relatedness and importance of story events." *Journal of Memory and Language* 24 (5): 595–611.

Van Herwegen, Jo, and Gabriella Rundblad. 2018. "A cross-sectional and longitudinal study of novel metaphor and metonymy comprehension in children, adolescents, and adults with autism spectrum disorder." *Frontiers in Psychology* 9: 945.

Van Tiel, Bas, and Marc Kissine. 2018. "Quantity-based reasoning in the broader autism phenotype: A web-based study." *Applied Psycholinguistics* 39 (6): 1373–1403.

Vicente, Agustín, and Ingrid L. Falkum. 2023. "Accounting for the preference for literal meanings in autism spectrum conditions." *Mind & Language*: 119–140.

Vicente, Agustín, and Isabel Martín-González. 2021. "The literalist bias in the autistic spectrum conditions: Review of existing accounts." *Studies in Psychology* 42 (2): 298–333.

Vicente, Agustín, Catrinel Michel, and Valentina Petrolini. 2023. "Literalism in autistic people: A predictive processing proposal." *Review of Philosophy and Psychology*: 1–24.

Vulchanova, Mila, and Valentin Vulchanov. 2022. "Rethinking figurative language in autism: What evidence can we use for interventions?" *Frontiers in Communication* 7: 910850.

Vulchanova, Mila, Daniela Saldaña, Sara Chahboun, and Valentin Vulchanov. 2015. "Figurative language processing in atypical populations: The ASD perspective." *Frontiers in Human Neuroscience* 9: 24.

Vulchanova, Mila, Emily Milburn, Valentin Vulchanov, and Giuseppe Baggio. 2019. "Boon or burden? The role of compositional meaning in figurative language processing and acquisition." *Journal of Logic, Language and Information* 28 (2): 359–387.

Walenski, Matthew, and Tracy Love. 2017. "The real-time comprehension of idioms by typical children, children with specific language impairment and children with autism." *Journal of Speech Pathology & Therapy* 3 (1): 130.

Wang, Qi, Dorothy J. Campbell, Suzanne L. Macari, Katarzyna Chawarska, and Frederick Shic. 2018. "Operationalizing atypical gaze in toddlers with autism spectrum disorders: A cohesion-based approach." *Molecular Autism* 9 (1): 25.

Westerveld, Marleen F., and Joanne M.A. Roberts. 2017. "The oral narrative comprehension and production abilities of verbal preschoolers on the autism spectrum." *Language, Speech, and Hearing Services in Schools* 48 (4): 260–272.

Westerveld, Marleen F., Pascale Filiatrault-Veilleux, and Jennifer Paynter. 2021. "Inferential narrative comprehension ability of young school-age children on the autism spectrum." *Autism & Developmental Language Impairments* 6: 23969415211035666.

Wetherby, Amy M., and C. Andrew Prutting. 1984. "Profiles of communicative and cognitive-social abilities in autistic children." *Journal of Speech and Hearing Research* 27: 364–377.

Whyte, Elisabeth M., and Keith E. Nelson. 2015. "Trajectories of pragmatic and nonliteral language development in children with autism spectrum disorders". *Journal of Communication Disorders*, 54: 2–14.

Wilson, Anna C., and Dorothy V.M. Bishop. 2020. "Registered report: Investigating a preference for certainty in conversation among autistic adults compared to dyslexic adults and the general population." *PeerJ* 8: e10398.

Wilson, Anna C., and Dorothy V.M. Bishop. 2021. "'Second guessing yourself all the time about what they really mean…': Cognitive differences between autistic and non-autistic adults in understanding implied meaning." *Autism Research* 14 (1): 93–101.

Wilson, Anna C., and Dorothy V.M. Bishop. 2022. "A novel online assessment of pragmatic and core language skills: An attempt to tease apart language domains in children." *Journal of Child Language* 49 (1): 38–59.

World Health Organization. 2022. *ICD-11: International Classification of Diseases (11th Revision)*. https://icd.who.int/en

Ying Sng, Christine C., Mark Carter, and Jennifer Stephenson. 2018. "A systematic review of the comparative pragmatic differences in conversational skills of individuals with autism." *Autism & Developmental Language Impairments* 3.

Young, Erin C., Jennifer J. Diehl, Deborah Morris, Susan L. Hyman, and Loisa Bennetto. 2005. "The use of two language tests to identify pragmatic language problems in children with autism spectrum disorders." *Language, Speech, and Hearing Services in Schools* 36 (1): 62–72.

Zanchi, Paola, and Laura Zampini. 2021. "The narrative competence task." *European Journal of Psychological Assessment* 37 (1): 15–22.

Zane, Emily, and Rebecca B. Grossman. 2023. "Analysis of noun phrase ambiguity in narratives reveals differences in referential establishment but not cohesion for older autistic children." *Journal of Speech, Language, and Hearing Research* 66 (8): 2802–2820.

Zeidan, Joe, Eric Fombonne, James Scorah, Ayesha Ibrahim, Maureen S. Durkin, Shekhar Saxena, Ayesha Yusuf, Andrew Shih, and Mayada Elsabbagh. 2022. "Global prevalence of autism: A systematic review update." *Autism Research* 15 (5): 778–790.

Elite multilingualism

Elisabeth Barakos
University of Vienna

1. Introduction

What are elites? What is eliteness? How do elites connect to language? What is elite multilingualism? In what ways does elite multilingualism differ from other types of multilingualism? How can we study elites, eliteness, and language? Why is it important and interesting to study elite multilingualism? And why and how is it significant to the field of pragmatics?

These are key questions that not only form the centre of this handbook chapter but also relate to long-standing concerns over the social study of language and questions over why some forms of multilingualism are valued differently than others. Globalisation, cosmopolitanism, increased transnational migration, evolving socio-political dynamics, and shifts in economic structures have led to a transformation in how multilingualism is perceived and valued. Previously viewed as a problem, multilingualism is now seen as a valuable and commodifiable resource and a distinguishing feature of one's educational, linguistic, social, and professional identity (Bourdieu 1984; Heller and Duchêne 2016; Ruiz 1984). This shift is fuelled by the recognition that in the linguistic marketplace, specific forms of multilingualism — elite multilingualism as one such phenomenon — play a crucial role in defining identity and affording status, privilege, power, and distinction. Within these constellations, a heightened emphasis on a language-centred elitism has emerged (Barakos and Selleck 2019: 286). As will be shown in this chapter, this elitism assigns varying degrees of importance to different forms and levels of multilingualism. These include an appreciation of a socially advantaged, largely White, middle-class group of speakers whose linguistic repertoire encompasses globally dominant international prestige languages and a devaluation of the repertoires of linguistically minoritized and racialised groups with working-class and other marginalised backgrounds (see section *Historical Developments*).

To fully address questions over such language-based inequalities and such growing language-centred elitism, both ends of the so-called class spectrum (Thurlow and Jaworski, 2017) need to be addressed in research. As Howard (2019) cogently captures, we are inclined to examine inequality "from the perspective of the one who suffers the consequences of the subordination or oppression, not the one who receives the benefits;

hence those who receive privilege are not in our focus" (Howard 2019: 180–181). Similarly, Waters (2018: 412) argues that scholars "pay insufficient attention to social elites and how they are made through and by educational institutions and the systems they represent." Piller (2016: 208) also encourages linguists interested in inequalities to grapple with "understanding linguistic privilege" as an important window to understand "linguistic domination."

In keeping with this line of thinking to 'study up', the point of departure for this chapter is that language, and for that matter multilingualism, is invested with a structuring mechanism that affords certain groups of people more status, power, and privilege than others, based on their differently valued semiotic resources. In light of this, elite multilingualism captures precisely a phenomenon that brings:

> Social and/or material capital, a sense of belonging, prestige, excellence, privilege, and access through the use of specific linguistic resources for certain social groups and individuals. Elite multilingualism is essentially a phenomenon where language serves as an access code to a local, national or global perceived elite (way of life) [for some members of society]. (Barakos and Selleck 2019: 362)

Whilst we have proposed the term "elite multilingualism", the term or label itself is of secondary importance compared to the range of concepts for which it enables analytical contemplation. The significance of studying elite multilingualism lies in its ability to open up new understandings of the ways in which language, speech and communication intersect with processes of privilege and distinction. Centrally, it opens up a perspective in pragmatics to illustrate analytically how and why people hierarchise language(s) and valorise some forms of multilingualism over others across different sites and domains of communication considered elite and non-elite.

In this chapter, I seek not only to chart the development of scholarship on elites, eliteness and language, but also to frame the key stakes of an elite multilingualism research perspective for the field of pragmatics. The chapter considers how some forms of multilingualism are considered elite, for whom exactly, and which consequences this has for the production of social boundaries and the formation of social and linguistic hierarchies and differentiation processes. For this purpose, the chapter lays out how social, cultural, political, and historical factors impinge on the discursive formation and practice of elites, eliteness, and multilingualism in privileged institutional sites of education, professional or social life. It attends to the role of language in elite institutions, the notion of eliteness as consumption such as travel, tourism, or food, eliteness as a marker of qualification, achievement, and aspiration, and the role of elite language in the professions and the labour market. Such orientations and fields of study are crucial for pragmatics researchers with a vested interest in the social and discursive conditions surrounding *language in use* and the complex of *language and inequality*. Ultimately, this chapter serves to show how a focus on elite multilingualism in pragmatics research is not just relevant but also crucial in visualising, if not interrupting, specific conceptions of language as a site where privilege, class distinction and inequality is reproduced and legitimated.

2. Key concepts and terms

2.1 Elite(s) and eliteness

There is an established body of research on elites, notably in education and sociology (of education), as groups of people that inhabit superior social positions of privilege and power in society (see Maxwell and Aggleton 2015; Savage et al. 2015; van Zanten 2018). Traditionally, research into elites have centred on analysing the strategies employed by social groups to attain or uphold their status and dominant positions, as well as exploring the ways in which these elites exert their influence and power. Whether to treat elites as a distinct social class has been questioned widely (e.g. Scott 2008). Research in elite studies has recently seen a resurgence in the social sciences – sociology in particular (Howard and Kenway 2015; Savage and Williams 2008), especially with a view to the necessity of recognising and confronting how capitalism propels societal transformation and shapes or reshapes the formation of elite groups. Of interest here is also an understanding of "how social locations (e.g., schools, workplaces, and communities) create and maintain privilege for certain groups (e.g., White, heterosexual, male, and affluent)" (Howard 2019: 18; following McIntosh 1988).

What, then, are elites and what is eliteness? These concepts are slippery, and their boundaries unclear. They have also come to be defined in different ways across sociological, educational and linguistic scholarship. The early twentieth century witnessed a particular focus on elites in sociology, social theory and political theory. Scholars primarily explored the dynamic interplay of power within institutions and individuals, as well as its connection to the political and national systems of the ruling class (Maxwell 2015). In the field of the sociology of education, there has been a robust interest in elite education and its correlation with social hierarchies and power structures on both national and global scales (e.g., Howard and Gaztambide-Fernandez 2010; Khan 2012; Maxwell 2015; van Zanten 2018). Much of this research is influenced by Bourdieu's work on language, capital and differentiation (1984, 1991), aiming to address the fundamental question of what defines elites and social class, and who and what determines the valuation and distribution of resources in society. Scholarship has also been inspired by Khan's (2012: 362) understanding of elite membership as linked to "the control over value of, and distribution of resources."

There are different entry points to defining elite(s). The term elite(s) is often fetishised in mundane and popular discourses about political elites, cultural elites, local/global elites and institutional elites (schools, universities, organisations etc.). In discussing the local politics of global English, Sonntag (2003) provides an insightful perspective from the field of political science, suggesting that elites should not be viewed as monolithic and unchanging but rather as multifaceted and dynamic. According to this perspective, there exist various interconnected clusters of elites (political, economic, cultural, linguistic and so forth), each employing different forms of capital to attain and maintain elite standing (Sonntag, 2003: 8). Similarly, Howard and Kenway (2015) detail different types of elites: global and local; political, cultural, super and top elites; ruling elites or hidden elites; old or new elites.

What these strands of research share is the idea that 'elites' are not monolithic entities, contrary to mundane discourses, and that elitism in particular is best understood as a practice, as exemplified and documented by Thurlow and Jaworski (2017). In essence, eliteness is "something people do, not something they have or are" (Thurlow and Jaworski 2017: 244). In that sense, eliteness is firmly rooted in the discourses and social practices of people. Drawing on Bourdieu's practice and resource-centred approach, it can further be established that:

a. Eliteness is not an asserted thing that people have or don't have but a social-relational process.
b. Eliteness manifests discursively and socially in what people do.
c. Eliteness intertwines with a sense of superiority, as well as power and influence.
d. Elites inherently involve processes of classification and hierarchisation.
e. Elites are shaped through social interactions, constituting a self-defined and perceived social group whose members share common characteristics based on perceived superiority, along with patterns of inclusion and exclusion.
f. Eliteness and elite(s) are part of a continuum that is shaped in and through individual and collective discourses and practices.

Such an understanding helps to avoid dichotomising and oversimplifying eliteness and non-eliteness, elites and non-elites as two homogenous groups in the sense of "the rich" and "the poor", with two distinctive and categorial ends. How, then, do these understandings of elites and eliteness link with language?

2.2 Language, elites and eliteness

As previously sketched, in the disciplines such as education and sociology (of education), there has been a key focus on examining the formation and practices of elites and eliteness. These fields have propelled the examination of social class and paralleled a revival of scholarship into elites (and their contestation). But how about language studies? The existence of current interests in language and elites in education (including elite multilingualism) is coupled with a long-standing concern in sociolinguistics, applied linguistics and linguistic anthropology in the connections between language, class and social stratification. Sociolinguistics and applied linguistics have long provided key scholarship on the connection between language and social class (see Block 2014, 2017 and Chun 2019 for a review; Eckert 2000; Heller 1995; Labov 1966; Rampton 2006; 2010; Rampton et al. 2008; Snell 2018).

In many of these linguistic enquiries, conceptual points of inspiration regarding 'class' stem largely from adjacent fields such as sociology and education (e.g. Bernstein 1971; Bourdieu 1984; Savage et al. 2015). So whilst conceptualisations of class abound in sociology or education, Bourdieu (1984: 102) has provided a common entry point to the sociolinguistic study of social class and classed identity as something relational, that is, not just marked by wealth, income, occupation or education but by social status, distinction, and attendant social practices (Block 2014: 52). As Block (2014) and Chun (2019) explain, this is due to the lack of conceptual clarity about 'class' in sociolinguistics itself, as well as an analytic tendency to categorize people into static occupational groups (e.g. working class vs. middle-class; blue-collar vs. white-collar workers). Over time, the initial interest in class within language studies has diminished, giving way to a stronger emphasis on language and identity as well as the so-called 'multi/pluri turn', as critiqued by Kubota (2014). This shift, at the time, has highlighted a growing focus on linguistic and cultural diversity and multiculturalism in applied linguistics. As a result, fields like SLA, multilingualism research and language education have been marked by "a generalized disengagement from and erasure of class" (Block 2014: 170).

Block (2014; 2018) has convincingly argued that the current resurgence of interest in social class and structural inequalities in language studies has been brought about by the growing stratification and inequality of the neoliberal knowledge economy and capitalist globalisation. This revived interest in the concept of social class (see e.g. Chun 2019; Park 2019; Rampton 2010) grapples with the connection between language and social inequality and the nature of power in society (Sunyol 2019). From the perspective of elitism and education, Sunyol (2019: 68) adds that the widening gap between rich and poor, coupled with the middle class moving closer to the lower end of the social class spectrum, may have contributed to the renewed interest in researching elites and eliteness in language studies.

In line with refreshed pledges to analyse class dynamics within sociolinguistics and discourse studies, new scholarship has emerged on the connection between language, elites and eliteness under the banner of 'elite discourse studies' (including aspects of elite multilingualism). This line of work mostly focuses on sites and topics such as tourism, mobility, travel and food discourse or different types of language worker such as artists, advertisers, dialect coaches and journalists (Mapes 2021; Thurlow 2020; Thurlow and Jaworski 2017) or, to a lesser extent, in bi- and multilingual education studies (see e.g., Barakos and Selleck 2019; De Mejía 2002; Selleck and Barakos 2019; Sunyol 2019). What these studies share is the examination of the ways in which language is treated and marketed as "an objective skill, acquired and possessed, that affords status, recognition legitimacy, and ultimately material remuneration, to those who possess it" (Block 2017: 6).

I have established earlier that eliteness, and elitism as a practice rather than a quality one has or does not have, has been examined and observed widely to manifest itself in privileged fields such as tourism, food discourse or work-related and social mobilities and in privileged educational sites. Importantly, it is also observable in the differing value allocations attached to multilingualism, favouring some forms more than others. Moreover, it is observable in the ways people change and adapt their language(s) and ways of speaking, including the use of multiple semiotic forms, in order to improve their social status (see *Current Contributions and Topics* for examples). The next section sketches the contours of elite multilingualism and considers its counterpart, that is, what is not considered elite.

2.3   The concept of elite multilingualism

As De Costa (2019: 454) explains for elite multilingualism, "the roots of its existence may be traced to a robust desire to distinguish individuals from each other." Linked to this is the understanding that not all types of multilingualism are treated on an equal basis. Multilingualism is linked to inequalities of access to linguistic and social resources in society, which connects to social hierarchisation and marginalisation. In that sense, as Ortega claims, "multilingualism is not only inequitable but also gradient" (Ortega 2018: 3), making some forms of multilingualism more acceptable and powerful than others in society. As a result, processes of "elite closure" (Myers-Scotton 1993: 149) may materialise as "a type of social mobilization strategy by which those persons in power establish or maintain their powers and privileges via linguistic choices."

As such, some types of multilingualism have become a symbol of privilege and high status for certain individuals, simultaneously resulting in vulnerability and injustices in accessing more privileged positions for others, particularly in specific socio-economic contexts (Selleck and Barakos 2019). De Costa adds that it is by default that "elite multilingualism lacks an inclusive dimension and bears a material dimension" (Shankar and Cavanaugh 2012, qtd. in De Costa 2019: 454). With these premises in mind, we need to ask how it comes that some forms of multilingualism are rendered more elite, prestigious or desirable in the linguistic marketplace than others? Of interest here is further why people tend to hierarchise languages (and for that matter, language users) in the first place.

In the contemporary landscape of changing geopolitical constellations, neoliberalism, and intensified migration, individuals become multilingual or pursue multilingualism for diverse reasons, contributing to a varied spectrum of motivations and conditions in the context of leisure, education and work. An emerging trend in the appreciation of language skills in today's society has become evident, which has been linked with the quest for creating a productive, creative, cosmopolitan, market-oriented and entrepreneurial self.

Coupled with this trend is a pervasive elitism that assigns varying degrees of value to different forms and levels of multilingualism (Barakos and Selleck 2019). These value allocations have significantly influenced the design of bilingual educational programs (García 2009), the dynamics of language-related work processes and the commodified potential of language skills (Heller and Duchêne 2016), as well as access to services and opportunities on the job market.

The context of foreign language education and language learning more generally serves as an exemplary terrain to document the different evaluations of multilingualism as more or less elite. Kramsch (2014) precisely captures a range of factors that bring elite multilingualism into being, ranging from modernist understandings of language, the one-language-culture-nation triad, persisting standard language norms and native speaker ideals:

> Modernity, a product of the 18th-century Enlightenment, is characterized by all the features that FL teachers take for granted: the existence of nation — states, each with their national language and their national culture; the existence of standardized languages with their stable grammars and dictionaries that ensure the good usage of the language by well-educated citizens that FL learners are expected to emulate; the superiority of national languages over regional dialects and patois; the clear boundaries between native and foreign languages and among foreign languages so that one can clearly know whether someone is speaking French, German, or Chinese, standard Spanish or regional Spanish; the codified norms of correct language usage and proper language use that language learners have to abide by for fear of not being understood or not being accepted by native speakers. Kramsch (2014: 297)

We can thus establish that there is always a degree of hierarchisation, valuation and prestige attached to different language varieties and language practices, tying such an understanding to Bourdieu's (1984) account of language, capital and distinction. In this respect, language ideologies come into play in all dimensions of looking at language, whether it concerns people's language use, perceived language competencies, normative teaching practices or in the context of a stratified multilingual labour market.

As shown earlier in Kramsch's quote, the phenomenon of elite multilingualism is thus interlocked with long-standing ideological concerns with linguistic norms and standardisation (e.g. seeking prestige by assimilating to the standard). It further connects to the idea that there are monolithic, fixed languages or language varieties (e.g., French, German, Chinese, British English or Indian English) with imagined homogenous speech communities linked to a nation state. But what, then, makes multilingualism elite?

The idea of a bounded and fixed language has been undergirded by the idea of the superiority of a standard language that acts as a norm-centred benchmark and enjoys greater prestige (Gal 2006; Hüning et al. 2012). Such assumptions inevitably lead to the devaluation of all other forms of language use that may be considered deviant from the norm (e.g. using 'non-standard' forms of language, using varieties considered less prestigious, having a 'thick' accent, mixing or switching codes). Such perceived deviations have led to the production of myths about which language(s) and language varieties are considered to be "good", "authentic" or "desirable" in language education or professional life (Davies 2003; Park 2010).

In sum, what makes multilingualism elite is not necessarily the imagined boundedness of language, but its very potential for linguistic commodification, classed and racialised hierarchisation and processes of distinction, including the resulting inequalities that attach to accessing prestige and distinction in the first place. At the same time, the very existence of elite multilingualism invokes the existence of a non-elite form of multilingualism. Or as De Costa (2019: 454) puts it: "For elite multilingualism to exist, however, it needs to have a counter discourse, one that contrasts and subsequently helps characterise elite multilingualism." The following overview, far from being exhaustive, tracks the historical developments of forms of elite and non-elite bi/multilingualism as captured in applied, sociolinguistic and linguistic anthropological scholarship.

3. Historical developments of elite multilingualism

In the earlier literature on elite bilingualism, eliteness is often depicted in somewhat contradictory and binary terms. There is, for example, a common distinction between "elite" and "folk" bilingualism that has been prominent (Fishman 1977; Paulston 1975). As far back as the 1970s, Paulston (1975: 5) captured "elitist bilingualism" as the privilege of middle-class and well-educated people, typically involving prestigious international languages. Paulston (1978) employs the term "elite bilinguals" to describe individuals who voluntarily become multilingual, typically through educational pursuits. In contrast, folk bilingualism, commonly associated with ethnic minorities, characterises a scenario in which individuals acquire a new language involuntarily for survival, often due to migration (see also Butler and Hakuta 2004). This differentiation is often based on the belief that elite bilingualism is untroublesome for the speaker, given that it arises from intentional choices (Rydenvald 2015: 214). Based on the social status of language, Fishman (1977) similarly classified bilinguals in terms of "folk" or "elite." Following this distinction, folk bilinguals are associated with linguistic minority communities where the minority language holds lower prestige compared to the majority language (Fishman 1977). Elite bilinguals can command a dominant language and may also speak another one which may afford them with additional advantages and benefits within society.

In the context of French-English bilingualism in Canada, Heller (2002: 49) captures elite bilingualism as "standard and monolingual forms and practices largely acquired through literacy." In foregrounding literacy and the standard form of language, Heller also highlights the pivotal role that educational institutions play in enabling an elite type of bilingualism. In essence, "the language of the educated and male middle/upper class — the definers of the nation and its uniformized, regimented language — becomes the standard against which other languages and language variants are made intelligible as substandard" (Heller 2020: 124). This more prestigious type of bilingualism has been premised on the idea of 'parallel monolingualism' or 'double monolingualism'. For Heller (2006: 83), 'double monolingualism' captures a situation in which "[l]anguages are still seen as autonomous systems; what is valued is multilingualism as a set of parallel monolingualisms, not a hybrid system" (Heller 2006: 5). Such language ideologies, then, suggest that keeping one's languages separate or even mastering them as a 'native' speaker is a marker of distinction in education, professional or social life and mapped with perceived superior competence and intelligence. These are the circulating ideologies that bring elite multilingualism into its very existence.

One seminal piece of work is De Mejía's *Power, Prestige and Bilingualism* (2002), in which she writes about the creation and dispersion of various types of bilingualism as they relate to power and prestige in international educational contexts, with a focus on South America. Taking Bourdieu's (1991) view of language as symbolic capital, she captures "elite bilingualism" as something that renders "a definite advantage, socially and economically" for people who choose to learn more than one language because of their "lifestyle, employment opportunities, or education" (De Mejía 2002: 41). This drive for developing an elite bi- or multilingual repertoire is interlocked with becoming a global citizen and developing a "new global identity" (De Mejía 2002: 51). Elite bilingualism enables "access to prestigious international languages for those upwardly mobile individuals and their families who need or who wish to be bilingual or multilingual" (De Mejía 2002: 5). If we follow Block (2014: 134) here, this quest is "very much a middle-class aspiration" linked to mobility and the accumulation of different forms of capital.

Taking a power-based perspective, De Mejía (2002) and Guerrero (2010) discuss a range of similar terms such as "elite vs. folk bilingualism", "optional bilingualism", "prestigious bilingualism" and "enrichment bilingualism", which characterise privileged circumstances of becoming bi- and multilingual. Such terms are grounded in the concept of "language choice", which allows individuals to become bilingual from a standpoint of privilege and power. Nevertheless, according to Guerrero (2010), elite bilingualism is not a voluntary occurrence in non-European, less developed nations such as China, South Africa and Colombia. In these places, children are compelled by circumstances to receive English instruction, a necessity driven by the pursuit of upward social mobility (Guerrero 2010: 174). In this sense, elite multilingualism oftentimes captures a mobility-, leisure- and lifestyle-related multilingualism (Codó 2018; Garrido 2017; Kubota 2011) that nurtures an internationally mobile workforce and a cohort of mobile learners. This focus stands in opposition to multilingualism in the context of political or forced migration, where language learning is mostly not a choice but an obligation for the purposes of citizenship, integration and access to services, education and the job market — so often "imposed by circumstances" (De Mejía 2002: 43).

Another type of terminology is offered by Jaspers (2009) who distinguishes between a "prestige" (or "pure") multilingualism and a "plebeian" (or "impure") multilingualism, which he defines as:

> The use of various languages by the mostly urban, mostly multi-ethnic, very often poorly-educated working class across Europe. It concerns first, second and third generation migrants with linguistic repertoires comprising varieties of national (or minority) languages (among others Moroccan Arabic, Berber, Turkish and Kurdish) of their countries of origin as well as proficiency in (very often regional) varieties spoken in the host country.
> (Jaspers 2009: 19)

With this binary distinction, Jaspers (2009) aims to capture the paradoxical situation of valuing some types of language(s) or linguistic varieties more than others. These valuations range from well-educated, mobile, transnational individuals proficient in predominantly Western European, prestigious global languages acquired through formal education or by choice, to less privileged, often working-class, urban, minority, heritage, and migrant communities whose linguistic repertoires are highly plural and frequently learned in less formal educational settings. Along the same lines, Blommaert (2011: 251) has tried to capture this distinction by describing a "multilingualism of the elite" and a "multilingualism of the poor."

In Heller's (2002) research about the commodification of bilingualism in Canada, she delves into the emergence of a so-called "bilingual elite" that is capable of interacting effectively with both monolingual anglophones in influential roles and more marginalised "working class" bilinguals. She specifically draws a distinction between "elite bilingualism", which signifies the dominance of "standard and monolingual forms and practices largely acquired through literacy" (Heller 2002: 49), and "working-class bilingualism", characterised by a reliance on mixed language forms and predominantly orally acquired practices. In Plöger and Barakos (2021) we distinguish between an "elite" and a more "precarious" type of multilingualism. This distinction tries to capture the ongoing hierarchisation processes affecting languages and speakers, based on the different perception, valuation and treatment of people's multilingual resources and repertoires. This, in turn, nurtures deficit perspectives and broader structural inequalities that, more often than not, are linked to migration (Plöger and Barakos 2021: 403).

From the perspective of colonialism and in the context of Hong Kong, Lin (2015: 19–23) uses the terms "egalitarian bi/multilingualism" and "hierarchical bi-/multilingualism" and contrasts "grassroots trans-semiotizing" (localised, creative, innovative and agentive linguistic practices) with an "elite bi/multilingualism", which is considered cosmopolitan and often favoured by the state. In the context of racialised learners, Flores et al. (2020: 2) differentiate between "white bilingualism as inherently valuable and racialized bilingualism as inherently deficient." They go on to explain that "a double standard" exists between these two types of bilingualism which dominate mainstream education policy discourse and practice (Flores et al. 2020: 2).

Aligning with de Mejía (2013: 4), such binary classifications "may have been useful in its original formulation to draw attention to the differing values and ideological assumptions associated with these two traditions." They may also indicate how individuals position themselves vis-à-vis multilingualism and capture their own dichotomous perceptions of different forms of multilingualism. At the same time, such binary distinctions may also miss the representation of the fluid nature of bi- and multilingualism and tend to homogenise groups of speakers as either privileged/elite/wealthy/pure/White or underprivileged/ undereducated/poor/impure/racialised. As earlier discussed, it may be more helpful to think about elite multilingualism along the lines of a continuum with two ends and treat it as a discursive, ideological, enacted, affective, and socially constructed phenomenon.

In addition, although financial or other material wealth can be one dimension of eliteness, it does not capture the full picture. Elite multilingualism can also serve as an aspiration, ambition, and an ideology that everyday individuals of all classes subscribe to. Having marketable language resources at one's disposal allows people to realise their aspirational desires such as gaining a specific qualification, accessing citizenship, or climbing up the social mobility ladder (for examples, see *Eliteness as qualification, achievement, and aspiration*).

The conceptual account of elite multilingualism offered so far in this chapter has provided a range of conceptual and theoretical avenues for scholars in pragmatics interested in the connects of language, elites, and elite multilingualism. In order to study elite multilingualism *in use* from a pragmatic orientation, the next section will offer empirical insights into the various facets of elite multilingualism in use. It showcases work ranging from the study of language in elite institutions, eliteness as consumption and lifestyle, eliteness as a qualification, achievement, and aspiration as well as the role of elite language(s) in the labour market.

4. Current contributions and topics

Despite the wealth of critical ethnographic research exploring multilingualism as a space marked by inequality and social injustice, there has been a recent surge in attention towards elite multilingualism as a factor that perpetuates social disparities. Recognising the intricate demands and aspirations associated with contemporary multilingualism, there is a need for alternative perspectives that prompt new research inquiries, particularly focusing on more privileged and aspirational groups in society. In the following, I will review current contributions and research domains related to elite multilingualism, with a primary emphasis on its manifestation in education and its impact on economic and social aspects of privilege. These contributions (albeit selective) showcase how elite multilingualism can be studied methodologically via research methods and procedures commonly adopted in pragmatics: ethnographic approaches that involve observational data collection procedures such as recordings of naturally occurring data or field notes, elicited procedures such as interviews or attitudinal surveys, as well as (multimodal and critical) discourse analytic or interactional approaches to map how language, elites and eliteness are tightly interwoven in localised spaces.

4.1 Elite institutions

Education has always been a key institution to provide or deny access to "valued symbolic resources, such as bilingualism" (De Mejía 2002: 37). To establish some premises, we can argue that institutional sites of education serves as a primary terrain for the formation, reproduction and enactment of elite(s) and eliteness. Work in this vein has looked at the nature of elite education and educational privilege, at education systems as mechanisms for social mobility and the reproduction of privilege, distinction, and status, but also at the discourses and resources that contribute to the formation of elite identities and status. Research has covered fields such as elite private schooling, international schools, elite university education, and global citizenship education (see e.g., Gaztambide-Fernández 2009; Khan 2012, 2016; Maxwell 2015; Vandrick 2011; van Zanten et al. 2015; 2018; Waters 2018). Class-making is an interwoven aspect of elite educational institutions. To exemplify, Tarc and Tarc (2015) show how international schools serve as "transnational spaces of agonist social class-making" (2014: 34). They lead to a shift in "national, cultural, and economic affinities" (2014: 36) and frequently become arenas of contention where "various historical and social factors… intersect, giving rise to moments of discontinuity" (2014: 42).

Focusing on secondary schools and higher education, van Zanten et al. (2015) demonstrate the formation of elites, privilege, and excellence and its connection to the production of inequality. They document the process of how globalising practices affect the trajectories, strategies, and identities of elite groups (institutions) and individuals (parents, students, graduates) and their negotiation of educational advantage. Vandrick's (2011) work examines the privileged identities of multilingual "Students of the New Global Elite" (SONGEs) who access American universities and are characterised by a distinct profile, having "lived and studied in at least three countries; … [being] affluent and privileged; and … [exhibiting] a sense of global membership" (Vandrick 2011: 160). Of interest here is the role of bi- and multilingualism as well as English in shaping elite SONGE identities, which enable students to shore up even more educational privilege.

Adopting critical sociolinguistic approaches, Codó and Sunyol (2019) discursively and ethnographically analyse the institutionalisation of a Mandarin Chinese programme in an elite school in Barcelona, which has re-branded itself as an international and multilingual school (see also Sunyol 2019). The offer of learning Chinese is constructed as a "distinction practice" (Codó and Sunyol 2019: 13) in an already competitive educational climate of Englishisation and the learning of Spanish and Catalan at this institution. In Relaño-Pastor and Fernández-Barrera's (2019) sociolinguistic ethnography of an elite model of bilingual education, a CLIL-programme (Spanish-English) in Spanish schools, we learn about a common strategy of establishing elitism in education: the use of English native speakers as "guarantors of educational elitism, distinctiveness, and linguistic prestige in the highly commodified market of English" (Relaño-Pastor and Fernández-Barrera 2019: 421). Findings also point to ingrained contradictions and disputes that using the native English teacher as an icon of eliteness entails.

Another example of how elitism manifest in education is offered by Liberali and Megale (2016). In their study of the expanding mode of elite bilingual (Portuguese-English) education in Brazil, they critique persistent monoglossic views of language. Their analysis of texts, curricula, and materials from Brazilian bilingual schools show that such sites are deemed "a convenient opportunity to achieve two important and necessary functions in the education of their children: a quality education and the teaching of a foreign language" (2016: 100).

In the context of European and international schools, Rydenvald's (2015) sociolinguistic survey reveals the language practices, perceptions, and attitudes of transnational and multilingual teenagers from a Swedish background with socially mobile middle-class trajectories. Whilst the teenagers share seemingly "uncomplicated" (Baker and Prys-Jones 1998) and voluntary elite multilingual profiles, characterised by their parents' "planned and purposeful" (Baker and Prys-Jones 1998: 15) educational choices, they face struggles over actively using the local majority language. In addition, the children tend to use more multilingual language practices (alongside Swedish) at home than expected but orient to largely English and monolingual interactions in group communication and with their peers.

4.2 Eliteness as consumption and lifestyle

Within the field of elite discourse studies, Thurlow and Jaworski (2017, 2019) orient their discourse-analytic research towards the aspirational, ideological, and relational character of eliteness. In their earlier work, which is mainly grounded in ethnography, multimodality, and critical discourse studies (e.g., Thurlow and Jaworski 2012, 2014), we learn more about elite status and luxury travel in an era marked by global mobility. They analyse how marketers and commercial entities utilise visual, spatial, material, and linguistic resources to showcase elitism and manipulate the visibility and invisibility of luxury labor (Thurlow and Jaworski 2014). In another line of work (Thurlow and Jaworski 2017, 2019) they explores how discourse plays a key role in mediating and legitimising class privilege and the formation of elite status, emphasising qualities of distinction, excellence, and superiority as they arise among groups with material wealth, political influence or socially privileged positions.

Additionally, research in this vein delves into how various groups and institutions, in specific moments, places, and ways lay claim to eliteness as a means to position themselves, or be positioned by others, as either elite or non-elite. In Thurlow (2020), analytic attention is centred on the specialist, elite activities of high-end language work conducted by so-called wordsmiths and professionals such as journalists, dialect coaches, judges, school principals, advertisers, translators, and publishers. Within the context of professional discourse studies and high-end language work, Mapes (2021, 2023) explores the concept of elite authenticity and distinction at the crossroads of language and social class. Using a multimodal critical-discourse analytic approach, she explores food and material culture consumption, authenticity, and elite food discourse (Mapes 2021), as well as the high-end language work of political speechwriters (Mapes 2023).

In a critical discourse-ethnography, Barakos (2019, 2022) traces the discourses, ideologies, and practices of freelance language trainers as mobile language workers. They are employed by an elite Austrian language education company which offers language and intercultural competence training. Focusing on affect and the emotional labour of language trainers, the results demonstrate that instructors, who appear to have privileged positions thanks to their native speaker status, find themselves navigating a delicate balance between elite and precarious employment conditions due to the freelance nature of their labour. The findings also demonstrate how private adult language schools play a significant role in the discursive production of elites and eliteness as part of a lifestyle and consumerist project: an aspirational elite groups of learners who acquire languages considered profitable, and native language trainers as gatekeepers of educational success. Results reveal the ways in which such institutions and the neoliberal ideologies and affects they (re)produce – here employability, profitability, self-enhancement, and native speaker norms and ideals – serve a fundamental role in producing elite status: namely by buying, selling, and consuming elite language classes.

In what follows, elite ways of thinking about the native speaker and standard language ideals as the reference model in teaching and learning continue to permeate the quest for a life-style related multilingualism. This quest is maintained by the private language education market and what Sunyol (2019: 78) captures as the ongoing "frenzy for developing elite multilingual repertoires." As Park (2016) adds, ideologies surrounding the way we sound and speak constitute a key factor in the formation of linguistic hierarchies. More often than not, such (aspirational) ideologies forms the basis for the creation of distinction and elite forms of multilingualism.

4.3 Eliteness as qualification, achievement, and aspiration

There is a bulk of critical applied, sociolinguistic, and linguistic anthropological scholarship that examines the formation and recreation of elite(s) in connection with transnational identity processes, social class, and language as an economic facilitator for a more privileged way of life. The bulk of these studies also showcases how eliteness manifests as a form of qualification, achievement and aspiration.

In the context of the Philippines, Reyes (2017) discusses the invention of (aspirational) elite identities, which include the categories of "Conyo" elites and other "middle-class" elites. The Philippine conyo is part of an affluent urban youth that is light skinned, wealthy, and materialistically oriented. Conyo also describes their distinct youth language, which is framed as a mix or fusion of American English and Tagalog. Conyos are characterised by modelling and reproducing colonial behaviour and power and sit at the interface between colonial identities and their Westernised middle-class counterparts. In a study of English as a medium of instruction (EMI) and the discursive construction of elite identity in Bangladesh (Jahan and Hamid 2019), we learn about elite formation through language and changing discourses of elitism in relation to debates regarding the use of English or Bangla as medium of instruction. Via an analysis of news media discourse, the authors reconstruct elite identity formation among English-medium students in the media via the axes of an exclusive communicative repertoire, high-quality global education, and a cosmopolitan sense of global mobility. Rather than passing down inherited social privilege, students perceive and construct English-medium education as a key mechanism "to transform elite privilege into qualifications and inheritance into achievement" (Jahan and Hamid 2019: 402) in a globalised world. These results are consistent with those of other studies, for example that of Sah and Karki (2023), who examine the elite appropriation of EMI policies and related inequalities in Himalayan schools.

In the context of Kenya, Bunyi (2008) shows that English remains key for educational access and social mobility. Bunyi (2008: 148) emphasises that "English was the official vehicle and the magic formula to colonial elitedom" (drawing on Ngũgĩ 1985: 115). This colonial legacy has created a gulf between an elite that is capable of speaking English and a non-elite that cannot access English-medium education and is largely literate only in their indigenous language. As such, non-elite parents aspire for their children to be taught in English from an early age, to gain access to a global resource.

Bae and Park's (2016) study *Becoming Global Elites Through Transnational Language Learning* takes the case of middle-class pre-university students in Korea, who undertake Early Study Abroad programmes in Singapore to learn key English language skills and prepare themselves for a competitive global marketplace (see also Pérez-Milans' (2014) study on language aspirations of students learning Mandarin Chinese in a working-class school in London). This type of work aligns with other studies that demonstrate the relationship between language ideologies, language learning, and economic value in the context of foreign language learning, for instance, those by Park (2010), Erling (2017), or Kubota (2011). They capture a mobility-, leisure- and lifestyle-related multilingualism (Codó 2018; Garrido 2017; Kubota 2011) that nurtures an internationally mobile workforce and a cohort of mobile learners.

Similar formations of an aspirational class of global elites, as captured by Vandrick (2011), can be found in Paquet and Levasseur's (2019) ethnographic study about adult newcomers to Montreal, Canada, who attend the francization programme as new speakers of French. The study used semi-structured interviews and participant observation in formal classrooms, informal encounters in hallways, the library, and coffee shops, to document the experience and practices of these newcomers. Results demonstrate that newcomer students actively invest in building an elite French-English bilingualism with the potential to access eliteness through the job market and social networks. At the same time, findings demonstrate the boundaries that these students face between an elite French/English bilingual and an aspirational non-elite multilingual group of speakers, whose plurilingual repertoire is not always considered valuable. After all, these newcomers are "expected to learn, master and use French as so-called native speakers" for the purposes of social inclusion (Paquet and Levasseur 2019: 11).

4.4 Elite language in the labour market

In the realm of professional prestige within the global workforce, Day and Wagner (2007) provide insights into the language dynamics experienced by individuals in the international job market. They coin the term "bilingual professional" to characterise the communication skills and behaviours of professionals who willingly relocate for career advancement, aiming to enhance their opportunities in both work and life (Day and Wagner 2007: 381). In the context of a critical sociolinguistic ethnographic study about a Luxembourg workplace at a multilingual European Union (EU) institution (Lovrits and de Bres 2021), we learn more about the ways in which native-English speaking trainees pursue "desired personal development towards a multilingual status" (Lovrits and de Bres 2021: 408), which would offer them access to a more privileged way of life and establish their cosmopolitan self. The trainees experienced their own ascribed native-speaker status as working against their desires of becoming an elite multilingual within the multilingual work context of the institution. In a similar European institutional context, Drewski (2023) explores the complex language dynamics within a group of EU officials, who are characterised by an emerging transnational elite of professionals. Whilst multilingualism serves as a marker of elite distinction, there are intra-group struggles and boundaries drawn over one's competency in English and French as the two major working languages.

Vessey and Nicolai's (2023) study of multilingual London nannies offers insights into the ways multilingualism affords access to this niche type of labour. Drawing on qualitative data based on interviews and focus groups involving 15 multilingual nannies based in the UK, the nannies' multilingual profiles and domestic language work is sustained by middle-class families who contribute to the (re)production of elitism by favouring specific linguistic repertoires offered by multilingual nannies. Lorente's (2017) critical sociolinguistic and ethnographic study of the labour migration of multilingual Filipino nannies sheds light on the centrality of prestige languages such as English for securing a job as a domestic worker.

Garrido (2017; 2021) delves into the professional activities and multilingual capabilities of transnational humanitarian elites who leverage their 'cosmopolitan capital' — a form of cultural capital involving solidarity, openness, and specific linguistic proficiencies — to attain and sustain an elite status. Coupling sociolinguistics with ethnography, Garrido problematises elite multilingualism within an international humanitarian organisation headquartered in French-speaking Switzerland (Geneva). She demonstrates that "not all the language varieties are valued equally in a certain construction of elite multilingualism, signalled by language ideological debates about their institutional status" (Garrido 2021: 54). Findings show that in order to access privileged delegate positions within this organisation, tensions and strategic debates arise over the different values attached to English as a global lingua franca, French as the official language in Geneva and an international working language, and the increasing value of other working languages such as Arabic, Pashto or Dari.

4.5 Elites, language, and social class

Frequently, people tend to use accent as a basis for forming judgements about intelligence or trustworthiness. This tendency can result in what linguists refer to as accent bias or linguistic discrimination. In the context of language, social class and mobility, the Accent Bias in Britain Project (https://accentbiasbritain.org/) examines accent bias in terms of accessing elite professions (e.g., in law, financial services, or medicine). Sharma et al. (2019) and Levon et al. (2021) trace the ways that accent bias is connected to the perceived professional competence of different candidates and whether and in what ways accent bias shapes the evaluation of job candidates. Findings suggest consistent patterns of accent discrimination against Black and White working-class London accents, compared to perceived "standard" accents such as Received Pronunciation (RP) that are considered elite and prestigious and signal class status.

As Britain (2018) reminds us though, the nature of RP as an elite accent or an accent of the elite is not homogenous or fixed: "whilst RP like accents are bound, nevertheless, to be influential, the elite group today is likely to have a more diffuse, variable accent than the 'old' upper class was supposed to have had" (Britain 2018: 7). Relatedly, elite groups, as previously discussed, are also not homogenous entities. Whilst this strand of work does not explicitly use the frame of elite multilingualism, it centres the connections between language and social class in elite professions. This line of work also flags the perennial issues of linguistic stratification and hierarchisation of modes of speaking, which generate (new) elite multilinguals and elitist ways of thinking about language varieties and speakers. In a linguistically stratified job and education market, such studies underline one of the key concerns in elite multilingualism research: what causes a particular way of speaking to be perceived as more prestigious and advantageous than another? And what are the palpable effects for which segments of society?

In the context of migration and diaspora, Sharma (2021) traces the formation of transnational elites by analysing the speech patterns of second-generation young British Asians who increasingly incorporate educated Indian English, as one form of symbolic capital, into their communicative practices. Drawing on sociolinguistic methods, Sharma documents this changing shift from Indian English as a variety traditionally marked by low status to one marked by growing global prestige in and beyond India. As Sharma (2021: 682) notes, for some British Asians "this new exogenous form of symbolic capital is an alternative to the struggle for class mobility within the British system."

5. Perspectives for the future

Current scholarship on elite multilingualism has begun to explore the ways in which language functions as a gateway to local, national, and globally perceived elite (aspirational) lifestyles and elite status. As shown in this chapter, contexts for this research vary widely: from English as a medium of instruction, to elite bilingual education, the role of multilingualism in language work and professional life, transnationalism and mobilities, eliteness in lifestyles and contexts of labour, international and private education, and language learning in the context of migration, as well as accent and social class studies.

Exploring elite multilingualism is, at heart, an interdisciplinary project that calls for sociolinguistic, discursive, ethnographic, and other critically oriented approaches and methodologies in the social study of language — across disciplines, distinct social, cultural, and political contexts and local and urban regions around the globe. As indicated by the developments charted in this chapter, a substantial portion of scholarly work has been influenced by interdisciplinary perspectives, drawing upon fields such as political theory, sociology, anthropology, and education studies, besides the study of language. The field of pragmatics would certainly benefit from future in-depth discourse and ethnographic studies on elite multilingualism (as showcased in this chapter) that extend into adjacent disciplines. Such varied perspectives allow to fully explore how the connection between eliteness and language is concretised in practice to create distinction. At the same time, the topics presented in this chapter (e.g. elitism in education, eliteness as a linguistic and social aspiration, or eliteness as consumption and lifestyle) lend themselves to be further examined from a pragmatic perspective. Indeed, as a perspective in the field of pragmatics, elite multilingualism contributes to the wider project of making visible and denaturalising language hierarchisation practices that are tied to linguistic norms, social class, standardisation, and named languages as fixed entities that can be measured, counted and commodified.

From a sociological perspective, Savage and Williams (2008) have argued for bringing together elite studies and social class analysis. If we follow their argument, it is important to overcome the separation between scholarship on elites and social class and focus on the "top 1%" (that is, wealthy elites) in social class analysis and a theorisation of elites in class analysis. In contrast, for researchers in the field of pragmatics, it may be more useful to not reduce enquiries into elite multilingualism to the top 1% of society. Rather, as shown with this overview chapter, sociolinguists and discourse analysts have long emphasised the discursive and relational nature of eliteness and the need for mapping elite status as something that is not confined to material capital but which could also be an aspiration, irrespective of one's material wealth. Future research may thus consider exploring common topics in pragmatics in areas that studies on elite multilingualism in this chapter have highlighted.

Having said this, there remains a need for intersectional approaches to fully understanding how elite multilingualism intertwines with issues of social class, race, ethnicity, and gender. More work is needed to understand the ways in which elites and social class, which have traditionally been viewed as two distinct areas of research, connect or disconnect. Additionally, exploring what novel methodological approaches could be developed to conduct an intersectional analysis of language and elites is crucial. I concur with Vandrick's (2011) long-argued point that the field of TESOL, for instance, has not substantially addressed language and social class. Similarly, Motha (2014: 148) calls on language education professionals to notice and address "the workings of race, empire, and language ideologies in our practice." Inspired by such calls for more research, further studies in pragmatics are required to establish in what forms different types of elite multilingualism may feature in the creation of class, racial or gendered distinction.

Relatedly, new theoretical and empirical insights also need to be garnered as to how distinct language resources may become an essential element in embodying eliteness (for some), and what role institutions (public or private) play in (re)producing and circulating eliteness and elitist stances, and with what effect. To exemplify, such elitist stances may comprise the persistent discursive construction of native speakerism and White privilege, as shown in Ruecker and Ives' (2015) study of advertising discourse for a range of language schools in Japan, Korea, Thailand, and other Asian countries. Elitist stances may also be reflected in sustaining standard language or raciolinguistic ideologies that uphold and reproduce the perceived linguistic deficit of marginalised students in schools "through norm-referencing idealized whiteness as the standardized linguistic benchmark" (Cushing 2022: 316; see also Flores 2020).

During a period of increasing disparities between linguistic and social privilege and precarity across various facets of social life, more research is also required regarding the links between the formation of elites, elite status, and eliteness and processes of supranationalism, imperialism, colonialism, and racialisation. It is these very processes that exacerbate sociolinguistic inequality, sociolinguistic hierarchies in institutional contexts, and unequal practices of elite multilingualism. Opting for (aspirational) elites and the formation of elite status as a focal analytic point offers a valuable perspective in pragmatics for conducting linguistic research on pressing language and social issues.

Further reading

De Mejía, Ana María. 2002. *Power, Prestige, and Bilingualism: International Perspectives on Elite Bilingual Education*. UK: Multilingual Matters Ltd. (This groundbreaking work stands out as one of the first to deal with elite bilingual education programmes, with a particular emphasis on South American countries).

References

Bae, Sohee, and Joseph Sung-Yul Park. 2016. "Becoming global elites through transnational language learning?: The case of Korean early study abroad in Singapore." *L2 Journal* 8 (2): 92–109.

Baker, Colin, and Sylvia Prys-Jones. 1998. *Encyclopaedia of Bilingualism and Bilingual Education*. Clevedon: Multilingual Matters.

Barakos, Elisabeth, and Charlotte Selleck. 2019. "Elite multilingualism: Discourses, practices, and debate." *Journal of Multilingual and Multicultural Development* 40 (5): 367–374.

Barakos, Elisabeth. 2019. "Multilingual language trainers as language workers: A discourse-ethnographic investigation." *Language and Intercultural Communication* 19 (2): 184–200.

Barakos, Elisabeth. 2022. "Language work and affect in adult language education." *Journal of Sociolinguistics* 26: 26–44.

Bernstein, Basil. 1971. *Class, Codes and Control Vol. 1: Theoretical Studies Towards a Sociology of Language*. London: Routledge.

Block, David. 2014. *Social Class in Applied Linguistics*. London: Routledge.

Block, David. 2017. "What on earth is 'Language commodification'?" In *Sloganizations in Language Education Discourse*, ed. by Susanne Breidbach, Lutz Küster, and Barbara Schmenk, 19–36. Bristol: Multilingual Matters.

Blommaert, Jan. 2011. "The long language-ideological debate in Belgium." *Journal of Multicultural Discourses* 6 (3): 241–256.

Bourdieu, Pierre. 1984. *Distinction: A Social Critique of the Judgement of Taste*. London: Routledge.

Bourdieu, Pierre. 1991. *Language and Symbolic Power*. 1st ed. Cambridge: Polity Press.

Britain, David. 2018. "Beyond the 'gentry aesthetic': Elites, received pronunciation and the dialectological gaze in England." In *Elite Discourse: The Rhetorics of Status, Privilege and Power*, ed. by Crispin Thurlow and Adam Jaworski, 46–56. London: Routledge.

Bunyi, Grace. 2008. "Constructing elites in Kenya: Implications for classroom language practices in Africa." In *Encyclopedia of Language and Education*, ed. by Nancy H. Hornberger. Boston, MA: Springer.

Butler, Yuko, and Kenji Hakuta. 2004. "Bilingualism and second language acquisition." In *The Handbook of Bilingualism*, ed. by Tej K. Bhatia and William C. Ritchie, 114–144. Oxford: Blackwell Publishing.

Chun, Christian W. 2019. "Language, discourse, and class: What's next for sociolinguistics?" *Sociolinguistics* 23: 332–345.

Codó, Eva. 2018. "The intersection of global mobility, lifestyle and ELT work: A critical examination of language instructors' trajectories." *Language and Intercultural Communication* 18 (4): 436–450.

Codó, Eva, and Anna Sunyol. 2019. "'A plus for our students': The construction of Mandarin Chinese as an elite language in an international school in Barcelona." *Journal of Multilingual and Multicultural Development* 40 (5): 436–452.

Cushing, Ian. 2022. "Word rich or word poor? Deficit discourses, raciolinguistic ideologies and the resurgence of the 'word gap' in England's education policy." *Critical Inquiry in Language Studies* 20 (4): 305–331.

Davies, Alan. 2003. *The Native Speaker: Myth and Reality*. Clevedon: Multilingual Matters.

Day, Dennis, and Johannes Wagner. 2007. "Bilingual professionals." In *Handbook of Multilingualism and Multilingual Communication*, ed. by Peter Auer and Li Wei, 391–404. Berlin: De Gruyter.

De Costa, Peter I. 2019. "Elite multilingualism, affect and neoliberalism." *Journal of Multilingual and Multicultural Development* 40 (5): 453–460.

De Mejía, Anne-Marie. 2002. *Power, Prestige, and Bilingualism: International Perspectives on Elite Bilingual Education*. Clevedon: Multilingual Matters.

De Mejía, Anne-Marie. 2013. "Elite/folk bilingual education." In *The Encyclopedia of Applied Linguistics*, ed. by Carol A. Chapelle, 1858–1863. Oxford: Blackwell Publishing.

Drewski, Daniel. 2023. "Language and symbolic boundaries among transnational elites: A qualitative case study of European commission officials." *Global Networks* 00: e12434.

Eckert, Penelope. 2000. *Linguistic Variation as Social Practice*. London: Wiley-Blackwell.

Erling, Elizabeth J. 2017. "Development aid, language planning and English education in Bangladesh." *Current Issues in Language Planning* 11 (4): 388–406.

Fishman, Joshua A. 1977. "The social science perspective." In *Bilingual Education: Current Perspectives*, ed. by Joshua A. Fishman, 14–62. Arlington: Center for Applied Linguistics.

Flores, Nelson, Amelia Tseng, and Nicholas Subtirelu (eds) 2020. *Bilingualism for All? Raciolinguistic Perspectives on Dual Language Education in the United States*. Bristol: Multilingual Matters.

Flores, Nelson. 2020. "From academic language to language architecture: Challenging raciolinguistic ideologies in research and practice." *Theory Into Practice* 59 (1): 22–31.

Gal, Susan. 2006. "Migration, minorities and multilingualism: Language ideologies in Europe." In *Language Ideologies, Policies and Practices*, ed. by Claire Mar-Molinero and Patrick Stevenson, 13–27. London: Palgrave Macmillan.

García, Ofelia. 2009. *Bilingual Education in the 21st Century: A Global Perspective*. Oxford: Blackwell Publishing.

Garrido, Maria Rosa. 2017. "Multilingualism and cosmopolitanism in the construction of a humanitarian elite." *Social Semiotics* 27 (3): 359–369.

Garrido, Maria Rosa. 2021. "The evolution of language ideological debates about English and French in a multilingual humanitarian organisation." *Language Policy* 21 (1): 47–73.

Guerrero, Carlos. 2010. "Elite vs. folk bilingualism: The mismatch between theories and educational and social conditions." *HOW, A Colombian Journal for Teachers of English* 17 (1): 165–179.

Gaztambide-Fernández, Rubén. 2009. "What Is an Elite Boarding School?" *Review of Educational Research* 79 (3): 1090–1128.

Heller, Monica, and Alexandre Duchêne. 2016. "Treating language as an economic resource: Discourse, data, debates." In *Sociolinguistics: Theoretical Debates*, ed. by Nikolas Coupland, 139–156. New York: Cambridge University Press.

Heller, Monica. 1995. "Language choice, social institutions, and symbolic domination." *Language in Society* 24 (3): 373–405.

Heller, Monica. 2002. "Globalization and the commodification of bilingualism in Canada." In *Globalization and Language Teaching*, ed. by David Block and Deborah Cameron, 47–63. London: Routledge.

Heller, Monica. 2006. *Linguistic Minorities and Modernity: A Sociolinguistic Ethnography*. 2nd ed. London: Continuum.

Heller, Monica. 2020. "Sociolinguistic frontiers: Emancipation and equality." *International Journal of the Sociology of Language* 263: 121–126.

Howard, Adam. 2019. "Enduring privilege: Schooling and elite formation in the United States." *Zeitschrift für Pädagogik* 65: 178–191.

Howard, Adam, and Rubén A. Gaztambide-Fernández. 2010. *Educating Elites: Class Privilege and Educational Advantage*. Lanham, MD: Rowman and Littlefield.

Howard, Adam, and Jane Kenway. 2015. "Canvassing conversations: Obstinate issues in studies of elites and elite education." *International Journal of Qualitative Studies in Education* 28 (9): 1005–1032.

Hüning, Matthias, Ulrike Vogl, and Olivier Moliner (eds). 2012. *Standard Languages and Multilingualism in European History*. Amsterdam: John Benjamins.

Jahan, Ismat, and M. Obaidul Hamid. 2019. "English as a medium of instruction and the discursive construction of elite identity." *Journal of Sociolinguistics* 23: 386–408.

Jaspers, Jurgen. 2009. "Inleiding [Introduction]." In *De klank van de stad: Stedelijke meertaligheid en interculturele communicatie [The Sound of the City: Urban Multilingualism and Intercultural Communication]*, ed. by Jurgen Jaspers, 7–32. Antwerp: Acco.

Khan, Shamus Rahman. 2012. "The sociology of elites." *Annual Review of Sociology* 38: 361–377.

Khan, Shamus Rahman. 2016. "The education of elites in the United States." *L'Année Sociologique* 66 (1): 171–192.

Kramsch, Claire. 2014. "Teaching foreign languages in an era of globalization: Introduction." *The Modern Language Journal* 98 (1): 296–311.

Kubota, Ryuko. 2011. "Learning a foreign language as leisure and consumption: Enjoyment, desire, and the business of Eikaiwa." *International Journal of Bilingual Education and Bilingualism* 14 (4): 473–488.

Kubota, Ryuko. 2014. "The multi/plural turn, postcolonial theory, and neoliberal multiculturalism: Complicities and implications for applied linguistics." *Applied Linguistics* 37: 474–494.

Labov, William. 1966. *The Social Stratification of English in New York City*. Washington, D.C.: Center for Applied Linguistics.

Levon, Erez, Devyani Sharma, Dominic J.L. Watt, Andréa Cardoso, and Yirong Ye. 2021. "Accent bias and perceptions of professional competence in England." *Journal of English Linguistics* 49 (4): 355–388.

Liberali, Fernanda Coelho, and Aline Helena Megale. 2016. "Elite bilingual education in Brazil: An applied linguist's perspective." *Colombian Applied Linguistics Journal* 18 (2): 95–108.

Lin, Angel. 2015. "Egalitarian bi/multilingualism and trans-semiotizing in a global world." In *The Handbook of Bilingual and Multilingual Education*, ed. by Wayne E. Wright, Sovicheth Boun, and Ofelia García, 17–37. Wiley-Blackwell.

Lorente, Beatriz P. 2017. *Scripts of Servitude: Language, Labor Migration and Transnational Domestic Work*. Bristol: Multilingual Matters.

Lovrits, Valéria, and Julia de Bres. 2021. "Prestigious language, pigeonholed speakers: Stances towards the 'native English speaker' in a multilingual European institution." *Journal of Sociolinguistics* 25: 398–417.

Mapes, Gwynne. 2021. *Elite Authenticity: Remaking Distinction in Food Discourse*. New York: Oxford University Press.

Mapes, Gwynne. 2023. "The life of a political speech(writer): Metadiscursive text trajectories in high-end language work." *Journal of Linguistic Anthropology* 33 (3): 264–284.

Maxwell, Claire. 2015. "'Elites': Some questions for a new research agenda." In *Elites, Privilege and Excellence: The National and Global Redefinition of Educational Advantage*, ed. by Agnès Van Zanten, Stephen Ball, and Brigitte Darchy-Koechlin, 15–28. London: Routledge.

Maxwell, Claire, and Peter Aggleton. 2015. *Elite Education: International Perspectives*. London: Routledge.

McIntosh, Peggy. 1988. White Privilege and Male Privilege: A personal account of coming to see correspondences through work in women's studies. (Working Paper 189). Wellesley, MA: Wellesley College Center for Research on Women.

Motha, Suhanthie. 2014. *Race, Empire, and English Language Teaching: Creating Responsible and Ethical Anti-Racist Practice*. New York: Teachers College Press.

Myers-Scotton, Carol. 1993. "Elite closure as a powerful language strategy: The African case." *International Journal of the Sociology of Language* 1993 (103): 149–164.

Ngũgĩ, wa Thiong'o. 1985. 'The language of African literature', *New Left Review*, 109–127.

Ortega, Lourdes. 2018. "SLA in uncertain times: Disciplinary constraints, transdisciplinary hopes." *Working Papers in Educational Linguistics* 33 (1): 1–30.

Paquet, Marianne, and Caroline Levasseur. 2019. "When bilingualism isn't enough: Perspectives of new speakers of French on multilingualism in Montreal." *Journal of Multilingual and Multicultural Development* 40 (5): 375–391.

Park, Joseph Sung-Yul. 2010. "Images of 'good English' in the Korean conservative press: Three processes of interdiscursivity." *Pragmatics and Society* 1 (2): 189–208.

Park, Joseph Sung-Yul. 2016. "Language as pure potential." *Journal of Multilingual and Multicultural Development* 37 (5): 453–466.

Park, Joseph Sung-Yul. 2019. "Rethinking class in sociolinguistics: Series introduction." *Journal of Sociolinguistics* 23 (4): 331.

Paulston, Christina Bratt. 1975. "Ethnic relations and bilingual education: Accounting for contradictory data." *Working Papers on Bilingualism* 6: 368–401.

Paulston, Christina Bratt. 1978. "Education in a bi/multilingual setting." *International Review of Education* 24 (3): 309–328.

Pérez-Milans, Miguel. 2014. "Mandarin Chinese in London education: Language aspirations in a working-class secondary school." *Language Policy* 14 (2): 153–181.

Piller, Ingrid. 2016. *Linguistic diversity and social justice: An introduction to applied sociolinguistics.* Oxford: Oxford University Press.

Plöger, Susanne, and Elisabeth Barakos. 2021. "Researching linguistic transitions of newly-arrived students in Germany: Insights from institutional ethnography and reflexive grounded theory." *Ethnography and Education* 16 (4): 402–419.

Rydenvald, Malin. 2015. "Elite bilingualism? Language use among multilingual teenagers of Swedish background in European schools and international schools in Europe." *Journal of Research in International Education* 14 (3): 213–227.

Rampton, Ben, Roxy Harris, James Collins, and Jan Blommaert. 2008. "Language, class and education." In *Kluwer Encyclopedia of Language and Education*, ed. by Nancy H. Hornberger, 71–81. Boston: Springer.

Rampton, Ben. 2006. *Language in late modernity. Interaction in an urban school.* Cambridge: Cambridge University Press.

Rampton, Ben. 2010. "Social class and sociolinguistics." *Applied Linguistics Review* 1: 1–22.

Relaño-Pastor, Ana María, and Ana Fernández-Barrera. 2019. "The 'native speaker effects' in the construction of elite bilingual education in Castilla-La Mancha: Tensions and dilemmas." *Journal of Multilingual and Multicultural Development* 40 (5): 421–435.

Reyes, Adrienne. 2017. "Inventing postcolonial elites: Race, language, mix, excess." *Journal of Linguistic Anthropology* 27 (2): 210–231.

Ruecker, Todd, and Laura Ives. 2015. "White native English speakers needed: The rhetorical construction of privilege in online teacher recruitment spaces." *TESOL Quarterly* 49: 733–756.

Ruiz, Richard. 1984. "Orientations in language planning." *NABE Journal* 8: 15–34.

Sah, Pramod K., and Jeevan Karki. 2023. "Elite appropriation of English as a medium of instruction policy and epistemic inequalities in Himalayan schools." *Journal of Multilingual and Multicultural Development* 44 (1): 20–34.

Savage, Mike, and Kevin Williams (eds). 2008. *Remembering Elites.* Oxford: Blackwell.

Savage, Mike, Niall Cunningham, Fiona Devine, Sam Friedman, Daniel Laurison, Lisa McKenzie, Andrew Miles, Helene Snee, and Paul Wakeling. 2015. *Social Class in the 21st Century.* Pelican.

Scott, John. 2008. "Modes of power and the re-conceptualization of elites." In *Remembering Elites*, ed. by Mike Savage and Kevin Williams, 27–43. Oxford: Blackwell.

Selleck, Charlotte, and Elisabeth Barakos. 2019. "Elite multilingualism." In *The Routledge Handbook of Linguistic Ethnography*, ed. by Karin Tusting, 286–298. London: Routledge.

Shankar, Shalini, and Jillian R. Cavanaugh. 2012. "Language and materiality in global capitalism." *Annual review of anthropology* 41 (1): 355–369.

Sharma, Devyani. 2021. "Social class across borders: Transnational elites in British ideological space." *Journal of Sociolinguistics* 25: 682–702.

Sharma, Devyani, Erez Levon, Dominic Watt, Yirong Ye, and Andréa Cardoso. 2019. "Methods for the study of accent bias and access to elite professions." *Journal of Language and Discrimination* 3 (2): 150–172.

Snell, Julia. 2018. "Solidarity, stance, and class identities." *Language in Society* 47 (5): 665–691.

Sonntag, Selma. 2003. *The Local Politics of Global English: Case Studies in Linguistic Globalization.* Lanham: Lexington Books.

Sunyol, Alícia. 2019. Multilingualism, Elitism and Ideologies of Globalism in International Schools in Catalonia: An Ethnographic Study. PhD dissertation.

Tarc, Paul, and Ana Tarc. 2015. "Elite international schools in the Global South: Transnational space, class relationalities and the 'middling' international schoolteacher." *British Journal of Sociology of Education* 36 (1): 34–52.

Thurlow, Crispin, and Adam Jaworski. 2012. "Elite mobilities: The semiotic landscapes of luxury and privilege." *Social Semiotics* 22 (5): 487–516.

Thurlow, Crispin, and Adam Jaworski. 2014. "Visible-invisible: The social semiotics of labour in luxury tourism." In *Elite Mobilities*, ed. by Thomas Birtchnell and Javier Caletrío, 176–193. London: Routledge.

Thurlow, Crispin, and Adam Jaworski. 2017. "Introducing elite discourse: The rhetorics of status, privilege, and power." *Social Semiotics* 27 (3): 243–254.

Thurlow, Crispin, and Adam Jaworski. (eds). 2019. *Elite Discourse: The Rhetorics of Status, Privilege and Power.* London: Routledge.

Thurlow, Crispin (ed). 2020. *The Business of Words: Wordsmiths, Linguists and Other Language Workers.* London: Routledge.

Vandrick, Stephanie. 2011. "Students of the new global elite." *TESOL Quarterly* 45 (1): 160–169.

Van Zanten, Agnès. 2018. *Elites in Education.* London: Routledge.

Van Zanten, Agnès, Stephen J. Ball, and Brigitte Darchy-Koechlin (eds). 2015. *World Yearbook of Education 2015: Elites, Privilege and Excellence: The National and Global Redefinition of Educational Advantage.* 1st ed. London: Routledge.

Vessey, Rachael, and Ellen Nicolai. 2023. "The language ideologies of multilingual nannies in London." *Journal of Sociolinguistics* 27: 221–244.

Waters, Johanna. 2018. "Elites." *British Journal of Sociology of Education* 39 (3): 412–419.

Formulaic language

Natalia Filatkina
University of Hamburg

1. Introduction

Formulaic language research has spanned phraseology, spoken language research/interactional linguistics, corpus linguistics, text and discourse studies, Construction Grammar as well as the framework of Discourse Traditions. Concepts developed in these areas enable an exchange of ideas, though only a few concepts have been included in this dialogue so far. The present chapter highlights the common aspects and the differences between these various concepts in the way they are discussed within the area of Germanic linguistics. The chapter aims at answering two questions: (a) in what sense these concepts can be regarded as related and (b) how the differences between them, if any, can be mediated. Section 2 focuses on the notion of formulaic language. Section 3 gives a brief outline of selected research directions that appear to provide a particularly promising connecting link to the concept of formulaic language. The selection presented in Sections 3.1–3.5 is guided by their comparability with the concept of formulaic language from the point of view of Germanic linguistics.[1] Section 4 sums up the findings.

2. Formulaic language: Starting point and a working definition

The existence of formulaic patterns in the widest sense (including phrasemes, constructions, non-literal units, and/or other prefabs) has been hypothesized for all languages of the world, even though predominantly only languages with a long written tradition and codified norms have been studied so far (for new data, cf. Piirainen et al. 2020). Erman and Warren (2000: 37) state that approximately 55% of all verbal utterances are so-called prefabs that consist of at least two words and are cognitively stable (cf. also Bybee and Torres Cacoullos 2002). Tomasello (2003), Behrens (2011), and Filatkina (2019) show to what extent these findings affect both L1 and L2 language acquisition processes.

---

1. For a more detailed analysis that is not restricted to linguistics only, cf. Filatkina (2018). See a recent overview also in Stein and Stumpf (2019).

Corpus linguistic studies were among the first to deliver empirical evidence for the formulaic nature of human communication and to suggest a shift of paradigms.[2] Languages generally provide their speakers with considerable freedom in how to achieve their communicative goals in the most effective way. The success of a communicative act depends not only on a good choice of single words and the correct application of grammatical rules, but also on an appropriate combination of words and rules with regard to the pragmatic aspects of a certain communicative situation. All forms of oral and written human interaction result from a large number of complex choices that Sinclair (1991: 110) described as "the open choice principle." This linguistic fact seems to be a truism now. Nevertheless, Sinclair also called attention to the fact that although some word combinations, sentences, and texts are the results of a complex choice based on linguistic freedom and creativity, others include "a large number of semi-preconstructed phrases that constitute single choices ("the idiom principle"), even though they might appear to be analysable into segments" (Sinclair 1991: 110). In this sense, "the open choice principle" meets "the idiom principle." In what follows, "the idiom principle" is addressed with the term *formulaic language/patterns*.

Despite this fact, there is no definitive answer to the question of what formulaic language is and what it is not. The term "formulaic language/formulaic patterns" is applied to a wide range of highly heterogeneous phenomena and unites very different (linguistic) approaches to language. By its very nature, the concept has fuzzy boundaries and has been criticized for this. However, as will be shown below, the fuzziness does not necessarily hamper the operationalization of the concept. On the contrary, it opens it up for manifold applications depending on the research questions involved. Formulaic language might include:

a. phrasemes (collocations, idioms, routine formulae, proverbs, and sayings) with different degrees of lexicalization (Sections 3.1–3.2),
b. conventionalized patterns in the micro- and macrostructure of text types (Sections 3.2–3.3),
c. conventional patterns of speech acts and argumentation at the level of discourse (Section 3.3), and
d. various types of constructions in the Construction Grammar sense (including abstract grammatical structures such as ditransitive or resultative constructions, Section 3.4),
e. as well as various realizations of general cultural traditions (Section 3.5).

---

2. Cf. Firth (1957), Stubbs (2001), Steyer's notion of habitual word combinations ("usuelle Wortverbindungen", Steyer 2013) and Bubenhofer's work on recurrent patterns of language use ("Sprachgebrauchsmuster", Bubenhofer 2009).

Even though there is no common definition of the term, a consensus has been reached with regard to the main criteria of formulaic patterns. These are: recurrence, conventional character, historicity, replicability, and adaptability to a specific situation of communication including variation and change (Stein and Stumpf 2019: 19). The existence of formulaic patterns in this broad sense has been hypothetically ascribed to all languages, even though predominantly only languages with a long written tradition and codified norms have been studied so far (for new data cf. Piirainen et al. 2020). Needless to say, any written or oral text can be considered formulaic with regard to these criteria. What types of formulaic patterns contribute to this characterization and how dominant they are in each individual text can vary considerably (cf. a novel vs. an employment contract). Due to the diverse nature of the phenomenon in question individual studies in the field of formulaic language normally do not aim to cover all aspects. Instead, they focus on selected criteria; cf. one of the earliest and well-received definitions in Wray (2002: 9), according to which a formulaic pattern is

> a sequence, continuous or discontinuous, of words or other elements, which is, or appears to be, prefabricated: that is stored and retrieved whole from memory at the time of use, rather than being subject to generation or analysis by the language grammar.
> (Wray 2002: 9)

At first glance, the definition does not suggest the inclusion of regular compositional units such as *large number* (as opposed to *great number*) in the concept of formulaic language. However, Wray (2002: 10 and 2013: 2200–2201) explicitly favors this inclusion in the same way as she includes units with a fairly high degree of lexical and morphosyntactic variation of their form, as in (1):

(1) NP$_i$ set + TENSE POSS$_i$ *sights on (V)* NP$_j$
 the teacher had set his sights on promotion
 I've set my sights on winning that cup

Additionally, the parenthesis "or appears to be" in the quotation above supports this inclusion as it leaves room for variation: formulaic patterns do not have to be holistic in that they are permanently subject to change. According to Wray (2002: 5), this is due to the changing needs of human communication that reflect changes in the society and are not necessary primarily linguistically motivated. Diachronically oriented studies of formulaic patterns show that this openness is the prerequisite that makes it possible to grasp emerging formulaic patterns in historical texts. The parenthesis, which might seem theoretically non-precise and difficult to operationalize, can easily be justified methodologically from a diachronic point of view. Based on the analysis of an extensive data set from older varieties of German, Filatkina (2018: 1 and 164) defines formulaic language in a broad sense. According to these studies, formulaic language

a. includes single words, typologically heterogeneous combinations of words, sentences, and texts
b. that might be understood holistically,
c. can show varying degrees of conventionalization (ranging from high to low) regarding their form, meaning and functions, but have a stable underlying syntactic and/or cognitive structure,
d. are based on and reflect the cultural and communicative traditions of the society they are used in, and
e. which can be characterized by a considerable degree of functionalization in the production and reception of a particular act of oral communication, written text (genre) or spoken discourse.

3. Many shades of formulaic patterns: A brief outline of related concepts

3.1 Phraseology

An early attempt to grasp the complex nature of formulaic language was undertaken within the framework of phraseology on the basis of Slavic, Romance, and Germanic languages and dates back to the 1960s. The term "formulaic language" was not used in this paradigm. Instead, the units under investigation were described as phrasemes. According to Burger (2015), phrasemes are polylexical items that must consist of at least two words, have a more or less stable form in which they are frequently reproduced by speakers and can (but do not have to) be idiomatic in meaning. Research was traditionally focused mainly on one type of polylexical word combination, namely idioms such as *spill the beans* or *break the ice*, because they fulfilled all the above-mentioned criteria. This focus was one of the reasons that prevented (a) the development of a strong theoretical framework within the sphere of phraseological research and (b) the inclusion of phraseological units in theoretical linguistic discussions. As Feilke (1994: 377) puts it, research into phraseology functions as "a receptacle of theoretically not clarified problems of linguistics."

By contrast, newer linguistic theories such as usage-based approaches to Construction Grammar (Section 3.4), corpus linguistics, or text and discourse studies (Section 3.3) show that the formulaic character of human communication reaches far beyond the items that can meet the criteria of phrasemes.[3] Furthermore, the pivotal role of formulaic patterns can be observed not only in modern languages but also at historical stages of language development (cf. Filatkina 2013; Filatkina and Hanauska 2010; Filatkina, Gottwald and

---

3. Language acquisition (Tomasello 2003) and language loss (Wray 2008, 2012) are strongly interwoven with formulaic patterns. Filatkina (2018: 38–45; 2019) provides an overview.

Hanauska 2009; Hanauska 2014; Gottwald and Hanauska 2013; Hoff 2012; Filatkina 2018 gives an overview of studies for languages other than German). These studies show that the criteria established for phrasemes on the basis of modern languages turn out to be static and therefore not applicable to the study of the diachronic dynamics of formulaic patterns. Polylexicality appears to be problematic from the outset because of the general lack of any (standardized mandatory) spelling norms in the language history. Stability is the exception rather than the rule in historical language use, frequency cannot be employed due to the fragmentary character of historical textual heritage (among other more substantial restraints), and idiomaticity often poses problems resulting from the temporal and cultural distance between today's researcher and the text under investigation.

Moreover, the research conducted for Old German (Filatkina 2018) shows that the accepted criteria with which we are familiar from existing theories of language change do not apply to the emergence and conventionalization processes of formulaic patterns in the same way as, e.g., to sound change, grammatical or even lexical change. Such criteria as frequency of use and codification/normatization seem to play a less significant role. By contrast, creative modification, irregularity as well as the role of cultural and textual/ discourse traditions in which a formulaic pattern is embedded are of crucial importance. Weber (2015) illustrates the latter for formulaic patterns with the example of *notwithstanding* in English. This loan pattern, which emulates French and Latin models, initially served above all to express a legal practice that had been adopted from papal practice, the so-called *non obstantibus*-formula. The adoption of a legal concept thus went hand in hand with the imitation of the corresponding patterns with indigenous means.[4]

3.2 Spoken language research

Parallel to phraseological research and strongly influenced by the sociological concept of communicative genres (cf. "*kommunikative Gattung*"), formulaic language was one of the central objects of research on spoken language (Coulmas 1981; Stein 1995) and oral poetry, and of ritual studies (Werlen 1984; Rauch 1992), conversation analysis and most recently interactional linguistics (Gumperz 1982; Selting and Couper-Kuhlen 2000; Fiehler et al. 2004; Deppermann 2004, 2007). For a long time, formulaicity was even reduced to spoken language and considered its main stylistic attribute. Luckmann (1986) defines communicative genres (e.g. greeting) as communicative processes that have become socially conventionalized. According to Günthner and Knoblauch (1994: 703), they are realized through the use of typical "combinations of different recurrent elements on both the paradigmatic and syntagmatic level." The recurrent elements include the prosodic design, choice of words, syntax, word combinations, selection of topics, rhetoric topoi, and figures of speech. Since then, chapters on formulaic patterns have

---

4. For more examples from different languages and dialects, cf. Dobrovol'skij and Piirainen (2021).

been a compulsory part of all linguistic introductions to spoken language (for German, cf. e.g. Schwitalla 2012). Koch and Oesterreicher (2011: 3–20) point out their importance for the language of immediacy as they contribute to the creation of such factors as privacy, intimacy, emotionality, dialogic nature, and spontaneity.[5] Oral poetry research explains the pivotal role of formulaic patterns predominantly through mnemonic necessity. The lack of written tradition dictates the formal design of texts by rhyme and rhythm, syntactic symmetries, phonetic assonances, and alliterations; it also influences the meaning of the formulaic utterances.

The underlying assumption of the more recent linguistically oriented research is that language use consists of solving communicative tasks, many of which are recurrent, and conventional communication forms/practices (Fiehler et al. 2004). The handling of such tasks can be facilitated if linguistic utterances do not have to be produced each time in a new way but can be reproduced as conventional formulaic patterns. Conventions of social linguistic interaction are historical phenomena by nature and can change in space and time. Language structures are therefore not to be understood as an abstract system containing specified individual elements that are combined into sentences, but as units that are actively (re)produced in a context-bound manner and adapted to the requirements of a given interaction. Thus, language structures are products of the consolidation of social interactions or, in interactional linguistic terms, products of sedimentation. The speakers' metalinguistic knowledge of the conventionalized communicative practices and individual formulaic patterns on the one hand and the ability to make the right choice from the variety of non-conventionalized utterances available to speakers on the other have been addressed in various studies under the term "communicative competence" (Hymes 1987: 35–71) or "conversational competence" (Deppermann 2004: 15–33).

3.3 Text and discourse linguistics

The functions of formulaic language have been studied within the scope of text and discourse linguistics. Under the influence of the findings of cognitive psychology on the pivotal role of schemes, frames, and scripts in the process of knowledge acquisition, storage, and use, text linguistics has adopted the notion of text production as a cognitive process and of texts as the results of dynamic mental processes. Since then, the notion of so-called global patterns, complex patterns, or text patterns (cf. German *"globale Muster," "komplexe Muster," "Textmuster"* in Heinemann and Heinemann 2002: 129–165) has been at the center of the text linguistic research program (Fillmore 1976; van Dijk 1980; Gumperz 1982; Antos 1989). Warnke (1999: 219) stresses the existence of the "standardized forms of

---

5. But formulaic patterns can also be shown to be of key importance for the language of distance, according to Koch and Oesterreicher's framework.

verbal interaction" that contribute to "the formal and semantic organization of linguistic actions with regard to their functions."

These concepts refer not only to the linguistic surface of texts or individual formulaic patterns but more so to larger schematic units in the macrostructure and layout of texts. They demonstrate that different text types can be formulaic to a different degree: a piece of literary fiction would show a different (and probably less formal) type of macrostructural formulaicity than an official letter, a recipe, an employment contract, or an invitation. For texts with a high degree of formulaic macrostructure, the text linguistic research suggests the term "formulaic text" (*"formelhafte Texte"*, cf. Dausendschön-Gay, Gülich and Kraft 2007). At the same time, global patterns are also understood as orientation schemes based on successful communicative experiences, which allow individuals to act and re-act appropriately while producing and interpreting texts (cf. also the concept of Discourse Traditions in Section 3.5). Global patterns thus also involve the speakers' knowledge of the specifics of text (type) design in agreement with the conventions established in a society. The conventional application of this knowledge appears to be necessary in the production of any text type, regardless of the degree and strength of its formulaic nature. Feilke (1994, 1996) puts this notion at the center of his concept of "common sense competence", which is based on the mechanism of *"idiomatische Prägung"* (Feilke 1994: 238 and 366). *"Idiomatische Prägung"* spans three main levels of human interaction.[6] At the syntagmatic level of word combinations, Feilke (1994: 376; 1996: 240–311) distinguishes syntactic coinage (*"syntaktische Prägung"* in his terms, cf. the examples in (2) taken from German); at the level of semantic conceptualization and denotation — semantic coinage (3), and at the level of social interaction and/or communicative performance — pragmatic coinage (4).

(2) [sentence 1]   *geschweige denn*
                    'let alone'
    [sentence 2];   *solange*
                    'as long as'
    [sentence 1], [sentence 2]; *Wenn ich dich richtig verstehe*
                    'if I understand you right' [...]

(3) *ab und zu*
    'now and then'
    ins Gras beißen
    'to kick the bucket'
    über den Berg sein
    'to be over the mountain'

---

6. Each type at each level is subdivided even further; cf. an overview in Feilke (1996: 217–320).

(4) *Ich liebe dich!*
'I love you',
Verstehen Sie mich nicht falsch
'Do not understand me wrong'

Thus, formulaic character gives a text its own cultural value, which Tophinke (1996: 103) describes as "cultural expressiveness." The link between a formulaic pattern and a context ensures that speakers resort to appropriate units in the process of communication (Stein 1995, 2003).[7] Evidence for such links has already been provided from different research perspectives (cf. Koch 1997; Stumpf and Filatkina 2018 for modern German; Filatkina 2018: 310–374 for Old German; Wray 2009: 36 and Wray and Perkins 2000: 7 for English), recently also within the model of Construction Discourse in Östman (2005, 2015; Section 3.4).

Formulaic patterns in a narrow phraseological sense (routine formulae, idioms, collocations, cf. Section 3.1) have traditionally been considered a constitutive part of global patterns even though they were not always explicitly addressed as such. For instance, explaining the term "text pattern," Heinemann and Heinemann (2002: 130–131) use almost exclusively phrasemes in the traditional phraseology sense (Section 3.1), without, however, explicitly drawing attention to their multi-word nature. Adamzik (1995: 28) speaks of communicative routines; Heinemann (2000a: 516) of style patterns or parts-of-text patterns (cf. German "Text-Teilmuster"); Heinemann (2000b: 356–369) and Gülich and Hausendorf (2000: 369–385) of patterns of text production ("*Vertextungsmuster*"), to name just a few terms. Expressions like *I would like to conclude, firstly, the following study aims at [...]* structure the text and facilitate the identification of different texts as examples of a certain type of text (here: scientific prose) (cf. Stein 2010; Linke 2001 for obituaries; Stein 2011 for advertisements).[8] One of the most important findings of the text linguistic approaches was the relativization of the role of frequency in the emergence of formulaic patterns (Feilke 1994: 226). A pattern becomes conventionalized not just due to its frequent use but only if it is sufficiently embedded in a specific text or discourse tradition, i.e. if a pattern satisfies the speakers' communicative/pragmatic needs in a certain communicative situation.

Discourse studies address the issue of formulaic language as recurrent regularities in language use ("*Regelmäßigkeiten im Sprachgebrauch*", cf. Busse 2005: 305; Busse and Teubert 2013: 13–30).[9] The detailed corpus-based analysis of such regularities should

---

7. Linke (2003) gives some examples from a diachronic perspective and analyzes the cultural boundedness of the collocation *Spaß haben* 'to have fun'. Cf. also Linke (2011).
8. Sabban (2007) uses the term "text production power" („*textbildende Potenz*") with regard to this function of individual formulaic patterns. Cf. also the function of discourse marking in Wray (2002: 101; Wray and Perkins 2000: 1–28).

allow conclusions to be drawn about collective knowledge, mentality, ways of thinking and feeling, aims, and goals of a certain society in a certain discourse.[10]

3.4 Construction grammars (CxG) and construction discourse (CxD)

Formulaic patterns provide evidence for the necessity of understanding language not as a system organized at different levels (e.g. lexicon and grammar) but as a continuum of different linguistic and extra-linguistic domains that have to be described in their entirety. Within the paradigm of Construction Grammar (CxG) (and Cognitive Grammar), formulaic patterns have played a central role from the very beginning (Fillmore, Kay, and O'Connor 1988 on *let alone*; Goldberg 1995; Langacker 1987). In fact, it was the inability of other (particularly formal) language theories to describe "exceptions," i.e. formulaic utterances as in (3–4), that led to the establishment of CxG.

One of its major principles is the assumption that a human language consists of signs representing conventionalized form/meaning correspondences that are not strictly predictable from the properties of their component parts or from other constructions. The term "construction" is generally applied to generalizations over typologically very different language instances, regular and irregular, ranging from morphemes and compounds (*door frame* or *lighthouse*) over idioms (*spill the beans*) and degree modifiers (*sort of/ kind of*) to abstract constructions such as caused-motion, ditransitive or resultative constructions. They differ with regard to their cognitive representations (from concrete verbal utterances to abstract cognitive schemas), but all tend to have a more or less restricted structure that has a certain meaning as well as different lexical slots whose specification can vary depending on the context (cf. examples in Stefanowitsch 2013; Stefanowitsch and Gries 2003). All these extremely heterogeneous constructions stand on equal footing in building the basis for human communication and understanding processes, without being ascribed exclusively to core grammar or to the lexicon. As Goldberg (2003: 223) puts it, "the network of constructions captures our knowledge of language in *toto* — in other words, it's constructions all the way down."

Even though CxG includes utterances like idioms, it nevertheless remains a theory of grammar, not of a language as a whole, mainly because the constructional analysis is hardly ever taken beyond the sentence level.[11] However, CxG acknowledges that language is intricately interwoven with most other aspects of human behavior (cotextual,

---

9. It should be mentioned that the term "discourse" does not refer to oral texts, but is used here in the research tradition of Germanic linguistics where it means a transtextual and epistemic debate on a certain topic (e.g. migration) that is conducted in a number of different texts, shared by social groups of different sizes and expressed by virtue of various verbal and visual means (Gardt 2007: 30).

10. Cf. selected contributions in Stumpf and Filatkina (2018: 283–375).

11. For a different approach, cf. Stumpf and Stein (2024).

contextual, or intertextual information; cf. Fillmore 1982). With its origins in Fillmore's research, the concept of Construction Discourse (CxD, Östman 2005, 2015) has been developed recently as a possible extension of CxG, not as an alternative to it, because

> [t]here is no ontological, methodological, nor cognitive basis for accepting morphemes and words as having constructions associated with them – as, indeed, being licensed by constructions – but not to accept combinations of sentences, paragraphs, and whole texts/discourses. Size does not matter. (Östman 2005: 127)

The grammar model that evolves out of this approach is much more encompassing than traditional conceptions of grammar. The main claims in favor of the incorporation of text and discourse into CxG are as follows: (1) much of discourse is conventionalized; (2) discourse is not in opposition to syntax – the two complement each other; therefore (3) discourse and syntax are parts of grammar, which is built upon various external contextual attributes with "discourse patterns" (dp) being one of them. Östman (2005: 131–132) defines discourse patterns as the "cognitive discourse correlate of 'meaning' on sentence level, […] conventionalized associations between text type and genre." They are form – meaning – function pairings with at least three values:

a. discourse frame (cognitively based, e.g. a prototype conceptualization of what a recipe should look like)
b. text type (structurally based, formal features of texts, e.g. narrative, instructive, descriptive, etc.)
c. activity mode (based on interactional and social activities; e.g. genre).

The claim and the major difference from text and discourse linguistic studies is that "conceptualization on discourse level [NF: for example, peoples' understanding of what a recipe should look like] takes place primarily in terms of discourse patterns, rather than (or, at least, in addition to) in terms of genre and text types" (Östman 2005: 132). Studies of this kind assume the existence of an inventory of multiple discourse patterns (e.g. dp recipe, dp letter of congratulation, dp contract, etc.) called "discursicon" (on analogy with "lexicon", "constructicon") that forms a part of the repertoire that competent speakers will be familiar with, and that they can refer to at will. It is therefore a part of the competent speakers' communicative competence. At the current stage of the research, the question concerning the relationship between the concepts of CxG and CxD on the one hand and text and discourse linguistics (Section 3.3) on the other has not been addressed in a systematic way yet (cf. Stumpf and Stein 2024 for first attempts).

3.5 Discourse traditions (DTs)

The framework of DTs has been well-received in the field of linguistic variation and change within contemporary Romance studies. However, it has received scant attention so far beyond these fields, e.g. in Germanic linguistics or in linguistics in general, particularly in the field of formulaic language studies (Filatkina 2023).

The concept of DTs (Coseriu 1981; Koch 1997; Oesterreicher 1997; Schlieben-Lange 1983; Kabatek 2015) is based on the notion that any language is deeply embedded in social and cultural life and linked to history. To use language in order to transmit messages and to be understood implies not just the correct application of grammatical rules and the appropriate choice of individual words. In order to achieve their communicative goals, speakers have to make complex choices from the repertoire of linguistic means available to them. On the one hand, the complex selection processes are determined by human creativity and linguistic freedom, and on the other hand by conventions of communication that competent speakers of a given language establish over time. The concept of DTs reflects this interconnectedness of languages with conventions, history and speakers' freedom to choose. It suggests that a language is shaped not just by its grammar and lexicon, but also by conventionalized formulations that are characteristic for various communicative situations. DTs can be considered one specific realization of general cultural traditions. They encompass conventionalized patterns at three levels that differ with regard to their degree of abstraction/complexity (Wilhelm 2001). They range from single formulaic utterances (e.g. forms of address or greeting expressions at the beginning of a dialogue) through patterns of oral and written text structure (e.g. a specific layout of a recipe, novel, telephone conversation, or private letter) to complex discourse universes (e.g. literature, everyday communication, science, or religion). The crucial underlying idea is fourfold. Firstly, all forms of written or oral texts are deeply rooted in (at least) one DT and this is why, secondly, DTs govern and determine the selection of specific linguistic elements and routines that, in their turn, are defined by DTs (Winter-Froemel et al. 2015: 4; Kabatek 2015: 55). For instance, the utterance *Mother drowned baby* might seem to be irregular or even grammatically incorrect from the point of view of modern Standard English, but it is completely appropriate as a title of a DT "newspaper article" and will be recognized as such by competent speakers of English. In this sense, DTs are elements of linguistic competence, which implies the correct usage of grammar and lexicon, but also allows for variation, in accordance with the conventionalized DTs. Thirdly, DTs are historical and culture-specific phenomena, but they are not (necessarily) confined to a given language. They are rather part of the external conditions of language use, language change and the speakers' metalinguistic knowledge (Aschenberg 2003: 7–8). Even though the textual and linguistic form of an official job application might vary significantly between languages, (adult) speakers of all languages have an external knowledge about the DT "job application" and its differences from the DT "private letter." Finally,

DTs are not static, they undergo diachronic changes that Koch (1997: 66–70) classifies as diversification, mixture, and convergence. DTs can also be a motor/catalyst of language change and affect even such core layers of language systems as grammar and syntax (cf. various examples in Winter-Froemel et al. (eds) 2015). The benefits of DTs have to be seen in the facilitation of communication, reduction of the complexity of choices speakers have to make and also in the modeling and schematization of social behavior. With regard to these four core features, the overlap between the concept of DTs and text and discourse linguistics (Section 3.3) appears to be most clear.

4. Formulaic language: Still an elephant in the room

The brief outline of the different understandings of formulaic language in Sections 2 and 3 leads to the questions of whether these concepts can be considered as related; how the differences between them, if any, can be mediated; and how an integrative approach to formulaic language can be implemented empirically when analyzing texts.

As shown in Section 3.1, the notion of phrasemes addresses a specific, rather small group of formulaic patterns below the level of the sentence. The difference between the terms *formulaic patterns* and *constructions* (3.4) is twofold: the former does not include morphemes but extends its scope to formulaic texts and discourse; the latter prototypically does not include texts (with the exception of CxD), but incorporates morphemes. Spoken language (3.2) and text linguistic (3.3) approaches, the DTs (3.5), and formulaic language represent integrative research dimensions that are necessary if the ultimate aim is to develop a full-fledged model of communication. They should be considered as empirically underpinned attempts at reaching a holistic view of how language works. Each of these concepts starts from a different theoretical premise and they have partially different goals. However, they all place conventionalization as well as cultural, historical, and cognitive roots of human communication at the center of research. They encompass heterogeneous utterance types with different degrees of conventionalization and at different levels of human interaction and may put them on an equal, complementary, or hierarchical (but not competitive!) footing. Much more research needs to be undertaken to provide a theoretical framework for the interconnectedness of these heterogeneous types of formulaic patterns. A dialogue between the concepts would appear to be an appropriate way to proceed. As Wray (2012: 239) puts it:

> To put all of this another way, we can rather easily assume that formulaic language is like the elephant differently described by blind men with access to different parts of its huge mass. We may imagine that in due course our work will join up and we will grasp the nature of the whole beast. But the point of the metaphor is that the blind men do not know if they are in fact describing aspects of the same thing, because they cannot see the elephant. And we, for the moment at least, cannot necessarily assume that there is a single

phenomenon at the heart of our different activities, or if there is, that there are not also a few small rodents skulking about in the room too, confusing the description of the elephant and, perhaps, also influencing how it behaves. We can describe what we find, and call it formulaic language. But the elephant in the room is that we do not know if there is just one elephant in the room.

References

Adamzik, Kirsten. 1995. "Aspekte und Perspektiven der Textsortenlinguistik." In *Textsorten — Texttypologie: Eine kommentierte Bibliographie*, ed. by Kirsten Adamzik, 11–40. Münster: Nodus.

Antos, Gerd. 1989. "Textproduktion: Ein einführender Überblick." In *Textproduktion*, ed. by Gerd Antos and Hans P. Krings, 5–57. Tübingen: Narr.

Aschenberg, Heidi. 2003. "Diskurstraditionen: Orientierungen und Fragestellungen." In *Romanische Sprachgeschichte und Diskurstraditionen*, ed. by Heidi Aschenberg and Raymond Wilhelm, 1–18. Tübingen: Narr.

Behrens, Heike. 2011. "Die Konstruktion von Sprache im Spracherwerb." In *Konstruktionsgrammatik III: Aktuelle Fragen und Lösungsansätze*, ed. by Alexander Lasch and Alexander Ziem, 165–179. Tübingen: Stauffenburg.

Bubenhofer, Noah. 2009. *Sprachgebrauchsmuster: Korpuslinguistik als Methode der Diskurs- und Kulturanalyse*. Berlin/New York: De Gruyter.

Burger, Harald. 2015. *Phraseologie: Eine Einführung am Beispiel des Deutschen*. Berlin: Erich Schmidt.

Busse, Dietrich. 2005. "Sprachwissenschaft als Sozialwissenschaft?" In *Brisante Semantik: Neuere Konzepte und Forschungsergebnisse einer kulturwissenschaftlichen Linguistik*, ed. by Dietrich Busse, Thomas Niehr, and Martin Wengeler, 21–43. Tübingen: Narr.

Busse, Dietrich, and Wolfgang Teubert. 2013. "Ist Diskurs ein sprachwissenschaftliches Objekt? Zur Methodenfrage der historischen Semantik." In *Linguistische Diskursanalyse: Neue Perspektiven*, ed. by Dietrich Busse and Wolfgang Teubert, 13–30. Wiesbaden: Wissenschaftliche Buchgesellschaft.

Bybee, Joan L., and Rena Torres Cacoullos. 2002. "The role of prefabs in grammaticization. How the particular and the general interact in language change." In *Formulaic Language. Volume 1: Distribution and Historical Change*, ed. by Roberta Corrigan, Edith A. Moravcsik, Hamid Ouali, and Kathleen M. Wheatley, 187–217. Amsterdam/Philadelphia: John Benjamins.

Coseriu, Eugenio. 1981. *Textlinguistik: Eine Einführung*, ed. by Jörn Albrecht. Tübingen: Narr.

Coulmas, Florian. 1981. *Routine im Gespräch: Zur pragmatischen Fundierung der Idiomatik*. Wiesbaden: Akademische Verlagsgesellschaft.

Dausendschön-Gay, Ulrich, Elisabeth Gülich, and Ulrich Kraft. 2007. "Phraseologische/formelhafte Texte." In *Phraseology: An International Handbook of Contemporary Research*, ed. by Harald Burger, Dmitrij Dobrovol'skij, Peter Kühn, and Neal R. Norrick, 468–480. Berlin/New York: De Gruyter.

Deppermann, Arnulf. 2004. "‚Gesprächskompetenz': Probleme und Herausforderungen eines möglichen Begriffs." In *Analyse und Vermittlung von Gesprächskompetenz*, ed. by Michael Becker-Mrotzek and Gisela Brünner, 15–33. Frankfurt a.M.: Lang.

Deppermann, Arnulf. 2007. *Grammatik und Semantik aus gesprächsanalytischer Sicht*. Berlin/New York: De Gruyter.

Dobrovol'skij, Dmitrij O., and Elisabeth Piirainen. 2021. *Figurative language: Cross-cultural and Cross-linguistic Perspectives*. Berlin/Boston: De Gruyter.

Erman, Britt, and Beatrice Warren. 2000. "The idiom principle and the open choice principle." *Text & Talk* 20: 29–62.

Feilke, Helmuth. 1994. *Common Sense-Kompetenz: Überlegungen zu einer Theorie „sympathischen" und „natürlichen" Meinens und Verstehens*. Frankfurt a.M.: Suhrkamp.

Feilke, Helmuth. 1996. *Sprache als soziale Gestalt: Ausdruck, Prägung und die Ordnung der sprachlichen Typik*. Frankfurt a.M.: Suhrkamp.

Fiehler, Reinhard, Birgit Barden, Mechthild Elstermann, and Barbara Kraft. 2004. *Eigenschaften gesprochener Sprache*. Tübingen: Narr.

Filatkina, Natalia. 2013. "Wandel im Bereich der historischen formelhaften Sprache und seine Reflexe im Neuhochdeutschen: Eine neue Perspektive für moderne Sprachwandeltheorien." In *Sprachwandel im Neuhochdeutschen*, ed. by Petra M. Vogel, 34–51. Berlin/New York: De Gruyter.

Filatkina, Natalia. 2018. *Historische formelhafte Sprache: Theoretische Grundlagen und methodische Herausforderungen*. Berlin/Boston: De Gruyter.

Filatkina, Natalia. 2019. "Musterhaftigkeit im Spracherwerb." In *Sprachliche Vorgeformtheit: Eine Einführung*, ed. by Stephan Stein and Sören Stumpf, 211–239. Berlin: Erich Schmidt.

Filatkina, Natalia. 2023. "Discourse traditions and formulaic language studies." In *Manual of Discourse Traditions in Romance*, ed. by Esme Winter-Froemel and Álvaro S. Octavio de Toledo y Huerta, 705–719. Berlin/Boston: De Gruyter.

Filatkina, Natalia, Johannes Gottwald, and Monika Hanauska. 2009. "Formelhafte Sprache im schulischen Unterricht im Frühen Mittelalter: Am Beispiel der so genannten „Sprichwörter" in den Schriften Notkers des Deutschen von St. Gallen." *Sprachwissenschaft* 34: 341–397.

Filatkina, Natalia, and Monika Hanauska. 2010. "Wissensstrukturierung und Wissensvermittlung durch Routineformeln: Am Beispiel ausgewählter althochdeutscher Texte." *Yearbook of Phraseology* 1: 45–71.

Fillmore, Charles J. 1976. "Pragmatics and the description of discourse." In *Pragmatik/Pragmatics II: Grundlegung einer expliziten Pragmatik*, ed. by Siegfried J. Schmidt, 83–104. München: W. Fink.

Fillmore, Charles J. 1982. "Frame Semantics." In *Linguistics in the Morning Calm*, ed. by the Linguistic Society of Korea, 111–137. Seoul: Hanshin.

Fillmore, Charles J., Paul Kay, and Mary Catherine O'Connor. 1988. "Regularity and idiomaticity in grammatical constructions: The case of *let alone*." *Language* 64: 501–538.

Firth, John R. 1957. "Modes of meaning." In *Papers in Linguistics 1934–1951*, ed. by John R. Firth, 190–215. Oxford: Oxford University Press.

Gardt, Andreas. 2007. "Diskursanalyse: Aktueller theoretischer Ort und methodische Möglichkeiten." In *Diskurslinguistik nach Foucault: Theorie und Gegenstände*, ed. by Ingo H. Warnke, 27–52. Berlin/New York: De Gruyter.

Goldberg, Adele E. 1995. *Constructions: A Construction Grammar Approach to Argument Structure*. Chicago/London: University of Chicago Press.

Goldberg, Adele E. 2003. "Constructions: A new theoretical approach to language." *Trends in Cognitive Sciences* 7: 219–224.

Gottwald, Johannes, and Monika Hanauska. 2013. "Formelhafte Sprache in den althochdeutschen und altsächsischen Beichten." *Sprachwissenschaft* 38: 445–476.

Gumperz, John J. 1982. *Discourse Strategies*. Cambridge: Cambridge University Press.

Gülich, Elisabeth, and Heiko Hausendorf. 2000. "Vertextungsmuster Narration." In *Text- und Gesprächslinguistik: Ein internationales Handbuch zeitgenössischer Forschun*, ed. by Klaus Brinker, Gerd Antos, Wolfgang Heinemann, and Sven F. Sager, 369–385. Berlin/New York: De Gruyter.

Günthner, Susanne, and Hubert A. Knoblauch. 1994. "*Forms are the food of faith*: Gattungen als Muster kommunikativen Handelns." *Kölner Zeitschrift für Soziologie und Sozialpsychologie* 4: 693–723.

Hanauska, Monika. 2014. "*Historia dye ist ein gezuyge der zijt ...*": Untersuchungen zur pragmatischen Formelhaftigkeit in der volkssprachigen Kölner Stadthistoriographie des Spätmittelalters. Heidelberg: Winter.

Heinemann, Wolfgang. 2000a. "Textsorte – Textmuster – Texttyp." In *Text- und Gesprächslinguistik: Ein internationales Handbuch zeitgenössischer Forschung*, ed. by Klaus Brinker, Gerd Antos, Wolfgang Heinemann, and Sven F. Sager, 507–523. Berlin/New York: De Gruyter.

Heinemann, Wolfgang. 2000b. "Vertextungsmuster Deskription." In *Text- und Gesprächslinguistik: Ein internationales Handbuch zeitgenössischer Forschung*, ed. by Klaus Brinker, Gerd Antos, Wolfgang Heinemann, and Sven F. Sager, 356–369. Berlin/New York: De Gruyter.

Heinemann, Margot, and Wolfgang Heinemann. 2002. *Grundlagen der Textlinguistik: Interaktion – Text – Diskurs*. Tübingen: Narr.

Hoff, Carina. 2012. "*Si sagent vns guode wort*: Formelhafte Sprache in den südwestdeutschen Nonnenviten des 14. Jahrhunderts." In *Aspekte der historischen Phraseologie und Phraseographie*, ed. by Natalia Filatkina, Ane Kleine, Marcel Dräger, and Harald Burger, 67–82. Heidelberg: Winter.

Hymes, Dell. 1987. "Communicative competence." In *Sociolinguistics: An International Handbook of the Science of Language and Society*, ed. by Ulrich Ammon, Norbert Dittmar, and Klaus Mattheier, 35–71. Berlin/New York: De Gruyter.

Kabatek, Johannes. 2015. "Warum die 'zweite Historizität' eben doch die zweite ist: Von der Bedeutung von Diskurstraditionen für die Sprachbetrachtung." In *Diskurse, Texte, Traditionen: Modelle und Fachkulturen in der Diskussion*, ed. by Franz Lebsanft and Angela Schrott, 49–62. Bonn: Bonn University Press.

Koch, Peter. 1997. "Diskurstraditionen: Zu ihrem sprachtheoretischen Status und ihrer Dynamik." In *Gattungen mittelalterlicher Schriftlichkeit*, ed. by Barbara Frank, Thomas Haye, and Doris Tophinke, 43–79. Tübingen: Narr.

Koch, Peter, and Wulf Oesterreicher. 2011. *Gesprochene Sprache in der Romania: Französisch, Italienisch, Spanisch*. 2nd edition. Berlin/New York: De Gruyter.

Langacker, Ronald W. 1987. *Foundations of Cognitive Grammar, Volume 1: Theoretical Prerequisites*. Stanford: Stanford University Press.

Linke, Angelika. 2001. "Trauer, Öffentlichkeit und Intimität: Zum Wandel der Textsorte 'Todesanzeige' in der zweiten Hälfte des 20. Jahrhunderts." In *Zur Kulturspezifik von Textsorten*, ed. by Ulla Fix, Stephan Habscheid, and Josef Klein, 195–223. Tübingen: Narr.

Linke, Angelika. 2003. "*Spaß haben*: Ein Zeitgefühl." In *Standardfragen. Soziolinguistische Perspektiven auf Sprachgeschichte, Sprachkontakt und Sprachvariation*, ed. by Jannis K. Androutsopoulos and Evelyn Ziegler, 63–79. Frankfurt a.M.: Lang.

Linke, Angelika. 2011. "Signifikante Muster: Perspektiven einer kulturanalytischen Linguistik." In *Begegnungen: Das VIII. Nordisch-Baltische Germanistentreffen in Sigtuna vom 11. bis 13.6. 2009*, ed. by Elisabeth Wåghäll Nivre and Constanze Ackermann, 23–44. Stockholm: Acta Universitatis Stockholmiensis.

Luckmann, Thomas. 1986. "Grundformen der gesellschaftlichen Vermittlung des Wissens: Kommunikative Gattungen." In *Kultur und Gesellschaft*, ed. by Friedhelm Neidhardt and René König, 191–211. Opladen: Westdeutscher Verlag.

Oesterreicher, Wulf. 1997. "Zur Fundierung von Diskurstraditionen." In *Gattungen mittelalterlicher Schriftlichkeit*, ed. by Barbara Frank, Thomas Haye, and Doris Tophinke, 19–41. Tübingen: Narr.

Östman, Jan-Ola. 2005. "Construction discourse: A prolegomenon." In *Construction Grammars: Cognitive Grounding and Theoretical Extensions*, ed. by Jan-Ola Östman and Miriam Fried, 121–144. Amsterdam/Philadelphia: John Benjamins.

Östman, Jan-Ola. 2015. "From construction grammar to construction discourse ... and back." In *Konstruktionsgrammatik V: Konstruktionen im Spannungsfeld von sequenziellen Mustern, kommunikativen Gattungen und Textsorten*, ed. by Jörg Bücker, Susanne Günthner, and Wolfgang Imo, 15–43. Tübingen: Narr.

Piirainen, Elisabeth, Natalia Filatkina, Sören Stumpf, and Christian Pfeiffer (eds). 2020. *Formulaic Language and New Data: Theoretical and Methodological Implications*. Berlin/Boston: De Gruyter.

Rauch, Elisabeth. 1992. *Sprachrituale in institutionellen und institutionalisierten Text- und Gesprächssorten*. Frankfurt a.M.: Suhrkamp.

Sabban, Annette. 2007. "Textbildende Potenzen von Phrasemen." In *Phraseologie: Ein internationales Handbuch der zeitgenössischen Forschung*, ed. by Harald Burger, Dmitrij Dobrovol'skij, Peter Kühn, and Neal R. Norrick, 237–253. Berlin/New York: De Gruyter.

Schlieben-Lange, Brigitte. 1983. *Traditionen des Sprechens: Elemente einer pragmatischen Sprachgeschichtsschreibung*. Stuttgart: Kohlhammer.

Schwitalla, Johannes. 2012. *Gesprochenes Deutsch: Eine Einführung*. 4th edition. Berlin: Erich Schmidt.

Selting, Margret, and Elizabeth Couper-Kuhlen. 2000. "Argumente für die Entwicklung einer 'interaktionalen Linguistik'." *Gesprächsforschung. Online-Zeitschrift zur verbalen Interaktion* 1: 76–95.

Sinclair, John McHardy. 1991. *Corpus, Concordance, Collocation*. Oxford: Oxford University Press.

Stefanowitsch, Anatol. 2013. "Collostructional analysis." In *The Oxford Handbook of Construction Grammar*, ed. by Thomas Hoffmann and Graeme Trousdale, 290–306. Oxford/New York: Oxford University Press.

Stefanowitsch, Anatol, and Stefan Th. Gries. 2003. "Collostructions: Investigating the interaction of words and constructions." *International Journal of Corpus Linguistics* 8: 209–243.

Stein, Stephan. 1995. *Formelhafte Sprache: Untersuchungen zu ihren pragmatischen und kognitiven Funktionen im gegenwärtigen Deutsch*. Frankfurt a.M.: Lang.

Stein, Stephan. 2003. *Textgliederung: Einheitenbildung im geschriebenen und gesprochenen Deutsch – Theorie und Empirie*. Berlin/New York: De Gruyter.

Stein, Stephan. 2010. "Versprachlichungsstrategien beim öffentlichen Reden über Tod und Trauer: Was Todesanzeigen verbergen – und offenlegen." *Sprachwissenschaft* 35: 369–407.

Stein, Stephan. 2011. "Strategien der Vertextung in Werbetexten." *Zeitschrift für angewandte Linguistik* 54: 33–56.

Stein, Stephan, and Sören Stumpf. 2019. *Muster in Sprache und Kommunikation: Eine Einführung in Konzepte sprachlicher Vorgeformtheit.* Berlin: Erich Schmidt.

Steyer, Kathrin. 2013. *Usuelle Wortverbindungen: Zentrale Muster des Sprachgebrauchs aus korpusanalytischer Sicht.* Tübingen: Narr.

Stubbs, Michael. 2001. *Words and Phrases: Corpus Studies of Lexical Semantics.* Oxford: Oxford University Press.

Stumpf, Sören, and Natalia Filatkina (eds). 2018. *Formelhafte Sprache in Text und Diskurs.* Berlin/Boston: De Gruyter Mouton.

Stumpf, Sören, and Stephan Stein (eds). 2024. *Konstruktionsgrammatik X: Textsorten und Textmuster als Konstruktionen?* Tübingen: Stauffenburg.

Tomasello, Michael. 2003. *Constructing a Language: A Usage-based Theory of Language Acquisition.* Cambridge: Cambridge University Press.

Tophinke, Doris. 1996. "Zwei Aspekte der Texttypik: Funktionalität und kulturelle Expressivität – ein historisches Fallbeispiel." In *Texte: Konstitution, Verarbeitung, Typik*, ed. by Susanne Michaelis and Doris Tophinke, 101–115. München/Newcastle: Lincom Europa.

van Dijk, Teun A. 1980. *Macrostructures: An Interdisciplinary Study of Global Structures in Discourse, Interaction, and Cognition.* Hillsdale: Lawrence Erlbaum Associates.

Warnke, Ingo. 1999. "Diskursivität und Intertextualität als Parameter sprachlichen Wandels: Prolegomena einer funktionalen Sprachgeschichtsschreibung." In *Schnittstelle Text/Diskurs*, ed. by Ingo Warnke, 215–222. Frankfurt a.M.: Lang.

Weber, Beatrix. 2015. "'the seid acte, statute or ordenaunce, or eny other made to the contrary, notwithstondyng': Zur Rolle der Faktoren 'Diskurstradition' und 'Sprachkontakt' bei der Etablierung der *notwithstanding*-Konstruktion im Englischen." In *Konstruktionsgrammatik* IV, ed. by Alexander Lasch and Alexander Ziem, 225–241. Tübingen: Stauffenburg.

Werlen, Iwar. 1984. *Ritual und Sprache: Zum Verhältnis von Sprechen und Handeln in Ritualen.* Tübingen: Narr.

Wilhelm, Raymund. 2001. "Diskurstraditionen." In *Language Typology and Language Universals: An International Handbook*, ed. by Martin Haspelmath, Ekkehard König, Wulf Oesterreicher, and Wolfgang Raible, 467–477. Berlin/New York: De Gruyter.

Winter-Froemel, Esme, Araceli López Serena, Álvaro Octavio de Toledo y Huerta, and Barbara Frank-Job. 2015. "Diskurstraditionen, Diskurstraditionelles und Einzelsprachliches im Sprachwandel: Zur Einleitung." In *Diskurstraditionelles und Einzelsprachliches im Sprachwandel / Tradicionalidad discursiva e idiomaticidad en los procesos de cambio lingüístico*, ed. by Esme Winter-Froemel, Araceli López Serena, Álvaro Octavio de Toledo y Huerta, and Barbara Frank-Job, 1–27. Tübingen: Narr.

Winter-Froemel, Esme, Araceli López Serena, Álvaro Octavio de Toledo y Huerta, and Barbara Frank-Job. (eds). 2015. *Diskurstraditionelles und Einzelsprachliches im Sprachwandel / Tradicionalidad discursiva e idiomaticidad en los procesos de cambio lingüístico.* Tübingen: Narr.

Wray, Alison. 2002. *Formulaic Language and the Lexicon.* Cambridge: Cambridge University Press.

Wray, Alison. 2008. *Formulaic Language: Pushing the Boundaries.* Oxford/New York: Oxford University Press.

Wray, Alison. 2009. "Identifying formulaic language: Persistent challenges and new opportunities." In *Formulaic Language*, ed. by Roberta Corrigan, Edith A. Moravcsik, Hamid Ouali, and Kathleen M. Wheatley, 27–51. Amsterdam/Philadelphia: John Benjamins.

Wray, Alison. 2012. "What do we (think we) know about formulaic language? An evaluation of the current state of play." *Annual Review of Applied Linguistics* 32: 231–254.

Wray, Alison. 2013. "Formulaic sequences." In *The Encyclopedia of Applied Linguistics*, ed. by Carol A. Chapelle, 2200–2205. Oxford: Oxford University Press.

Wray, Alison, and Michael R. Perkins. 2000. "The functions of formulaic language: An integrated model." *Language and Communication* 20: 1–28.

Nils Erik Enkvist

Jan-Ola Östman & Tuija Virtanen
University of Helsinki | Åbo Akademi University

1. Life and overview

Nils Erik Enkvist (1925–2009) is best known as one of the forerunners in linguistic stylistics and in text linguistics, fields of research which he more or less single-handedly introduced to students of language and literature in the Nordic countries in the 1960s (stylistics), and in the early 1970s (text linguistics). His close contacts with text linguists in Eastern Europe also made him an important instrument in making contemporary text linguists in Czechoslovakia and in East Germany better known world-wide. In his home country Finland as well as to a large extent also in the other Nordic countries he soon became the core representative of a linguistics that went "beyond the sentence".

Enkvist was born into a bilingual (Swedish and Finnish) family, and throughout his life he functioned just as well in Finnish as in Swedish, but English was to become his main academic language; a prominent British linguist in the mid-1970s said of Enkvist that he is one of those foreigners who speaks better English than any Englishman. Having studied English and phonetics a couple of years at the University of Helsinki, he left for the University of Michigan in 1945, receiving an MA from there in 1948 — with Charles C. Fries as one of his teachers. (He financed his studies not only as an assistant in the phonetics laboratory, but also as a jazz pianist in the evenings.)

In his research, Enkvist distinguished himself not only as a linguist, but also as a literary scholar. His 1951 doctoral dissertation from the University of Helsinki was in English literature (*Caricatures of Americans on the English Stage prior to 1870*), and up until the mid-1960s most of his publications dealt with literary topics; cf. in particular *American Humour in England before Mark Twain* (1953), *The Seasons of the Year. Chapters on a Motif from Beowulf to the Shepherd's Calendar* (1957), and his textbook on Chaucer in 1964 (cf. Enkvist 1964a).

As the only professor of English language and literature at the Swedish-language Åbo Akademi University, Enkvist continued being extremely versatile — working on literature, phonetics, and applied linguistics in addition to establishing himself as a world-wide expert on stylistics and text linguistics. For a personal account of his formative experiences of a multilingual life, see Enkvist (2001).

During his long and influential career, Enkvist published about a dozen books and over 300 scholarly articles — mostly (but not exclusively) in English, Swedish, and Finnish. In the overview below, we focus on some of the concepts and ideas that are especially relevant to pragmatics, and where he either made a lasting impression in the field or where he was among the first to take the field in a new direction.

2. Stylistics

Borderland research curiosities seem to have been of special interest for Enkvist. He was a pioneer in bridging the gap between theoretical and applied linguistics, especially so in Finland and the other Nordic countries. But it was the idea of joining together his linguistic and literary interests that truly made a world-wide impact. The 1964 book on *Linguistics and Style*, written together with John Spencer and Michael Gregory, consists of two parts, of which the first is written by Enkvist, and called "On defining style". Both in theory and in practice, this book established the very field of linguistic stylistics.

Enkvist's (1964b: 28) original definition of the style of a text as "the aggregate of the contextual probabilities of its linguistic items" might today seem somewhat awkward if not dated, but it was a first important step in the direction of defining style as (text producers') *choice*, and as variation within different types of text. In addition to a large number of articles on stylistics, he published the influential *Linguistic Stylistics* in 1973, where he defines style as "that type of linguistic variation which correlates with context in a wide sense of the term, including both textual context and situational context" (1973a: 17). His Swedish-language *Stilforskning och stilteori* was published in 1974 and became the standard work of reference especially in Sweden.

In the early and mid-1970s, Enkvist's main interest became that of text and discourse studies, but he never forgot stylistics. In 1984–1988 he brought stylistics and text linguistics tightly together in his Academy of Finland (the National Science Foundation of Finland) funded research group Style and Text. This research group was also special in that it included scholars beyond English and the Nordic languages, in particular scholars like Martina Björklund, who investigated narrative strategies and point of view in the works of Čechov (see e.g. Björklund 1993).

2.1 Literary pragmatics

Literary pragmatics is another good illustration of how themes and topics that interested Enkvist in stylistics have been received, applied, and further extended. His continued interest in literature and style was of crucial importance for fostering studies in the newly founded subdiscipline of literary pragmatics in the 1980s. This line of research has brought together Enkvist's literary and linguistic concerns, particularly his thoughts on literature in relation to discourse analysis and pragmatics.

Work on literary pragmatics was especially continued by Enkvist's successor at Åbo Akademi University, Roger Sell (cf. Sell 1991, Sell and Verdonk 1994). Within his Literary Pragmatics Project, Sell in 1988 hosted the first international symposium in the field. In this and other symposia on literary pragmatics, Enkvist gave presentations in which he addressed pragmatic issues, drawing particular attention to the link between interpretability and contextualization, both in language use more generally and within literary communication more particularly (cf. Enkvist 1991).

Sell has continued to take up literary pragmatic issues, moving from a historical literary pragmatics towards an all-embracing account of literature as one among other forms of communication (cf. Sell 2020), an approach that has been centrally prompted by aspects of Enkvist's work.

3. Text linguistics

Even though there had indeed been many studies that went beyond the sentence, especially in the U.S.A. (Zellig Harris in the early 1950s: cf. Harris 1952; Kenneth Lee Pike in his tagmemics: cf. Pike 1954; and in particular Robert E. Longacre's studies on the grammar of discourse – summarized later in Longacre 1983), the impact of transformation-generative grammar became widespread also in the Nordic countries. This started to change in the late 1960s (also enhanced by the advent of Generative Semantics in the U.S.A., which gradually grew into pragmatics), and especially so in the early 1970s. Studies had very early on showed that word order was extremely important in languages like Czech, and especially the question of what triggered the use of different word orders to stand for, basically, the same propositional content.

3.1 Promoting text linguistics

Largely due to his well-established contacts with scholars from the rest of Europe, Enkvist soon realized that what he had been doing within stylistics was also very relevant for the newly founded field of text linguistics. As early as in 1975 Enkvist published his Finnish-language textbook *Tekstilingvistiikan peruskäsitteitä*, where he introduced the new field to scholars in Finland.

At the same time, he received funding from the Academy of Finland to establish what he was to call the Text Linguistics Research Group (1974–1977). This group of researchers soon became the major hub for research in text linguistics in Europe and beyond, with the book series *Reports on Text Linguistics* publishing studies on English, on Old English, on Swedish, and on Finnish by the members of the research group.

Invitations were readily extended to scholars from other countries to visit and discuss text-linguistic issues with the group. This line of work was continued in the research group Style and Text (see above), where e.g. Tuija Virtanen (1992a) discussed the effects of text strategies and information structuring on the use of adverbials in English, and where Brita Wårvik (1993) modeled grounding criteria for narratives. Jan-Ola Östman and Tuija Virtanen (1999) systematized the theoretical bases of the jungle of concepts related to information structuring in sentences and texts.

One of the important innovative features of Enkvist's 1970s research group was his early introduction of computational and statistical methods in the analysis of the textual triggers that influence the use of particular word orders in the languages dealt with in the research group. Here Enkvist continued his interest in stylostatistics (e.g. Enkvist 1973a), and applied his earlier insights to text-linguistic challenges; cf. Andersson (1978), Hakulinen et al. (1980), and the collection edited by Enkvist and Kohonen (1976). The details of the research group's coding system were especially developed by Viljo Kohonen in his 1978 study on Old English word order (see Section 5 below).

3.2 Cohesion and coherence

One of the early important questions that Enkvist was engaged in was the difference between cohesion and coherence. M.A.K. Halliday and Ruqaiya Hasan published their influential book on *Cohesion in English* in 1976, and even though this was a major landmark for text linguistics, it focused on the explicit markers of cohesion: reference, substitution, ellipsis, conjunction, and lexical relations. What was lacking were the *reasons* for what it is that makes a collection of sentences a text proper. Among Enkvist's most famous examples of this difference was the sequence of sentences given in (1), which on the surface looks like a text, and it can be shown to have all the lexical and referential elements that bind the sentences together. Still, it is not a text proper — because it lacks coherence.

(1) I bought a Ford. The car in which President Wilson rode down the Champs Elysées was black. Black English has been widely discussed. The discussions between the governors ended last week. A week has seven days. Every day I feed my cat. Cats have four legs. The cat is on the mat. Mat has three letters. (Enkvist 1978: 110–111)

Enkvist (1978) talks about such texts as being *pseudo-coherent*. He is here clearly moving in the direction of pragmatics and seeing texts as what we today would rather talk about in terms of discourse. In the Text Linguistics Research Group *coherence* was used to stand for all kinds of semantico-functional phenomena which collaborate to give as output a contextually acceptable and adequate text, whereas *cohesion* was used for denoting the textual tightness which is manifested by morpho-syntactic, lexical-similarity, and/or metrical means. And as Enkvist (1978) shows, we can have cohesive texts which are not coherent, and vice versa; non-cohesive coherent texts were called *pragmatically coherent* by Enkvist.

3.3 Interpretability and textual worlds

In the last resort, according to Enkvist, one's *perspective* overrides everything else: coherence is something that text producers and text receivers themselves bring into the discourse. In this way, Enkvist (1989) theoretically extended his understanding of coherence by including the notions of textual worlds and interpretability. In particular, coherence, he argues, depends "on our ability of specifying the worlds evoked by, and surrounding, a text" (Enkvist 1989:162). Here he also discusses one of his favorite aspects of interpretability, i.e., processes involved in incremental text comprehension, where his ideas come close to textual interpretation in terms of what Charles Fillmore called frames of understanding (cf. e.g. Fillmore 1982).[1]

Connexity is the term Enkvist uses for *cohesion plus coherence*; the notion of connexity he regards as the sum of the qualities of a text which make it interpretable: "a text is interpretable to all those who can, under prevailing circumstances, build around that text a text world in which that text seems plausible" (Enkvist 1990:21). Text worlds are specific and usually highly constrained, so "to construe text worlds, we must know universes of discourse" (Enkvist 1989:184) which contain knowledge about the world at large. Drawing on the relevant bits of our encyclopaedic knowledge of the world facilitates the inferencing processes needed to interpret textual coherence. But inferencing, of various kinds, "is based on human laziness, or in a prettier phrase, on the avoidance of needless effort in communication between people who share certain assumptions about the world" (Enkvist 1990:18). The processes of interpreting texts are thus closely tied to situational and socio-cultural contexts as well as to people's understandings of text categories of various kinds.

In a number of studies from 1973, Enkvist developed his ideas concerning *theme dynamics* as he related text-linguistic analyses of the links found between the beginnings or endings of successive sentences in a small corpus of literary and non-fiction texts to matters of style (cf. e.g. Enkvist 1973b). This procedure yielded two major stylistic trends: a thematically iterative, *static* style and the *dynamic* style of theme progression displaying frequent shifts in thematic material. Rather than involving a series of microanalyses of connexity between sentence pairs or sequences, the focus of identifying such *textual style markers* was on long stretches of text.

Enkvist's interest in linearization matters led him to single out a small number of common *text strategies* and to investigate their uses in texts of different types through a *parametric* view of word order (see e.g. Enkvist 1985b, 1986b, 1987b). Hence, *communicative*

---

1. Enkvist's favorite examples of incremental text comprehension were versions of utterances like *The horse raced past the barn ... fell*, where — when read and understood incrementally — the expectation is that the utterance stops after *barn*, but then *fell* is added, and the interpretation of the whole utterance changes — from the horse racing to somebody else (i.e. a non-expressed rider) being the Agent of the sentence.

success might at times be grounded in strategy-marking adverbials placed initially at textual boundaries and strings of references of various kinds to main participants in the thematic position. Such actual choices of expression serve to indicate the hierarchy of the perforce linear text, but they also show the outcome of the *conflicts and conspiracies* that may be assumed to have gone into its production (see e.g. Enkvist 1985b). In this light, Virtanen (1992a) explored the discourse functions of sentence-initial adverbials of time and place in written narratives and procedural place descriptions.

Early on, Enkvist had related characteristic weighting patterns of text-strategic parameters to text categories of different kinds, as well as to styles and communicative situations, essentially contrasting *evocative* texts with *operational* ones. Virtanen (1992b) devised a two-level model of text and discourse types, explicating their internal relations by matches and mismatches between form and function. What Enkvist showed was that texts can be well-formed, acceptable, as well as socially and stylistically appropriate; yet, their possible connexity must be subsumed under processes of interpretability involving incremental constructions of text worlds with their specific constrained states of affairs.

4. Studies on interaction

Ethnomethodological conversation analysis had barely reached linguists in the Nordic countries in the early 1970s. But seeing spoken language as *text* was nothing new. Enkvist himself, with his background in phonetics, published early and important studies on the prosody of paragraphs and paragraph boundaries, e.g. in news reports (cf. Enkvist and Nordström 1978).

4.1 Impromptu speech

Enkvist also more generally showed an interest in spoken interaction. In the early 1980s he organized a symposium with the title *Impromptu Speech*, and a volume with that title was published under his editorship in 1982 (cf. Enkvist 1982a). This book contains studies on discourse strategies, on challenges of segmentation in impromptu speech, on pragmatic particles, on cross-language hazards, etc., with contributions by renowned scholars from different countries (Eddy Roulet, Jan Svartvik, Itamar Even-Zohar, David Brazil, etc.) discussing a large variety of languages. Especially members Auli Hakulinen and Jan-Ola Östman of the Text Linguistics Research Group went on to publish books and articles on interactional phenomena (cf. e.g. Östman 1981) throughout the following decades. Östman continued to work on narrowing whatever gap there might have been between discourse analysis and pragmatics (cf. Östman 1986), and Hakulinen was somewhat later to be in charge of the first grammar of Finnish based on text-linguistic principles, including detailed information about conversational Finnish (cf. Hakulinen et al. 2004).

4.2 The CIF principle

As an addendum to the Czech notion of *communicative dynamism*, where the general principle was that one starts an utterance with old/given information and gradually moves toward what is to be focused and new, Enkvist in the early 1980s added versatility to this rather static notion; his views in this respect would later become very important in studies of interaction (cf. Section 4.1). He called one of his principles the *CIF Principle*, i.e., *The Crucial Information First Principle* (cf. e.g. Enkvist 1981, 1984, 1987b, 1989). In many contexts, especially in spoken interaction, you have to start with the most crucial information (i.e. the *focus*), in order to get your addressee's attention. Thus, when Shakespeare's Richard III was in dire straits, he did not use (what in text linguistics of the 1970s and 1980s was seen as) the prototypical theme-rheme progression and start with a known element like *I* as in (2a), but he started with the most crucial information of needing a horse, as the first element; see (2b).

(2) a. I offer my Kingdom to anyone who can bring me a horse!
    b. A horse, a horse, my Kingdom for a horse!

Today, the idea of putting crucial information first is nothing exceptional, but within text-linguistic research in the 1980s it was quite a new insight.

It is always difficult to know who the first scholar was to suggest an insight. This is so today, but even more so at the time before Google and other search engines: ideas get thrown around at conferences, scrutinized and molded in informal discussions. There were thus no doubt others, too, who had realized the importance of what Enkvist called the CIF Principle; even Jespersen (1949: 54) suggested a Principle of Actuality. Nevertheless, Enkvist was a master at making new and difficult concepts easily understandable, accessible, and directly usable in linguistic analyses. This was so all through his discussions of text production and text comprehension as he crystallized complex matters into a few central concepts (e.g. text/discourse strategies), principles (e.g. the CIF Principle) or text-linguistic models explicating multifaceted phenomena such as interpretability.

5. Old English

Enkvist's interest in and knowledge of earlier periods of English also made him return to poems like *Beowulf* and look at them from the point of view of them having been produced in a spoken format. In his work on the Old English pragmatic particle *þa*, he showed in Enkvist (1986a) that it is not only an action marker (as he had argued in Enkvist 1972), but that "*þa* does its main job or jobs at text and discourse level" (Enkvist 1986a: 301), as a marker of foregrounding. This line of thinking was further developed in the work of Style and Text member Brita Wårvik (cf. Enkvist and Wårvik

1987; Wårvik 2013; cf. also Östman and Wårvik 1994 on the Finnsburg narrative) on the relative foregrounding and backgrounding of textual elements — also across time, discussing whether this has to do with a typological shift or style shift (i.e. in relation to the development of genres), thus continuing Paul Hopper's and Sandra Thompson's (1980) influential work on grounding and transitivity in grammar and discourse.

Another very prominent direction of study on Old English from a text-linguistic perspective was Kohonen's (1978) study of Old English word order, which — as mentioned above — appropriately brought quantitative text-linguistic analysis into the realm of historical linguistics. Kohonen's study of information structure not only took into account formal factors like constituent length but also textual motivations like topicalization and cohesion. Kohonen's work was not the first to use statistical methods to get a better understanding of Old English text structure, but whereas earlier work had mostly focused on (combinations of) lexical items, his study joined quantitative methods and historical linguistics with insights from Enkvist's text linguistics. In the mid-1980s, Enkvist talked about *historical text linguistics*, a forerunner of today's historical pragmatics.

6. Iconicity

One aspect of a text that was not paid much attention to at the time — and still is not getting enough attention — is the impact of iconicity on the production and understanding of text.

Enkvist's Finnish-language textbook from 1975 includes a chapter on *iconic cohesion*, i.e. factors influencing the cohesion of a text which rely on some part of the text being an image of another part of the same text. This iconic isomorphism, he shows, can be phonetic, phonological, or syntactic in nature, and in more abstract forms it can indeed be found on any level of a text, literary or otherwise. Enkvist's influential article in the first issue of the journal *TEXT* (1981) dealt with "experiential iconicism in text strategy" of four kinds: instances where the temporal, spatial, causal, or socially conditioned order in the text conforms to people's experience of the world. This kind of isomorphy that obtains between the text and our picture of the world is reminiscent of the *ordo naturalis* of the rhetorical tradition, and is applicable to both clausal and textual (strings of) elements.

At more or less the same time (in 1980), John Haiman had published his renowned articles about iconicity, isomorphism, and economic motivation in syntax. With Enkvist's background in poetics and stylistics, iconicity was nothing unfamiliar to him as he applied these concepts to text and discourse generally. According to Enkvist, iconicity and isomorphism can make a seemingly incoherent text coherent by the very surface similarities between sentences strung together, thus contributing to the interplay of the different forces that go into the construction of a text strategy. To speak with Enkvist (1986b: 257), experiential iconicity "may make the text into an icon or picture of its universe of discourse"; in syntactic iconicity, again, texts exhibit parallel structures which become icons of one another for various purposes, aesthetic or other. In her work on the discourse functions of adverbial placement in narratives and descriptive texts, Virtanen (1992a) identifies *structural iconicity* in instances where the number, size, and/or information status of sentence-initial strategy markers reflect the size of the textual boundary that they serve to signal, thus helping to indicate the hierarchy of text structure. This kind of iconicity is also in line with Givón's (1985) ideas on iconicity and isomorphism in syntax.

7. Applied linguistics

Enkvist was constantly concerned about the applicability of academic work. He was one of the founders of AFinLA, the Finnish Association of Applied Linguistics, and he served in several state committees that worked out principles for how to improve university education in languages. For instance, his report (Enkvist 1970) on basic challenges for language centers at universities had the effect that every Finnish university saw the importance of establishing a language center of its own.

But he also did important research in the field of what he saw as applied linguistics. In fact, the 1964 book on stylistics was published in an Oxford University Press book series on applied linguistics. Moreover, he considered the field of rhetoric to be applied text linguistics.

One study that particularly stands out from this point of view is the collection *Coherence and Composition*, which he edited in 1985 in order to stimulate inter-Nordic co-operation in the application of text and discourse linguistics to the teaching of composition (Enkvist 1985a). The volume is based on a symposium he had organized in 1984 and formed the starting point of *The Nordtext Project*, a dynamic network of writing scholars from four Nordic countries whose well-attended symposia continued into the 1990s. In his introduction to the volume Enkvist emphasized the importance of the new perspectives into the study of cohesion and coherence in composition which linguistic stylistics, and text linguistics and discourse analysis can offer. As a shared goal he also raised the issue of improving contacts between theorists and practitioners of composition. Enkvist's view of applied linguistics as a wide and eclectic discipline offering a flow of information between theory and practice is evident in many of his writings dealing with the new vistas opened up by applications of text and discourse linguistics, as well as of linguistic stylistics, to different aspects of language teaching and learning; witness, for instance, his (1987a) discussion of text linguistics for the applier, his (1990) exposition of fundamental problems in the study of discourse aimed at students of writing, and his (1982b) survey of situational contexts from the perspective of stylistics. He also often returned to the issue of theorizing in contrastive linguistics as the basis of applications of concepts and models (see e.g. Enkvist 1984).

At his department at Åbo Akademi University he was seconded in his research on applied linguistics by Håkan Ringbom, who focused his research on the challenges of living with three languages (Swedish, Finnish, and English) in a bilingual (Finnish – Swedish) nation like Finland (cf. e.g. Ringbom 1987) – an experience that he and Enkvist and most of their students were confronted with at Åbo Akademi University. Of special interest for Enkvist in the 1970s was the then challenging technique of cloze testing (cf. e.g. Enkvist and Kohonen 1978).

8. Academic administration, honors, and legacy

In addition to his scholarly work, Enkvist was skilled and efficient in university management, not only as Head of his department, but also as Dean of the Faculty of Arts (1961–1964), as Rector (1966–1969), and as Chancellor (1991) – all at Åbo Akademi University. He was research professor at the Academy of Finland for two periods, and he received the distinguished title of Academician in 1990 (as one of its twelve Finnish Fellows, and the first from a language subject). His memberships in learned academies included the Finnish Society of Sciences and Letters, as well as The Royal Swedish Academy of Letters, History and Antiquities. He was a truly international scholar and active in several associations, his presidencies including those of the European Linguistic Society (SLE), the Modern Humanities Research Association (MHRA), and the International Federation of Modern Languages and Literatures (FILLM). He was awarded four honorary doctorates (in the U.S.A., in Poland, and in Sweden), and he received a Festschrift for his 50th birthday (cf. Ringbom 1975).

Nils Erik Enkvist was extremely well-travelled in comparison to other scholars at the time, from the 1960s until his retirement and beyond. Both as a teacher generally, and as presenter at conferences and as guest lecturer, he was notorious and unusually exciting. But despite – or maybe because of – his varied interests and his desire to see connections and to find an ever deeper and more general understanding of the humanities, he did not focus on promoting *one* single concept that academia would remember him for. He was rather – and always – part of ongoing academic discussions, part of the dynamic process of doing linguistics, and text and discourse linguistics in particular.

His scholarly profile was thus *not only* in some ways enrichingly old-fashioned *but also* in other ways far ahead of his time. Enkvist was a flexibly minded polymath whose perhaps most important legacy was to stress the importance of the mediation of up-to-date knowledge about language, and with this he built the foundation for modern linguistics in Finland and beyond.

References

Andersson, Erik (ed). 1978. *Working Papers on Computer Processing of Syntactic Data*. Turku: Åbo Akademi University.

Björklund, Martina. 1993. *Narrative Strategies in Čechov's The Steppe: Cohesion, Grounding and Point of View*. Turku: Åbo Akademi University Press.

Enkvist, Nils Erik. 1951. *Caricatures of Americans on the English Stage prior to 1870*. Helsinki: Societas Scientiarum Fennica, Commentationes Humanarum Litterarum, 18, 1.

Enkvist, Nils Erik. 1953. *American Humour in England before Mark Twain*. Turku: Åbo Akademi University. Acta Academiae Aboensis, Humaniora, 21, 3.

Enkvist, Nils Erik. 1957. *The Seasons of the Year. Chapters on a Motif from Beowulf to the Shepherd's Calendar*. Helsinki: Societas Scientiarum Fennica, Commentationes Humanarum Litterarum, 22, 4.

Enkvist, Nils Erik. 1964a. *Geoffrey Chaucer*. Stockholm: Natur och kultur.

Enkvist, Nils Erik. 1964b. "On defining style: An essay in applied linguistics." In *Linguistics and Style*, by Nils Erik Enkvist, John Spencer and Michael Gregory, 1–56. Oxford: Oxford University Press.

Enkvist, Nils Erik. 1970. *Kielipalveluopetuksen peruskysymyksiä* [*Basic issues for language center teaching*]. Turku: Åbo Akademi University. Working Papers from the Department of English, Åbo Akademi University, no. 3.

Enkvist, Nils Erik. 1972. "Old English adverbial þa – an action marker?" *Neuphilologische Mitteilungen* LXXIII: 90–96.

Enkvist, Nils Erik. 1973a. *Linguistic Stylistics*. The Hague: Mouton.

Enkvist, Nils Erik. 1973b. "'Theme dynamics' and style: An experiment." *Studia Anglica Posnaniensia* 5: 127–135.

Enkvist, Nils Erik. 1974. *Stilforskning och stilteori* [*Research on style, and the theory of style*]. Lund: Gleerup.

Enkvist, Nils Erik. 1975. *Tekstilingvistiikan peruskäsitteitä* [*Basic concepts in text linguistics*]. Helsinki: Gaudeamus.

Enkvist, Nils Erik. 1978. "Coherence, pseudo-coherence, and non-coherence." In *Reports on Text Linguistics: Semantics and Cohesion*, ed. by Jan-Ola Östman, 109–127. Turku: Åbo Akademi University.

Enkvist, Nils Erik. 1981. "Experiential iconicism in text strategy." *TEXT* 1: 97–111.

Enkvist, Nils Erik. (ed). 1982a. *Impromptu Speech: A Symposium*. Turku: Åbo Akademi University.

Enkvist, Nils Erik. 1982b. "Categories of situational context from the perspective of stylistics." In *Surveys 1: Eight State-of-the-Art Articles on Key Areas in Language Teaching*, ed. by Valerie Kinsella, 58–79. Cambridge: Cambridge University Press.

Enkvist, Nils Erik. 1984. "Contrastive linguistics and text linguistics." In *Contrastive Linguistics: Prospects and Problems*, ed. by Jacek Fisiak, 45–67. Berlin: Mouton.

Enkvist, Nils Erik. (ed). 1985a. *Coherence and Composition*. Turku: Åbo Akademi University.

Enkvist, Nils Erik. 1985b. "A parametric view of word order." In *Text Connexity, Text Coherence: Aspects, Methods, Results*, ed. by Emel Sözer, 320–336. Hamburg: Helmut Buske.

Enkvist, Nils Erik. 1986a. "More about the textual functions of the Old English adverbial þa." In *Linguistics across Historical and Geographical Boundaries. Vol 1: Linguistic Theory and Historical Linguistics. Vol 2: Descriptive, Contrastive, and Applied Linguistics*, ed. by Dieter Kastovsky and Aleksander Szwedek, 301–310. Berlin: Mouton de Gruyter.

Enkvist, Nils Erik. 1986b. "Linearization, text type, and parameter weighting." In *Language and Discourse: Test and Protest*, ed. by Jacob L. Mey, 245–260. Amsterdam: John Benjamins.

Enkvist, Nils Erik. 1987a. "Text linguistics for the applier: An orientation." In *Writing Across Languages: Analysis of L2 Text*, ed. by Ulla Connor and Robert B. Kaplan, 23–43. Reading, MA: Addison-Wesley.

Enkvist, Nils Erik. 1987b. "Text strategies: Single, dual, multiple." In *Language Topics: Essays in Honour of Michael Halliday*, ed. by Ross Steele and Terry Treadgold, 203–211. Amsterdam: John Benjamins.

Enkvist, Nils Erik. 1989. "Connexity, interpretability, universes of discourse, and text worlds." In *Possible Worlds in Humanities, Arts and Sciences: Proceedings of Nobel Symposium 65*, ed. by Sture Allén, 162–186. Berlin: de Gruyter.

Enkvist, Nils Erik. 1990. "Seven problems in the study of coherence and interpretability." In *Coherence in Writing: Research and Pedagogical Perspectives*, ed. by Ulla Connor and Ann M. Johns, 9–28. Alexandria, VA: TESOL.

Enkvist, Nils Erik. 1991. "On the interpretability of texts in general and of literary texts in particular." In *Literary Pragmatics*, ed. by Roger D. Sell, 1–25. London: Routledge.

Enkvist, Nils Erik. 2001. "Reminiscences of a multilingual life: A personal case history." In *Reflections on Multiliterate Lives*, ed. by Diane Belcher and Ulla Connor, 51–59. Clevedon: Multilingual Matters.

Enkvist, Nils Erik, and Viljo Kohonen (eds). 1976. *Reports on Text Linguistics: Approaches to Word Order*. Turku: Åbo Akademi University.

Enkvist, Nils Erik, and Viljo Kohonen (eds). 1978. "Cloze testing: Some theoretical and practical aspects." *AFinLA Yearbook* 8: 181–206.

Enkvist, Nils Erik, and Hans Nordström. 1978. "On textual aspects of intonation in Finland-Swedish newscasts." *Studia Linguistica* 32: 63–79.

Enkvist, Nils Erik, and Brita Wårvik. 1987. "Old English þa, temporal chains, and narrative structure." In *Papers from the 7th International Conference on Historical Linguistics*, ed. by Anna Giacalone Ramat, Onofrio Carruba and Giuliano Bernini, 221–237. Amsterdam: John Benjamins.

Fillmore, Charles J. 1982. "Frame semantics." In *Linguistics in the Morning Calm*, ed. by the Linguistic Society of Korea, 111–137. Seoul: Hanshin.

Givón, Talmy. 1985. "Iconicity, isomorphism, and non-arbitrary coding in syntax." In *Iconicity in Syntax*, ed. by John Haiman, 187–219. Amsterdam: John Benjamins.

Haiman, John. 1980. "The iconicity of grammar: Isomorphism and motivation." *Language* 56: 515–540.

Hakulinen, Auli, Fred Karlsson, and Maria Vilkuna. 1980. *Suomen tekstilauseiden piirteitä: Kvantitatiivinen tutkimus* [On the characteristics of sentences in text in Finnish: A quantitative study]. Helsinki: University of Helsinki, Department of General Linguistics; Publications 6.

Hakulinen, Auli, Maria Vilkuna, Riitta Korhonen, Vesa Koivisto, Tarja Riitta Heinonen, and Irja Alho. 2004. *Iso suomen kielioppi* [The large Finnish grammar]. Helsinki: Suomalaisen Kirjallisuuden Seura.

Halliday, M. A. K., and Ruqaiya Hasan. 1976. *Cohesion in English*. London: Longman.

Harris, Zellig S. 1952. "Discourse analysis." *Language* 28: 1–30.

Hopper, Paul J., and Sandra A. Thompson. 1980. "Transitivity in grammar and discourse." *Language* 56: 251–299.

Jesperson, Otto. 1949. *A Modern English Grammar on Historical Principles. Part VII: Syntax*. Copenhagen: J. Jørgensen & Co.

Kohonen, Viljo. 1978. *On the Development of English Word Order in Religious Prose Around 1000 and 1200 A.D.: A Quantitative Study of Word Order in Context*. Turku: Åbo Akademi University.

Longacre, Robert E. 1983. *The Grammar of Discourse*. New York: Plenum Press.

Östman, Jan-Ola. 1981. *You know: A Discourse-Functional Approach*. Amsterdam: John Benjamins.

Östman, Jan-Ola. 1986. Pragmatics as Implicitness. PhD dissertation, University of California, Berkeley. https://escholarship.org/uc/item/5kg7s881

Östman, Jan-Ola, and Brita Wårvik. 1994. "The Fight at Finnsburh: Pragmatic aspects of a narrative fragment." *Neuphilologische Mitteilungen* XCV: 207–227.

Östman, Jan-Ola, and Tuija Virtanen. 1999. "Theme, comment, and newness as figures in information structuring." In *Discourse Studies in Cognitive Linguistics*, ed. by Karen van Hoek, Andrej A. Kibrik and Leo Noordman, 91–110. Amsterdam: John Benjamins.

Pike, Kenneth Lee. 1954. *Language in Relation to a Unified Theory of the Structure of Human Behavior*. Ann Arbor, MI: Summer Institute of Linguistics.

Ringbom, Håkan (ed). 1975. *Style and Text: Studies Presented to Nils Erik Enkvist*. Stockholm: Skriptor.

Ringbom, Håkan. 1987. *The Role of the First Language in Foreign Language Learning*. Bristol: Multilingual Matters.

Sell, Roger D. (ed). 1991. *Literary Pragmatics*. London: Routledge.

Sell, Roger D. (ed). 2020. *Literary Communication as Dialogue: Responsibilities and Pleasures in Post-Postmodern Times*. Amsterdam: Benjamins.

Sell, Roger D., and Peter Verdonk. (eds). 1994. *Literature and the New Interdisciplinarity: Poetics, Linguistics, History*. Amsterdam: Rodopi.

Virtanen, Tuija. 1992a. *Discourse Functions of Adverbial Placement in English: Clause-Initial Adverbials of Time and Place in Narratives and Procedural Place Descriptions*. Turku: Åbo Akademi University Press.

Virtanen, Tuija. 1992b. "Issues of text typology: Narrative — a 'basic' type of text?" *TEXT* 12: 293–310.

Wårvik, Brita. 1993. *On Grounding in Narrative: Survey of Models and Criteria*. Turku: Department of English, Åbo Akademi University.

Wårvik, Brita. 2013. *Perspectives on Narrative Discourse Markers: Focus on Old English þa*. Turku: Åbo Akademi University.

See also: *Prague School, Stylistics, Literary Pragmatics, Text and Discourse Linguistics, Text linguistics, Text structure*

Indirectness

Nicolas Ruytenbeek
KU Leuven

1. Introduction

Since the late 1970s, scholars in pragmatics have given a lot of attention to the phenomenon of indirectness (also referred to as *indirect communication*), with a clear focus on indirect directives or indirect requests (IRs) (see, e.g., Ruytenbeek 2021). In the present article, I will address the most important definitions of speech act indirectness that have been proposed in the literature since the early work by Austin (1962) and Searle (1975) in the speech act theoretic tradition. In addition, I will critically review available experimental data bearing on the processing of different types of indirectness.

Since the majority of studies on the production side of indirectness have documented the realization of specific speech act types, such as requests, apologies, refusals, etc., it seems appropriate to discuss these studies separately, in a dedicated Handbook entry (see, for example, the recent contributions on complaining (Rodriguez 2022) and directives (Ruytenbeek 2023)). Therefore, in Section 4 of this article, I have instead chosen to address the cognitive dimension of the mechanisms of indirection by reviewing experimental research in psycho- and neurolinguistics that attempts to identify the characteristics specific to indirection, rather than the peculiarities of the processing or production of different types of speech acts. Thus, unlike previous review articles focusing on IRs such as Walker (2013), I will not discuss in detail here the bulk of the empirical research that has been devoted to the forms that (direct and indirect) speech acts (SAs) take across different languages (but see Section 2.2.3 for a short overview) or communicative genres.

This contribution is structured as follows. I will first review the major notions of indirectness that co-exist in the literature, starting from the original notion of an indirect speech act to eventually consider degrees of indirectness (Section 2). I will then address, in Section 3, the view that indirectness is motivated by politeness considerations, as well as other reasons for opting for indirect communication. In Section 4, I will review experimental work bearing on the processing of ISAs, ranging from offline paraphrase acceptability judgments to neurolinguistic and psychophysiological studies. In Section 5, I will conclude and outline promising directions for future research on the topic of indirectness.

2. What is indirectness?

Two recurring issues with indirectness are, on the one hand, that different notions are used in the literature to refer to the direct or indirect mode of realization of SAs and, on the other hand, that authors do not always make explicit what notion of indirectness they are endorsing (Grainger and Mills 2016: 34). In addition, scholars such as Kiesling and Johnson (2010) have developed broader, interaction-oriented notions of indirectness (or what they called *indirection*) that largely depart from the traditional, speech act theoretic view of *speech act* indirectness (see also Lempert 2012 for a discussion). The goal of this section is therefore to identify the different notions of speech act indirectness on the market, with a focus on whether they consist in a binary distinction between direct and indirect SAs (Section 2.1), or, rather, conceive of SAs in terms of a continuum of (in)directness (Section 2.2).

2.1 Binary notions

2.1.1 *Indirectness and non-literalness*

According to Searle's (1969) speech act theory (SAT), the assignment of a speech act (or illocutionary act) to a particular utterance depends on the mood of the sentence uttered.[1] It is the morpho-syntactic features of the sentence (the *illocutionary force indicators*) that determine illocutionary force (Searle 1979: 30; Vanderveken 1990: 15–16). This theory is often called "literalist" because it postulates a one-to-one correspondence relationship between sentences containing such illocutionary force indicators and their illocutionary meaning when they are used in the performance of literal SAs. In other words, for SAT, sentence-types encode illocutionary forces — a view called the *Literal Force Hypothesis*. (For more details, see Ruytenbeek 2021, Chapter 1 and Meibauer 2019)

In SAT, in addition to the SA that can be predicted on the basis of the sentence-type, an utterance can result in the performance of another SA. For example, the interrogative sentence in (1) would constitute, at the literal level, the performance of a request for information about the addressee's (A) ability to close the door.

(1) Can you shut the door?

In many situations, this interrogative construction is uttered by the speaker (S) to indirectly request that A close the door, without S actually intending A to provide them with an answer to the question asked. In that case, the only thing that would matter to S is whether A will comply with their request for action. According to SAT, the request

---

1. Following the speech act theoretic tradition, I will use the phrase *illocutionary act* or, for short, *speech act*, to refer to the action performed by a speaker who utters a sentence with an illocutionary force and a propositional content.

achieved by means of the utterance in (1) is regarded as indirect in the sense that it is performed *by means of, and in addition to*, the literal SA associated with the interrogative sentence type instantiated by (1), namely a polar question about A's ability to close the door. To infer that S did not want them to take the utterance of (1) as a literal question about their abilities, A has to use Gricean principles of conversational cooperation, as well as contextual information (Grice 1975). This inferential reasoning allows A to come to the conclusion that the literal question about their abilities is irrelevant in the current conversational context. A will then use the literal meaning of S's utterance as a starting point to uncover S's illocutionary intention beyond that literal meaning (Searle 1975, 1979: 113–114).

The original speech act theoretic definition of indirectness thus is closely related to the notion of non-literalness. It cannot, however, satisfactorily be equated with it (Grainger and Mills 2016: 35–37). In SAT, indirectness constitutes a subset of the category of non-literalness. Non-literal language use – for example, irony and metaphor – and indirectness are similar in the sense that the content of the SA that S primarily intends to perform is not identical with the content of the SA encoded by the sentence-type of the utterance (sentence mood). ISAs, however, are characterized by the double performance of a direct SA and an indirect SA, the latter being performed not instead of, but in addition to the former (Searle 1979: 114–115; 143–144). By contrast, in the case of a (non-literal) ironic or metaphorical utterance, S means something different from what they literally express. It is therefore possible for an utterance to convey both a non-literal SA and another, distinct, ISA. Accordingly, the interrogative utterance in (2) could be intended as a request in a context where A is making a lot of noise.

(2) Could you make any more noise?

With (2), S would be requesting that A keep it down. According to SAT, such an ironic request would count two times as non-literal: S is not asking whether it is possible for A to make more noise, and neither are they actually requesting that A make more noise.

In SAT, there is a one-to-one relationship between each of the three sentence-types and the major English SA types (Searle 1979; Searle and Vanderveken 1985; Vanderveken 1990). According to the literalist view assumed by SAT, illocutionary forces are encoded at the level of sentence-types. Declaratives encode the illocutionary force of asserting, imperatives the force of requesting action, and interrogatives the force of requesting information. A straightforward consequence of this view regarding the scope of indirectness is that, as soon as the actual illocutionary force of an utterance departs from its direct illocutionary force, the SA counts as indirect. So, any request for action performed by means of a sentence that is *not* imperative, any request for information performed by means of a sentence that is *not* of the interrogative type, and any assertive SA that is *not* performed by means of a declarative sentence fall within the category of indirectness. For instance, the good wishes performed with the imperative utterance in

(3) would be considered indirect, i.e., performed by means of, and in addition to, the literal directive SA encoded by the imperative sentence-type. (For a more detailed discussion of the indirect uses of imperatives, see, e.g., Ruytenbeek 2021)

(3) Sleep well!

As we will see in Section 2.2, in the aftermath of SAT, several scholars have extended the notion of indirectness to cases that do not fit the literalist dimension of the initial theory.

2.1.2 Indirectness and the locutionary/illocutionary distinction

The speech act theoretic notion of indirectness introduced by Searle (1975) can be traced back to Austin's (1962) distinction between locutionary and illocutionary acts. To simplify somewhat, according to Austin (1962: 94–98), performing a locutionary act boils down to producing a meaningful utterance; the performance of an illocutionary act necessarily entails the performance of a locutionary act. An example is (4), which, at the illocutionary level, would be a request to shut the door.

(4) You could shut the door.

The locutionary act performed with (4) can be referred to by using reported speech, as in *S said that A could close the door* (Austin 1962: 95). In the case of the imperative in (5), the locutionary act would be that *S told A to shut the door*:

(5) Shut the door.

Thus, according to Austin, the three major English sentence-types, i.e., declarative, interrogative, and imperative encode different types of locutionary acts (see also Recanati 2013). While different SAs are possible at the illocutionary level, such as the assertion that A could shut the door for (4), only one locutionary act of saying is associated with the utterance.

As in Austin's (1962) approach, the definition of indirectness proposed by Recanati (1987) builds on the distinction between locutionary and illocutionary acts associated with the utterance of a sentence. For Recanati, it is crucial to discern the illocutionary act *indicated* by an utterance, or its potential illocutionary force, and the illocutionary act that is actually *performed* by means of the utterance. According to Recanati, the locutionary act corresponds to the illocutionary act indicated by an utterance. In this view, it is possible for the illocutionary act indicated by a sentence (locutionary act) and the illocutionary act that the utterance is meant to perform (actual illocutionary act) to differ. This is what happens with ISAs. In (4), for example, at the locutionary level, S is saying that A is able to shut the door. The illocutionary act that is indicated by the utterance of the sentence (4) is thus an assertive. However, on some occasions, in uttering (4), S performs an illocutionary act that does not match the one indicated by the sentence uttered, i.e., a request that A shut the door.

Another way to approach indirectness in reference to the locutionary/illocutionary opposition has been proposed by Kissine (2013: 118–122). This time, the distinction concerns the propositional content of the locutionary act and of the illocutionary act, respectively. As Kissine (2008, 2013) suggests, in the case of an ISA such as (4), the propositional content of the locutionary act of *saying that* (i.e., that A is able to shut the door) is different from the propositional content of the illocutionary act of requesting, i.e., that A shut the door.

(4) You could shut the door. (repeated)

For Kissine (2013: 98–100, 118–122), the illocutionary act performed by uttering a sentence should be considered indirect only if its propositional content is not identical to that of the locutionary act that is performed with the utterance.

2.1.3 Indirectness and secondariness

Thus far, we have discussed definitions of indirectness from a formal point of view, i.e., by differentiating levels of meaning associated either with the type of sentence used or with the type of SA performed or indicated. Now I would like to consider ISAs from a more cognitive point of view, by giving a central role to distinctions involving the perspective of the interpreter. One such distinction concerns the primary vs. secondary status of the SAs that can be performed by the uttering of a sentence. For instance, according to Recanati (2004: 74–75), an illocutionary meaning (or SA) would be *secondary* in the sense that its interpretation requires the derivation of another, more basic, *primary* meaning that is implied by the utterance act. Understanding the secondary meaning of an utterance thus involves an inferential path taking the primary meaning as a starting point. Secondary illocutionary meanings meet Recanati's (2004: 42–44) availability condition, according to which language users are aware of the distinction between primary and secondary meanings, and of the inference from the primary meaning to the secondary meaning. Whether an IR performed by means of, for example, (1)–(4) would meet the availability condition is unclear.

(1) Can you shut the door? (repeated)

(4) You could shut the door. (repeated)

This question boils down, in part, to asking whether the interpreters would also infer the meaning of a question (1) or statement (4) about their ability to shut the door. If the availability condition is not met, the SA will qualify as primary. (The experimental evidence discussed in Section 4 suggests that this is indeed often not the case and hence, that many of such SAs qualify as primary.) By contrast, it seems safer to hypothesize that, in the case of the remark about the negative state of affairs in (6), the primary meaning of a statement would be available to the interpreter.

(6) It's cold in here.

The idea is that A would be able to reflect afterwards on the reason why S made a comment about the temperature in the room. The IR in (6) would thus be considered secondary in the sense that it meets the availability condition.

In Ruytenbeek (2021: Chapter 1), I pointed out an ambiguity in Recanati's primary/secondary distinction. Based on Recanati's writings, it is possible to interpret the distinction in terms of a logical relationship. According to another interpretation, the distinction concerns the temporal relationship between the two levels of meaning: an illocutionary meaning would be secondary because it is derived *after* the primary illocutionary meaning. This is precisely the definition that Kissine (2013) adopted. According to him, a SA counts as secondary if its understanding necessitates the prior interpretation of another, primary SA. Under this chronological definition, the IR performed with the remark in (6) would be considered secondary because A first has to interpret the remark as a statement about the temperature before being able to understand it as a request.

To return to the question of the definition of indirectness, we can conclude that the direct or indirect nature of an illocutionary act can be distinguished from the fact that it is primary or secondary. An indirect SA can thus be secondary, that is, interpreted without the utterance being understood as a direct (and primary) SA (Recanati, 1987: 165–167; see also Kissine 2013: 111–122). Accordingly, recent experimental work on the processing of indirect requests (IRs) such as Ruytenbeek et al.'s (2017) study indicates that the SA of requesting can be performed in an indirect manner without being interpreted as a secondary illocutionary meaning. (More on this in Section 4.1.)

2.1.4 *Conventional indirectness: Binary or categorical?*

The notion of indirectness that was originally proposed by Searle (1975) is associated with the distinction between conventional and non-conventional ISAs. As pointed out by Searle (1969, 1975), a general observation about ISAs is that the content of many sentences used in their performance is conceptually related to their felicity conditions. For instance, in the case of directives, the following IR constructions refer to different types of felicity conditions (cf. Searle 1975: 64–67, 71–72).

(1) Can you shut the door? (repeated)

(7) You will shut the door.

(8) I would like you to shut the door.

For instance, (1) concerns the preparatory condition for the performance of a directive SA, i.e., A's ability to carry out the action expressed in the propositional content of the utterance. (7) refers to the propositional content condition according to which A will perform a future action. As a statement to the effect that S wants A to do the action of shutting the door, (8) concerns the sincerity condition for the performance of requests. Searle (1975: 66) noted that many sentences used in the performance of ISAs have a "generality of form." What he was hinting at is that the syntactic structure of the constructions instantiated in, for example, (1), (7), and (8) includes a modal verb (i.e., *can* and *will/would*), the second-person pronoun *you* to single out the addressee and a verbal phrase (VP) corresponding to the action to be performed by A. In the literature, ISAs performed by uttering such sentences with a generality of form are called *conventional* (and also, albeit less frequently, *conventionalized*) ISAs (e.g., Searle 1975; Morgan 1978). What these constructions have in common is that they all instantiate a more abstract construction, i.e., modal verb + *you* + VP.

Clark (1979: 432–433) is more precise than Searle when it comes to explaining what it means for an ISA construction to be "conventionally" indirect. He explains that conventional ISAs involve different *conventions of means*, i.e., conventions about the strategies that can be used to perform ISAs. According to him, a convention of means "specifies a semantic device by which an indirect speech act can be performed" (Clark 1979: 433). An example of a convention of means is making a reference to the preparatory conditions that have to be met for the performance of the intended SA to be felicitous. From that perspective, the utterance in (9) would qualify as a conventional ISA – a conventional IR, to be more accurate – as it refers to a convention of means aligned with the preparatory condition for directives (cf. Searle 1975: 61–62).[2]

(9) Could you tell me the price for a fifth of Jim Beam? (Clark 1979: 448)

By contrast, unlike (9) and the constructions in (7)–(8), the polar interrogative sentence in (10) does not involve the convention of means about the preparatory conditions for directives (nor any other convention of means related to the felicity conditions for directives, more generally).

(10) Does a fifth of Jim Beam cost more than £5? (Clark 1979: 448)

That being said, Clark claims that even though it is a non-conventional IR, (10), which expresses a question about the price of a fifth of Jim Beam, can still be used to request that A tell S how much a fifth of Jim Beam costs. IRs performed by means of sentences that do not express the expected action are also often referred to as "non-conventional" ISAs. An example is (6), which expresses a reason for A to perform some action.

(6) It's cold in here. (repeated)

---

2. Panther and Thornburg (1998) reinterpreted Searle's notion of conventionality of means through the lens of *metonymic illocutionary scenarios*, which outline how the propositional content of constructions used as IRs relate to the conceptual content of the SA of requesting. Within their cognitive linguistic framework, the components of the request scenario are a reinterpretation of SAT's felicity conditions.

Searle (1975: 66) pointed out that, even though it has not the generality of form discussed above, under proper circumstances (6) can serve as a request (for example, to shut the window or turn on the heating).

It seems to me that, despite the fact that sentences such as (6) do not explicitly mention the specific action that is requested from A, such utterances would nonetheless qualify as *conventional* ISAs: while unrelated to the felicity conditions of the SA, a relevant convention of means involves A's reasons for complying with the directive (or S's reasons for performing the directive). I fail to see why the notion of conventionality of means should be limited to the categories of sentences that *both* have a generality of form and refer to felicity conditions of a particular SA type. In Ruytenbeek (2021), I proposed to extend the scope of this notion not only to remarks such as (6) (the convention is the expression of a negative state of affairs), but also to imperative directives. In the latter case, the convention of means is expressing the content of the requested action using a force-dynamic pattern. I therefore believe that the right question to ask is not whether a construction used to perform an ISA is conventional or non-conventional; rather, it is about which convention of means is instantiated by a particular ISA utterance. Conventionality of means can thus be conceived of as a categorical criterion according to which a SA of a particular type can be performed by choosing from a list of strategies. In fact, this view does justice to Searle's observation that not all the sentences of the group "Sentences concerning reasons for doing [the action]" have a generality of form. As will also become clear from the discussion offered in Section 2.2.1, whether an ISA construction is related to a convention of means for the performance of ISAs and whether it has a generality of form are two different questions that should not be confused. Because the bulk of research devoted to the relationship between SA performance and conventionality of means to date has focused exclusively on directives, another issue that remains open for further investigation is the extent to which the notion of conventionality of means can be applied to non-directive SAs.

2.2 Graded notions

2.2.1 *Standardization*

In addition to the binary notion of indirectness and the categorical notion of conventionality (of means), what Clark (1979: 433) calls *conventionality of form* is also useful for distinguishing between the variety of indirect realizations of SAs:

> There are [...] conventions of form — conventions about the wording of indirect speech acts. *Can you pass the salt?* and *Could you pass the salt?*, for example, are highly conventional, or idiomatic, forms in English for requesting the salt. *Is it possible for you to pass the salt?* and *Are you able to pass the salt?* are less idiomatic, and *Is it the case that you at present have the ability to pass the salt?* is not at all idiomatic.

Within a single convention of means, constructions differ in terms of the degree to which they make their indirect illocutionary meaning available for interpretation. Consider the following two constructions, both of which concern A's ability to shut the door.

(1) Can you shut the door? (repeated)

(11) Are you able to shut the door?

While their literal meaning is identical (if one interprets modal *can* in the ability sense) and both can, in theory, felicitously be used as a request to shut the door, (1) is more strongly associated to the performance of an IR compared to (11). In other words, relative to (11), (1) has a stronger degree of *standardization* as an IR expression. Accordingly, ISAs performed by means of constructions such as (1) are referred to as *standardized* ISAs, while ISAs performed with constructions such as (11) are labeled *non-standardized* ISAs, referring to different positions on a cline of standardization. The notion of standardization relates to Morgan's (1978) conventions of usage, according to which natural inferential schemes have "conventionalized" over time, giving rise to short-circuited inferences.

A similar view was advocated by Bach and Harnish (1979:198), who proposed, following Morgan (1978), that the frequency of use of an IR construction such as (1) with a directive illocutionary meaning has resulted in the "compression of the inference" from the literal meaning of the utterance — the question about A's abilities — to its indirect directive meaning. For them, considering that a given ISA construction is highly standardized for the performance of a type of ISA means that the inferential path from the literal to the indirect illocutionary meaning of the expression has been short-circuited; this enables, in the case of a *Can you VP?* IR, A to infer "[S's] requestive illocutionary intent without having to identify the literal intent of questioning" (Bach and Harnish 1979:198).

Following Bach and Harnish (1979), to avoid any confusion, I will not employ *conventionality* in two different senses. Rather, I will only use *conventional(ity)* to refer to conventions of means and *standardization* to refer to differences in the degree to which an ISA construction makes its ISA meaning more or less transparent for the interpreter.[3]

In addition to the two criteria that we have discussed above, i.e., conventionality of means and standardization, a third notion is required to satisfactorily account for the variety of constructions that can be used in the performance of ISAs. To illustrate, while the following two utterances involve the same convention of means about A's abilities and are elaborations on the same *Can you...?* construction, they differ in the extent to which they make their indirect request illocutionary meaning salient.

(1) Can you shut the door? (repeated)

(12) Can you shut the door, please?

---

3. Note that Brown and Levinson (1987:132; 290), following Morgan (1978), use the term *conventionalization* to refer to the diachronic process of standardization.

This is what I called *illocutionary force salience* (Ruytenbeek 2021: Chapter 3). The idea is that, while the propositional content of these two utterances is identical, the presence of the request Illocutionary Force Indicating Device (IFID) *please* in (12) makes its IR meaning more salient compared to that of (1) (this prediction was experimentally demonstrated in Clark's (1979) studies about IR interpretation by local merchants over the phone). Interestingly, the notion of illocutionary force salience both applies to direct and indirect SA realizations. For example, considering the pair of utterances in (5)–(13), it can be argued that the presence of *please* makes the request meaning of the construction more salient in the sense that the same utterance without the particle does not leave out other possible interpretations, such as a command or a piece of advice.

(5) Shut the door. (repeated)

(13) Shut the door, please.

More recently, Holtgraves and Robinson (2020) have shown that the presence of an emoji can help interpreters disambiguate utterances with a potentially sarcastic meaning. This suggests that emoji can function as IFIDs, thus increasing the degree of salience of the (possibly indirect) illocutionary meaning of utterances.

2.2.2 Degrees of indirectness

At this stage, regardless of the exact definition of indirectness that we assume, a SA either is direct or indirect. However, there is also a graded notion of indirectness available in the literature (see, for instance, Leech 1983; Blum-Kulka and Olshtain 1984; Blum-Kulka 1987; and Blum-Kulka et al. 1989). According to this view, *direct* and *indirect* refer to different positions on a scale of (in)directness. If we apply this notion to the SA of request, for example, the direct SA constructions according to the original speech act theoretic definition, i.e., imperative requests, would be considered as "more direct" compared to the request forms originally classified as indirect, such as *Can you VP?*.

A scholar who adopted this view is Leech (1983: 108), who was interested in the effect of "using a more and more indirect kind of illocution" on the degree of perceived politeness.[4] The focus was thus on how participants perceived varying degrees of (in)directness (Blum-Kulka 1987: 132). The rationale for a scale of request indirectness was that "forms [can be] ordered approximately according to [...] the obviousness of the directive" (Ervin-Tripp 1976: 29) or to their "degree of illocutionary transparency" (Blum-Kulka 1987: 133). Accordingly, the longer "the inferential path needed to arrive at an utterance's illocutionary point," the more indirect the SA performed with this utterance

---

4. Contrary to what Blum-Kulka (1987: 133) claimed, while Searle (1975) suggested that the amount of interpretative work can be expected to be higher for requests performed by means of, for example, negative state remarks compared to ability questions, he never explicitly endorsed a graded notion of (in)directness. Nor did Brown and Levinson (1987) assume that indirectness comes by degrees.

(Blum-Kulka 1987: 133). A positive correlation is thus postulated between the degree of indirectness and the amount of inferential work for the interpreter. In the case of the most direct SA realizations, the illocutionary force is indicated, for example, at the level of the sentence-type used, while for the most indirect forms the illocutionary force has to be inferred.

Following the view that (in)directness comes in degrees, a variety of IR realizations were arranged on a cline of increasing indirectness, ranging from imperatives to negative state remarks, with standardized IR constructions of the *Can you VP?* type in between. While early proposals distinguished between only six request realization types (Ervin-Tripp 1976: 29–45), later classifications included eight (House and Kasper 1981: 163–164) or nine categories (Blum-Kulka 1987: 133).

Despite its apparent appeal, the operationalization of (in)directness in terms of relative degrees faces a number of problems. From the perspective of the amount of inferential work for the interpreter, some contrasts do indeed seem a priori plausible; imperative requests, for example, should be easier to interpret as requests relative to negative state remarks (cf. the category of hints in Ervin-Tripp (1976: 42–45) and House and Kasper (1981: 163)). For other contrasts, however, it is less clear whether one construction, e.g., ability interrogatives, should be perceived as more indirect than the other, e.g., want declaratives. In fact, the defendants of what can be called the *graded indirectness hypothesis* rarely made explicit the criteria they used to position different constructions on the (in)directness scale. This is understandable in Blum-Kulka's (1987) study, as relative positions on the cline of (in)directness were determined on the basis of respondents' directness ratings.

Directives set aside, the definition of (in)directness that has been applied to the SA of complaining in previous work (House and Kasper 1981: 160–161; Trosborg 1995: 315–372) proves even more problematic. As pointed out by Decock and Depraetere (2018), in addition to the notion of the transparency with which the illocutionary meaning is conveyed (assuming greater inferential work for more indirect SA realizations), the "assumed degree of face-threat" (2018: 35) for the recipient of the complaint also plays a role. For instance, according to House and Kasper (1981: 160–161), the complaint performed by means of (14) is more indirect compared to that performed with (15).

(14) You have ruined my blouse.

(15) You are really mean.

While, as House and Kasper proposed, in both (14) and (15) S indeed *explicitly asserts* something, the propositional content of (15) does not express the complainable, i.e., the negative event that S is complaining about. In face-threat terms, (15) is more likely to be perceived by A as being offensive — at least in Western cultures — (Decock and Depraetere 2018: 35), but that has nothing to do with the degree of illocutionary transparency or the hypothesized amount of interpretative work for A. In the same vein,

Trosborg (1995: 314) draws a contrast between a "straightforward accusation" (direct complaint) and utterances that "only indirectly express [S's] ill feelings towards [A]." Here, the propositional content of the intended complaint SA is different in both cases, which makes an (in)directness-based comparison irrelevant. The upshot of this discussion is that complaint (in)directness, as adopted by House and Kasper (1981) and Trosborg (1995), is a (largely unclear) combination of illocutionary meaning transparency and face-threat considerations. A possible solution would be to replace it, as Decock and Depraetere (2018) did, with a graded notion of illocutionary transparency of the complaint meaning.

A third issue is that the graded notion of (in)directness only seems viable if it is operationalized in a context-dependent manner. That is, unlike the traditional binary definition of indirectness, it is virtually impossible to determine a priori all possible contrasts in terms of relative (in)directness between candidate constructions. Moreover, the validity of a particular scale of (in)directness would require systematic empirical investigation. That being said, the view that different realizations of a given SA type can be ordered on a cline of (in)directness has made an important contribution by allowing testable predictions about the degree of interpretive effort associated with different SA realizations.

2.2.3 Cross-cultural research on indirectness

Under the impulse of Brown and Levinson (1987) and Blum-Kulka et al. (1989), scholars have explored the (in)direct realizations of different speech acts across different languages. Most, if not all, of the studies that I will briefly address below adopt a graded view of (in)directness, whether at the level of individual SA realizations or at the level of groups of speakers. Using either authentic data from corpora or natural interactions or data from discourse completion tasks, these authors document speakers' preference for more or less (in)direct speech act realizations. In these studies, indirectness is often approached as a type of politeness strategy (Brown and Levinson 1987; more on this in Section 3).

A tendency in cross-cultural pragmatic research on indirectness has been to include an English lingua-culture as a standard of comparison (e.g., Kerkam 2015 on Arabic; Ngor-To Yeung 2000 on Chinese; Larina 2008 on Russian; Ogiermann 2009 on German, Polish and Russian; Spees 1994 on Japanese; Tannen 1981 on Greek; Hidalgo-Downing et al. 2014 and Márquez Reiter et al. 2005 on Spanish). However, such a reference to English is not systematic and there also exist monocultural studies, such as Le Pair (2005) and Schouten (2007) on Dutch and Pizziconi (2009) on Japanese. In addition, the last few years have seen a growing number of studies adopting a cross-cultural comparative perspective, such as Chen and Wang (2021), who investigated indirectness in the speech of Chinese and Korean speakers, and Venuti (2020), who focused on IRs in German and Italian (see also Rygg (2012) on Norwegian and Japanese).

A large body of research specifically concerns (in)directness in directives (Benzdira 2023 on Algerian Arabic; Ngor-To Yeung 2000; Zhang 1995 on Chinese; Byon 2006 and Yu 2011 on Korean; Lwanga-Lumu 1999 on Luganda; Upadhyay 2003 on Nepali; Ruytenbeek 2019, 2020 and Manno 2002 on French; Marti 2006 on Turkish; Ruzickova 2007 on Spanish; Wierzbicka 2003: Chapter 2 on Polish). Here, too, cross-cultural comparisons can be found: De Geer and Tulviste (2002) documented IRs (and requests in general) in Swedish and Estonian, Veres-Guśpiel (2020) IRs in Polish and Hungarian, Márquez Reiter (2002) in Uruguayan and Peninsular Spanish, and Marsily (2018) in French and Spanish. Another example is Yu (2011), who analyzed the relationship between (in)directness and politeness in request realizations in English, Hebrew, and Korean. In Sifianou (1993), off-record indirectness was investigated both in Greek and in English. In the footsteps of Ogiermann (2009), Urbanik (2017) explored directives in Polish and Norwegian. As far as other SA types are concerned, in Chinese, for instance, indirectness has been investigated in general (Zhou and Zhang 2022), as well as in evaluations (Chen and Wang 2021), proposals, and disagreements (Ngor-To Yeung 2000). The indirectness of both requests and criticisms has been analyzed in Russian (Kulbayeva 2020).

Although not exhaustive, this overview shows that empirical studies on the topic of SA indirectness in the world's languages are far from systematic. Hopefully, the coming years will see more comparative work between distant languages and cultures, as well as research targeting different types of SA within specific lingua-cultures.

3. The reasons for indirectness

Before asking why speakers might resort to indirectness, we must first qualify the idea that indirectness is necessarily the result of a strategic choice on their part. Although this view lies at the heart of Brown and Levinson's (1987) influential politeness theory, according to which the use of indirectness in positive, negative, and off-record politeness strategies allows speakers to minimize the emotional costs of their utterances (see also Searle 1975), it has been the subject of debate in recent years. I will return to it shortly.

According to Brown and Levinson (1987), SAs constitute, for the most part, a threat to the speaker's and/or to the addressee's face(s). Specifically, directive acts endanger the negative face of addressees, as they reduce their freedom of action. Thus, the imperative request (5) exerts some degree of psychological pressure on A to perform this action, regardless of their actual volitional state.

(5) Shut the door. (repeated)

On the other hand, illocutionary acts that imply a negative evaluation of A's person or actions, such as criticisms, reproaches, and insults, damage A's positive face, i.e., A's desire to be approved of. This is the case, for example, with (16), which damages A's public self-image and reputation.

(16) You did a terrible presentation.

To minimize the threat to A's negative face, S could phrase their request in an indirect manner involving, for example, a negative politeness strategy consisting in giving A options. In (12), by using modal *can* and an interrogative construction, S makes it easier for A not to comply.

(12) Can you shut the door? (repeated)

Instead of openly criticizing A's performance with a negative, devaluing judgment as in (16), S could also produce an ambiguous utterance like (17), which is likely to be understood as an excuse for the underachievement if the presentation turns out to be of poor quality (or if A believes it to be so) (Holtgraves 1998).

(17) It's difficult to give a good presentation.

A number of empirical studies have shown that (standardized) indirect SA realizations are not necessarily associated with a higher degree of perceived politeness compared to direct SA realizations (e.g., Blum-Kulka 1987; Ogiermann 2009; Upadhyay 2003; Wierzbicka 1985). Against the background of graded indirectness, we can conclude that there is no positive correlation between degree of indirectness and degree of perceived politeness. For instance, very indirect and complex SA realizations can decrease perceived politeness, as they require too much inferential work from A (Manno 2002). They can also be perceived as *overpolite*, which has a negative overtone (Culpeper 2011: 100–103). One should therefore not assume that less standardized ISAs, such as hints, are necessarily more polite than more standardized ones. These findings make it all the more necessary to identify other possible motivations for the use of SA indirectness.

In situations where politeness considerations are not the reason why S formulate their utterances in an indirect manner, the main motivations for indirectness are the wish to avoid committing oneself to the very performance of the SA, the desire to convey multiple meanings at once and the creation or the reinforcement of the intimacy between S and A (Ruytenbeek 2021: Chapter 5).

Regarding the first reason, the more unlikely the direct illocutionary meaning of a pragmatically ambiguous utterance, the more likely that the interpreter will infer its indirect meaning (Clark 1979). For example, if A was unaware of the current temperature in the room where S and A were sitting at the time of the utterance, A may very well interpret (6) at face value, i.e., as a mere comment about the cold temperature.

(6) It's cold in here. (repeated)

This type of ISAs belongs to Brown and Levinson's (1987: 211) category of off-record indirectness, which is characterized by the impossibility to attribute a clear illocutionary intent to S. Because of their truly ambiguous nature, off-record SAs require higher inferential work on the part of the interpreter. Obviously, illocutionary commitment avoidance and politeness considerations are not incompatible motivations for indirectness, as the former enables S to protect themself (including their positive face) from the potentially negative consequences of their utterances. In fact, off-record indirectness offers the best cost/benefit ratio when it comes to performing high-risk SAs such as attempting to bribe a person or making sexual advances, which are central to the *strategic speaker model* (Lee and Pinker 2010; Pinker 2011; Pinker et al. 2008). According to this model, off-record indirectness makes it possible for S to maximize the success of their communicative goals while minimizing the negative consequences of their intended ISAs, such as negative emotions, social awkwardness, and legal costs. This is because off-record utterances allow for plausible deniability of S's illocutionary intent: S cannot be considered to be committed to the performance of the SA they nonetheless intended to convey.

Another advantage of resorting to indirectness is that it helps convey multiple illocutionary meanings at the same time, instead of having to get them across using separate utterances. This is also true of (6), a declarative sentence depicting a negative state of affairs. It can, in addition to its literal meaning about the temperature, be a means for S to convey their dissatisfaction and/or to request that A do something about the current state of affairs. Terkourafi (2011, 2014) proposed that off-record indirectness can, on some occasions, be used to create or reinforce a feeling of intimacy between the conversational participants. This is because S, in leaving implicit a range of illocutionary meanings, may count on the fact that A will be able to figure these out by themself. In doing so, S would emphasize and strengthen the common ground they shared with A, i.e., the set of mutual assumptions and beliefs that they are relying on when drafting their utterance, and which will be invoked by A to make sense of the same utterance. The high amount of inferential work necessary for A to identify the meanings that S indirectly communicates is thus offset by the positive socio-emotional effects of relationship reinforcement.

4. Experimental evidence on the processing of indirectness

In order to understand what it means for an utterance to constitute an ISA, it is necessary to take a closer look at available experimental data. In what follows, I will therefore critically discuss experimental studies that have explored the processing of indirectness. As the majority of previous studies concern directive SAs, with a clear focus on requests, the generalizability of their results remains fairly limited. Nevertheless, we will also see that recent years have witnessed the publication of studies examining other speech acts such as indirect responses and indirect refusals.

4.1 Indirectness and secondariness

Following Grice's (1975) and Searle's (1975) explanation of how the intended meaning of an ISA expression can be inferred by an interpreter, deriving the direct SA of an ISA utterance is the starting point of an inference leading to the recognition of the intended ISA. As Searle (1975: 62–63) himself pointed out, an explanation along these lines is not meant as a psychological theory of utterance interpretation, but rather as a possible rational reconstruction of the inferential steps involved in ISA understanding. Based on the classic speech act theoretic analysis, a sequential model of ISA interpretation was developed: the Standard Pragmatic Model or, for short, SPM. A central tenet of the SPM is that an ISA is by definition secondary, as it is inferred on the basis of, and in addition to, the primary illocutionary meaning of the utterance. For instance, according to the SPM, the IR interpretation of *Can you VP?* is predicted to be the result of an inferential procedure anchored in the recognition of the direct SA performed with the utterance, i.e., the question about A's abilities. In other words, the derivation of this direct meaning is necessary to access the intended IR meaning of the utterance.

Gibbs (1979) conducted a case study to assess the reliability of the SPM. Participants were shown brief stories concluding with a specific utterance, such as (18), framed either as an IR or a direct question. In another experimental condition, the construction was presented without any accompanying contextual narrative.

(18)   Must you open the window?

Following their reading of the target utterance, participants were asked to determine whether a subsequent sentence, such as (19)–(20), accurately paraphrased the utterance they had just read.

(19)   Need you open the window?

(20)   Do not open the window.

In instances where the target utterances were presented without prior context, participants were quicker to process paraphrases like (19), corresponding to the direct question interpretation, compared to the request paraphrases such as (20). This suggests that the direct interpretation of such IR expressions was readily available. However, when a context preceded the utterance, responses were faster for interpreting the IR paraphrases such as (20). This suggests that if a suitable context precedes a structure commonly used as an indirect request, whether it is used as a direct speech act or as an indirect request does not increase the time needed to understand it and judge its paraphrase as (in)correct. These findings challenge the validity of the SPM, which posits that expressions used as indirect requests, which are secondary by definition, should require more time to process compared to their direct uses. Subsequent experiments employing varied methodologies and/or different forms of indirect requests corroborated this finding.

What these studies show is that, regardless of whether the direct meaning of an IR construction gets activated during comprehension, ISAs that are contextually supported do not increase response times compared to direct alternatives.

4.2 Direct and indirect interpretations of ISA constructions

A more systematic approach to the empirical study of indirectness is to compare the comprehension of the direct vs. the indirect meaning of a particular ISA construction. For instance, one would contrast the ability question meaning of the IR construction *Can you VP?* with its indirect meaning of a request to VP. The underlying assumption is that it is possible to conceive of a context in which the ISA construction, such as *Can you VP?*, is truly ambiguous between its direct and its indirect interpretation. An example of such experimental approaches is Abbeduto et al.'s (1989) pioneer study, where IR constructions of the *Could you VP?* type were presented to participants. The properties of the physical items used in the lab where the experiment took place created the conditions necessary to make constructions such as (21)–(22) contextually ambiguous.

(21) Could you open the scissors?

(22) Could you roll the shoebox?

The results of this study indicate that, when they had doubts regarding whether or not it was possible to perform the action mentioned in the utterance, the participants responded only to the direct meaning of the utterance.

In Shapiro and Murphy's (1993) study, participants were presented with questions such as (23)–(24). Their task was to indicate whether or not the question contained a plausible direct meaning, i.e., the meaning of a request for information for (23)–(24).

(23) Can you stop whistling?

(24) Do you have any money?

To avoid any interference due to the presence of an indirect meaning, such as a request for action in (23) or a request for money in (24), participants were explicitly instructed to ignore the possible indirect meanings of the utterances. Provided you can whistle, it is very easy to stop whistling; this makes the ability question meaning of (23) quite unlikely. By contrast, the direct meaning of (24), i.e., that of a request for information, is more likely to be associated with the expression. This study reveals that the presence of a plausible indirect meaning increases response times for deciding whether the direct meaning is plausible, as is the case in (24). The experiment was then replicated with a twist; this time, participants were not instructed to assess the likelihood of the direct illocutionary meaning, but, rather, they were asked to answer pragmatically ambiguous questions similar to those in (23)–(24). The results of the experiment indicate that participants did not take longer to answer a question when one or two meanings were plausible. In addition, their response times were similar regardless of whether it was the direct or the indirect meaning of the utterance that was the only plausible interpretation. This suggests that it is not the direct or indirect nature of an illocutionary meaning, but, rather, whether or not it is a likely continuation of a conversation that impacts its processing times.

Using event-related potentials (ERPs) to measure electrical neural activity during stimulus processing, Coulson and Lovett (2010) compared the comprehension of negative state remarks such as (25) intended as a direct statement or as an IR for another bowl of soup.

(25) My soup is too cold to eat.

The participants in their study had to indicate whether a remark such as (25) was an expected continuation of the scenario or not. Coulson and Lovett found, for these negative state remarks, different patterns of brain activity for the direct and indirect interpretations. When the remark was meant as an IR, it gave rise to more positive waveforms between the second word (*soup*) and the sixth word (*to*) compared to its interpretation as a direct statement. For the authors, this finding was an indication of decreased processing effort for the utterance when it was meant as an IR. However, it can also be explained by the observation that, compared to the literal statement reading, the IR interpretation of the negative state remarks was more natural in the conversational contexts used in Coulson and Lovett's experimental scenarios (see also Boux et al. 2023: 3 and Ruytenbeek 2021: Chapter 4).

Another study pertaining to the processing of negative state remarks is van Ackeren et al.'s (2012), which investigated the activation of brain regions associated with motor action during the processing of negative state remarks such as (26) used as IRs.

(26) It is very hot here.

The authors first displayed a picture of a scene on the computer screen; then they presented a spoken utterance to the participants. The participants' task was to listen attentively to the utterances and decide whether or not the speakers wanted their addressees to perform some action. In 15% of the trials, they were also asked whether the utterance was a request. The key finding of this study is that, despite the fact that the literal meaning of negative state remarks such as (26) does not include any lexical reference to motor action, processing them as IRs elicited increased activation in the cortical motor areas. In addition, negative state remarks meant as IRs gave rise to a stronger activation of two brain regions typically associated with Theory of Mind (ToM): the medial prefrontal cortex (mPFC) and the temporo-parietal junction (TPJ). This latter result can be explained by the need for extra activation in the ToM areas for the successful comprehension of less standardized ISA expressions, the processing of which relies heavily on the mental states the interpreter attributes to S. These findings thus reveal extra processing costs for IRs of the negative state remark type, as these were associated with a higher level of activation in specific brain regions. Importantly, other experimental studies found similar ToM brain networks to be activated during the processing of indirect replies in English and Japanese (e.g., Bašnáková et al. 2014; Bendtz et al. 2022; Feng et al. 2021; Shibata et al. 2011; see Boux et al. 2023 for a discussion).

Using the pupillometry technique, Tromp et al. (2016) measured changes in pupil size during the interpretation of negative state remarks. With a design comparable to van Ackeren et al.'s (2012), they found that negative state remarks increased pupil diameter only when they were used as IRs. Assuming that changes in pupil size reflect changes in processing load (see e.g., Piquado et al. 2010 for a review), this finding could indicate that IRs of the negative state remark type are more effortful to process compared to their direct counterparts. This conclusion should, however, be qualified: as in van Ackeren et al.'s (2012) study, the IR uses of the negative state remarks in Tromp et al.'s (2016) experiment were compared to a different SA type, i.e., statements (assertive type) (Egorova et al. 2014). It therefore remains possible that the brain activation and pupil size patterns found in these studies reflect, at least in part, processing differences for distinct SA types.

The experimental studies reported on in Ruytenbeek et al. (2017) were designed in such a way that French IR constructions, such as *Can you VP?* (*Pouvez-vous VP?*) and *Is it possible to VP?* (*Est-il possible de VP?*), could be interpreted either as a polar question or as an IR in exactly the same context. The authors designed a grid containing geometrical shapes of different types (square, circle, etc.) and colours (red, green, etc.), with some boxes in the grid being empty. A response button with *yes* and *no* as options was featured just below the grid containing the coloured shapes. One experiment consisted in the audio presentation of recorded utterances played through headphones. At the same time, the grid containing the coloured geometrical shapes and the response buttons was displayed on the screen of the testing computer. The participants were instructed to react to the stimuli either by answering with *yes* or *no* or by moving a shape to another box in the grid. It was only possible to displace a shape if the final position was empty so that the shape would fit it.

In the first experiment, the stimuli included imperative instructions, IR expressions that could only be responded to with *no*, IR expressions that both could be responded to with *yes* or by displacing a shape in the grid, and control items. In the first experiment, IR utterances and controls were of the interrogative type, whereas in the second experiment their declarative counterparts (and a *true/false* response button) were used instead:

(27)   Can you move the red circle to the left of the yellow rectangle?

(28)   Is it possible to move the red circle to the left of the yellow rectangle?

(29)   You can move the red circle to the left of the yellow rectangle.

(30)   It is possible to move the red circle to the left of the yellow rectangle.

For half of the IR expressions, there were two possible response options: either clicking on the *yes* button or moving the shape to another box in the grid (it was technically impossible for participants to provide both responses to a particular stimulus; it was thus a forced choice). The following measures of IR interpretation were collected: type of response (answering yes/no or moving a shape), response times, and eye fixations.

An interesting finding in this study is that ability interrogatives and declaratives resulted in longer response times not when they were processed as IRs, but when they were understood as direct questions and statements, respectively. A plausible explanation is that the IR meaning associated with these expressions competed with the direct interpretation reflected in the *yes/true* responses, causing interference. Another finding is the absence of eye fixations on the *yes/true* response buttons for trials where a stimulus was interpreted as an IR. This suggests, against the SPM discussed in Section 4.1, that the IR interpretations of these stimuli were primary and not secondary. It was also found by Ruytenbeek et al. (2017) that the request interpretations were more frequent for the highly standardized *Can you VP?* and *You can VP* compared to the less standardized *Is it possible to VP?* and *It is possible to VP*. This result provides empirical evidence for the impact of degrees of standardization on the likelihood of an indirect interpretation. Finally, it is quite striking that the direct interpretations of the pragmatically ambiguous ability interrogatives and declaratives outnumbered their IR interpretations by a ratio of two to one. A plausible reason for the high frequency of direct interpretations of the IR stimuli in Ruytenbeek et al.'s (2017) experiments has to do with politeness considerations. As we saw in Section 3, politeness is sometimes a reason for using indirectness. In the context of Ruytenbeek et al.'s (2017) studies, however, no real interaction took place between the speakers who had recorded the spoken utterances and the actual participants in the experiments. The latter were therefore unlikely to attribute to the former any intention to be polite that would explain their use of indirectness.[5] Another possible reason why participants more often interpreted the IR constructions as direct SAs is that it was easier for them to do so: clicking on the *yes/true* button took less time than selecting and moving a shape to another box in the grid.

In a recent study, Boux et al. (2023) investigated the cognitive properties of the interpretation of indirect replies. The stimuli in their experiment consisted of question-answer pairs such as (31a)–(32) and (31b)–(32):

(31) a. Is your cat hurt?
 b. Are you bringing your cat to the vet?

---

5. An anonymous reviewer remarked that since politeness can also occur between strangers, prior interaction is not a precondition for it. A possible explanation for the presence of indirectness in the instructions of this study could be a default expectation that instructions are formulated *in a polite manner*; of course, further empirical work will be needed to verify this hypothesis.

(32)   It got wounded.

Here, the SA performed in the first part of the pair is a request for information; both the direct and the indirect replies provide information to the question asked. The study also included pairs constituted by an information query (33a) or an indirect offer/proposal (33b) followed by a reply such as (34).

(33)   a.   Have you decided on a destination?
       b.   Shall I buy the train tickets?

(34)   We are not sure where to go yet.

While (34) provided information to the question asked in (33a), the same expression consisted of the rejection of the offer/proposal in (33b). Three key findings are worth commenting on here. First, participants rated the indirect replies as being less predictable compared to their direct counterparts, which can be explained by the fact that there were fewer constraints on the propositional content of indirect replies compared to *yes* and *no* direct replies. Second, indirect replies were perceived as less semantically similar to the questions and less coherent with the preceding context in comparison with direct replies. This lower degree of coherence with the context is consistent with the analysis of indirect replies following information queries and declinations of offers as violations of the relation maxim (Grice 1975). And third, participants considered the interpretation of indirect replies to be less certain compared to that of direct replies. It is important to note that these different measures displayed a very high positive correlation rate. It therefore makes sense to operationalize off-record indirectness using such a set of cognitive features that should, in all likelihood, also be reflected by neuro-psychological correlates (cf. Tomasello 2023).

4.3   Summary

Let us take stock. The experimental studies discussed in this Section invalidate the hypothesis, presented in Section 2, that standardized IRs are necessarily secondary. Concerning the processing times associated with indirectness in requests, available evidence shows that highly standardized IRs do not systematically take longer to process relative to their imperative counterparts or their direct interpretations. In other words, the comprehension of an IR does not necessarily entail the activation of its direct meaning. Whether these results also apply to less standardized IR expressions, such as negative state remarks, remains to be demonstrated. In future experimental studies, one should indeed remain aware that indirectness is not a homogenous pragmatic category, as it both encompasses idiomatic, highly standardized ISA constructions and less standardized ISA constructions also referred to as off-record indirectness. Regarding the neuro-cognitive correlates of indirectness, while little is known about highly standardized ISAs, available experimental data indicate that negative state remarks and indirect replies, both of which can be motivated by considerations of politeness, result in a higher activation in the brain network associated with Theory of Mind.

5. Conclusions and future directions

When I opened this article, I asked the following question: *What is indirectness?* To answer it, I put forward the idea that two types of notions should be distinguished in the literature: binary definitions, on the one hand, and a graded notion, on the other hand. In doing so, I reduced the complexity of the picture drawn by authors such as Grainger and Mills (2016: 34–35), while acknowledging the substantial body of cross-cultural pragmatic studies on (in)directness across different languages and varieties of languages. I also pointed to the theoretical difficulties encountered by the hypothesis of a continuum of (in)directness. I believe that the terminological clarification and the discussion of available definitions offered in this article will "support, guide, but also challenge the interpretation of psycholinguistic and neurolinguistic studies on indirectness" (Boux et al. 2023: 22). This research will make it possible to test a higher number of predictions depending on the theoretical background one assumes. For instance, I expect the processing effort for different SA interpretations – and the likelihood that an ISA will be primary or secondary – to be shaped by a combination of parameters including, among others, conventionality of means, standardization, and salience of illocutionary meaning. Following the impulse of the neurolinguistic and psycholinguistic studies carried out in the last decade, more recent experimental studies involving psychophysiological methods are needed to document the brain activity and the cognitive and emotional correlates of various forms of indirectness (Tomasello 2023), while remaining aware that speakers' motivation for using indirectness may very well influence how their utterances are perceived and processed. I hope that, complemented by a systematic consideration of the socio-cultural variables influencing SA comprehension, the notions and approaches discussed in this article will pave the way for more studies on SA interpretation in general, and on indirectness in particular both in specific world's languages and as part of cross-cultural comparative research.

Funding

This chapter was written during a research stay at the Jean Nicod institute in November-December 2023, funded by KU Leuven (reference ZKE3026 – STG/22/010).

Open Access publication of this chapter was funded through a Transformative Agreement with KU Leuven.

References

Abbeduto, Leonard, Laurie Furman, and Betty Davies. 1989. "Identifying speech acts from contextual and linguistic information." *Language and Speech* 32 (3): 189–203.

Austin, John L. 1962. *How to Do Things with Words*. Oxford: Clarendon Press.

Bach, Kent, and Robert M. Harnish. 1979. *Linguistic Communication and Speech Acts*. Cambridge: MIT Press.

Bašnáková, Jana, Kirsten Weber, Karl Magnus Petersson, Jos Van Berkum, and Peter Hagoort. 2014. "Beyond the language given: The neural correlates of inferring speaker meaning." *Cerebral Cortex* 24 (10): 2572–2578.

Bendtz, Katarina, Sarah Ericsson, Josephine Schneider, Julia Borg, Jana Bašnáková, and Julia Uddén. 2022. "Individual differences in indirect speech act processing found outside the language network." *Neurobiology of Language* 3 (2): 287–317.

Benzdira, Halima. 2023. Cross-cultural Realization of the Speech Act of Requests: Case Study of Algerian Ph.D. Students. PhD dissertation, Manchester Metropolitan University.

Blum-Kulka, Shoshana. 1987. "Indirectness and politeness in requests: Same or different?" *Journal of Pragmatics* 11 (2): 131–146.

Blum-Kulka, Shoshana, Juliane House, and Gabriele Kasper (eds). 1989. *Cross-Cultural Pragmatics: Requests and Apologies*. Norwood: Ablex.

Blum-Kulka, Shoshana, and Elite Olshtain. 1984. "Requests and apologies: A cross-cultural study of speech act realization patterns (CCSARP)." *Applied Linguistics* 5: 198–212.

Brown, Penelope, and Stephen Levinson. 1987. *Politeness: Some Universals in Language Usage*. Cambridge: Cambridge University Press.

Boux, Isabella P., Konstantina Margiotoudi, Felix R. Dreyer, Rosario Tomasello, and Friedemann Pulvermüller. 2023. "Cognitive features of indirect speech acts." *Language, Cognition and Neuroscience* 38 (1): 40–64.

Byon, Andrew Sangpil. 2006. "The role of linguistic indirectness and honorifics in achieving linguistic politeness in Korean requests." *Journal of Politeness Research* 2 (2): 247–276.

Chen, Xi, and Jiayi Wang. 2021. "First order and second order indirectness in Korean and Chinese." *Journal of Pragmatics* 178: 315–328.

Clark, Herbert H. 1979. "Responding to indirect speech acts." *Cognitive Psychology* 11: 430–477.

Coulson, Seana, and Christopher Lovett. 2010. "Comprehension of non-conventional indirect requests: An event-related brain potential study." *Italian Journal of Linguistics* 22 (1): 107–24.

Culpeper, Jonathan. 2011. *Impoliteness: Using Language to Cause Offence*. Cambridge: Cambridge University Press.

De Geer, Boel, and Tiia Tulviste. 2002. "Behaviour regulation in the family context in Estonia and Sweden." *Pragmatics* 12(3): 329–346.

Decock, Sofie, and Ilse Depraetere. 2018. "(In)directness and complaints: A reassessment." *Journal of Pragmatics* 132: 33–46.

Egorova, Natalia, Friedemann Pulvermuller, and Yury Shtyrov. 2014. "Neural dynamics of speech act comprehension: An MEG study of naming and requesting." *Brain Topography* 27 (3): 375–392.

Ervin-Tripp, Susan. 1976. "Is Sybil there? the structure of some American English directives." *Language in Society*. 5: 25–66.

Feng, Wangshu, Hongbo Yu, and Xiaolin Zhou. 2021. "Understanding particularized and generalized conversational implicatures: Is theory-of-mind necessary?" *Brain and Language* 212: 104878.

Gibbs, Raymond W. 1979. "Contextual effects in understanding indirect requests." *Discourse Processes* 2: 1–10.

Grainger, Karen, and Sara Mills. 2016. *Directness and Indirectness Across Cultures*. Springer.

Grice, Herbert P. 1975. "Logic and Conversation." In *Syntax and Semantics, Vol. 3: Speech Acts*, ed. by Peter Cole and Jerry L. Morgan, 41–58. New York: Academic Press.

Hidalgo-Downing, Laura, Raquel Hidalgo-Downing, and Angela Downing. 2014. "Strategies of (in)directness in Spanish speakers' production of complaints and disagreements in English and Spanish." In *The Functional Perspective on Language and Discourse: Applications and Implications*, ed. by María Angeles Gómez González, Francisco José Ruiz de Mendoza Ibáñez, Francisco Gonzálvez García, and Angela Downing Rothwell, 261–284. Amsterdam: John Benjamins.

Holtgraves, Thomas. 1998. "Interpreting indirect replies." *Cognitive Psychology* 37 (1): 1–27.

Holtgraves, Thomas, and Caleb Robinson. 2020. "Emoji can facilitate recognition of conveyed indirect meaning." *PloS one* 15(4): e0232361.

House, Juliane, and Gabriele Kasper. 1981. "Politeness markers in English and German." In *Conversational Routine*, ed. by Florian Coulmas, 157–185. The Hague: Mouton.

Kerkam, Zainab M. 2015. A comparison of Arabic and English Directness and Indirectness: Cross-Cultural Politeness. PhD dissertation, Sheffield Hallam University.

Kiesling, Scott F., and Elka Gosh Johnson. 2010. "Four forms of interactional indirection." *Journal of Pragmatics* 42 (2): 292–306.

Kissine, Mikhail. 2008. "Locutionary, illocutionary, perlocutionary." *Language and Linguistics Compass* 2 (6): 1189–1202.

Kissine, Mikhail. 2013. *From Utterances to Speech Acts*. Cambridge: Cambridge University Press.

Kulbayeva, Aisulu. 2020. "Balancing power and solidarity through indirectness: A case study of Russian and Kazakh meeting chairs." *Journal of Politeness Research* 16 (2): 159–191.

Larina, Tatiana. 2008. "Directness, imposition and politeness in English and Russian." *Cambridge ESOL: Research Notes* 33: 33–38.

Le Pair, Rob. 2005. "Politeness in The Netherlands: Indirect requests." In *Politeness in Europe*, ed. by Leo Hickey, and Miranda Stewart, 66–81. Bristol, Blue Ridge Summit: Multilingual Matters.

Lee, James J., and Steven Pinker. 2010. "Rationales for indirect speech: The theory of the strategic speaker." *Psychological Review* 117 (3): 785–807.

Leech, Geoffrey. 1983. *Principles of Pragmatics*. London: Routledge.

Lempert, Michael. 2012. "Indirectness." In *The Handbook of Intercultural Discourse and Communication*, ed. by Christina Bratt Paulston, Scott F. Kiesling, and Elizabeth S. Rangel, 180–204. Oxford: John Wiley & Sons.

Lwanga-Lumu, Joy Christine. 1999. "Politeness and indirectness revisited." *South African Journal of African Languages* 19 (2): 83–92.

Manno, Giuseppe. 2002. "La politesse et l'indirection: Un essai de synthèse." *Langage & Société* 100 (2): 5–47.

Márquez Reiter, Rosina. 2002. "A contrastive study of conventional indirectness in Spanish: Evidence from Peninsular and Uruguayan Spanish." *Pragmatics* 12 (2): 135–151.

Márquez Reiter, Rosina, Isobel Rainey, and Fulcher, Glenn. 2005. "A comparative study of certainty and conventional indirectness: Evidence from British English and Peninsular Spanish." *Applied linguistics* 26 (1): 1–31.

Marsily, Aurélie. 2018. "Directness vs. indirectness: A contrastive analysis of pragmatic equivalence in Spanish and French request formulations." *Languages in Contrast* 18 (1): 122-144.

Marti, Leyla. 2006. "Indirectness and politeness in Turkish–German bilingual and Turkish monolingual requests." *Journal of Pragmatics* 38 (11): 1836–1869.

Meibauer, Jörg. 2019. "What is an indirect speech act?" *Pragmatics and Cognition* 26 (1): 61–84.

Morgan, Jerry L. 1978. "Two types of convention in indirect speech acts." In *Syntax and Semantics. Vol 9, Pragmatics*, ed. by Peter Cole, 261–280. New York: Academic Press.

Ngor-To Yeung, Lorrita. 2000. "The question of Chinese indirectness: A comparison of Chinese and English participative decision-making discourse." *Multilingua* 19 (3): 221–264.

Ogiermann, Eva. 2009. "Politeness and in-directness across cultures: A comparison of English, German, Polish and Russian requests." *Journal of Politeness Research* 5: 189–216.

Panther, Klaus-Uwe, and Linda Thornburg. 1998. "A cognitive approach to inferencing in conversation." *Journal of Pragmatics* 30 (6): 755–769.

Pinker, Steven. 2011. "Indirect speech, politeness, deniability, and relationship negotiation: Comment on Marina Terkourafi's "The puzzle of indirect speech". *Journal of Pragmatics* 43 (11): 2866–2868.

Pinker, Steven, Martin A. Nowak, and James J. Lee. 2008. "The logic of indirect speech." *PNAS* 105 (3): 833–838.

Piquado, Tepring, Derek Isaacowitz, and Arthur Wingfield. 2010. "Pupillometry as a measure of cognitive effort in younger and older adults." *Psychophysiology* 47 (3): 560–569.

Pizziconi, Barbara. 2009. "Stereotyping communicative styles in and out of the language and culture classroom: Japanese indirectness, ambiguity and vagueness." In *Pragmatics Applied to Language Teaching and Learning*, ed. by Gomez Moron, Reyes, Manuel Padilla Cruz, Lucia Fernandez Amaya, and Maria De la O Hernandez Lopez, 221–254. Cambridge: Cambridge Scholars Publishing.

Recanati, François. 1987. *Meaning and Force: The Pragmatics of Performative Utterances*. Cambridge: Cambridge University Press.

Recanati, François. 2004. *Literal Meaning*. Cambridge: Cambridge University Press.

Recanati, François. 2013. "Content, mood, and force." *Philosophy Compass* 8: 622-32.

Rodriguez, Andrea. 2022. "Complaining." *Handbook of Pragmatics* Online 25: 66–90.

Ruytenbeek, Nicolas. 2019. "Lexical and morpho-syntactic modification of student requests: An empirical contribution to the study of im/politeness in French e-mail speech acts." *Lexique* 24: 29–47.

Ruytenbeek, Nicolas. 2020. "Do indirect requests communicate politeness? An experimental study of conventionalized indirect requests in French email communication." *Journal of Politeness Research* 16 (1): 111–142.

Ruytenbeek, Nicolas. 2021. *Indirect Speech Acts*. Cambridge: Cambridge University Press.

Ruytenbeek, Nicolas. 2023. "Directives (with a special emphasis on requests)." In *Handbook of Pragmatics* Online 26: 67–93.

Ruytenbeek, Nicolas, Ekaterina Ostashchenko, and Mikhail Kissine. 2017. "Indirect request processing, sentence-types and illocutionary forces." *Journal of Pragmatics* 119: 46–62.

Ruzickova, Elena. 2007. "Strong and mild requestive hints and positive-face redress in Cuban Spanish." *Journal of Pragmatics* 39 (6): 1170–1202.

Rygg, Kristin. 2012. "Direct and indirect communicative styles: A study in sociopragmatics and intercultural communication based on interview discourse with Norwegian and Japanese business executives." PhD dissertation, University of Bergen.

Schouten, Barbara C. 2007. "Self-construals and conversational indirectness: A Dutch perspective". *International Journal of Intercultural Relations* 31 (3): 293–297.

Searle, John R. 1969. *Speech Acts: An Essay in the Philosophy of Language.* Cambridge: Cambridge University Press.

Searle, John R. 1975. "Indirect speech acts." In *Syntax and Semantics, vol. 3: Speech Acts*, ed. by Peter Cole and Jerry L. Morgan, 59–82. New York: Academic Press.

Searle, John R. 1979. *Expression and Meaning: Studies in the Theory of Speech Acts.* Cambridge: Cambridge University Press.

Searle, John R., and Daniel Vanderveken. 1985. *Foundations of Illocutionary Logic.* Cambridge: Cambridge University Press.

Shapiro, Amy M., and Gregory Murphy. 1993. "Can you answer a question for me? Processing indirect speech acts." *Journal of Memory and Language* 32 (2): 211–229.

Shibata, Midori, Jun-Ichi Abe, Hiroaki Itoh, Koji Shimada, and Satoshi Umeda. 2011. "Neural processing associated with comprehension of an indirect reply during a scenario reading task." *Neuropsychologia* 49 (13): 3542–3550.

Sifianou, Maria. 1993. "Off-record indirectness and the notion of imposition". *Multilingua* 12 (1): 69–80.

Spees, Hiroko. 1994. "A cross-cultural study of indirectness." *Issues in Applied Linguistics* 5(2): 231–253.

Tannen, Deborah. 1981. "Indirectness in discourse: Ethnicity as conversational style." *Discourse Processes* 4 (3): 221–238.

Terkourafi, Marina. 2011. "The puzzle of indirect speech." *Journal of Pragmatics* 43: 2861–2865.

Terkourafi, Marina. 2014. "The importance of being indirect." *Belgian Journal of Linguistics* 28: 45–70.

Tomasello, Rosario. 2023. "Linguistic signs in action: The neuropragmatics of speech acts." *Brain and Language* 236: 105203.

Tromp, Johanne, Peter Hagoort, and Antje S. Meyer. 2016. "Pupillometry reveals increased pupil size during indirect request comprehension." *Quarterly Journal of Experimental Psychology* 69: 1093–1108.

Trosborg, Anna. 1995. *Interlanguage Pragmatics: Requests, Complaints, and Apologies.* Berlin: Mouton de Gruyter.

Upadhyay, Shiv R. 2003. "Nepali requestive acts: Linguistic indirectness and politeness reconsidered." *Journal of Pragmatics* 35 (10–11): 1651–1677.

Urbanik, Pawel K. 2017. "Requests in Polish and Norwegian informal conversation: A comparative study of grammatical and pragmatic patterns." PhD dissertation, University of Oslo.

Vanderveken, Daniel. 1990. *Vol. 1, Meaning and Speech Acts.* Cambridge: Cambridge University Press.

Van Ackeren, Markus J., Daniel Casasanto, Harold Bekkering, Peter Hagoort, and Shirley-Ann Rueschemeyer. 2012. "Pragmatics in action: Indirect requests engage theory of mind areas and the cortical motor network." *Journal of Cognitive Neuroscience* 24 (11): 2237–2247.

Venuti, Ilaria. 2020. "Politeness, indirectness and efficacy in Italian and German requestive speech acts." PhD dissertation, Università Ca' Foscari Venezia.

Veres-Guśpiel, Agnieska. 2020. "Social contexts of indirect requests in Polish and Hungarian." *New Horizons in English Studies* 5 (1): 24–47.

Walker, Traci. 2013. "Requests." In *Handbook of Pragmatics: Pragmatics of Speech Actions*, ed. by Marina Sbisà and Ken Turner, 445–466. Berlin: De Gruyter.

Wierzbicka, Anna. 1985. "Different cultures, different languages, different speech acts. *Journal of Pragmatics* 9: 145–178.

Wierzbicka, Anna. 2003. *Cross-cultural pragmatics: The semantics of human interaction*. Berlin: Mouton de Gruyter.

Yu, Kyong-Ae. 2011. "Culture-specific concepts of politeness: Indirectness and politeness in English, Hebrew and Korean requests." *Intercultural Pragmatics* 8 (3): 385–409.

Zhang, Yanyin. 1995. "Indirectness in Chinese requesting." In *Pragmatics of Chinese as a Native and Target Language*, ed. by Gabriele Kasper, 69–118. Honolulu: University of Hawaii Press.

Zhou, Ling, and Shaojie Zhang. 2022. "A multifunctional analysis of off-record indirectness in Chinese interactions." *Language Sciences* 90: 101459.

Indexicality

Tomi Visakko & Heini Lehtonen
University of Helsinki

1. Introduction

In the study of language, the term *indexicality* typically refers to a realm of meaning that is not based on the symbolic contents of linguistic signs *per se*, but on the context-dependent configurations and effects of linguistic signs in use. These effects are at work, for example, when German is used in car advertisements (*Volkswagen. Das Auto.*) and restaurants all around the globe are named with French looking/sounding names. There is nothing about the structure of German language that makes it especially suitable for selling cars. It is the indexicality of *Deutsch* that invokes associations with advanced technology, functionality, and reliability, in the same way as *français* is associated with culinary pleasures and culture (Hornikx et al. 2013).

In particular, the theorization of indexical phenomena has sought to explain how language use is inherently intertwined with social activities, groups and categories. Indexicality, in other words, deals with the social effects of language use. As Agha (2007a: 14) puts it: "[T]he social effects mediated by speech are highly context-bound or *indexical* in character: they are evaluated in relation to the context or situation at hand, including those aspects of the situation created by what has already been said or done."

While the social effects of language use become actualized in specific events as the sum of many contextual variables, indexicality often relies on widely recognized cultural models, schemata, or stereotypes that link features of language with social categories. Indexicality, thus, requires the analyst to pay attention to the details of events of language use as well as socially transmitted models of indexicality. Indexicality, then, is a way of understanding in analytical detail how rough distinctions between "micro-level" linguistic details and "macro-level" social categories become linked at different *scales* of social interaction (see Blommaert 2007a; Carr and Lempert 2016).

Agha (2007a: 14) specifies that "we may speak, in particular, of social indexicality when the contextual features indexed by speech and accompanying signs are understood as attributes of, or relationships between, social persons." The term social indexicality thus foregrounds the indexical effects that are in play when linguistic resources become associated with recognizable social identities, styles, or interactional stances. For instance, several studies from late modern European cities show how resources emerging from ethnic minorities come to index urban youth styles, and a streetwise stance (e.g. Aarsæther 2010; Knudsen 2010; Nørreby 2015; Lehtonen 2016a; Gadet 2022; Gross and Boyd 2022; Quist 2022; Svendsen 2022).

In this article, we explore indexicality in the broad sense as the contextual conditions and effects of language use. Our aim is to show that a broad attention to indexical relations is a useful way to understand and to critically evaluate the embeddedness of linguistic meaning in and across contexts (of usage). That is, indexicality here covers all the different ways in which linguistic forms become linked to and derive their meaning from context-bound sociocultural practices. Thus, indexicality offers a view on processes of contextualization, a concept developed in interactional sociolinguistics that has evolved in parallel with the theories of indexicality (Gumperz 1982, 1992; Silverstein 1992). The indexical phenomena we center on include registers and enregisterment, genres and genre formation, interdiscursivity, voice, and stylized performances. They all illuminate in different ways how linguistic signs "point to" different dimensions of context, thus contributing to the social organization of the event.

Indexicality as a term has a long history in Western philosophy and semiotics. For the linguistic uses of the term, Charles Peirce's (1839–1914) (see *C. S. Peirce*) synthesis of the preceding philosophical and semiotic traditions is an inescapable starting point, for it was a Peircean view of indexicality that was imported to linguistics by pioneers, such as Roman Jakobson (1896–1982) (see *Roman Jakobson*) and his student Michael Silverstein (1945–2020). In Peircean semiotics, indexicality denotes a specific type – or ground – of meaning that is based on the contiguity of the object and the sign. That is, indexical meanings derive from a perceived relationship of causality or co-occurrence between the sign and the object of which the sign conveys information. Classical examples include, for example, smoke as an index of fire, a weather vane as an index of wind direction, or a pointing finger as an index of an object or a direction (Lee 1997a: 119; Parmentier 1994: 4–5; Mertz 1985: 4). In the study of language, indexicality draws attention to the emergent coordination of events of language use (see Silverstein 2023: 22). Different co-occurring (linguistic and non-linguistic) elements of the event bring about an experience of a specific kind of social context. As Silverstein (2023: 23) puts it: "This cause-and-effect 'bringing about' is, from a semiotic perspective, a mode of what Charles Sanders Peirce termed indexicality." Indexical meaning, in other words, unfolds temporally, across events of sign production and sign interpretation. The import of such a view for the study of language is, among other things, that it forces one to look at language in terms of a contextual interpretative process, instead of an abstract lexico-grammatical system alone.

One phenomenon that forced linguists to theorize an indexical level of meaning early on are shifters, such as deictic pronouns or adverbs (e.g. *you*, *this*, *here*). Their referents, or denotata, cannot be reckoned independent of their context of usage (sometimes called referential indexicality) (see *Deixis*; see also *Roman Jakobson*). In other words, it is necessary for an interpreter to infer — relying on other co-present signs and contextual knowledge — how the shifters "point" to the ongoing event (see Silverstein 1976; Hanks 1992). In shifters, the indexical component is part of their symbolic meaning. The same requirement of contextual inference, however, applies to any pragmatic act of reference and predication (see *Reference and descriptions*), to different layers of pragmatic implication (see *Conversational implicature*) or to speech acts (see *Speech act theory*). Ultimately, any utterance may be viewed as shifter-like in the sense that its ulterior interpretation depends on the numerous ways in which it is seen as presupposing and entailing different aspects of context (see Lee 1997a: 90–94). Broadly speaking, then, indexicality can be seen to cover the entire field of "pragmatic" meanings that arise when linguistic symbols become embedded in and interpreted in relation to actual co-texts and contexts of use. The discussion on shifters falls outside the scope of this article.

The focus of this article lies on discourse-level phenomena, and it is positioned at the crossroads of linguistic anthropology, discourse studies, and variational sociolinguistics. In recent years, these three fields of linguistic research have in many ways moved closer to one another, although it has always been somewhat arbitrary to draw strict boundaries between them, since they have common roots and overlapping interests. Indexicality as a theoretical notion and the empirical study of different kinds of indexical meanings is precisely one of the major overlapping areas of interest between these traditions. In our discussion, we have focused on some influential theorists of indexicality in these fields: Michael Silverstein, Asif Agha, Richard Bauman, Jan Blommaert, Elinor Ochs, and Penelope Eckert. Our aim is to show links between the approaches that might seem distant to each other at the first glimpse, and to illustrate different ways in which the notion of indexicality has been applied in these fields.

The scope of phenomena included in any overview of indexicality is necessarily entwined with the specific empirical and epistemological interests of different research traditions as well as their metatheoretical conceptions of what constitutes language and meaning. Our discussion sets off from the premise that all processes of language use and meaning-making turn heavily on indexicality, making the notion of indexicality central to the study of language. In real-life social interactions, linguistic signs become continuously interpreted as indexical of, for example, the genre of the ongoing language-mediated interpersonal encounter, of specific social categories projected on the participants, such as gender or class, or of mental states, such as stances, beliefs, affects, or attitudes (see also Kockelman 2013: 68–74). Indexicality, thus, allows analysts to observe the fundamental social essence of language. Indexicality draws attention to the so-called *total linguistic fact*. The designation was coined by Silverstein for what he viewed as the "central datum for a science of language." The total linguistic fact refers to "an unstable mutual interaction of meaningful sign forms contextualized to situations of interested human use, mediated by the fact of cultural ideology" (Silverstein 1985: 220). In other words, an indexically-minded analyst must pay attention to the dialectical and dynamic relations between linguistic structure, practice, and ideology across historical trajectories. From another perspective, the theory of indexicality offers means to empirically operationalize the Bakhtinian concepts of dialogism, polyphony, and heteroglossia (Bakhtin 1981; see Silverstein 2023: 137; *Heteroglossia, Polyphony, M.M. Bakhtin*). Meaning in any event of language use emerges out of indexical relations to past and future forms of language use and to others' voices.

Our aim is to show how a variety of phenomena that have been of interest to linguists are indexically organized. That is, they turn upon contextually emergent patterns of language use and their social effects. One of the core questions relates to the regularities of indexical interpretation: How is it that many people across different events of language use are able to recognize the same social effects? How does a specific utterance or event of language use become recognized as a unique token of a general type? For instance, language users' ability to interpret an utterance as "polite", say, as deferring to the addressee, presupposes some knowledge of a register of politeness, or of mutually competing registers. Interpreting a register-mediated effect, e.g. hearing a segment of speech as "polite", means that the participant is able to recognize a specific indexical pattern in the temporally unfolding event and is able to link it to a stereotype or model of indexicality. The formation of relatively stable and recognizable types of language use, such as registers or genres, then, is central to our discussion.[1] As was shown by Silverstein, such indexicality is interdiscursive in nature. The typification of utterances as similar to or different from antecedent utterances relies on indexical links across events of language use. Therefore, we include interdiscursivity and intertextuality in our discussion. Wherever possible, we refer to existing handbook articles for more detailed discussion of specific phenomena.

For an individual, the importance of indexical phenomena also lies, for example, in performances of identity and questions of group belonging. Finding the kind of social voice that enables inclusion in a specific group requires the mastery of suitable

---

1. The distinction between types and tokes has its equivalent in Peircean semiotics. Indexical relations may be viewed either as relatively unique (or *singular*), or as instances of general types, which Peirce called *legisigns*, based on their (metaphorically) "law-like" nature (see e.g. Lee 1997a: 121–124; Kockelman 2013: 51–53). General types may, on the one hand, be products of experience-based inductive reasoning: interpreters generalize their particular experiences into stereotypes, that is, they infer the features of a type based on cases they encounter (see Kockelman 2013: 7–8, 143). On the other hand, general types are learned: they circulate as socially transmitted cultural models or schemata (Agha 2007a: 77–81, 145–146; Silverstein 2003), coordinating meaning-making in semiotic communities. Indexicality, thus, relies on "law-like" legisigns that shape, at a general level, indexical interpretation in particular events of language use. Under different indexical legisigns, the same sign may lead to completely different indexical interpretations. Consequently, different types or models of interpretation may compete with one another and become differentially valued in or accessible for different communities.

resources as well as an ability to anticipate and manage competing or unwanted interpretations. Stylized performances, for instance, illustrate the complex and layered nature of the effects of indexicality: they employ existing resources of social indexicality, and at the same time, potentially contribute to the processes that create new forms of social indexicality. Voice performances also show how indexical effects are subject to diverging interpretations and valuations. Wherever possible, we have drawn attention to the ideologically ordered and hierarchical nature of indexicality.

Our presentation proceeds as follows: Section 2 presents some of the basic theoretical dimensions of indexicality, such as indexical presupposition and entailment, register formation or enregisterment, genre formation and interdiscursivity in general. We aim to show how these concepts have been developed in linguistic anthropology and adopted in discourse studies and sociolinguistics. Section 3 unravels the role of indexical phenomena in the sociolinguistic study of language variation and change, following the three waves of variation study from Labovian surveys to a more qualitative understanding of the links between linguistic variation and social identities. We illustrate the application of the concepts and their interrelations to empirical analysis with two examples based on our own research. Example 1 (Section 2.3) deals with the interpretation of voice in a written text in a specific genre context, making use of text analysis and questionnaire data. Example 2 (Section 3.4) looks at the interactional functions of pronoun variation in a stylized performance in face-to-face conversation. In Section 4, we sum up our discussion and suggest some ways in which the broad notion of indexicality remains useful as a heuristic and critical tool for linguists.

2. From linguistic anthropology to discourse studies

In Silverstein's seminal linguistic anthropological work (see Silverstein 2023 for a summary), which has also been adopted into many forms of sociolinguistics and discourse studies (see e.g. Blommaert 2005), the notion of indexicality draws attention to the inseparable links between language use and socio-cultural contexts, or language *in* culture and society. In other words, for an analyst, the role of indexicality is to illuminate the total linguistic fact (see Section 1) by highlighting the concrete, empirically observable links between specific linguistic patterns, the sociocultural practices and interactions in which they are embedded, and the underlying language ideologies that shape their usage and interpretation. An understanding of indexicality is needed to explain how a configuration of linguistic signs can "bring about" a specific social effect or "evoke" a specific macro-sociological category. In Silverstein's theoretical account (e.g. 2003: 194, 202–203), the term *ethnometapragmatics* designates the semiotic dimension of ideologically informed cultural models that construe indexical links between language forms and socio-cultural categories. The prefix *ethno-* in the term marks such constructs as *emic* ones that circulate and evolve in specific communities and semiotic practices and are shaped by local language ideologies (see also Silverstein 1979; Kroskrity 2000; *Language ideologies*). Metapragmatic categories cannot, therefore, be taken as a given, but as an object of empirical, ethnographic inquiry (see e.g. Blommaert 2001; Blommaert and Jie 2010: 8–9; see also *Ethnography*, Section 3.3). Metapragmatic models have also been called *metaindexical* (e.g. Lee 1997a: 164–167; Nakassis 2018: 297–298; Silverstein 2023: 157), as they regiment at a higher level (*meta-*) the formation of indexical relations, or more generally as *metasemiotic* (e.g. Agha 2007a: 21–23; Silverstein 2023: 15), as they often model a broad variety of signs, including non-linguistic ones. It is, then, essential to keep in mind that the indexical effects of language use involve many semiotic modalities, although this aspect is not foregrounded in our discussion.

As indexicality deals with contextually emergent meanings, the indexical functions of linguistic signs need to be approached in terms of temporally unfolding steps: the event before and after the effect the indexical sign brought about. In Silverstein's (2003) theoretical account, indexical meanings arise from a dialectic of indexical *presupposition* and *entailment*. Any indexical sign presupposes aspects of the co-text and context of its occurrence as part of the comprehensibility of the sign (see also Silverstein 2023: 156). That is, a sign has to be "fitted" into whatever semiotic configuration has been established previously in the ongoing event of social interaction. The indexical entailment of the sign, in turn, refers to the effect of the sign, that is, to the creative, context-transforming consequences of the use of the sign. As the indexical effects of a sign are mediated – or enabled and constrained – by metapragmatic models, they are *ordered*. On the one hand, models that are, relatively speaking, shared and stable within a community give rise to similar (e.g. "ordered") interpretations across events of language use. On the other hand, several metapragmatic models may be superimposed one on another and may compete or conflict with one another at any given level or order of interpretation: a first order indexical fact (e.g., that an interlocutor in an everyday conversation has dropped a technical term, requiring expertise in some academic domain) may become ideologically contested at a second order of interpretation (e.g., divergent stances on whether that makes the interlocutor intellectual, condescending, or conceited and how to respond accordingly) (see Silverstein 2003: 193, 206; see also Section 3.1). The "meaning" of an indexical sign does not, thus, arise in any straightforward manner from the sign itself, but is mediated by orders of metapragmatic models in different communities and fields or domains of discourse (see Blommaert 2007b: 116–118; see also Sections 3.3 and 3.4).

Silverstein's theoretical account, thus, models indexicality as a temporally unfolding, dialectic, and cumulative process of sign production and interpretation. Another way of putting this is to say that the proper unit of analysis of indexicality is a text-in-context, that is, a stretch of many signs, whether spoken or written, that become interpreted together. The term *entextualization* has been used to refer to the process of producing a "text", or a pattern of signs that becomes interpreted as a meaningful whole so that each segment can be interpreted in relation to one another and to the whole (Silverstein 1993; see also Bauman and Briggs 1990). Entextualization, then, leads to *text-level indexicality* (Agha 2007a: 24–25) that pertains to the ways in which co-textually co-present signs cumulatively interact with each other, for example, reinforcing or canceling out each other's effects. Entextualized sign patterns may be viewed both as *denotational* text, as patterns of reference and predication, and as *interactional* texts, as patterns of contextualized social action between participants (see also 3.3). The coherence of entextualization relies on, for instance, deictic, anaphorical, and other cohesive means as well as on metrical patterning of signs into recognizable adjacency pairs between participants or genred macrostructures reflecting specific cultural models of staged discursive action (see e.g. Silverstein 2023: 156; see also *Cohesion and coherence; Text structure*). An understandable "text", where different pieces fall into place coherently, is, in itself, then, one kind of indexical achievement. At further levels of interpretation, an entextualized stretch may become recognized as an instance of a type of discursive activity, a genre, which we will discuss in 2.2, or it may become interpreted as indexical of a particular social persona, identity, or voice, which we turn to next.

2.1 Enregisterment of indexicality and emblems of identity

Based on the previous discussion of indexical presupposition and entailment, this section elaborates on the conditions of how a specific social category becomes indexable through language use. Following Agha (2007a), the question will be discussed in terms of *emblems* and *enregisterment*. The aim of these concepts is to explain what makes it possible for a set of linguistic signs to indexically entail or "bring about" a social effect, such as an experience of a "polite", "refined", "dramatic" or "masculine" persona (as already touched upon in the introduction). The key to the question lies in metapragmatic models that link linguistic signs to what Agha (2007a: 76, 169, 235) calls *icons* or *images of personhood*. An *emblem* of social identity, correspondingly, is a set of signs more or less unambiguously linked to an image of personhood. Its social effect can be characterized by designators that describe categories of personhood, such as (some sub-type of) "masculine". In Agha's terms, an emblem indexes a *social persona*, a figure of personhood that participants can inhabit in interaction (2007a: 235–237). Social indexicality, thus, requires metapragmatic models that turn specific patterns of signs into performable and "readable" manifestations of social personae. In the process of interpreting an unfolding text, whether written or spoken, any entextualized sign pattern may become interpreted as an emblem of social identity (only) insofar as a particular metapragmatic model links the signs to social effects. The notion of emblematicity, then, guides the analyst to pay attention to the conditions of social indexicality and the characterizability of indexical effects as mediated by metapragmatic constructs (cf. Kockelman 2013: 74–79, 164–167; see also the discussion on indexical fields in 3.3).

Some such effects are contingent on relatively unique, emergent sign patterns or situation-specific metapragmatic models and may not be readily transferrable from a particular event of language use to other contexts (see Agha 2007a: 237, 255–257). However, a central concern in linguistic anthropology has been to explain the regularity of indexical effects across events of language use. The notion of *enregisterment* of indexicality aims to explain how specific signs become widely recognized in a community as indexing specific social categories across events of language use. That is, notion of enregisterment explains how *registers* – seemingly stable metapragmatic models that link sign types with social types – emerge in socio-historical and ideological processes. Agha's (2007a: e.g. 167–171) theoretical account emphasizes the reflexive nature of register formations: registers are metapragmatic models or stereotypes of indexicality that link a *repertoire* (specific linguistic and/or other signs) with a *social range* (images of personhood, persona types, types of social relationship) for specific *social domains*, that is, for those language users who recognize the register or are competent in its use. A register-mediated emblem, then, involves a socially transmitted, widely recognized *stereotype of personhood*.

While registers serve to coordinate indexical meaning-making within social domains, their interpretation and valuation are ordered and subject to fractional divergence and ideological contestation. For instance, a specific register may be understood as an index of a positively valued form of masculinity by those who commit to and identify with the register, but, at the same time, it may be viewed as a "toxic" form of masculinity by ideological rivals. Both interpretations, nevertheless, share an enregistered order of interpretation that links a specific repertoire of signs with a specific social (gender) category.

As register models organize the interpretation and evaluation of social personae and identities, from a language user's perspective, register models, are important resources of *voice* construction (see e.g. Agha 2005; Blommaert 2008; Section 2.3). The notion of enregistered indexicality, in fact, explains, from a specific standpoint, the complex field of classic Bakhtinian *heteroglossia*, or the sociocultural realm of recognizable voices and their dialogical relations, situated in time and place (Silverstein 2023: 137; Agha 2007a: 165; see also *Heteroglossia*). For a language user, identification with a specific social category or group often requires competence in a corresponding register that enables a public identity performance or a group membership. Registers, thus, become entangled in processes of social differentiation, identity politics, and the naturalization of ideological imagery (see Agha 2007a; Irvine and Gal 2000; Gal and Irvine 2019). Differences in competence and valuation may also turn registers into "scarce goods" (Agha 2007a: 131) or "prestige commodities" (Agha 2007a: 216). That is, registers, like all semiotic resources, have particular systems of "distribution" in societies and, therefore, position different social types differentially in terms of access to such resources. Enregisterment processes – indexical stereotyping, valuation, and access – are, then, closely related to questions of economic and political power and inequality (Blommaert 2007b: 117–120).

Register-mediated voice performances may also indexically presuppose several register models simultaneously and entail effects that are composite, intermediate, instable, or labile (see also the discussion on indexical fields in 3.3). In addition to congruent, stereotype-conforming usages, register models, thus, also allow for *tropes* of various kinds: gradient, hybrid, or ironic usages in context-specific patterns of entextualization (Agha 2005: 48; 2007a: 265–268) (see the example of "caring" or "motherly" masculine speech in 3.1). If such context-specific, creative or strategic, usages become interdiscursively taken up in subsequent events of language use and by other language users, they may gradually become enregistered into new metapragmatic models. In other words, a previously entextualized emblem may be indexically presupposed and effectively recontextualized across events of language use. In propitious conditions of enregisterment, it may become "gelled" into a new metapragmatic model and re-scaled into a widely recognized one (e.g., through mass-mediated discourses, institutional regulation, or influential individuals) (Agha 2007a: e.g. 150–154; Silverstein 2003: 222; Urban 2001: e.g. 224–227, 237–242).

2.2 Genres and interdiscursivity as indexical phenomena

Another indexical phenomenon that has preoccupied linguistic anthropologists and discourse analysts alike is *genre formation*, a process in many ways analogous to enregisterment. The notion of genre explains how individual (denotational and interactional) texts become interpreted as representing a *type* of text, indexically linked to others with similar characteristics (see *Genre; Intertextuality*). Bauman (2004: 4), for instance, draws attention to "generic framing devices," recognizable, genre-specific textual traits, that "carry with them sets of expectations concerning the further unfolding of the discourse, indexing other texts." Such expectations, then, "constitute a framework for entextualization" (ibid.). What Bauman describes is a temporally unfolding dialectic between entextualized signs and metapragmatic models (cf. Sections 2 and 3.3). Participants, in other words, produce and interpret individual texts in light of appropriate genre models. Genre models function as indexically presupposable metapragmatic models that link individual texts with a generalized understanding of the event of language use (e.g., its typical purposes or functions, social roles, and intended consequences on different time scales). Thus, genre models — like register models — contribute to the social, intersubjective coordination of events of language use.

Genres are a case of what Silverstein (2005: 9) calls *type-sourced* interdiscursivity. In such forms of interdiscursivity, a general type of discourse is indexically presupposed as a "source" that frames the ongoing event of language use as a token or instance of the type. In *token-sourced* interdiscursivity, in contrast, a specific instance of language use — that is, a particular text rather than a genre — becomes indexically presupposed as a "source" in another event of language use. In both cases, there is a perceived iconic likeness between events of language use and, consequently, an indexical relationship is formed between those events. They are seen as co-occurring within a specific frame of likeness. In other words, the indexically linked texts are interpreted in relation to one another, as somehow similar. This iconic similarity can pertain to both structural and functional similarities. Genres as presupposed metapragmatic models may regiment textual structures and denotational or stylistic choices as well as the perceived purpose of the text and the default participant roles. In such cases, an emerging text becomes entextualized and contextualized in light of previous instances of discourse. Interdiscursivity is, then, inherently *chronotopic*, situated in time and place, as it turns on links across events of language use (Blommaert 2015, 2018; De Fina and Perrino 2020; see also *Chronotope*).

To rephrase, in interdiscursive processes, two levels of indexicality are in play: the *intra*-discursive indexical patterning of a text (level 1) indexes recognizable *inter*-discursive relations across events of language use (level 2). This results in intertextual relations, or *intertexts*, in which texts-in-context become viewed as the same in some respects (Silverstein 2005: 7). This perceived likeness can be used in different ways to entail indexical effects, for instance, evoking past texts or modeling future ones. Different *techniques of interdiscursivity*, thus, become "deployable as role strategies of the participants" (Silverstein 2005: 7). For instance, tokens of previous discourse can be sourced and treated it *as if* they represented a genre. Such interdiscursive strategies contribute to "traditionalization", or the creation of an impression of textual tradition (see Briggs and Bauman 1992: 147–148). In contrast, elements that are, from the interpreter's standpoint, recognizably linked to actual textual traditions can be used to imbue the text with historical or political associations and textual authority (ibid.). Such indexical effects, which localize a text in some world of discourse, then, depend on the context-bound interdiscursive techniques employed. Interdiscursive techniques may consolidate into *metadiscursive practices*, or ideologically driven systems in which specific types of discourse become routinely juxtaposed and processed in relation to one another. For instance, Bauman and Briggs (2003) describe in detail the European discursive practices through which oral folk traditions became re-worked into "modern" nationalist emblems in the 19th century, simultaneously othering and marginalizing the voices of the original "pre-modern" sources, thus constructing indexical orders for the voices, registers, and genres involved.

In the light of the previous discussion, the Bakhtinian notion of *dialogism* (Bakhtin 1981) may be approached in terms of interdiscursive indexicality. Any event of language use is inevitably situated in the indexical fields of different worlds of discourse (Silverstein 2005: 9). The processes of entextualization and (re-)contextualization necessarily result in intertextual relations, evoking past or future texts, voices, or stances. Interdiscursivity, then, is a ubiquitous form of indexicality that explains the formation of types of discourse.[2] In addition, interdiscursivity draws attention to how events in time

---

2. Moreover, Silverstein's discussion extends the notion of interdiscursivity even to regularities of denotational meaning and pragmatic acts of referring, that is, to the fundamental linguistic processes in which participants infer the referents that words "point to". In this view, intensional meanings, or denotational stereotypes (Agha 2007a: 119–121), as the metapragmatic models discussed above, accumulate or "grow" out of chains of previous usage. Silverstein bases his discussion, among others, on Putnam's (see *Analytical philosophy*) and Kripke's (see *Reference and descriptions*) views.

and place become indexically interlocked through language-in-use so that the resulting intertexts may be used to construct images of (a)temporality and (dis)continuity.

2.3 Example: The dynamic emergence of indexical meanings in the interpretation of written text

Our examples aim to highlight the fact that the dynamic emergence of indexical meanings is not bound to any specific mode of language production, although the entextualization and contextualization processes of different forms of speech and writing differ. The differences pertain, for example, to the participants' connectedness "through signs at varying degrees of separation by criteria of co-presence, directness, intermediation, mutual awareness, and the capacity to respond to each other" (Agha 2007a: 10). In many forms of writing, entextualized patterns of signs are relatively lasting and visible. The contiguity of co-textually co-present signs is, then, repeatedly observable and re-readable, as in the following example that illustrates some of the concepts presented in the previous sections. The chunk of writing below (Example 1) is a segment from a Finnish-language online dating advertisement from the year 2007 (for details see Visakko 2015). For the sake of brevity, the excerpt only contains the first lines of the text. Even this short excerpt, however, allows us to focus on some of the most important aspects of the indexical interpretation of this kind of written text.

First of all, since such texts are encountered on specific sites and via specific search criteria that intertextually group similarly categorized texts with one another when browsing through the search results, the indexical path of access in itself activates the question of genre: what links these texts together in terms of purposes, participant roles, and patterns of entextualization?

(1) Finnish online dating advertisement 2007. Translation by author 1.
Haluan miehen joka on tyytyväinen itseensä
Haluan miehen joka tietää mitä halua[a]
Haluan miehen joka haluaa rakastaa
Haluan miehen joka osaa näyttää tunteensa
Haluan miehen joka osaa keskustella
Haluan miehen joka on itsenäinen, mutta kaipaa kumppania
Haluan miehen joka tyytyväinen siihen mitä näkee peilistä olematta kuitenkaan liian itserakas
[Onko tällaisia? –]

I want a man who is satisfied with himself
I want a man who knows what he wants
I want a man who wants to love
I want a man who can show his feelings

> I want a man who can have a conversation
> I want a man who is independent, but longs for a companion
> I want a man who is satisfied with what he sees in the mirror but without being too vain
> [Are there men like this? —]

The primary purpose of such texts is the presentation of self in an idealized form, simultaneously describing or implying what the ideal respondent is like. This explains the central referents in the denotational text of the excerpt (the first-person indexicals; the recurrence of the noun *mies* 'man'). Whatever the writer entextualizes (or does not), then, becomes in one way or another read in terms of what type of person the writer represents and what kind of reader should reply. The emerging interactional text — the negotiated alignment between the writer and reader — is, in other words, shaped by the indexically presupposed genre model. (Any user who indiscriminately replies to anyone has not understood the game of indexical selectivity involved in the genre.) At a wider level of indexical orders, the generic activity is linked, for example, to cultural understandings of where the line between acceptable idealization and exaggerated, false "puffery" is drawn.

In terms of token-level interdiscursivity, however, the genre is only loosely conventionalized. The entextualization of individual texts is quite varied. In fact, it has been suggested that this is often the case with "promotional" genres of different kinds: the intertextual "gap" between individual texts may be intentionally wide (see Briggs and Bauman 1992; Halmari and Virtanen 2005), as the aim is to differentiate oneself from others. As was noted earlier, a defining feature of the dating ad genre is that the textual patterning in itself becomes a central index of voice and identity.

Let us now concentrate on the textual structure of the excerpt, a list of seven parallel sentences, each one typographically placed on a separate line. Each of the seven sentences has the same syntactic structure. The matrix clause denotes a mental process of 'wanting' and its object (the NP *miehen*, 'man' in the accusative). Each instance of the noun 'man' is qualified with a relative clause. That is, the varying part in the parallel structure describes the ideal respondent from seven different angles. The repetition binds the seven sentences together into a metrical pattern, which evokes a rhythmic pattern so that "the reality of the discourse object is felt as well as cognized" (Urban 2001: 100). This pattern of co-textual contrasts contributes to the interpretation of the writer's voice in a number of ways. Agha (2007b) describes voices as segmentable contrasts within a text that can be biographically individuated, as the voice of a specific person, or "socio-demographically" characterized, as the voice of a *type* of person. As will be seen shortly, such characterizations also include "views of subjectivity" (Lee 1997b: 366) or "mind styles" (Semino 2007), that is, ideas about the mental disposition of the voiced person.

To see how indexical interpretations arise and differ according to the interpreter, elicited data from actual interpreters is one methodological option. In a questionnaire administered to 27 university students, the respondents were asked to describe up to three different impressions that three dating ads, the one discussed here included, stirred and to justify them with concrete linguistic or contextual features. In the questionnaire answers, the excerpt above received a lot of attention. The characterizations can be divided roughly into two main groups, which are not mutually exclusive, but based on a different interpretative logic. Some characterized the writer as "demanding" (or in similar terms). Such respondents pointed to the repetition of the expression of desire and sometimes to other traits, such as the indicative mood ('I want' instead of, say, 'I would like to'). This, tentatively, may be viewed as a "quantitative" interpretation that is based on the number of expressions of desire within the text. As the text unfolds and the expressions recur often enough to become significant, they become an entextualized emblem of identity and incorporated in the writer's voice.

There is, however, another line of characterizations that emphasizes the "dramatic" nature of the writer's voice. These respondents justify their interpretations by characterizing the foregrounded pattern of expressions of desire as "poetic" or "poem-like". In such interpretations, the writer is perceived as interdiscursively type-sourcing a pre-existing model of entextualization. The voicing effect, in other words, does not rely on cumulative repetition but on a recognizable "poem-like" metrical pattern, which the writer is deemed capable of mastering to some degree. This line of interpretation can, then, more readily be analyzed in terms of enregistered emblems of identity, as it involves stereotypic, recognizable notions of "poetic" language use and associated imagery of "dramatic" personhood that become projected on the writer's voice.

In the first line of interpretations, the parallel patterning becomes interpreted as "quantitatively" intensifying the denoted mental process. In the second line of interpretations, the patterning "qualitatively" contextualizes the event as a "dramatic" mode of subjectivity, implying a degree of difference from everyday voices and experiences. These two interpretations ("demanding" vs. "dramatic") also differ in terms of how they may be further evaluated in light of cultural conceptions of, for example, what constitutes acceptable expression of desire and reasonable demands for idealized others. Subsequent steps of indexical interpretation often become merged in the characterizations. For instance, when a respondent characterizes the writer as "trying to be artistic and original", the description presupposes several orders of interpretation: recognizing a poetic pattern, inferring its perceived underlying motive in the genre context, and evaluating the outcome (as unsuccessful).

We see, then, that the writer's voice is both perceived differently by differentially positioned interpreters and constituted as the total effect of many dimensions of indexical interpretation. As always, such dimensions of interpretation are conditioned by ideologically and socio-politically organized orders of indexicality.

We will return to the emergent nature of indexical meanings in the analysis of stylized performances in our second Example (3.3). Before that, in the following sections, we discuss how theories of indexicality have contributed to the sociolinguistic research of language variation and change.

3. Indexicality in sociolinguistic variation studies

In the previous section, we stated that the role of indexicality in linguistic anthropological theorizing has been to explain the linkage between micro-level social interaction and macro-sociological categories. Considering this, it is no wonder that sociolinguists, too, have increasingly turned to linguistic anthropological theories of indexicality. Ever since its emergence in the 1970s, the central focus of variationist sociolinguistics (see *Variationist sociolinguistics, Sociolinguistics*) has been to explain the ways in which linguistic variants are linked to particular speakers and to social patterns of variation: what makes people — groups and individuals — vary and change the way they speak? Variation studies observes and explains the connections between language and social identity, and it is almost impossible not to arrive at social mechanisms of indexicality when explaining these connections. In fact, Silverstein (2003: 193) opens his introduction to indexical order by stating: "'indexical order' is the concept necessary to showing us how to relate the micro-social to the macro-social frames of analysis of any sociolinguistic phenomenon." In addition to explaining the role of attitudes, ideologies, and perception in language change, theories of indexicality contribute to the sociolinguistic approaches to style and stance (see Jaffe 2016).

Eckert (2012) identifies three waves of variation studies that differ from each other in their focus and methodologies. These three waves are relevant to the topic of indexicality, as they illustrate how the focus of attention shifts from etic variables to emic understandings of social practice, where the *social meaning* — that is, social indexicality — of linguistic resources plays a central role. It is important to point out that these waves overlap and do not necessarily follow each other chronologically (cf. Eckert 2012: 88). The theory that became relevant in the third wave has largely existed and been developed in linguistic anthropology since the 1970s. However, the quantitative Labovian variation analysis (1st wave) occupied such a dominant position in sociolinguistics that variation analysis almost became a synonym for sociolinguistics. The turn to the theories of social indexicality and ethnographic methodologies is evident in the field as a whole as well as in the trajectories of individual researchers. We have structured this section to loosely follow the three waves, although this is only one way of describing the interactions between sociolinguistic variation studies and linguistic anthropology.

3.1 Indicator, marker, and stereotype and the indexical order

According to Eckert (2012), the first wave of variation studies begins with Labov's (1966, 1972) quantitative analysis of urban variation in terms of age, gender, and social class, using large data samples and etic variables. Although quantitatively oriented, the distinctions he draws between *indicator, marker,* and *stereotype* have been extremely influential in later conceptualizations of indexicality (see Eckert 2008: 463–464). In his theory of indexical order (see Section 2), Silverstein (2003) discusses the Labovian concepts as examples of indexical processes and relates the notion of orders of indexicality to these Labovian concepts. One influential example of the kind of sociolinguistics that draws both on the Labovian concepts and on Silverstein's notion of indexical order is the analysis of the social indexicality of Pittsburghese by Johnstone et al. (2006).

As indicated in Section 2, the basic idea behind Silverstein's (2003) notion of indexical order is that any linguistic resource that functions as a social indexical (of the first order) can potentially, through recontextualization, receive a new interpretation and be reappropriated in a new context (second, third, etc. orders of indexicality). A similar idea was already present in Labov's work, as the increasing role of metapragmatic evaluation determines whether an indicator becomes a marker or a stereotype. For indicators, there exists a largely subconscious indexical relationship between the linguistic variant and a group of people, such as an age group (Labov 1972: 134). This relationship is quantitatively observable in a large sample of data, and at least some speakers are aware of it, although it often remains uncommented. Silverstein (2003: 217) concludes that an indicator is "a reliably presupposing index of such [category] membership of a speaker."

Markers "will produce regular responses in subjective reaction tests" (Labov 1972: 314). That is, speakers comment on the indexical relationship between the variants and the group. This reflexive metapragmatic action makes it possible to use the variant for strategic stylization (Bakhtin 1981; Rampton 2006: 27, 224; Coupland 2007: 149–155; see also *Style and styling, Crossing*). To understand variation and change, the realization of linguistic variation and people's evaluations of that variation (i.e. reflexive metapragmatics) must be seen as two sides of the same coin.

Stereotypes, according to Labov (1972: 314) are "socially marked forms, prominently labelled by society," and in Silverstein's (2003: 220) wording, "markers that have tilted in the direction of ideological transparency, the stuff of conscious, value-laden, imitational inhabitance — consciously speaking 'like' some social type or personified image." In Agha's (2007a) terms, they have become enregistered into widely recognized metapragmatic models (registers) that often have a name or a well-known label. A stereotype may receive a new interpretation and be used to refer to certain characteristics or a "type" of people in a new context (cf. Agha 2007a: 235–237; Woolard 2008). A classic example of an indexical feature that is used as a "stereotype" in a new context can be found in Ochs' (1992) article *Indexing gender*. In her terms, there exists a "direct" indexical link between mothers, feminity, and certain linguistic features used in interactions with babies. Once a new, "indirect" indexical link has been established whereby these linguistic forms are in turn associated with acts of care and tenderness, male speakers can use them to express a "caring" and "motherly" stance. Ochs (1992: 341–345) calls this characteristic of indexicality *constitutiveness*.

For decades, Labovian variation analysis remained the dominant methodology in the field of variation studies.[3] Due to its quantitative nature and use of large data samples, it has been able to explain the co-dependence between certain linguistic variants and groups organized around certain background variables, but its explanatory power does not extend to individuals, situational variation, or the relationship between individuals and groups.

3.2 From stylistic practices to emic social meaning

The second wave of variation studies still focused largely on the same variables as the first wave, but also included qualitative methods such as participant observation, which allowed the researcher to get a handle on the local social categories that explain group internal variation (Eckert 2012). A holistic understanding of style enters the stage and leads to conceptualization of style as social practice (Quist 2008; see also *Style and styling*). Eckert's classic study of the "jocks" and "burnouts" in a US high school is a classic example, in which variation patterns are analyzed on the basis of opposing styles identified through ethnographic methods (Eckert 1989, 2000). These styles are not just researcher's categories, but also recognized by the participants themselves. The ethnographic data show that the participants recognize certain semiotic characteristics of these styles, such as clothing or engagement in certain activities, and are able to comment on them. However, this metapragmatic commentary does not necessarily extend to language. We can assume that there is a social indexical relationship between the frequency of certain variants and a particular style, but without reflexive metapragmatic data it is difficult to unravel the layers of indexicality involved. Thus, in the second wave, the linguistic variables are still chosen by the researcher, and metapragmatic negotiations about them are not a part of the data. This is where the third wave differs from the second wave.

In the third wave, we see a shift from "classic" variables to a reconceptualization of linguistic features as semiotic resources that are meaningful to the participants (Eckert 2012). Any linguistic feature can carry social meaning, that is, function as a social indexical. In the third wave, the variationist path finally arrives at enregisterment. Eckert (2008: 456) writes:

> Styles associated with types in the social landscape bear an important relation to class, but not a direct one. They are the product of *enregisterment* (Agha 2003) and I might call them *registers* were it not for the common use of the term in sociolinguistics to refer to a static collocation of features associated with a specific setting or fixed social category.

---

3. Nevertheless, the waves overlap and do not necessarily follow each other chronologically.

Since then, many sociolinguists have adopted Agha's notions of register, enregisterment, and social indexicality (see e.g. Woolard 2008; Madsen et al. 2015; Johnstone 2016; Lehtonen 2016b).

In exploring the "meaning" of sociolinguistic variants in the light of the theories of social indexicality, Eckert (2008: 39) proposes the concept of *indexical field*:

> I argue that the meanings of variables are not precise or fixed but rather constitute a field of potential meanings — an indexical field, or constellation of ideologically related meanings, any one of which can be activated in the situated use of the variable. The field is fluid, and each new activation has the potential to change the field by building on ideological connections.

The analytical utility of the concept lies in its ability to explain how the same variant of a sibilant /s/ can in different contexts be associated with urbanity, femininity, or gay men (Halonen et al. 2020; cf. Calder 2019). All of these "meanings" are part of the sign's indexical field, and a single occurrence will foreground one of the ideological-indexical connections (although there is usually some interdependence between the different dimensions).

3.3 Reflexivity and perception in language variation and change

Agha's theory of enregisterment accentuates the role of reflexivity and perception in language variation and change. This is not "all new" to variational sociolinguistics, as folk linguistics and perceptual dialectology have focused on metalanguage, language attitudes, and perception for decades (Niedzielski and Preston 2000). The intertwining of attitudes and variation has been observed in the tendency of certain groups to systematically avoid features associated with negative attitudes (stigma) and to favor features associated with positive attitudes (prestige).

Although these patterns of (de)identification can be observed in quantitative surveys, survey data tell us little about how speakers move from perception to attitude and (dis)identification: what is the voice (Bakhtin 1981) or the social persona (Agha 2007a: 14) that the speakers associate with a linguistic feature in a particular context (Rampton 2006: 227)?[4]

---

4. The dynamics of how the interlocutors determine the relevant context for interpretation of what is said in interaction has been the focus of contextualization theory, developed by the pioneer of interactional sociolinguistics, John Gumperz (1982). Revisiting his central theory, Gumperz (1992) discusses the essence of contextualization cues as indexical signs and metapragmatic phenomena. In the same volume, Silverstein (1992: 55) points out that "the phenomena of 'contextualization' are inherently indexical ones" and stresses the role of metapragmatics in contextualization. Indeed, contextualization cues, such as the act of code-switching or a change in prosody or voice quality, participate in indexical

The question of how linguistic sign-forms are linked to ideological interpretations of different types of social personae, is at the heart of the third wave variation studies. To include perception and reflexivity in the analysis, the analyst needs metapragmatic data, that is, speech commenting on speech and action commenting on action. The metapragmatic commentary may be explicit: for instance, an interviewee may bring up a categorization and directly associate certain ways of speaking with that social category. However, interactional sociolinguistics (Gumperz 1982; see also *Interactional sociolinguistics, John Gumperz*) has developed tools to uncover more implicit types of metapragmatic commentary. In particular, sequences of interaction in which language itself becomes the centre of attention offer interesting data. These sequences can be staged performances, or other "performance-like" stretches of talk (Coupland 2007: 146). Bell and Gibson (2011: 555) point out that staged performances "have the potential to trigger significant sociolinguistic effects," because they agentively build on existing social meanings. In everyday talk-in-interaction, sociolinguists have focused on sequences that are marked both linguistically and extra-linguistically as performances (e.g., through contextualization cues; Gumperz 1982). These performances differ from the surrounding speech, and such sequences are often studied under the notion of stylization. Stylizations bring about an "image of another's language" (Bakhtin 1981) and can thus function as a metapragmatic commentary (Rampton 2006: 27, 224; Coupland 2007: 149–155; Johnstone et al. 2006: 99).

3.4 Example: The variation and the social indexicality of *minä* ('I') in spoken interaction

In the following example we will focus on one linguistic form, the Finnish first-person pronoun *minä* 'I' or 'me', and its functions in a stylized performance. The first-person singular pronoun is one of the most commonly studied variables in Finnish variation analysis. Its variants in spoken dialects include *mä, mää, mie, meä, mi, mnää* and *minä* (Kettunen 1940: 113). In spoken dialects, *minä* often alternates with other variants, with *minä* being used for used for stress and contrastive functions (cf. Paunonen 1995[1982]: 162; Lappalainen 2004: 71–72). Although *minä* is/was the dominant variant only in some areas, it was enregistered as the only variant for the written standard. In written Finnish, it is furthermore possible (and often stylistically preferable) to omit the first-person pronoun, as the person is expressed with the verb conjugation. In most varieties of spoken Finnish, the written standard variant is used only for limited functions. In the capital area, where the example was collected, the most common variant in the spoken language is *mä : mu-*, while *minä : minu-* is only used for stress and contrastive func-

---

processes by indexing stretches of talk that offer a metapragmatic evaluation of an indexical relationship between the lexico-grammatical form and the social personae (see Gumperz 1992: 50).

tions (cf. Paunonen 1995[1982]: 162; Lappalainen 2004).[5] In Finnish as a second language textbooks, however, *minä* is overused (cf. Tanner 2012). Similarly, in teacher talk directed to language learners, *minä* is explicitly used in non-stressed and non-constrastive functions as well (Ahtosalo 2012). As a result, it has become associated with learner language (cf. Lehtonen 2011, 2015, 2016b). As a consequence of this enregisterment process and the resulting indexical relationship between *minä* and repertoires associated with language learning, *minä* alone can in certain stylizations be sufficient to contextualize the speech as the voice of Finnish learner or a "non-Finn" (although it mostly occurs in bundles with other features that together signal the social persona associated with Finnish learning). The repetitive use of *minä* and its association with Finnish as a second language textbooks is also an example of the indexical process of genre-formation (see Section 2.2).

Our Example (2) comes from a research interview conducted as a part of a linguistic ethnography project in Helsinki, Finland (Lehtonen 2015, 2016a, 2016b). In this sequence, Mary, a 15-year-old girl, her two friends, and the ethnographer-interviewer are discussing stylizations which the ethnographer had observed before. In the excerpt, Mary talks about possible situations where such stylizations could occur. Mary has moved from Kenya to Finland as a child.

(2) *Interview. I = interviewer, ethnographer-researcher; M = Mary. The variants of the first-person singular pronoun are in bold.*

```
01 M: mull_on kaverit jotka- (.) sillon kum mä muutin Suameem mä olin
      I-ADE (mulla)                        I (mä)              I (mä)
      I have friends that- (.) when I moved to Finland I was on a
02    niikuv valmistaval luakal,
      like preparatory class,
03 I: joo.
      yes.
04 M: ja- (.) me- (.) tutustuin siäl niij joskus me vaam mu<
      and- (.) we- (.) I got to know them there so sometimes we just re-
05    muistellaa et joo muistaksä mitem me puhuttii sillom
      remember back like yeah do you remember how we talked back then
06    me ei osattu suamee, (.) mä oon sille joo-o, (.) no esim
      we didn't know Finnish, (.) I'm like yeah, (.) well like
                                 I (mä)
07    vaikka ha ha ha [minä em puhus suamee voitko sinä
                       I (minä) NEG-1s speak Finnish can-2s you
      for instance ha ha ha I don't speak Finnish can you
08 I:                 [mhyhy.
09    autta m(h)inua [ha nis sillee.
      help I-akk (minua)
      help m(h)e     [ha like that
10 I:                 [mhyhy.
```

---

5. *minu-* ~ *mu-* represent the stem that the conjugation builds on. The *minu-*stem *(minun, minulta, minulle)* is the "written standard" variant, *mu-* *(mun, multa, mulle)* is common in spoken varieties.

There are 5 instances of *minä: minu-* ~ *mä: mu-* variable (bolded), and the "standard" variant *minä: minu-* only appears in the passage where Mary performs the way she and her friends used to speak "when they didn't know Finnish". This is not a coincidence: in all the interviews conducted for the project, the main variant was *mä: mu-*, and the most common function of *minä: minu-* was stylizations like the one in the excerpt.

The passage *minä en puhu suamee voitko sinä autta m(h)inua* "I don't speak Finnish can you help m(h)e' is framed as a performance through several cues. First, Mary explicitly states that this is the way she and her friends used to speak before, and the passage is preceded by the quotation marker *mä oon sillee* 'I'm like'. Second, laughter marks the passage as something that deviates from the routine flow of speech (Rampton 2006: 227). Mary clearly brings in another voice (even though in this case the voice is "her own voice" from before). Linguistically, this voice is brought to life by *minä: minu-* and the second-person singular pronoun *sinä*, which follows the similar variation pattern as *minä (sinä: sinu-* ~ *sä-: su)*, as well as by ignoring the quantitative opposition of long and short vowels in *autta* 'help' (pro *auttaa*). The voice is referred to as the voice of someone who does not yet know Finnish, and this framing is explicitly repeated in the stylization itself. The "standard" variants *minä: minu-, sinä: sinu-* are almost the only linguistic features that are used to index that voice in the stylization. It is possible for them to carry so much weight because they have been associated with learner repertoires through the enregisterment process rooted in textbook Finnish and teacher talk.

Stylizations and performances like this are a form of metapragmatic commentary. When Mary adopts the voice of "someone who does not know Finnish" through stylization, she is using signs that she herself recognizes as typical for that voice. She probably also assumes that the other participants are at least to some extent able to interpret their indexicality. In doing so, she relies on the social indexical relationship connecting a linguistic form to a social persona (someone who does not speak Finnish) and at the same time, she re-constitutes and recreates the indexical relationship. In this way, she participates in a speech-chain or an enregisterment process (Agha 2007a).

One of the analytical strengths of social indexicality theory is its ability to explain how speakers deploy social indexicality in social positioning in interaction. For instance, in our example, Mary positions herself vis-a-vis her former self and those who "do not know Finnish". She shows that the stylization is the "voice of another", not her current self, and takes a stance to express that she now belongs to those who "know Finnish".

In this sense, social indexicality overlaps with stance (see *Stance*), and stance is constitutive of social indexicality (Jaffe 2009, 2016). Kiesling (2009) goes as far as to argue that stance precedes variation, because "stance is the main interactional meaning being created" (Kiesling 2009: 173). In her study of possessive *me* (pro *my*), Snell (2010) uses the notions of stance and style for examining how they are associated with identity categories in interaction and posits "a chain of indexicality" that illustrates the dialogical and reflexive mechanisms of social indexicality. Snell concludes (2010: 650):

I am suggesting, then, a circular chain of indexicality in which meaning flows from local interactional stances to styles, personas and macro-level identity categories, and then back to local interactional use. Metapragmatic activity, including explicit metadiscourse, may highlight particular points in the chain as being salient.

The idea of a chain brings us back to the notions of enregisterment (see Sections 2.1, 3.2, 3.3) and constitutiveness (Ochs 1992; see also Section 3.1): in these "flows", recurring local interactional stances may lead to enregisterment, and registers may in turn be used to express new kinds of stances building on stereotypical social personae (see also 2.1).

4. Conclusion

In our discussion, we have looked at the theorization of indexical phenomena from the standpoint of different fields of linguistic research. We have shown how linguistic anthropological theoretical constructs and conceptualizations of indexical phenomena have been gradually adopted in different ways and at different stages in both discourse studies and variational sociolinguistics. Although our discussion is necessarily selective and limited to certain basic dimensions of language use and a few key theorists, the range of indexical phenomena covered above is wide. In fact, it has been our aim to show that "meaning" in its many different forms at all levels of language use is inherently a matter of indexical relations: the study of indexical processes explains the ever-changing links between linguistic sign-forms and their interpretative potential in different social contexts. Even denotational meanings, documented in dictionaries, result from long sociohistorical chains of discursive practices and enregisterment processes.

Admittedly, the other side of the constitutive and ubiquitous role of indexical semiosis is that the broad notion of indexicality in and of itself is hardly sufficient to describe or explain the wide range of particular phenomena it covers. As has been seen above, different dimensions of indexicality require specific theorization and methodology of their own (e.g., registers, genres, chronotopes, styles, voices, different forms of interdiscursivity, and many others not touched upon in this article). Moreover, in some interactional events indexicality is more obvious and transparent for the analyst than in others. However, it would be a simplification of the notion of indexicality to limit the empirical observations to the most obvious, emblematic cases. The analysis should embrace the ambivalence of indexicality. To observe the different ways in which indexicality works, different methods are needed.

It has been our aim to define indexicality at a general level, but its various empirical manifestations sometimes seem to escape description due to the dialogical and constitutive nature of indexicality: indexicality keeps re-inventing itself. As Nakassis (2018) points out in his critical reflection, indexicality is inherently constitutive and dialogical, and it is an oversimplification of an ambivalent phenomenon to "split" or reify indexicality into clear-cut classes, "orders", or distinctions between "direct" and "indirect". To become a "direct" index in the first place, such indexes must have gone through a complex socio-historical and dialogical process that naturalizes the links between contextual features and (linguistic) signs.

However, it is our belief that the fundamental notion of indexicality is useful as a heuristic tool that brings the analyst back to basic questions: What kinds of relations between linguistic signs and their contexts of use are crucial to the phenomenon under investigation? It also enables a critical evaluation of existing approaches: Have such phenomena been previously theorized to a sufficient degree? Are conventional methods adequate to reach into the depths of such phenomena? What is the relationship between emic (language users') and etic (analysts') understandings of the phenomena in question? Returning to the basic notion of indexicality, thus, ideally, helps researchers to deconstruct and re-evaluate naturalized conceptions of the study of language use, language variation, and the complex semiotic processes of meaning formation. In addition, indexicality offers common ground for different fields of context-sensitive linguistic analysis as well as for interdisciplinary efforts centered around socio-cultural meaning.

Transcription and glossing symbols

(.)	micropause
-	level intonation
,	slightly falling intonation
.	falling intonation
[	overlapping speech begins
e<	a word or the flow of speech interrupted
ADE	adessive case
AKK	accusative case
NEG-1S	negative verb, first person singular

References

Aarsæther, Finn. 2010. "The use of multiethnic youth language in Oslo." In *Multilingual Urban Scandinavia. New Linguistic Practices*, ed. by Pia Quist and Bente Ailin Svendsen, 111–126. Bristol: Multilingual Matters.

Agha, Asif. 2003. "The social life of cultural value." *Language & Communication* 23 (3–4): 231–273.

Agha, Asif. 2005. "Voice, footing, enregisterment." *Journal of Linguistic Anthropology* 15 (1): 38–59.

Agha, Asif. 2007a. *Language and Social Relations*. Cambridge: Cambridge University Press.

Agha, Asif. 2007b. "Recombinant selves in mass mediated spacetime." *Language & Communication* 27: 320–335.

Ahtosalo, Milja. 2012. Minän monet muodot: Yksikön 1. persoonan pronominin variaatio neljän suomi toisena kielenä -opettajan puheessa. [Many forms of minä: The variation of the first-person singular pronoun in the speech of four Finnish as a second language teachers.] Master's thesis, University of Helsinki.

Bakhtin, Mikhail. 1981. *The Dialogic Imagination. Four Essays*. Austin: University of Texas Press.

Bauman, Richard. 2004. *A World of Others' Words. Cross-cultural Perspectives on Intertextuality*. Malden, MA: Blackwell Publishing.

Bauman, Richard, and Charles Briggs. 1990. "Poetics and performance as critical perspectives on language and social life." *Annual Review of Anthropology* 19: 59–88.

Bauman, Richard, and Charles Briggs. 2003. *Voices of Modernity. Language Ideologies and the Politics of Inequality*. Cambridge: Cambridge University Press.

Bell, Allan, and Andy Gibson. 2011. "Staging language: An introduction to the sociolinguistics of performance." *Journal of Sociolinguistics* 15 (5): 555–572.

Blommaert, Jan. 2001. "Context is/as critique." *Critique of Anthropology* 21 (1): 13–32.

Blommaert, Jan. 2005. *Discourse. A Critical Introduction*. Cambridge: Cambridge University Press.

Blommaert, Jan. 2007a. "Sociolinguistic scales." *Intercultural Pragmatics* 4 (1): 1–19.

Blommaert, Jan. 2007b. "Sociolinguistics and discourse analysis: Orders of indexicality and polycentricity." *Journal of Multicultural Discourses* 2: 115–30.

Blommaert, Jan. 2008. "Bernstein and poetics revisited: Voice, globalization and education." *Discourse & Society* 19: 425–51.

Blommaert, Jan. 2015. "Chronotopes, scales, and complexity in the study of language in society." *Annual Review of Anthropology* 44: 105–16.

Blommaert, Jan. 2018. "Are chronotopes helpful? Why do we need another word for context?" *Working Papers in Urban Language and Literacies* 243: 1–9.

Blommaert, Jan, and Dong Jie. 2010. *Ethnographic Fieldwork: A Beginner's Guide*. Bristol: Multilingual Matters.

Briggs, Charles, and Richard Bauman. 1992. "Genre, intertextuality, and social power." *Journal of Linguistic Anthropology* 2 (2): 131–172.

Calder, Jeremy. 2019. "From Sissy to sickening: The indexical landscape of /s/ in SoMa, San Francisco." *Linguistic Anthropology* 29 (3): 332–358.

Carr, Summerson E., and Michael Lempert. 2016. *Scale: Discourse and Dimensions of Social Life*. Oakland: University of California Press.

Coupland, Nikolas. 2007. *Style. Language Variation and Identity*. Cambridge: Cambridge University Press.

De Fina, Anna, and Sabina Perrino. 2020. "Introduction: Chronotopes and chronotopic relations." *Language & Communication* 70: 67–70.

Eckert, Penelope. 1989. *Jocks and Burnouts: Social Categories and Identity in the High School*. New York: Teachers College Press.

Eckert, Penelope. 2000. *Linguistic Variation as Social Practice*. Oxford: Blackwell.

Eckert, Penelope. 2008. "Variation and the indexical field." *Journal of Sociolinguistics* 12 (4): 53–76.

Eckert, Penelope. 2012. "Three waves of variation study: The emergence of meaning in the study of sociolinguistic variation." *Annual Review of Anthropology* 41: 87–100.

Gadet, Françoise. 2022. "Youth vernaculars in Paris and surroundings." In *Urban Contact Dialects and Language Change*, ed. by Paul Kerswill and Heike Wiese, 264–281. New York: Routledge.

Gal, Susan, and Judith Irvine. 2019. *Signs of Difference. Language and Ideology in Social Life.* Cambridge: Cambridge University Press.

Gross, Johan, and Sally Boyd. 2022. "Sweden: Suburban Swedish." In *Urban Contact Dialects and Language Change*, ed. by Paul Kerswill and Heike Wiese, 246–263. New York: Routledge.

Gumperz, John. 1982. *Discourse Strategies.* Studies in Interactional Sociolinguistics 1. Cambridge: Cambridge University Press.

Gumperz, John. 1992. "Contextualization revisited." In *The Contextualization of Language*, ed. by Peter Auer and Aldo di Luzio, 39–54. Amsterdam: John Benjamins Publishing Company.

Halmari, Helena, and Tuija Virtanen. 2005. "Towards understanding modern persuasion." In *Persuasion Across Genres*, ed. by Helena Halmari and Tuija Virtanen, 229–244. Amsterdam: John Benjamins, Amsterdam.

Halonen, Mia, Sami Nyström, Heikki Paunonen, and Johanna Vaattovaara. 2020. *Stadin syntinen s.* [The sinful s of Helsinki City.] Helsinki: Art House.

Hanks, William. 1992. "The indexical ground of deictic reference." In *Rethinking Context. Language as an Interactive Phenomenon*, ed. by Alessandro Duranti and Charles Goodwin, 43–76. Cambridge: Cambridge University Press.

Hornikx, Jos, Frank van Meurs, and Robert-Jan Hof. 2013. "The effectiveness of foreign-language display in advertising for congruent versus incongruent products." *Journal of International Consumer Marketing*, 25 (3), 152–165.

Irvine, Judith, and Susan Gal. 2000. "Language ideology and linguistic differentiation." In *Regimes of Language*, ed. by Paul Kroskrity, 35–83. Santa Fe: School of American Research Press.

Jaffe, Alexandra. 2009. "Introduction: The sociolinguistics of stance." In *Stance: Sociolinguistic Perspectives*, ed. by Alexandra Jaffe, 1–28. New York: Oxford University Press.

Jaffe, Alexandra. 2016. "Indexicality, stance and fields in sociolinguistics." In *Sociolinguistics: Theoretical Debates*, ed. by Nicolas Coupland, 86–112. Cambridge: Cambridge University Press.

Johnstone, Barbara. 2016. "Enregisterment: How linguistic items become linked with ways of speaking." *Language and Linguistics Compass* 10 (11): 632–643.

Johnstone, Barbara, Jennifer Andrus, and Andrew E. Danielson. 2006. "Mobility, indexicality, and the enregisterment of 'Pittsburghese'." *Journal of English Linguistics* (34) 2: 77–104.

Kettunen, Lauri. 1940. *Suomen murteet III A. Murrekartasto.* [Finnish dialects III A. Dialect maps.] Helsinki: Finnish Literature Society. http://kettunen.fnhost.org/?i=1

Kiesling, Scott F. 2009. "Style as Stance." In *Stance: Sociolinguistic Perspectives*, ed. by Alexandra Jaffe, 171–194. New York: Oxford University Press.

Knudsen, Jan Sverre. 2010. "'Playing with words as if it was a rap game': Hip-hop street language in Oslo." In *Multilingual Urban Scandinavia. New Linguistic Practices*, ed. by Pia Quist and Bente Ailin Svendsen, 156–169. Bristol: Multilingual Matters.

Kockelman, Paul. 2013. *Agent, Person, Subject, Self. A Theory of Ontology, Interaction, and Infrastructure.* New York: Oxford University Press.

Kroskrity, Paul V. (ed.). 2000. *Regimes of Language: Ideologies, Polities, and Identities.* Santa Fe: School of American Research Press.

Labov, William. 1966. *The Social Stratification of English in New York City.* Washington D.C.: Center for Applied Linguistics.

Labov, William. 1972. *Sociolinguistic Patterns.* Oxford: Blackwell.

Lappalainen, Hanna. 2004. *Variaatio ja sen funktiot. Erään sosiaalisen verkoston jäsenten kielellisen vuorovaikutuksen tarkastelua.* [*Variation and its functions. Examining the linguistic interactions of members of a social network.*] Helsinki: Finnish Literature Society.

Lee, Benjamin. 1997a. *Talking Heads. Language, Metalanguage, and the Semiotics of Subjectivity.* London: Duke University Press.

Lee, Benjamin. 1997b. "Metalanguages and subjectivities." In *Reflexive Language. Reported Speech and Metapragmatics*, ed. by John Lucy, 365–392. Cambridge: Cambridge University Press.

Lehtonen, Heini. 2011. "Developing Multiethnic Youth Language in Helsinki." In *Ethnic Styles of Speaking in European Metropolitan Areas*, ed. by Friederike Kern and Margaret Selting, 291–318. Amsterdam: John Benjamins.

Lehtonen, Heini. 2015. Tyylitellen. Nuorten kielelliset resurssit ja kielen sosiaalinen indeksisyys monietnisessä Helsingissä. [Stylizing. The linguistic resources of adolescents and the social indexicality of language in multiethnic Helsinki.]" MA thesis, University of Helsinki. http://hdl.handle.net/10138/155659

Lehtonen, Heini. 2016 a. "What's up Helsinki? New linguistic diversity among adolescents." In *Linguistic Genocide or Superdiversity. New and Old Language Diversities*, ed. by Reetta Toivanen and Janne Saarikivi, 65–90. Bristol: Multilingual Matters.

Lehtonen, Heini. 2016b. "Troping on prejudice. Stylised "bad Finnish" performances among adolescents in Eastern Helsinki." *AILA Review* 29 (1): 15–47.

Madsen, Lian Malai, Martha Sif Kaerrebaek, Janus Spindler Møller (eds.). 2015. *Everyday Languaging: Collaborative Research on the Language Use of Children and Youth.* Trends in Applied Linguistics. Berlin: Mouton de Gruyter.

Mertz, Elisabeth. 1985. "Beyond symbolic anthropology: Introducing semiotic mediation." In *Semiotic Mediation: Sociocultural and Psychological Perspectives*, ed. by Elisabeth Mertz and Richard J. Parmentier, 1–19. Orlando: Academic Press.

Nakassis, Constantine V. 2018. "Indexicality's Ambivalent Ground." *Signs and Society* 6 (1): 281–301.

Niedzielski, Nancy A., and Dennis Richard Preston. 2000. *Folk Linguistics.* Berlin: Mouton de Gruyter, 2000.

Nørreby, Thomas. R. 2015. "Ethnic identifications in late modern Copenhagen." In *Everyday Languaging. Collaborative Research on the Language Use of Children and Youth*, ed. by Lian Malai Madsen, Martha Sif Karrebæk, and Janus Spindler Møller, 199–218. Berlin: De Gruyter Mouton.

Ochs, Elinor. 1992. "Indexing gender." In *Rethinking context. Language as an Interactive Phenomenon*, ed. by Alessandro Duranti and Charles Goodwin, 335–358. Cambridge: Cambridge University Press.

Parmentier, Richard. 1994. *Signs in Society. Studies in Semiotic Anthropology.* Bloomington: Indiana University Press.

Paunonen, Heikki. 1995 (1982). *Suomen kieli Helsingissä. Huomioita Helsingin puhekielen taustasta ja nykyvariaatiosta.* [*Finnish in Helsinki. Observations on the history and current variation of the spoken language in Helsinki.*] Helsinki: Helsingin yliopiston suomen kielen laitos.

Quist, Pia. 2008. "Sociolinguistic approaches to multiethnolect: Language variety and stylistic practice." *International Journal of Bilingualism* 12 (1–2): 43–61.

Quist, Pia. 2022. "Denmark: Danish urban contact dialects." In *Urban Contact Dialects and Language Change*, ed. by Paul Kerswill and Heike Wiese, 186–205. London: Routledge.

Rampton, Ben. 2006. *Language in Late Modernity. Interaction in an Urban School.* Cambridge: Cambridge University Press.

Semino, Elena. 2007. "Mind style twenty-five years on." *Style* 41 (2): 135–173.

Silverstein, Michael. 1976. "Shifters, linguistic categories, and cultural description." In *Meaning in Anthropology*, ed. by Keith Basso and Ellen Selby, 11–56. Albuquerque: University of New Mexico Press.

Silverstein, Michael. 1979. "Language structure and linguistic ideology." In *The Elements: A Parasession on Linguistic Units and Levels*. Chicago: Chicago Linguistic Society.

Silverstein, Michael. 1985. "Language and the culture of gender." In *Semiotic Mediation: Sociocultural and Psychological Perspectives*, ed. by Elisabeth Mertz and Richard J. Parmentier, 219–259. Orlando: Academic Press.

Silverstein, Michael. 1992. "The indeterminacy of contextualization: When is enough enough?" In *The Contextualization of Language*, ed. by Peter Auer and Luzio di Aldo, 55–76. Amsterdam: John Benjamins Publishing Company.

Silverstein, Michael. 1993. "Metapragmatic discourse and metapragmatic function." In *Reflexive l Language. Reported Speech and Metapragmatics*, ed. by John Lucy, 33–58. Cambridge: Cambridge University Press.

Silverstein, Michael. 2003. "Indexical order and the dialectics of sociolinguistic life." *Language & Communication* 23: 193–229.

Silverstein, Michael. 2005. "Axes of evals: Token versus type interdiscursivity." *Journal of Linguistic Anthropology* 15 (1): 6–22.

Silverstein, Michael. 2023. *Language in Culture. Lectures on the Social Semiotics of Language.* Cambridge: Cambridge University Press.

Snell, Julia. 2010. "From sociolinguistic variation to socially strategic stylization." *Journal of Sociolinguistics* 14 (5): 630–656.

Svendsen, Bente Ailin. 2022. "Norway: Contemporary urban speech styles." In *Urban Contact Dialects and Language Change*, ed. by Paul Kerswill and Heike Wiese, 206–222. London: Routledge.

Tanner, Johanna. 2012. "Rakenne, tilanne ja kohteliaisuus. Pyynnöt S2-oppikirjoissa ja autenttisissa keskusteluissa". [Structure, situation and politeness. Requests in Finnish as a second language textbooks and authentic conversations.] PhD Dissertation, University of Helsinki. http://hdl.handle.net/10138/32474

Urban, Greg. 2001. *Metaculture. How Culture Moves through the World.* Minneapolis: University of Minnesota Press.

Visakko, Tomi. 2015. Self-promotion as Semiotic Behaviour. The Mediation of Personhood in Light of Finnish Online Dating Advertisements. Phd Dissertation, University of Helsinki. http://hdl.handle.net/10138/156288

Woolard, Kathryn A. 2008. "Why dat now?: Linguistic-anthropological contributions to the explanation of sociolinguistic icons and change." *Journal of Sociolinguistics* 12 (4): 432–452.

Intervision

Marie Jacobs
Universiteit Gent

1. Introduction

An intervision is a type of meeting in which colleagues come together and share professional experiences, issues, and ideas. Such meetings are often organized to support employees and to boost their professional development (van Baarle et. al. 2022). The sessions take the form of what Wierda and Barendsen (2011:149) call a "collegial consultation", in which equals can counsel each other in a safe space without encountering judgments. This chapter argues that intervisions can be an inspiration or a source of information for linguists interested in studying professional practices, workplace discourse, or institutional communication. In doing so, it aims to show the affordances as well as the drawbacks of using intervision as a tool in qualitative studies. Following the congruous research loop between research design, collection/analysis and dissemination which characterizes bottom-up research processes (Maryns and Jacobs 2021), the chapter explores the role intervision might play at different stages throughout a research project. When designing the research project, issues raised during intervisions can for example help set or finetune the research agenda. This research-practitioner collaboration ensures the professional relevance of the research agenda, specifically, and translates into greater societal relevance of the knowledge gains, in general. Secondly, intervision might create opportunities for recruiting participants or negotiating (further) access. They can also constitute the empirical object of sociolinguistic analysis in their own right, as inquiries into problem-solving in a particular professional sphere can generate rich insights on hierarchies, tensions and ideologies that are present in a particular "Community of Practice" (Wenger 2011). Lastly, in the dissemination phase of a research project, intervisions can become fruitful arenas for checking or sharing research findings.

In what follows, this contribution will first discuss "intervisions" as a practice by drawing on pedagogical, psychological, and organisational literature. In doing so, Section 2 will formulate a comprehensive working definition of "intervisions" as a professional activity, differentiate intervision from other types of workplace talk and distinguish the different speaker roles and types of reflection that characterize the event. Section 3 dives into intervision in the workplace setting, by explaining the context in which intervisions are organized and by elaborating on how these contexts might influence the shape they take. In Section 4, the chapter moves on to scrutinise the value of intervisions as a tool for language researchers, specifically for those who work with qualitative and embodied linguistic methodologies such as pragmatics, sociolinguistics, and linguistic ethnography. Following the research loop described in Maryns and Jacobs (2021), Section 4.1 investigates how intervisions can help inform a project's research design, Section 4.2 explores the connection between intervisions and opportunities for data collection/analysis and Section 4.3 focuses on the dissemination phase. In doing so, the chapter investigates the type of knowledge generated through moments of collegial consultation and the way in which it can shape linguists' (access to) understandings of professional discourse.

2. Towards a definition

Numerous types of brainstorms, discussion groups and reflection meetings are organized in professional contexts. To distinguish "intervisions" from other types of workplace interaction, this chapter draws on the five rigid criteria laid out by Tietze's seminal dissertation research (2010). The ingredients of an intervision concern the relatively structured nature of the meeting (Kühl and Schäfer 2019) of which fixed speaker roles (criterium 1) and a set focus on professional issues (2) are essential parts. The bottom-up, non-hierarchical nature of intervisions is also defining: the peer-led character of the group discussion (3), the fact that there is no external stakeholder who facilitates the process (4) and the interchangeability of the conversation roles (5) complete the criteria list. The focus on symmetric relationships between the participants is what distinguishes intervisions from supervision or feedback sessions. This focus on peer-feedback, rather than on intervention by external experts, is informed by the idea that the participants in a particular problem are also often the experts of the problem's solution (Staempfli and Fairtlough 2019). Professionals can learn from relying on their peers to gain insight into certain types of work issues (Bellersen 2022). Organisations often have a lot of internal experience and expertise available, but co-workers do not necessarily see each other extensively nor do they spontaneously engage in knowledge sharing if such an opportunity does present itself. Taking the context of a school as an example, it is easy to see that there is common ground between different teachers and that it would be an added value if logistic, class management or interpersonal advice would circulate freely. At the end of the day, however, each class is an island in the sense that there is little opportunity for teachers to have a direct sense of what goes on in other teachers' classrooms and how colleagues are managing similar problems to the ones they are experiencing.

Teachers can seek advice and share experiences in the staff room and during breaktime, but providing designated time and space in the form of "arrangements in which peers provide critical and supportive feedback on a mutual basis" (Van Emmerik 2012: 86), ensures equal access and promotes more frequent and sustained knowledge-sharing practices. When diving into the interactional dynamics of intervisions, the pedagogical and organizational literature makes a distinction between three types of speaker roles and three types of reflection. In terms of speaker roles, there is a presenter, an audience, and a moderator. As indicated above, these roles are interchangeable and can rotate within an intervision or over the course of several of these meetings. The presenter (also called the "case provider," Bellersen 2022) is the one who volunteers an issue, an anecdote, or a challenge to be discussed. The audience (or the "reflecting team", Staempfli and Fairtlough 2019) offers their responses, advice, and experiences on this particular matter. The facilitator, finally, has a rather "structural role" (Angouri and Marra 2010). Much like a chair does in a corporate meeting, the facilitator moderates and guides the discussion (Bellersen 2022). Van Emmerick (2012: 86) explains the facilitator's crucial, yet non-hierarchical role as follows: "For the facilitator, the main focus point is how to keep the right balance between structure and *nothingness*, between words and silence. There need to be borders and there needs to be free space." The facilitator is, in other words, not expected to bring an objective stance or a solution to the table (Epprecht 2011). According to Bellersen and Kohlmann (2016) the group reflection instigated through intervision methods can take place on multiple levels: the case level, the characteristic actions level, and the views level. In the first category, the group reflection stays close to the specific case at hand. The group's considerations are not scaled up nor connected to other workplace dynamics. The second level concerns more in-depth contemplation and focuses on participants' approaches to issues rather than on the problem itself. The last level digs even deeper: the peer-consultation explores the participants' "hidden drivers" (Bellersen 2022), their beliefs, assumptions, and ideologies. This description underscores how intervision is a performative, social process in which knowledge is co-created during interaction (Van Emmerik 2012).

3. Workplaces and intervisions

More and more work contexts are becoming invested in reflexivity culture (Kühl and Schäfer 2019). One of the ways to pursue this is by means of intervisions, as a method of giving a platform to the exploration of workers' dilemmas, experiences, and challenges with regards to their job. These intervisions can be initiated or accommodated top-down by the management of private companies or public organizations (Van Baarle et al. 2022) or organized bottom-up by employees who perceive a need for more collaborative reflection and knowledge-sharing. The intervision method is most appropriate for work contexts in which standardizing or uniformizing professional practices is not advisable, desirable, or possible. These contexts are often characterized by issues and dilemmas that lack formalized or straightforward solutions, making collaborative reflection and advice from colleagues who have faced similar situations valuable. The fact that there are no clear-cut rules available within these professional contexts, foregrounds the need for reflection and deliberation. Examples are social work (Tietze 2010), education (Franzenburg 2009) or advocacy settings (Maryns and Jacobs 2021). Still, in recent years, (business) administration settings also show interest in organizing intervisions and promote self-learning (Kühl and Schäfer 2019). Bellersen's (2022) non-exhaustive yet divergent list of communities of practice who employ the method includes notaries, consultants, lawyers, teachers, vocational experts, physicians, managers, and accountants. She also emphasizes that the method is mainly used in continental Europe (The Netherlands, Belgium, and Germany — with a lot of foundational scholarship written in German) and Canada, although one could argue that similar practices might circulate in other professional contexts under a different name.

The main theoretical strands that underpin "intervisions" as a professional activity come from humanistic psychology. This discipline envisions employees as reflective subjects (Epprecht 2011) able to self-organise, to identify and articulate their own learning needs (Kühl and Schäfer 2019), and to self-actualise (Franzenburg 2009). The format of the intervisions is designed to boost collaborative reflection that can help to engage with individual and organizational problems. Intervision can thus be a considered a *tool* which can turn a free, colloquial discussion into a helpful instrument for coping with challenges in the workplace or a *system* that supports employees' reflection needs. Despite the strong theoretical embeddedness of intervisions (Tietze 2010) and its relatively widespread use (Bellersen 2022), there is "narrow evidence base for intervision in terms of both quantity and quality" (Staempfli and Fairtlough 2019: 1259) and no reason to assume regular intervision sessions would lead to better job performances (Wierda and Barendsen 2011). Outside of the realm of actual job performance, however, positive consequences of intervision are reported in the scholarly literature. Joint reflection is for example argued to help employees recognise the underlying structures of a problem (Van Baarle et al. 2022). When used in an educational context with students, intervisions train learners questioning and listening skills as well as their integrated thinking capacities (Staempfli and Fairtlough 2019). The students who participated in this latter research project also reported that they felt more confident about their (prospective) job performances because of their engagement in the intervision sessions. Bailey et. al (2014), finally, argue that the multitude of perspectives that are present during intervisions help to counter one-dimensional thinking in social work settings.

The remainder of this chapter explores how intervision can function as a tool in qualitative studies. The text is structured based on different research stages, dealing with design in Section 4.1, with data collection/analysis in Section 4.2 and with dissemination in Section 4.3. In these three sections, I will refer to methodological and empirical work from pragmatic, sociolinguistic and linguistic-ethnographic studies as well as to my own research experiences. These latter reflections reveal that the clear-cut definition and criteria of intervisions that is used in pedagogical and managerial literature is less rigid in practice. Not all practices that are labeled as "intervisions" by stakeholders live up to Tietze's (2010) theoretical standards. As workplace activities do not take place in a theoretical vacuum, the practice develops locally while holding on to the broadly recognizable structure of intervisions (King 2017). The examples from my own research clearly illustrate how operationalizing the theory of intervisions in practice entails a level of discretion to adapt practices to what one sees fit in a particular context, at a particular point in time.

4. Intervisions throughout a research project

4.1 Intervision as a tool at the stage of research design

When designing a research project that aims to analyse the intricacies of professional practices and discourse in a particular workplace, it can be of interest to formulate research questions in dialogue with the participants under discussion. This "joint problematization" (Roberts and Sarangi 1999) ensures that research efforts are dedicated in ways that are "recognised as helpful by practitioners" (Lefstein and Israeli 2015: 205). Workplace intervisions, which center around practitioner-provided challenges, can be relevant in this pursuit as they shed light on what issues characterize a particular setting and reveal how the community analyses the problem in their own terms. The concerns that are raised among colleagues are particularly interesting for researchers in the sense that they are of an "emic" nature (Pike 1967), defined and recognized as relevant by the field (and not merely by academics sitting behind their desk or observing a setting in which they have never played an active role). This makes intervisions a goldmine for scholars who conduct bottom-up research and are keen to understand practices "from within" (as is for example the tradition in linguistic ethnography: Rampton et al. 2004; Copland and Creese 2015). In this way, intervisions can play a crucial role in shaping or refining the research design of a project. Moreover, a "participatory" dimension (Matras and Robertson 2017), in the form of a collaborative engagement between researchers and practitioners, ensures not only the professional pertinence of the research agenda itself but also enhances the broader societal significance of the knowledge acquired. Research designs that are informed by workplace intervisions thus contain a practical application to social problems and hold the potential to bring about "real change" (Schaefer and Rivera 2013: 69).

In finetuning a research design, it is, however, essential to maintain a delicate balance between fundamental and societal relevance of the project. While sensitivity to the concerns of practitioners and collaborative definition of research areas are highly valuable, the literature underscores the existence of tensions arising from the different, and at times conflicting, orientations of researchers and practitioners (Bartunek and Rynes 2014; Maryns and Jacobs 2021). Academics often seek contextualized, nuanced, and non-normative understandings of "institutional life," while practitioners, influenced by the managerial or neoliberal structures they work in, prioritize efficiency optimization of the "institution" (Palomares and Poveda 2010). The challenge thus lies in reconciling the outcome-oriented interests of workplaces with the academic-scientific pursuits of researchers before embarking on the project. Numerous examples from institutional (Maryns and Jacobs 2021) and administrative/business contexts (as discussed in Bartunek and Louis 1996) demonstrate how a fruitful collaboration between practitioners and scholars is possible and can yield intricate and compelling insights into institutional phenomena. This chapter advises to find a balance between relevance and rigor at the stage of research planning and not merely at the dissemination phase. This is in line with recent calls to frontload research by paying more attention to evaluating the design of a research project at the very beginning of the project (Piller 2022).

As an example of how intervision can be used as a tool to finetune one's research design, I will be drawing on my own doctoral research project. At the beginning of my PhD on the role of language in legal counselling for asylum seekers, I attended an intervision that focused on 'Language and Credibility in the Asylum Procedure.' The session was organised by the Council of the Flemish Bar Associations, within the framework of ongoing professional development for asylum lawyers and legal experts. Just like the teachers in the hypothetical example provided in Section 2, lawyers' professional practices are highly similar, yet they rarely have the chance to see their colleagues in action — making an intervision a unique and necessary opportunity for knowledge sharing. The practitioners volunteered to take part in this specific session on this particular topic, but they are in fact formally obliged to follow a certain amount of professionalization training throughout their career. Lawyers are allocated points based on the training they undertake, which formally attests their engagement. As a scholar, socialized into linguistic ethnography and interested in language, legal counselling, and migration settings, I was highly interested to "hear from the field." The session was labeled and advertised as an 'intervision' by the organisers and participants. Its set-up conformed to Tietze's (2010) definition in the sense that the session served as a forum for reflective discussion on professional practices, that the participants' relationships were symmetrical and democratic and that speaker roles were interchangeable yet defined. The role of the facilitator was allocated to an asylum lawyer employed by an NGO, whose structural role (Angouri and Marra 2010) included welcoming everyone and closing the session. Apart from this she otherwise acted as a "regular" participant, as part of the "audience." A point of difference with the rigid theory on intervisions is that there were academics (me and a colleague) present in the room as participant-observers.

Throughout the session, practitioners raised issues they encountered in the workplace and in doing so they identified language-related challenges that stood out to them as problematic and that warranted further investigation. This list included: the recruitment and training of interpreters, particularly for minority languages, the linguistic proficiency of interactants in the asylum procedure, challenges in handling government documents within linguistically diverse contexts, the impact of non-verbal communication in intercultural communication settings, and the complexities introduced by video-conferencing tools (for more information see Maryns and Jacobs 2021). The lawyers' arguments and examples about how specific language-related challenges can impede asylum seekers' rights to a fair asylum procedure, directly fed into the research questions of my (post-)doctoral investigations. Their emic perspectives on the linguistic dimension of asylum determination helped finetune my research design and ensured that my research efforts responded to a concrete need in the field. In establishing such a "close and interactive relationship between scholarship and practice", I responded to Byrne and Gammeltoft-Hansen's call for fostering an "open dialogue and cross-fertilization" between academics and practitioners active in the realm of refugee law – an approach which they frame as a "major strength for any field engaged in empirically based and problem-solving research" (2020: 194–195).

4.2 Intervision as a tool at the stage of data collection and analysis

Linguistic-pragmatic research, interested in workplace interaction benefits from a profound level of engagement and cooperation between researchers and practitioners. Ethnography even inherently thrives on collaboration and embodies a participatory essence by consistently seeking the involvement of individuals (Budach 2020). In this context, intervision might pose opportunities for recruiting participants or negotiating (further) access. A research agenda based on issues that are identified as problematic in the field (during intervisions), has an increased potential to convince practitioners to collaborate in academic research, as "improving everyday institutional practice is a shared concern of researchers and practitioners alike" (Maryns and Jacobs 2021: 148). In my own research, while attending the intervision described above, it became clear that practitioners were looking for ways to have their voice heard, to raise issues. Franzenbrug (2009) reports – based on research on intervisions with teaching staff – that intervisions benefit workplaces by revealing shared struggles, which provides the employees with "a sense of coherence" (Antonovosky 1987) about their job. A similar dynamic seemed at stake here: airing frustration about migration policy and procedural injustice had a cathartic effect on the participants. Within the context of the intervision they were, however, preaching to the choir. Asylum lawyers who informed my research, by providing information, participating in interviews, or becoming a fieldwork participant, saw potential for impact beyond their own professional sphere in the prospects of my research project (Maryns and Jacobs 2021). They, in other words, believed that joining forces between practice and academia might have a chance to resonate on a policy level. All in all, my efforts to come up with a research agenda that met needs present in the field and to recruit participants who took part in the intervision, proved a valuable strategy for convincing asylum practitioners to partake in the research project.

Intervisions do not only present an opportunity for recruiting research participants. The event can also constitute interactional data in its own right. Researchers interested in workplace discourse and professional practices within a company or institution find rich data in intervision sessions as their object of analysis. The way in which topics are initiated and discussed during intervisions can reveal the hierarchies, tensions and ideologies present in a particular professional context. When it comes to analysing the interaction during an intervision, approaching the participants as behaving according to the principles of a "Community of Practice" (CoP) proves to be a relevant lens, as they form a group of people who "share a concern or a passion for something they do and learn how to do it better as they interact regularly" (Wenger 2011:1). The CoP concept was coined by Lave and Wenger (1991), further theorized by Wenger (1998) and introduced into sociolinguistics by Eckert and McConnell-Ginet (1992). The term plays a prominent role in the examination of language in the workplace (Holmes and Stubbe 2015; Angouri and Marra 2011). An alternative framework for conceptualizing intervision participants can be found in the notion of an "affinity space" (Gee 2005). Sociolinguistic descriptions such as "social network" (Milroy 1992) or "speech community" (Creese 2005) are, however, less fitting, as membership in these categories is not necessarily of a conscious or agentic nature. In contrast, the concept of CoP foregrounds members as active agents (cf. Eckert 2012 to see how this contrast reflects the distinction between the second and third waves of variation studies and how sociolinguistic work envisions the connection between language and society, or more specifically, meaning and agency). The conceptual emphasis on social learning (Meyerhoff and Strycharz 2013), also sets CoP apart from the other conceptualizations. It is exactly this focus on how members aim to reach a shared goal through a "jointly negotiated enterprise"(Meyerhoff 2004:528) that makes the CoP framework particularly suitable for analyzing intervision interaction.

Pedagogical research has described one of the outcomes of intervisions as the construction of "a common language" or "a shared professional discourse" to identify and address struggles as they unfold (Wierda and Barendsen 2011). Findings from CoP research tie in with this, as access to a shared repertoire, with jargon and shortcuts, is described as a crucial condition for membership in a CoP (Meyerhoff and Strycharz 2013). Analysing the intervision data that I collected within my own research project foregrounded how lawyers did not only identify legal problems but also pinpointed linguistic issues within the asylum procedure. What, however, stood out to me is the way in which these language problems were positioned against a legal rights framework rather than discussed in their own right. This was a recurring discursive move across the different members of the CoP: communicative issues, such as the use of non-certified interpreters within the asylum procedure were framed against asylum seekers' entitlement to a fair procedure. This finding, based on the intervision data, stimulated me as a linguistic-pragmatic researcher to not only delve into interactional dynamics and strategies to locally optimize multilingual management but to take into account the legal context and the human rights framework in which these interactions take place. Broadening the scope of my linguistic inquiry towards the legal-administrative context made relevant by the participants, allowed me to arrive at more holistic understandings. In this way, the analysis of the emic perspective of the lawyers during the interviews influenced the tone and content of my linguistic ethnographic thesis.

4.3   Intervision as a tool at the stage of research dissemination

Lastly, in the dissemination phase of a research project, intervisions can become fruitful arenas for checking or sharing research findings. Although intervision as a pedagogical tool is not very open to intervention from sources outside of the workplace, it does happen in practice that externals are involved. Important for intervisions' goal of knowledge-sharing is, however, that the event remains of a non-hierarchical nature.

This disposition is in line with how most (socio)linguists have come to see their own role. Having moved on from prescriptive linguistics, "a vertical and fundamentally authoritative enterprise" which presupposes an asymmetry between the linguist and its participants, modern-day linguists usually take on a less normative, more descriptive point of view (Jaspers and Meeuwis 2013: 728). The research process may involve some evaluative aspects, but the scholar does not position themselves as an external authority who prescribes actions to practitioners. Rather, the researcher adopts a reflexive and collective approach, which differs from an audit or consultancy model as used in corporate contexts (Jones and Stubbe 2004). In this way, the involvement of a researcher within the context of a workplace intervision does not necessarily become transformational to the activity's structure. When approaching the intervision session as a social learning process of a CoP, the researcher can position themself as a learner rather than a teacher, even when disseminating research findings and insights.

Together with a colleague, I reported back about my research on language and legal counselling in the context of asylum during an intervision much like the one described above. In doing so, we raised discussion points and showed patterns and interpretations based on the data set, rather than spelling out what should or should not happen in practice. Having attended intervisions before and having analyzed the event and its participants in terms of the CoP framework, I was familiar with the shared professional discourse that characterized the meetings (Wierda and Barendsen 2011) and aware of the lawyers' specific interests. In order to minimize my outsider role, I actively translated my research findings into the practitioners' repertoire, avoided the use of academic terminology and even occasionally used legal jargon. Building a dissemination event on an existing initiative (i.e., the intervisions organized by the professional community), helped me reach my audience and report back to those who have been involved and studied in the research project. Again, a shared perspective on the research issues and findings helped me sustain the practitioner-researcher relationship throughout the dissemination phase. As made explicit in research interviews, the lawyers envision it as their professional duty to safeguard the rights of asylum seekers. As a researcher in the realm of refugee law, I aligned with a similar stance, as it is a "a natural extension of the field's subject matter" to entertain a dual incentive of advancing scholarly knowledge and optimizing the asylum procedure, in a way that promotes the rights of refugees as it feels "fundamentally difficult to justify research into situations of extreme human suffering unless the alleviation of that suffering is an explicit objective of one's research agenda"(Byrne and Gammeltoft-Hansen, 2020: 189; Maryns and Jacobs 2021). The shared hopes to put language-related, procedural problems on the (inter)national policy agenda created a sense of alliance. This too leveled out the practitioner-scholar relationship into an egalitarian one.

5. Concluding thoughts

In this chapter, I have shown how intervisions, i.e., collegial consultations in which colleagues discuss and advise each other on workplace issues, can function as a tool for (socio)linguistic-pragmatic inquiry into professional contexts. In doing so, I started from the definition of intervisions by referring to pedagogical and organizational literature on the topic. These theoretical descriptions foregrounded the symmetrical, non-hierarchical nature of the activity and the conversational focus on professional practices as defining characteristics. Juxtaposing the literature on intervisions with linguistic-ethnographic data on intervisions in the sphere of immigration law foregrounded, however, how the theoretically clear-cut rules of what makes an intervision an intervision are less strict in practice. Following the structure of the research loop as put forward in Maryns and Jacobs (2021), the chapter showed how intervisions can be an added value throughout the (socio)linguistic-pragmatic research process.

Having described in detail in the discussion above how using intervision as a research tool can play out in the phase of research design, data cooperation/analysis and dissemination, I would like to highlight the circular nature of the research loop as a concluding thought. When looking at the role that intervisions played in my own research experiences, it becomes clear that the distinct affordances of the intervision organically tie in with one another — a certain boomerang effect seems to be at play: it is the research design that came into being in collaboration with the field that instigated research participation of people who took part in the intervision. It is the analysis of the intervision interaction that shapes the repertoire used in dissemination events in order to get an academic message across to practitioners. And finally, to come full circle, it is the comments, critiques, and reaction of stakeholders during dissemination that informs new research ideas and designs. This shows how researchers who engage with intervisions can use it to establish long-lasting scholar-practitioner relations and collaborations.

References

Angouri, Jo, and Meredith Marra. 2010. "Corporate meetings as genre: A study of the role of the chair in corporate meeting talk." *Text & Talk* 30(6): 615–636.

Angouri, Jo, and Meredith Marra. 2011. "'OK one last thing for today then': Constructing identities in corporate meeting talk." In *Constructing Identities at Work*, ed. by Jo Angouri and Meredith Marra, 85–100. Basingstoke: Palgrave Macmillan.

Antonovsky, Aaron. 1987. *Unraveling the Mystery of Health. How People Manage Stress and Stay Well.* San Francisco: Jossey-Bass.

Bailey, Ruth, Karen Bell, Wouter Kalle, and Manohar Pawar. 2014. "Restoring meaning to supervision through a peer consultation group in rural Australia." *Journal of Social Work Practice* 28(4): 479–495.

Bartunek, Jean Marie, and Meryl Reis Louis. 1996. *Insider/Outsider Team Research.* Thousand Oaks: Sage Publications.

Bartunek, Jean Marie, and Sara Lynn Rynes. 2014. "Academics and practitioners are alike and unlike: The paradoxes of academic–practitioner relationships." *Journal of Management* 40(5): 1181–1201.

Bellersen, Monique, and Inez Kohlmann. 2016. *Intervision: Dialogue Methods in Action Learning.* Zeist: Vakmedianet.

Bellersen, Monique. 2022. "The added value of intervision: Its effect on management consultants' professional practice." *Management Consulting Journal* 5 (1): 7–18.

Budach, Gabriele. 2020. "Collaborative ethnography". In *The Routledge Handbook of Linguistic Ethnography*, ed. by Karin Tusting, 198–210. London: Routledge.

Byrne, Rosemary, and Thomas Gammeltoft-Hansen. 2020. "International refugee law between scholarship and practice." *International Journal of Refugee Law* 32 (2): 181–199.

Copland, Fiona, and Angela Creese. 2015. *Linguistic Ethnography: Collecting, Analysing and Presenting Data.* London: SAGE.

Creese, Angela. 2005. "Mediating allegations of racism in a multiethnic London school: What speech communities and communities of practice can tell us about discourse and power." In *Beyond Communities of Practice*, ed. by David Barton and Karin Tusting, 55–76. Cambridge: Cambridge University Press.

Eckert, Penelope. 2012. "Three waves of variation study: The emergence of meaning in the study of sociolinguistic variation." *Annual review of Anthropology* 41: 87–100.

Eckert, Penelope, and Sally McConnell-Ginet. 1992. "Think practically and look locally: Language and gender as community-based practice." *Annual Review of Anthropology* 21(1): 461–488.

Epprecht, Christoph. 2011. "Intervision: A group-based peer-supervision project by EMCC Switzerland." In *Coaching and Mentoring Supervision: Theory and Practice: The Complete Guide to Best Practice*, ed. by Tatiana Bachkirova, Peter Jackson, and David Clutterbuck, 265–272. Maidenhead: Open University Press.

Franzenburg, Geert. 2009. "Educational intervision: Theory and practice." *Problems of Education in the 21st Century* 13(1): 37–43.

Gee, James Paul. 2005. "Semiotic social spaces and affinity spaces: From the age of mythology to today's schools." In *Beyond Communities of Practice*, ed. by David Barton and Karin Tusting, 214–232. Cambridge: Cambridge University Press.

Holmes, Janet, and Maria Stubbe. 2015. *Power and Politeness in the Workplace: A Sociolinguistic Analysis of Talk at Work*. London and New York: Routledge.

Jaspers, Jürgen, and Michael Meeuwis. 2013. "Away with linguists! Normativity, inequality and metascientific reflexivity in sociolinguistic fieldwork." *Multilingua* 32(6): 725–749.

Jones, Deborah, and Maria Stubbe. 2004. "Communication and the reflective practitioner: a shared perspective from sociolinguistics and organisational communication." *International Journal of Applied Linguistics* 14 (2): 185–211.

King, Brian. 2017. "Communities of practice." In *The Routledge Handbook of Language in the Workplace*, ed. by Bernadette Vine, 101–111. New York: Routledge.

Kühl, Wolfgang, and Erich Schäfer. 2019. "Intervision in the context of VUKA-World and new work." *Organisationsberatung, Supervision, Coaching* 26: 471–484.

Lave, Jean, and Etienne Wenger. 1991. *Situated Learning Legitimate Peripheral Participation*. Cambridge: Cambridge University Press.

Lefstein, Adam, and Mirit Israeli. 2015. "Applying linguistic ethnography to educational practice: Notes on the interaction of academic research and professional sensibilities." In *Linguistic Ethnography: Interdisciplinary Explorations*, ed. by Julia Snell, Sara Shaw, and Fiona Copland, 187–206. London: Palgrave Macmillan.

Maryns, Katrijn, and Marie Jacobs. 2021. "Data constitution and engagement with the field of asylum and migration." *Journal of Pragmatics* 178: 146–158.

Matras, Yaron, and Alex Robertson. 2017. "Urban multilingualism and the civic university: A dynamic, non-linear model of participatory research." *Social Inclusion* 5(4): 5–13.

Meyerhoff, Miriam. 2004. "Communities of practice." In *The Handbook of Language Variation and Change*, ed. by Jack Chambers, Peter Trudgill, and Natalie Schilling-Estes, 526–548. New Jersey: Wiley-Blackwell.

Meyerhoff, Miriam, and Anna Strycharz. 2013. "Communities of practice." In *The Handbook of Language Variation and Change*, ed. by Jack Chambers and Nathalie Schilling, 428–447. New Jersey: John Wiley & Sons.

Milroy, James. 1992. "Social network and prestige arguments in sociolinguistics." In *Sociolinguistics Today: International Perspectives*, ed. By Kingsley Bolton and Helen Kwok, 146–162. London and New York: Routledge.

Palomares, Manuel, and David Poveda. 2010. "Linguistic ethnography and the study of welfare institutions as a flow of social practices: The case of residential child care institutions as paradoxical institutions." *Text & Talk* 30(2): 193–212.

Pike, Kenneth. 1967. "Etic and emic standpoints for the description of behavior." In *Language in Relation to a Unified Theory of the Structure of Human Behavior*, ed. by Kenneth Pike, 37–72. The Hague: Mouton & Co.

Piller, Ingrid. 2022. "What exactly does an editor do?". *Multilingua*, 41(6): 629–637.

Rampton, Ben, Karin Tusting, Janet Maybin, Richard Barwell, Angela Creese, and Lytra Vally. 2004. "UK linguistic ethnography: A discussion paper." Online: https://www.lancaster.ac.uk/fss/organisations/lingethn/documents/discussion_paper_jan_05.pdf

Roberts, Celia, and Srikan Sarangi. 1999. "Hybridity in gatekeeping discourse: issues of practical relevance for the researcher." In *Talk, Work and Institutional Order: Discourse in Medical, Mediation and Management Setting*, ed. by Srikant Sarangi and Celia Roberts, 473–503. Berlin: Mouton de Gruyter.

Schaefer, Mary Beth, and Lourdes Rivera. 2013. "The prickly embrace of engaged scholarship: What it means to do research in an urban secondary (6–12) school." *Tamara Journal for Critical Organization Inquiry* 11(4): 67–78.

Staempfli, Adi, and Anna Fairtlough. 2019. "Intervision and professional development: An exploration of a peer-group reflection method in social work education." *The British Journal of Social Work* 49 (5): 1254–1273.

Tietze, Kim-Oliver. 2010. *Wirkprozesse und personenbezogene Wirkungen von kollegialer Beratung*. Wiesbaden: Verlag füt Sozialwissenschaften.

Van Baarle, Eva, Laura Hartman, Sven Rooijakkers, Iris Wallenburg, Jan-Willem Weeninck, Roland Bal, and Guy Widdershoven. 2022. "Fostering a just culture in healthcare organizations: experiences in practice." *BMC Health Services Research* 22(1): 1–7.

Van Emmerik, Ine. 2012. "Whitespace, intervision and shared agency." In *Pathways of Literacy to Nonviolent Life: Shared Leaderships*, ed. by Cláudia Múrias and Marijke de Koning, 83–89. Porto: Livpsic.

Wenger, Etienne. 1998. "Communities of practice: Learning as a social system." *Systems Thinker*, 9(5): 2–3.

Wenger, Etienne. 2011. *Communities of Practice: A Brief Introduction*, 1–7. http://hdl.handle.net/1794/11736

Wierda, Roelina, and Ronald Marc Barendsen. 2011. "Online intervision to enhance workplace learning for student teachers: Online professional development of student teachers in an international context." *Ubiquitous Learning* 3.2: 149.

Posthumanism and pragmatics

Leonie Cornips, Ana Deumert & Alastair Pennycook
KNAW, Maastricht University | University of Cape Town |
University of Technology Sydney

1. Introduction: Provincialising humans

Posthumanism, simply put, shifts the focus of research and politics away from humans; like Chakrabarty's (2000) call to 'provincialize Europe', it pushes humans to the margins. The challenges posed by human destructiveness, environmental degradation, climate change, population growth, resource scarcity, urbanization, diminishing resources, our treatment of animals, as well as major shifts in technology and communication present a range of ethical and political concerns to which posthumanism responds by decentring the human. While there are many strands to this thinking, for pragmatics it raises a central question: What would the pragmatics of communication look like if humans are either peripheral or even absent from the communication? Put another way, how can we understand communication if we decentre human language as commonly conceived, and instead look at humans and other animals, animals and other animals, humans and machines, machines and machines, animals and machines, and any of these in relation to other possible actants – plants, rocks, spirits, rivers, or forests? If pragmatics has always assumed human actors as central to its endeavour, what does this mean if humans and their language are provincialized? What might a more-than-human pragmatics start to look like? To pursue this, we will look firstly at the background of posthumanist thought and why it matters, and then focus on general issues for communication from this perspective, including ideas such as distributed language and communication.

We will then look at two topics which allow us to develop the contours of a more-than-human pragmatics: specifically at interspecies communication, with a particular focus on the dairy cow, as well as forms of communication with the spiritual world (such as spirits, ancestors and other absent presences). Clearly in such communicative contexts pragmatic norms and constraints will be very different, so we focus in these sections on communication that involves *attunement* to diverse others. Critical and politically engaged research, Brigstocke and Noorani, (2016: 2) suggest, "has often been described in terms of giving voice to marginalized subjects" but what happens "when we attempt to attune ourselves to forms of agency that do not possess a conventionally recognized voice to be amplified?" According to Carbonell et al. (2021), attunement calls "for a different kind of listening [that] entails an attentive listening which reaches beyond just linguistic meaning to become receptive to the unknown, the elusive, and the unfamiliar." They raise the question of "how can we tune into otherness in an open-ended way? How can we 'listen otherwise' and simply stay with something, receptive or engaging, experiencing the resonance in the world without translation?" (ibid). Ideas such as attunement give us a way of grasping how different species and entities as an assemblage of more-than-human relations, as embodied historical accretions engage with each other. An understanding of how different communicative actants attune to each other has implications for a broader understanding of pragmatics to which we return in the conclusion.

2. Posthumanism and communication

Posthumanism is best seen not so much as an identifiable philosophy, a fixed body of thought, but rather as an umbrella term, a navigational tool for understanding a present undergoing massive change, a way of responding to the need to rethink what it means to be human in the 21st century. Posthumanism includes several different, though at times overlapping, orientations. A central concern has been with the tenets of humanist political philosophy, questioning the foundations of the universalised category of *humanity* and its supposed inclusivity. From the long-standing decolonial critique that pointed to the hypocrisy of European claims to be *for* humanity while desecrating people, places and ways of thinking (Césaire 1955; Jackson 2013) to feminist and anti-racist challenges to the centrality of 'man' (Braidotti 2022; Wynter 2003), humanism has been a category to be confronted, changed or rejected. This posthumanist orientation confronts *also* the long history of intertwined images of Blackness and animality (Jackson 2020). A very different interest in transformations to what it means to be human brought about by changing technologies (sometimes called *transhumanism*) is "predicated upon a profound dissatisfaction with the current human condition and 'the biological chains' that keep human beings from actualizing their fullest potential" (Huberman 2021: 22). This raises questions about what it now means to be human (not so much a biological given as an improvable body), the rise of AI-based speech production (such as ChatGPT) being just another step in the challenge to the biological primacy of humans.

Beyond these concerns with humanist assumptions and interactions with and through new technologies, two particular strands of posthumanist thought are important for this paper, a new materialist approach to objects and artefacts and a turn towards understanding humans as one among many types of creatures. The new materialist orientation recalibrates the relations between humans and the non-human world. This line of thinking questions the boundaries between what is seen as inside and outside, where thought or language occur, and what role a supposedly exterior world may play in thought, action and language. The point is not to discount humans in the search for a more object-oriented ontology but to reconfigure where humans sit as *entangled* and *implicated* in other things. From this perspective, things, objects, artefacts are not seen as separate from humans or each other but as part of integrated wholes. Such *assemblages* address the ways that different things, people, objects and ideas come together in particular and often momentary constellations as "happenings" that are "greater than the sum of their parts" (Tsing 2015: 23), as "ad hoc groups of diverse elements, of vibrant material of all sorts" (Bennett 2010: 23).

New materialist perspectives allow us to rethink the relative weight given to different aspects of the material world, how they are related, and where humans may (or may not) fit into this picture. Putting these different factors together — a decentring of humans so that human/non-human boundaries become porous, a questioning of language as a unique property of some humans (from a Eurocentric perspective) (Deumert and Storch 2020; Jackson 2020), and an expanded vision of what counts as actants — language shifts from the brain to become a more distributed phenomenon (Pennycook 2018; Lamb 2019, 2024; Demuro and Gurney 2021). Language from this perspective is an emergent property deriving from the interactions and interrelations between human and other-than-human actors, including spatial resources and things usually seen as inanimate. As Pennycook (2018: 51) puts it, distributed language is: "a concept that challenges the idea of languages as internalized systems or individual competence and suggests instead an understanding of language as embodied, embedded and distributed across people, places and time." This distributional or relational approach suggests the open research question *what is happening* (Law and Mol 2008: 83)?

Instead of focussing on linguistic code(s) and/or speakers' practices (Deumert and Storch 2020), the focus can then turn to intraspecies and interspecies interaction (Cornips and van den Hengel 2021; Cornips 2022) or interartefactual communication (Otsuji and Pennycook 2024). An understanding of language as distributed allows for new perspectives on nonhuman animals as producers of a meaningful world through semiotic resources. Hence, animals, like humans, draw on semiotic resources that are embodied (Bucholtz and Hall 2016; Mondada 2016), and multimodal (Fricke 2013; Goodwin 2017), including sounds, bodily gestures and facial expressions, actions, movements, sensorial practices of meaning-making through tasting, touching, listening, seeing and smelling (Pennycook and Otsuji 2015), as well as the mediation of embodiment by material objects, spaces, and environments. A posthumanist perspective, in particular the concepts of entanglements and assemblages, helps to understand the multiple ways in which animals (and other non-human entities) are enmeshed in linguistic, social, cultural, material, and political relations. It expresses a multi-species interest "in better understanding what is at stake — ethically, politically, epistemologically — for different forms of life caught up in diverse relationships of knowing and living together" (Van Dooren, Kirksey, and Münster 2016: 5).

Such a focus in applied linguistics addresses two urgent research problems in the era of climate change and loss of biodiversity: first, how to decentre the human, hence, centre the animal (and other non-human entities), both theoretically and methodologically, especially within the strongly asymmetrical animal and human power relations, and second, how to fill the gap of knowledge in linguistics about the animal's interactional and communicative expressions (Meijer 2019). Tsing (2013: 33) for example emphasizes that our exclusive focus on human sociality as for example in linguistics "really hurts us. (…) If we want to know something about environmental change, we need to know about the social worlds other species help to build" and that we have to "[bring] more-than-human sociality into our understandings of the social" (2013: 35). In linguistic theories, there is as yet generally no eye for the sociality of animals, for what animal subjects make relevant in their intraspecies and interspecies interactions and for power relations concerning humans and other species. Posthumanism asks what our relation is to the planet, to other animals, to the objects around us, and re-evaluates ideas such as human agency, human nature, human language, or universalism.

In a long line of thinking that has decentred the position of humans, so they are no longer seen as separate from the other animals (Darwin), in control of their history (Marx) or in charge of their own minds (Freud), posthumanism continues this work of repositioning humans where they belong, not as monarchs of all they survey, but as equal cohabitants of the earth. It also therefore shares many ideas with, and indeed draws in multiple ways on, forms of Indigenous thinking on relations to land, people, place and animals (Topa (Four Arrows) and Narvaez 2022). The challenge is to disidentify from anthropocentric norms and the unearned privileges that have come with humanist assumptions. Both posthumanism and *first knowledges* (Neale, 2021) question the centrality and exceptionalism of humans as actors on this planet, the relationship to other inhabitants of the earth, and the role of objects and space in relation to human thought and action. This is a question of a *relational* approach to being: posthumanism is not therefore so much anti-human as it is opposed to *human hubris*. This has major implications for research on communication and pragmatics, requiring a shift from assumptions about mutual understanding between human actors towards a focus on forms of attunement among people, other animals, spirits, and the world around.

3. The animal turn in linguistics

This section provides a brief overview of ways a focus on the animal in linguistics challenges an anthropocentric view of language, communication, and interaction that can help us see non-human animals, and what they have to contribute, say, or express, differently. A focus on the animal in (applied) (socio)linguistics is not of course new. Kulick (2017) historicizes human – animal communication from diverging but also overlapping themes present in approaches from cognitive, psychic, psychological, interactional, ontological, and ethical dimensions. Many studies show that the animal serves as an interactional resource among humans. Humans talk to animals, especially to companion animals sharing households with 'their' humans. Tannen (2004), for example, draws attention to how family members sharing a household with a dog use her as a resource in mediating their interactions with each other, to mitigate emerging tensions or convey affection for each other (see also Mondémé 2018). A more recent example concerns Lamb's (2019) ethnographic research on human discursive practices surrounding problematic human-environmental relations, in particular, sea turtle conservation and ecotourism in Hawai'i.

One branch of research compares animal-directed talk to child-directed talk as it happens in Western society. Mitchell (2001), for instance, compared humans' talk to dogs during play interactions with previous studies about talk to infants. Features that overlap in American English are "a high-pitch register, a low mean length of utterance, high frequencies of grammatically acceptable utterances, present-tense verbs, repetitiveness, and attention-getting devices." Kulick (2017) and Szczepek Reed (2023) provide short overviews of the most recent studies focussing on animal-oriented talk by humans which might overlap with elderspeak, that is, 'babytalk' to institutionalized aged people.

Animals that have been studied in interactions with humans include also therapy horses and guide dogs (Mondémé 2023), companion birds (Harjunpää 2022), and dairy cows (Cornips 2022). Mondémé (2011) identifies various human forms of addressing their companion dogs during interaction. Harjunpää (2022) analyses how a human caretaker is sequentially responsive to her dog's 'woof's sound production with 'woof woof' or matches her vocal responses to the parrot's sound production. Mondémé (2018) discusses how humans may accommodate to how the companion animal is supposed to express herself. In addition to companion animals, De Malsche and Cornips (2021) show how humans talk to goats in a goat petting/dairy farm, while Szczepek Reed (2023) provides an in-depth interactional study focussing on phonology revealing how horse-riding coaches design talk to both horse and human rider simultaneously.

An animal, however, is more than an 'object' to talk to or a material and/or interactional resource used to manage human-centred interpersonal relationships. Simonen (2023) analyses the pragmatic meaning co-produced by a human and two dogs in social play when throwing and catching a ball, respectively. The embodied responses of the two dogs involved reveal how they react to human utterance and activity. Mondémé (2023: 307) analyses how a dog's or horse's gaze while interacting with humans is "followed by the human participant's uptake (mostly verbal, but sometimes solely embodied), evidencing the turn-allocational function of the animal's gaze on human participation". Similarly, Cornips et al. (2023) analyse how a cat sharing a household with humans employs deictic cues such as gaze and vocalization in order to coordinate attention of a human to a common object as a proxy for the event, e.g., providing food in the bowl and opening the door to go outside. Domestic cats also purr — showing a frequency peak with a range between 220 and 520 Hz — to solicit urgently food interacting with 'their' humans (McComb, Taylor, Wilson et al. 2009). Simonen and Lohi (2021: 424) show that dogs have implicit knowledge of their owners, on the basis of which dogs "have access to the principal ways in which human interaction is organized." Cornips (2022) and Nilsson and Norrthon (2024) analyse how interspecies greeting routines between cows and horses/dogs, respectively, and humans are organized.

Linguists also analyse animal, animal interactions like bonobos and chimpanzees (Fröhlich et al. 2016), with a particular perspective on human language evolution (Genty et al. 2020; Kulick 2017; Rossano 2013). Mondada (2018: 103; Mondada and Meguerditchian 2022) argues that multimodal transcripts of baboon-baboon interactions using conversation analysis (CA) evidence their mutual organization, and show that baboons' interactions are "methodically, sequentially, and temporally smoothly ordered". De Rijk and Cornips (2024) analyse play fighting behaviour of piglets in intensive barns. Their CA analysis shows how play fighting relies on monitoring the other party's continued willingness to engage, which is sequentially achieved through mutually constructed opening and closing sequences, floor yielding, and locally negotiating the rules for play.

Cornips (2019, 2022) explicitly makes a case for an animal turn in postcolonial (socio)linguistics as a way of critically engaging with language ideologies towards animal speakers, and how they create unequal relations of power. Drawing on long-term ethnographic fieldwork in various industrial dairy farms she shows that a dairy cow is a linguistic actor, who understands human vocalizations: calves can learn to respond to their individual name given to them by humans (Lange, Bauer, Futschik et al. 2020). A dairy cow (1) may open the interaction with a human (newcomer) in 'her' barn (Cornips 2022), (2) understands gaze withdrawal as turn-taking (Cornips and van Koppen 2024), (3) becomes aware that humans understand her request for a 'cookie', and alert to this, varies her recurrent vocalizations (Cornips 2024), (4) opens an interaction with the farmer by gaze and vocalizing but comes to know that the farmer doesn't gather the meaning of her multimodal interaction, and as a result, starts to articulate in a more pronounced way (Cornips and van Koppen 2024). Thus, not only so-called companion animals and/or higher primates but also dairy cows as so-called food animals are semiotically capable as co-beings who show "the ability to use language to convey a specific communicative meaning in a given context" (Parola et al. 2021: 7).

The animal turn in applied linguistics may lead to a new interspecies ethics, i.e. in "respectfully engaging in new rituals with them [that] can function as a gateway to further political interaction and extended conversations" (Meijer 2019: 214). But, "[p]erhaps, the most important question is not what kind of knowledge we can produce in the 'animal turn' [in (socio)linguistics], but what we do with this knowledge — that is; how we put it to work, and for whose benefit." (Pedersen 2014: 16). Such a turn has evident implications for language studies, expanding what is meant by language from the narrow, human-oriented considerations that have dominated linguistics to date, and opening up possibilities for a wider understanding of what is at stake in communication across a range of interactions that include humans and other animals, nonhuman animals, and animals and their wider environment. For Lamb (2024: 194) studies of *multispecies discourse* "multiply our perspectives of what language and discourse are, perspectives which will necessarily be as diverse as the multispecies relations from within which we are able to learn about them." The animal turn in sociolinguistics, therefore, is far more than a niche interest in understanding non-human animal communication; it suggests instead a need to rethink how we understand *all* communication, and questions the divisions that have been created between humans and the worlds they co-habit. This rethinking needs an attentive and unfolding listening "that aims to *attune*, to go beyond, that what does 'not hear' and is 'not here': a listening that is not subjected to anthropocentric sensorial and sense-making structures (…) but has a capacity to perceive the non-human: a listening that is (…) open and sets free" (Mandic 2023: 25–26). The phrase 'what is not here' leads us to another area of interest, communication with worlds that are not present in a naïve empiricist sense (as argued by Law 2007) but that are nevertheless able to affect us. They are 'absent presences' in the sense of Derrida (1994).

4. Communicating with other-worlds-of-being

The second domain of communication to be considered here concerns interaction with other-worlds-of-being, including communication with spirits, ancestors, and ghosts (questions of terminology are a challenge here, and writing in English limits our understanding of locally meaningful more-than-human presences, see Pels 2014).

Remaining agnostic about whether spiritual beings exist or not, the point is that communication occurs between people and other worlds-of-being. Moreover, many people believe that the communication also occurs in the opposite direction — spiritual entities that may include animals, trees, stones, recently deceased family, ancestors, or gods, communicate with people too. However, academics have long been skeptical of such claims. Possibly because terms such as 'shamanism', 'witchcraft', the 'occult', 'totem', 'mana', and 'taboo' were predominantly brought into being "to define an antithesis of modernity: a production of illusion and delusion that was thought to recede and disappear as rationalization and secularization spread throughout society" (Pels 2003: 4). Furthermore, it appears that a large percentage of psychologists, scientists, and philosophers self-identify as atheists and are thus not particularly welcoming to those who report experiences with more-than-human worlds (Yaden and Newberg 2022). This is also reflected in a recent survey which suggests that Anglophone philosophers generally see consciousness as being limited to humans and cohabitating animals such as cats (around 90% of philosophers assigned consciousness to adult humans and cats), with much smaller percentages considering the possibility of consciousness for other material entities (such as plants or particles), let alone other-worlds-of-being, such as ghosts, spirits, or ancestors. Thus, panpsychism — even though it has been discussed positively in established journals such as *Scientific American* (Hunt 2018; Goff 2022) — does not yet have a strong foothold among most Anglophone philosophers.

It is perhaps this skepticism which makes it difficult for many academics, including sociolinguists, to recognize the experiential reality of other-worlds-of-being (for examples of this skepticism, see Thomason and Poser 2020; Pablé 2022; as well as, on a regular basis, articles in *Skeptical Inquirer*). Anthropology, however, is an exception to the rule: there exists a long tradition of studying diverse forms of human-spirit interactions, albeit within a tradition that has, historically, been heavily invested in practices of 'othering' (Opler 1958; Crapanzano 1980; Lambek 1981; Stoller 1989; Motta 2022; Good et al. 2022; for reflections on 'a sociolinguistics of the spectre', see Deumert 2022). Such work notwithstanding, there seems to be a deep resistance to consider the ontological possibilities of other-worlds-of-being: "Away from such sympathetic fora, the prevalent academic response to supernatural belief remains one of unease" (Stevens and Tolbert 2018: 42; also MacKian 2011). Yet, given the prevalence of spiritual experiences across the world, it is helpful to adopt the agnostic perspective of William James who, in *Varieties of Religious Experience* (1917), documented — without any judgement about their 'reality' — the reports that people gave of such interactions. In other words, the focus should be on documenting and understanding spiritual experience, not to judge the validity of these claims.

Noetic feelings of panpsychic oneness (often combined with heightened emotions and sensory abilities), as well as a wide variety of spiritual experiences, are well-attested. Various statistics suggest that globally more than half of those surveyed had 'anomalous' experiences (which markedly differ from 'ordinary' experiences) at least once during their life (Cardeña et al. 2017). A study that focused on the US, India, and China found that between 20% and 30% of people regularly engage with those who have departed, and around 50% reported the experience of extra-sensory perception (such as precognition, clairvoyance or realistic dreams, Lau et al. 2020); in some sociocultural contexts the percentages exceed 90% (Lindsay et al. 2022). The ordinariness of such experiences was emphasized by James Hillman (in conversation with Sonu Shamdasani, 2013: 40) when he notes: "I think people already know all of this. They have their synchronic moments, they have their cautionary hunches and senses, and they have a no-no that comes up every so often."

While spiritual experiences have been documented globally, cultural specificities shape the identification and interpretation of such experiences (see, for example, Monteiro de Barros et al. 2022 for Brazil; Lindsay et al. 2022 for New Zealand). To recognize that for many people these experiences are real speaks to the ontological turn in the social sciences: while Western science might marginalize, if not vilify, spirituality and alterations of consciousness, other traditions might extol them (and render them intelligible), and acknowledge them as ontologically real (on the ontological turn, see Holbraad and Petersen 2017).

As posthumanist sociolinguists (that is, as scholars interested in communication beyond the human), we cannot ignore the fact that for many people communication is not limited to being in the presence of other humans: communication happens with non-human animals, material entities (including, for example, our engagement with art and the natural world), as well as absent-presences, from spiritual beings to ancestors. To understand these complexities, we need to radicalize empiricism; that is, to include not only what we can see, hear, touch, taste, or smell (and document with cameras and other tools), but also what we feel inside our bodies and minds. These experiences are real even if we struggle to incorporate them into existing academic frameworks. As Feld (2020:18) commented in a recent interview, "in linguistics or music we notate what humans do. And like anything else that's co-sounding or co-present or in the mind of the person who is speaking or sounding is not in the transcription!" Feld uses this moment of reflection to complicate Bakhtin's concept of citationality (that the word in language is always someone else's) beyond human citationality. He suggests that before we rush to fill this position ('someone else') with another human, we might want to ask, 'who is someone else?', 'who could be someone else?' (see also Motta's 2022, ethnographic work on possession, that is, spirits who communicate through, and cohabitate with, human bodies). As Feld notes, it could be "a cicada, not a person!" (2020:20).

According to Feld our soundings reflect an intervocalic engagement with the world, including the more-than-human world. For example, one might engage intervocalically with the sounds of cicadas, displaying an urge "to sound, to participate in whatever the cicada's sentence is, whatever the cicada's phrasing is, that world that is all around" (2020:21). In this context one could also consider Tuvan throat singing, which seeks to create intervocalic relations between the singer and the world. Or the South African practice of *umngqokolo*, another type of overtone singing which, in this case, establishes relations between the materiality and sound of the *umrhube* bow and the human voice (Dargie 1991). Here the 'word' is not that of another human, but of the natural world, or of an instrument (whose sound is experienced as spiritual, intoning other worlds). And sometimes our own sociolinguistic and semiotic practices are shaped not by what is present in a realist-physical way, but what we see as present in a spiritual way.

To illustrate this with an example, back in 2018, Ana was sharing her early ideas about other-worlds-of-being in a conversation with an acquaintance, who responded immediately, telling her about some research their family has been doing and how they — an amaXhosa family — found out that they had a German ancestor. Upon discovering this, they decided to hold a ritual, to bring him (it was a male ancestor) back into the family. In order to conduct the ritual correctly it was important that they could speak to him. As they were unsure of whether he would understand isiXhosa, they started learning German; not in-depth, but enough so that they could salute him and welcome him. An unusual case of motivation for learning a second language to say the least.

Staying with the idea of speaking with ancestors, Nokuzola Mndende (2002) refers to it as *ukuthetha*. This is not an arcane word in isiXhosa: it means 'speaking' and can also refer to human communication. However, in the context of ancestral communication *ukuthetha* is transformed and complexified: it shows heightened intensity, polyphonic semantics, a special vocabulary, a range of ritual speech acts, and draws on verbal as well as non-verbal forms of communication. It is a speech act within a world that contains two worlds, the physical, present world, and an other-world-of-being; a speech act that is characterized by a complex interplay of presences and absences. Not only do humans communicate with ancestors, but the latter are also actors in their own right, communicating with humans through a wide range of non-verbal signs. They might use, for example, dreams, visions, animals, and life events to reach out communicatively. Mndende comments:

> The language of the deceased can take the form of persistent illness among members of the clan, disharmony or misfortune, and can also manifest itself as strange behaviour by domestic animals such as dogs, goats or cattle, and wild animals such as bees, *uxam* (Nile monitor) or *umcelu* (small bird). (2002:30)

It is not humans who initiate such communication, but the ancestors: 'human beings are the recipients and respondents, and have to react in accordance with the needs of the ancestors ... amaXhosa ritual speech is [a] special form of communication whose authorship either originates from, or is endorsed, in the spiritual world' (2002: 189–190; 196).

All this points to the cohabitation of humans with other-worlds-of-being, a point that was made emphatically by Marc Motta (2022:276), reflecting on what he calls 'enmeshment', a term that links up with the notion of attunements discussed above:

> [As] long as I considered the spirits as ontologically exterior to the human world ... I would not be able to account for the way in which they were actually in relation with human beings ... how ordinary these spirits' voices are, how they are embedded in the everyday lives of people.

Thus, by turning to what is more-than-human we can actually learn something about what it means to be human; about human sociabilities beyond the engagement with other humans; and about the complexities of voice (with spirits demanding recognition because they are so often denied it), and about the need to attune to the other, to listen beyond the sounds of conventional language.

5. Implications for pragmatics

From a pragmatic perspective, it is easy to agree with Canagarajah's (2013: 32) view that the meaning-making potential of language "emerges through processes of alignment and adaptation, and does not reside in the system of language or cognition." To the extent that we arrive at forms of understanding (by no means a given) through interaction, this is achieved not so much by passing back and forth mutually agreed signs, but by negotiating meaning, adapting our communication, and finding forms of alignment. Once we see communication and pragmatics in these terms — not as add-ons to the more basic forms of communication that rely on the prior efficacy of language narrowly conceived but as the essentials of communication — it is not a great leap to consider communication beyond the human in terms of attunement. Once we take ideas such as enmeshment (Motta 2022) or entanglement (Pennycook 2020) seriously, it is clear that humans operate in a world of others — other animals, spirits, artefacts, environments — and that communication within and across such socio-material spaces is a process of aligning and attuning to what is going on. Hence, attunement, as defined by Ramshaw "demands openness, an ever-openness to the 'other': to sounds, persons, and ways of being" which "bridges the hearing/listening divide and is both grounded in the material/corporeal (hearing), yet also reaches or *strains* beyond such hearing to the unknown or as the as-of-yet-unheard (listening)" (2023: 89–90).

Drawing on various lines of posthumanist thought, this paper has used the idea of attunement as a way of thinking about how people, animals, spirits and other possible actants tune in to each other (rather than alignment — aligning with each other — or understanding — implying mutual comprehension). The implications for pragmatics more generally can be understood in several ways. The study of pragmatics beyond the human requires new sociolinguistic research tools. To adopt such an approach raises questions for the project of sociolinguistics (and linguistics more broadly): Do our existing sociolinguistic methods, such as conversation analysis, variationism, or discourse analysis, allow us to capture these interactions? Do we need new tools and approaches to document, and understand, communication beyond the human? Does such work allow us to broaden our understanding of language and communication? What does an ethnography of speaking or a 'unit' such as turn-taking look like if it takes into account diverse communicative encounters (see also Mondémé 2022)? It might be that we cohabit the world not only with objects and other animals, but also with diverse other consciousnesses, or at least many people act according to such a reality. This requires us to interrogate the methods we use; to transcend a purely human-focused sociolinguistics, not only in our thinking but also in our ordinary practices such as, for example, listening beyond hearing, and transcription.

There are also implications for pragmatics more broadly. Studying the pragmatics of animal or other-worldly communication not only requires new tools and approaches in itself but also suggests new directions for studies of human pragmatics. While much of the literature on animal interactions using conversation analysis is based on what animal participants in the interaction themselves make relevant (as evidenced by their observable behaviour), the focus on a set of observable communicative behaviours nevertheless misses the importance of semiotic and material affordances in making sense of the world (Lamb and Higgins 2020: 351). Once we understand communication within this larger framework that looks at material affordances, entanglements, and assemblages, at a wider totality of things brought together in an instance of communication, it becomes clear that such an approach applies to all communicative events: Interactions between humans are never limited only to the interface between two human minds and their languages. As Jackson (2013) reminds us, this is not merely a temporal move (the 'after' of the 'post'-human) but a geopolitical one, the relocation of communication in other spaces. This also suggests the need for new alliances, not just between pragmatics and other domains of language studies, but also with a range of other types of social and material investigation. What is at stake is "a kind of haptic sense-making and listening that allows for a co-existence with otherness, the makeup of which we sometimes know we know, know we don't know, or we don't know we don't know" (Carbonell et al. 2021). The bodily, artefactual, and spiritual dimensions of communication are never absent, and for a more comprehensive pragmatics, therefore, a wider set of possibilities needs to be considered.

References

Bennett, Jane. 2010. *Vibrant Matter: A Political Ecology of Things*. Durham: Duke University Press.

Braidotti, Rosi. 2022. *Posthuman Feminism*. Cambridge: Polity.

Brigstocke, Julian, and Tehseen Noorani. 2016. "Posthuman attunements: Aesthetics, authority and the arts of creative listening." *GeoHumanities* 2 (1): 1–7.

Bucholtz, Mary, and Kira Hall. 2016. "Embodied sociolinguistics." In *Sociolinguistics: Theoretical Debates*, ed. by N. Coupland, 173–197. Cambridge: Cambridge University Press.

Canagarajah, Suresh. 2013. *Translingual Practice: Global Englishes and Cosmopolitan Relations*. London: Routledge.

Carbonell, Isabelle, Anna Tsing, and Yen-Ling Tsai. 2021. "Attunements." *Fieldsights*, September 14. https://culanth.org/fieldsights/attunements

Cardeña, Etzel, Steven J. Lynn, and Stanley Krippner. 2017. "The psychology of anomalous experiences: A rediscovery." *Psychology of Consciousness: Theory, Research, and Practice* 4: 4–22.

Césaire, Aimé. 1955. *Discours sur le colonialisme*. Paris: Présence Africaine.

Chakrabarty, Dipesh. 2000. *Provincializing Europe: Postcolonial Thought and Historical Difference*. Princeton: Princeton University Press.

Cornips, Leonie, and Louis van den Hengel. 2021. "Place-making by cows in an intensive dairy farm: A sociolinguistic approach to nonhuman animal agency." In *Animals in Our Midst: The Challenges of Co-existing with Animals in the Anthropocene*, ed. by Bernice Bovenkerk and Jozef Keulartz, 177–201. Cham: Springer.

Cornips, Leonie, and Marjo van Koppen. 2024. "Multimodal dairy cow — Human interaction in an intensive farming context." *Language Sciences* 101: 101587.

Cornips, Leonie, Marjo van Koppen, Sterre Leufkens, Kristine Melum Eide, and Ronja van Zijverden. 2023. "A linguistic-pragmatic analysis of cat-induced deixis in cat-human interactions." *Journal of Pragmatics* 217: 52–68.

Cornips, Leonie. 2019. "The final frontier: Non-human animals on the linguistic research agenda." In *Linguistic in the Netherlands* 36 (1): 13–19, ed. by Janine Berns and Elena Tribushinina. Amsterdam: John Benjamins.

Cornips, Leonie. 2022. "The animal turn in postcolonial (socio)linguistics: The interspecies greeting of the dairy cow." *Journal of Postcolonial Linguistics* 6: 210–232.

Cornips, Leonie. 2024. "How (dairy) cows and human intertwine languaging practices: Recurrent vocalizations are not the same." In *Language as an ecological phenomenon. Languaging and bioecologies in human-environment relationships*, ed. by Sune Vork Steffensen, Martin Döring, and Stephen Cowley. London: Bloomsbury Publishing.

Crapanzano, Vincent. 1980. *Tuhami*. Chicago: Chicago University Press.

Dargie, David. 1991. "Umngqokolo: Xhosa overtone singing and the song Nondel'ekhaya." *African Music: Journal of the International Library of African Music* 7: 33–47.

Demuro, Eugenia, and Laura Gurney. 2021. "Languages/languaging as world-making: The ontological bases of language." *Language Sciences* 83: 1–13.

Derrida, Jacques. 1994. *Spectres of Marx: The State of Debt, the Work of Mourning and the New International*. London: Routledge.

De Malsche, Fien, and Leonie Cornips. 2021. "Examining interspecies interaction in light of discourse analytic theory: A case study on the genre of human-goat communication at a petting farm." *Language and Communication* 79: 53–70.

De Rijk, Lynn, and Leonie Cornips. 2024. "The detailed work of negotiating play: Studying pig interaction using conversation analysis." *Interaction Studies*, to appear.

Deumert, Ana, and Anne Storch. 2020. "Introduction: Colonial linguistics — Then and now." In *Colonial and Decolonial Linguistics: Knowledges and Epistemes*, ed. by Ana Deumert, Anne Storch, and Nick Shepherd, 1–21. Oxford: Oxford University Press.

Deumert, Ana. 2022. "The sound of absent-presence: Towards formulating a sociolinguistics of the spectre." *Australian Review of Applied Linguistics* 45 (2): 135–153.

Feld, Steven, Meghanne Barker, and Constantine V. Nakassis. 2020. "Spectral Signage." *Semiotic Review* 9. https://semioticreview.com/ojs/index.php/sr/article/view/63

Fricke, Ellen. 2013. Towards a unified grammar of gesture and speech: a multimodal approach. *Body — Language — Communication* ed. by Cornelia Müller, Jana Bressem, Silva H. Ladewig. Berlin: De Gruyter. Pp 733–754.

Fröhlich, Marlen, Kuchenbuch, Paul, Müller, Gudrun, Fruth, Barbara, Furuichi, Takeshi, Wittig, Roman M., & Pika, Simone. 2016. Unpeeling the layers of language: Bonobos and chimpanzees engage in cooperative turn-taking sequences. *Scientific Reports*, 6(1), 25887.

Genty, Emilie, Heesen, Raphaela, Guéry, Jean-Pascal, Rossano, Frederico, Zuberbühler, Klaus, & Bangerter, Adrian. 2020. How apes get into and out of joint actions: Shared intentionality as an interactional achievement. *Interaction Studies*, 21(3), 353–386.

Goff, Philip. 2022. "Does consciousness pervade the universe?" *Scientific American, Special Edition* 31: 124.

Good, Byron J., Andrea Chiovenda, and Sadeq Rahimi. 2022. "The anthropology of being haunted: On the emergence of an anthropological hauntology." *Annual Review of Anthropology* 52: 437–453.

Goodwin, Charles. 2017. *Co-Operative Action*. Cambridge: Cambridge University Press.

Harjunpää, Katariina. 2022. "Repetition and prosodic matching in responding to pets' vocalizations." *Langage & Société* 176 (2): 69–102.

Hillman, James, and Sonu Shamdasani. 2013. *Lament of the Death: Psychology of Jung's Red Book*. New York/London: W.W. Norton & Company.

Holbraad, Martin, and Morten Axel Pedersen. 2017. *The Ontological Turn: An Anthropological Exposition*. Cambridge: Cambridge University Press.

Huberman, Jennifer. 2021. *Transhumanism: From Ancestors to Avatars*. Cambridge: Cambridge University Press.

Hunt, Tamlyn. 2018. "The Hippies were right: It's all about vibrations, man! A new theory of consciousness." *Scientific American*. https://blogs.scientificamerican.com/observations/the-hippies-were-right-its-all-about-vibrations-man/

Jackson, Zakiyyah Iman. 2013. "Animal: New directions in the theorization of race and posthumanism." *Feminist Studies* 39 (3): 669–685.

Jackson, Zakiyyah Iman. 2020. *Becoming Human*. New York: New York University Press.

James, William. 1917. *The Varieties of Religious Experience: A Study in Human Nature*. New York: Longmans, Green & Co.

Kulick, Don. 2017. "Human-animal communication." *Annual Review of Anthropology* 46: 357–378.

Lange, Annika, Lisa Bauer, Andreas Futschik, Susanne Waiblinger & Stephanie Lürzel. 2020. Talking to cows: Reactions to different auditory stimuli during gentle human-animal interactions. *Frontiers in psychology* 11, Article 579346.

Lamb, Gavin Mitchell, and Christina Higgins. 2020. "Posthumanism and its implications for discourse studies." In *The Cambridge Handbook of Discourse Studies*, ed. by Anna De Fina and Alexandra Georgakopoulou, 350–370. Cambridge: Cambridge University Press.

Lamb, Gavin Mitchell. 2019. "Towards a green applied linguistics: Human-sea turtle semiotic assemblages in Hawai'i." *Applied Linguistics* 2019 (0/0): 1–26.

Lamb, Gavin Mitchell. 2024. *Multispecies Discourse Analysis: The Nexus of Discourse and Practice in Sea Turtle Tourism and Conservation*. London: Bloomsbury.

Lambek, Michael. 1981. *Human Spirits: A Cultural Account of Trance in Mayotte*. Cambridge: Cambridge University Press.

Lau, Elsa, Clayton McClintock, Marianna Graziosi, Ashrita Nakkana, Albert Garcia, and Lisa Miller. 2020. "Content analysis of spiritual life in contemporary USA, India, and China." *Religions* 11: 286.

Law, John, and Annemarie Mol. 2008. "The actor-enacted: Cumbrian sheep in 2001." In *Material Agency: Towards a Non-Anthropocentric Approach*, ed. by Carl Knappett and Lambros Malafouris, 57–78. Springer.

Law, John. 2007. "Making a mess with method." In *The Sage Handbook of Social Science Methodology*, ed. by William Outhwaite and Stephen P. Turner, 595–606. Thousand Oaks: Sage.

Lindsay, Nicole, Deanna Haami, Natasha Tassell-Matamua, Pikihuia Pomare, Hukarere Valentine, John Pahina, Felicity Ware, and Paris Pidduck. 2022. "The spiritual experiences of contemporary Māori in Aotearoa New Zealand: A qualitative analysis." *Journal of Spirituality in Mental Health* 24: 74–94.

MacKian, Sara. 2011. "Crossing spiritual boundaries: Encountering, articulating and representing otherworlds." *Methodological Innovations Online* 6: 61–73.

Mandic, Danilo. 2023. "Introduction." In *Hear*, ed. by Danilo Mandic, Caterina Nirta, Andrea Pavoni, and Andreas Philippopoulos-Mihalopoulos, 1–11. Law and the Senses Series. London: University of Westminster Press.

McComb, Karen, Anna M. Taylor, Christian Wilson, and Benjamin D. Charlton. 2009. "The cry embedded within the purr." *Current Biology* 19 (13): R507–R508.

Meijer, Eva. 2019. *When Animals Speak: Toward an Interspecies Democracy*. New York: New York University Press.

Mitchell, Robert. 2001. "Americans' talk to dogs: Similarities and differences with talk to infants." *Research on Language and Social Interaction* 34 (2): 183–210.

Mndende, Nokuzola. 2002. Signifying Practices: AmaXhosa Ritual Speech. Unpublished PhD dissertation, University of Cape Town.

Mondada, Lorenza, and Adrien Meguerditchian. 2022. "Sequence organization and embodied mutual orientations: Openings of social interactions between baboons." *Philosophical Transactions of the Royal Society B* 377 (1859): 20210101.

Mondada, Lorenza. 2016. "Challenges of multimodality: Language and the body in social interaction." *Journal of Sociolinguistics* 20 (3): 336–366.

Mondada, Lorenza. 2018. "Multiple temporalities of language and body in interaction: Challenges for transcribing multimodality." *Research on Language and Social Interaction* 51 (1): 85–106.

Mondémé, Chloé. 2011. "Animals as subject matter for social sciences: When linguistics addresses the issue of a dog's 'speakership'." In *Non-Humans in Social Science: Animals, Spaces, Things*, ed. by Petr Gibas, Katerina Paukneroká, and Marco Stella, 87–105. Červený Kostelec: Pavel Mervart.

Mondémé, Chloé. 2018. "How do we talk to animals? Modes and pragmatic effects of communication with pets." *Langage et Société* 163 (1): 77–99.

Mondémé, Chloé. 2022. "Why study turn-taking sequences in interspecies interactions?" *Journal for the Theory of Social Behaviour* 52 (1): 67–85.

Mondémé, Chloé. 2023. "Gaze in interspecies human–pet interaction: Some exploratory analyses." *Research on Language and Social Interaction* 56 (4): 291–310.

Monteiro de Barros, Maria Cristina, Frederico Camelo Leão, Homero Vallada Filho, Giancarlo Lucchetti, Alexander Moreira-Almeida, and Mario Fernando Prieto Peres. 2022. "Prevalence of spiritual and religious experiences in the general population: A Brazilian nationwide study." *Transcultural Psychiatry*.

Motta, Marco. 2022. "The fragility of voice: Hosting spirits in urban Zanzibar." *Current Anthropology* 63: 270–288.

Neale, Margo. 2021. "First knowledges: An introduction." In *Country: Future Fire, Future Farming*, ed. by Bruce Pascoe, Bill Gammage, and Margo Neale, 11–14. First Knowledges Volume 2. Melbourne: Thames and Hudson Australia.

Nilsson, Jenny, and Stefan Norrthon. 2024. "Opening interspecies encounters – Greetings between humans and nonhuman animals." *Journal of Pragmatics*. 229:40–55.

Opler, Morris E. 1958. "Spirit possession in a rural area of north India." In *Reader in Comparative Religion*, ed. by William A. Lessa and Evon Z. Vogt, 553–566. New York: Harper and Row.

Otsuji, Emi, and Alastair Pennycook. 2024. "Reassembling meaning while shopping." In *Multimodality and Social Interaction in Online and Offline Shopping*, ed. by Gitte Rasmussen and Theo Van Leeuwen, 85–103. London: Routledge.

Pablé, Adrian. 2022. "Linguistics for the apocalypse." *Language & Communication* 86: 104–110.

Parola, Alberto, Ilaria Gabbatore, Laura Berardinelli, Rogerio Salvini, and Francesca M. Bosco. 2021. "Multimodal assessment of communicative-pragmatic features in schizophrenia: a machine learning approach." *npj Schizophrenia* 7(28): 1–9.

Pedersen, Helena. 2014. "Knowledge production in the 'animal turn': Multiplying the image of thought, empathy and justice." In *Exploring the Animal Turn: Human-Animal Relations in Science, Society and Culture*, ed. by Erika Andersson Cederholm, Amelie Björck, Kristina Jennbert, and Ann-Sofie Lönngren, 13–18. Lund: Pufendorfinstitutet.

Pels, Peter. 2003. "Introduction: Magic and modernity." In *Magic and Modernity: Interfaces of Revelation and Concealment*, ed. by Birgit Meyer and Peter Pels. Stanford: Stanford University Press.

Pels, Peter. 2014. "Magic." In *Encyclopedia of Aesthetics*, ed. by Michael Kelly, 233–237. Oxford: Oxford University Press.

Pennycook, Alastair, and Emi Otsuji. 2015. "Making scents of the landscape." *Linguistic Landscape* 1 (3): 191–212.

Pennycook, Alastair. 2018. *Posthumanist Applied Linguistics*. London/New York: Routledge.

Pennycook, Alastair. 2020. "Translingual entanglements of English." *World Englishes* 39 (2): 222–235.

Ramshaw, Sara. 2023. "The song and silence of the sirens." In *Hear*, ed. by Danilo Mandic, Caterina Nirta, Andrea Pavoni, and Andreas Philippopoulos-Mihalopoulos, 87–142. Law and the Senses Series. London: University of Westminster Press.

Rossano, Frederico. 2013. Sequence organization and timing of bonobo mother-infant interactions. *Interaction Studies*, 14(2), 160–189.

Simonen, Mika, and Hannes Lohi. 2021. "Interactional reciprocity in human-dog interaction." In *Intersubjectivity in Action: Studies in Language and Social Interaction*, ed. by Jan Lindström, Ritva Laury, Anssi Perakyla, and Marja-Leena Sorjonen, 397–428. Amsterdam: John Benjamins.

Simonen, Mika. 2023. "Dogs responding to human utterances in embodied ways." *Journal of Pragmatics* 217: 69–84.

Stevens, Vanessa, and Jeffery A. Tolbert. 2018. "Beyond metaphorical spectrality: For new paranormal geographies." *New Directions in Folklore* 16: 27–57.

Stoller, Paul. 1989. *Fusion of the World: An Ethnography of Possession Among the Songhay of Niger*. Chicago: Chicago University Press.

Szczepek Reed, Beatrice. 2023. "Designing talk for humans and horses: Prosody as a resource for parallel recipient design." *Research on Language and Social Interaction* 56 (2): 89–115.

Tannen, Deborah. 2004. "Talking the dog: Framing pets as interactional resources in family discourse." *Research on Language and Social Interaction* 37 (4): 399–420.

Thomason, Sarah, and William Poser. 2020. "Fantastic linguistics." *Annual Review of Linguistics* 6: 457–468.

Topa, Wahinkpe (Four Arrows), and Darcia Narvaez (eds). 2022. *Restoring the Kinship Worldview: Indigenous Voices Introduce 28 Precepts for Rebalancing Life on Earth*. Penguin Random House.

Tsing, Anna Lowenhaupt. 2013. "More-than-Human Sociality." In *Anthropology and Nature*, edited by K. Hastrup, 27–42. New York: Routledge.

Tsing, Anna Lowenhaupt. 2015. *The Mushroom at the End of the World: On the Possibility of Life in Capitalist Ruins*. Princeton, NJ: Princeton University Press.

Van Dooren, Thom, Eben Kirksey & Ursula Münster. 2016. Multispecies studies. Cultivating arts of attentiveness. *Environmental humanities* 8(1): 1–23.

Wynter, Sylvia. 2003. "Unsettling the coloniality of being/power/truth/freedom: Toward the human, after man, its overrepresentation – An argument." *CR: The New Centennial Review* 3 (3): 257–337.

Yaden, David B., and Andrew B. Newberg. 2022. *The Varieties of Spiritual Experience: 21st Century Research and Perspectives*. Oxford: Oxford University Press.

Poststructuralist discourse theory

Jan Zienkowski
Université Libre de Bruxelles

1. Introduction: The 'theory' in discourse theory

The label 'discourse theory' can be used in at least three ways. First, it may designate theories of discourse that render assumptions about what discourses are and/or should be explicit. This means that the term could refer to 'discourse theories' of authors as varied as Saussure, Bakhtin, Wittgenstein, Lacan, Benveniste, Ducrot, Goffman, Wodak, Fairclough, Foucault, Habermas, Laclau, Butler, or Žižek (see Angermuller, Maingueneau, and Wodak 2014b). Second, the field of discourse studies can be conceptualized as a transdisciplinary meeting ground for 'discourse theorists' interested in the way discourse relates to power, subjectivity, and truth on the one hand, and 'discourse analysts' with a more linguistic or textual orientation who aim to understand how language, identity, and context conspire to generate meaning on the other hand (Angermuller, Maingueneau, and Wodak 2014a). While this may be a useful schematic distinction, the boundaries between discourse theory and analysis have proven to be rather soft and porous. Self-identified discourse theorists venture regularly into empirical analyses of (multimodal) texts and communicative phenomena (e.g. Phelan and Dahlberg 2011; Van Brussel, Carpentier, and De Cleen 2019), social practices (e.g. Marttila 2016), sociopolitical and historical change (e.g. Howarth, Norval, and Stavrakakis 2000), organisations, and institutions (e.g. Marttila 2019). Moreover, discourse theorists have set out to develop heuristic principles or methodological reflections to counter the so-called methodological deficit of poststructuralist discourse theory (Glynos et al. 2021; Torfing 2005; Howarth 2005). In many ways, the distinction between 'theory' and 'analysis' is misleading because the sensitizing concepts of discourse theory serve as tools for social and political analysis. At the same time discourse analysts — especially those who put a critical spin on their work — frequently venture into the domains of political philosophy and social theory to engage with questions of power, (in)equality and/or (in)justice (Zienkowski 2019; Flowerdew and Richardson 2020).

One could argue that all discourse studies are based on implicit and explicit theoretical assumptions and principles. Considered this way, it makes little sense to restrict the label 'discourse theory' to a specific type of discourse studies. All discourse scholars share an interest in the ways meanings get 'fixed' or stabilized but they develop very different vocabularies and explanations to explain this phenomenon (Zienkowski 2017: 92). Nevertheless, the label 'discourse theory' is frequently reserved for the approach initially developed in the context of the Ideology and Discourse Analysis program of the University of Essex. This type of discourse theory builds upon the political philosophy of Ernesto Laclau and Chantal Mouffe and is often referred to with acronyms such as DT (Discourse Theory), PDT (Post-structuralist Discourse Theory) and/or PDA (Post-foundational Discourse Analysis). The approach is also known as Essex-style discourse theory (see Critchley and Marchart 2004: 4). This chapter focuses on discourse theory in this third sense of the word.

The earliest iteration of this type of poststructuralist discourse theory can be found in *Hegemony and Socialist Strategy: Towards a Radical Democratic Politics* (Laclau and Mouffe 1985: 105–114). Reserving the label 'theory' for a specific approach to discourse can be considered pretentious when this implies a dismissal or reduction of other approaches to potentially useful toolboxes that may or may not be used by 'real' theorists, as if these approaches cannot provide relevant theoretical input for poststructuralist discourse theory. A more sympathetic reading would be that poststructuralist scholars claim the term 'theory' because they seek to provide an explanative framework for social and political phenomena rather than a method for analysing texts or utterances. The distinction between discourse theory and analysis is nevertheless becoming blurry as crossovers between 'theory' and 'analysis' have become more commonplace since the 2000s (see Marttila 2019; Glynos et al. 2021).

Essex-style discourse theory was initially developed as a research program inspired by post-Marxist and post-structuralist political philosophy. In this chapter, we use the label poststructuralism to refer to thinkers who share "a decentred conception of structure and of subjectivity, developed within the context of a systematic engagement with language and the symbolic dimensions of political practices" (Norval 2015: 156). This description applies to Laclau and Mouffe, who rejected the types of economic determinism and reductionism that characterizes orthodox and neo-Marxist thought (Mouffe 1979; Barret 1994). In their book, Laclau and Mouffe challenged key presuppositions of classic and neo-Marxist thought, while remaining dedicated to a critical ethos (see Jacobs 2018). Their political goal was articulated in the subtitle of their book: *Towards a Radical Democratic Politics*. The emergence of new social movements articulating identities, demands, and projects not anchored in notions of class could not be explained primarily or exclusively with reference to an economic logic, not even in the last instance. The radically democratic project of Laclau and Mouffe imagines and explains the articulation of emancipatory projects into a common democratic imaginary (see Smith 1998; Laclau 1996).

In their seminal work, Ernesto Laclau and Chantal Mouffe were not interested in the analysis of language use, texts, or interactions. The authors of *Hegemony and Socialist Strategy* (Laclau and Mouffe 1985) set out to develop a theory that could explain how (the meaning of) political identities, hegemonic claims, and strategic alliances, get fixed as performative effects of practices of articulation (Howarth and Stavrakakis 2000). They relied on Saussurean, Derridean, Lacanian, and Foucauldian terminology and ideas to develop an anti-essentialist ontology of the political that could account for the historically contingent, non-arbitrary, and antagonistic formation of political identities and alliances (see Howarth 2000).

If their book is now seen as a milestone for the linguistic turn within political philosophy, their discourse theory was initially designed to enable a post-Marxist account of hegemony and socialist strategy, in the service of a radical democratic imaginary. Discourse scholars expecting to find a model for linguistic or textual analysis in the work of Laclau or Mouffe are bound for a disappointing journey. The Essex concept of discourse cannot be reduced to language use — not even multimodal langue use. While it is possible, feasible, and useful to put the poststructuralist notion of discourse as articulation to work in combination with methodological and conceptual frameworks developed in other schools of discourse theory and analysis such as CDA (e.g. Montesano Montessori 2011; Fairclough and Chouliaraki 1999), corpus linguistics (e.g. Borriello and Mazzolini 2018), or linguistic pragmatics (e.g. Zienkowski 2017, 2012), the Essex approach was designed to account for the way subjects relate to discursive reality while engaging in vain but productive attempts to fix the meanings of self and other in necessarily provisional ways. Discourse theorists attempt to answer questions such as:

> What is the nature of 'politics' and 'the political'? To what extent is 'society' possible? How might we conceive of the subject? How is social and cultural 'identity' constructed? How might we draw the borders of 'community'? How can the relation between 'power' and the social world be conceptualized? What is the nature, if there is one, of 'order', of 'representation', of 'ideology'? How can we rethink notions of 'freedom' and 'equality'? And can we revive our ideas of 'democracy' and of 'emancipation'?
> (Critchley and Marchart 2004: 1)

Discourse theorists have developed sensitizing concepts (see Carpentier et al. 2010) that may appear rather abstract or mystifying to scholars accustomed to a less fuzzy jargon for analysing linguistic, textual and multimodal forms, functions and performances. The strength of Essex style discourse theory lies elsewhere, in its critical and explanative account of political subjectivity, ideology and hegemony (e.g. Howarth, Norval, and Stavrakakis 2000; Glynos et al. 2021). DT provides a theory of political identities and the articulation of political demands while explaining the ultimate failure of any political identity to establish (a final sense of) stability or ontological security for subjects. One might argue that DT starts out with a macro perspective on the ideological functions of Discourse(s) with a capital 'D' (e.g. 'socialism' or 'liberalism'), whereas the starting point of much discourse analytical work is a meso- or micro perspective on discourse with a small 'd' appearing in the form of concrete (multimodal) speech and text(s) (see Gee 2015; Carpentier and De Cleen 2007).

In what follows, I first present articulation as the core concept of Essex-style discourse theory. I then move on to a discussion of related concepts such as the field of discursivity, the nodal point, the empty signifier, and the logics of equivalence and difference, as well as a brief introduction the Lacanian approach to discourse and subjectivity. The third section of this chapter discusses new tendencies in poststructuralist discourse theory. Special attention goes to the subfield of fantasy studies, to inquiries into the logics of populism, as well as to theoretical and empirical explorations of the discursive-material knot. The final section of this chapter provides a brief discussion of the way linguistic pragmatics and poststructuralist thought might be articulated together and enrich each other. If linguistic pragmatics offers insight into the pragmatic dimension of articulatory practices, highlighting the importance of reflexive awareness, choice-making, and indexicality in discourse (Verschueren 2011, 1999; Robinson 2006), discourse theory offers a powerful explanative framework for the human impulse to find meaning in productive but vain attempts to fix the boundaries of identities, groups, and entire societies.

2. Articulation as the core concept of Essex-style discourse theory

Laclau and Mouffe approach discourse as an outcome of articulatory practices. The concept of articulation lies at the basis of their imaginary of social structure and change (see also Kortesoja 2023). Their starting point is that all social phenomena and objects acquire meaning through discourse (Carpentier and De Cleen 2007: 267). They state that "every object is constituted as an object of discourse", but this does not imply that they reduce reality to discourse (Laclau and Mouffe 1985: 108). Their point is rather that we can only make sense of reality discursively. They do not question the existence of reality, but argue that the way we make sense of an event, such as a brick falling on someone's head (e.g. as the result of coincidence or witchcraft), depends on how we articulate that event in discourse. At the same time, they follow Foucault in his refusal to reduce discourse to a linguistic phenomenon (Laclau and Mouffe 1985: 105–108; Foucault 1969: 40).

Laclau and Mouffe "call articulation any practice establishing a relation among elements such that their identity is modified as a result of the articulatory practice" (Laclau and Mouffe 1985: 105). Discourse is defined as "the structured totality resulting from that practice" (Laclau and Mouffe 1985: 105). The elements that can be quilted together, as 'moments' in a discourse, are accessible to us as signifiers. We need signifiers in our attempt to fix the meaning(s) of objects, identities, symbols, practices, narratives, and/or ideologies. Signifiers need not necessarily take a — purely — linguistic form. They may take the shape of sounds, images, statues, buildings, or performances. Laclau and Mouffe argue that meaning is established through the articulation of signifiers, and not in relation to a stable overarching structure. This explains why these thinkers must be considered *post*-structuralist, although much of their vocabulary draws on structuralists such as Saussure or Althusser. They do not consider structures irrelevant, but argue that the meaning(s) and boundaries of structures such as identities, groups, or societies can only be partially fixed in unstable practices of articulation.

Laclau and Mouffe take the Saussurean idea that signs acquire meaning in relations of difference, but reject the idea that language and discourse are stable totalities with fixed boundaries. They reject the idea that signs have fixed or stable positions within an overarching system. Linguistic and non-linguistic discursive structures exist by grace of practices through which structures are generated, reproduced, and changed. If all meaning is relational and dependent on the way signifiers get articulated with each other, no meaning can be ultimately fixed. There is nevertheless the possibility of a *partial* fixation of meaning.

Laclau and Mouffe's discourses exist as attempts to stop "the sliding of signs in relation to one another and hence to create a unified system of meaning" (Jørgensen and Philips 2002: 27). Discourse enables *and* reduces possibilities for interpretation and decision-making. To make their point, Laclau and Mouffe distinguish between the temporary and partial fixation of meaning(s) in discourse on the one hand, and the multiplicity of potential articulations on the other hand. To designate this realm of potentiality they coin the term *field of discursivity*. This field is conceptualized as a reservoir of 'surplus meaning' that surrounds any specific discourse (Laclau and Mouffe 1985: 111). It functions as an archive of excluded discursive elements. For Laclau and Mouffe "a discourse is always constituted in relation to what it excludes, that is, in relation to the field of discursivity" (Jørgensen and Philips 2002: 27). This implies that the "unity of meaning is in danger of being disrupted by other ways of fixing the meaning of the signs" (2002: 27).

Social actors routinely engage with reality *as if* they can fix the meanings of particular words, values, and identities. Discourses and identities are usually constructed *as if* the boundaries between classes, societies, or civilizations could be fixed or determined in a definitive way. This fading into the background of the contingent character of articulations is what discourse theorists call *ideology* (Torfing 1999; Barret 1994). Poststructuralist discourse theorists reject ideology understood as a form of false consciousness. They do not seek to uncover a reality masked by ideological presuppositions. Discourse theorists argue that all social reality has an ideological dimension. Rather than rejecting the notion of ideology as Foucault did, they propose a post-Marxist re-interpretation of the term. The analysis of the ideological function(s) of discourse, understood as an articulatory practice, involves a deconstruction of "the mechanisms which secure the imaginary essence of the community, without falling back on naturalistic fictions" (Norval 2015: 160–161). If ideology conceals anything, it is the contingent character of our social reality.

Social reality is generated through political decisions that fix (the meanings of) identities, norms, values, and practices in specific ways. Over time, such decisions crystallize into seemingly fixed conventions, rituals, and institutions, whose contingency is no longer recognized. The political origin of social objects and practices fades into the background, as our social reality sediments into a seemingly tangible reality. Any politicization of the ideological character of social reality implies a reactivation of sedimented and reified articulations. This is what Laclau and Mouffe mean when they assert the ontological *primacy of the political* over the social. Their discourse theory is less a theory of language use than an ontological and epistemological framework for thinking the political.

3. The conceptual framework of discourse theory

Laclau and Mouffe point out that even though no discourse functions as a closed totality, it remains possible to signify discourses *as if* they have clearly delineated boundaries. They write that discourse can be understood as an attempt "to dominate the field of discursivity, to arrest the flow of differences, to construct a centre." Going beyond a "banal constructionism" asserting that reality is defined and framed by discourse (Glynos and Stavrakakis 2004: 48), discourse theory turns to Lacanian psychoanalysis to conceptualize discourse as a productive but necessarily failing attempt to connect with the Real.

3.1 Discourse, subjectivity and the Real

The Lacanian Real can be described as a domain of raw experience, unmediated by representations and symbols, inaccessible to interpretation. According to Lacan, our access to the Real is paradoxically barred *because* of the symbols and images we rely on to make sense of our world. As soon as human beings start to imagine themselves as unified wholes, as soon as they start to develop a sense of self, from the moment they appropriate the pronoun 'I', while being inserted into the system of names and pronouns, any unmediated connection to the Real is irrevocably lost. According to Lacan, this process is triggered by our confrontations with reflections seen in the eyes of others and in mirrors. As soon as we construct our own Gestalt, we enter the realm of the Imaginary.

Because our reflections return different images to us, they do not provide a solid ground for identification though. Driven to establish a more coherent sense of self, the child will therefore enter into the Symbolic, which coincides more or less with its entry into the Imaginary (Stavrakakis 1999: 17–19; Lacan 1994). As we go through this mirror stage, our access to the Real is lost:

> What is lost is all unmediated access to the real. Now we can only try to encounter the real through symbolisation. We gain access to reality, which is mainly a symbolic construct, but the signified of the signifier 'reality', the real itself, is sacrificed forever. No identification can restore it or recapture it for us. But it is exactly this impossibility that forces us to identify again and again. We never get what we were promised but that's exactly why we keep longing for it. (Stavrakakis 1999: 34)

Because of their entry into the Symbolic — the realm of discourse — and their simultaneous separation from the Real, human beings strive for meaning and identification through discourse. Lacanian discourse theorists take the view that fantasy supports (our sense of) reality (Stavrakakis 1999: 62). Conceived in this way, political discourses offer competing accounts of reality and the fantasy of a common-sensical relation to our (national or ethno-cultural) identities as well as to society in general.

At the same time the identifications of subjects will always be incomplete *because* they rely on discourse to fix meaning. From a Lacanian point of view, the main function of the ego is to misrecognise 'the impossibility of fullness' or closure of any concrete identity, subject position and/or discourse. The ego's need for coherence and meaning pushes subjects to fill the lack at the centre of subjectivity (Laclau and Zac 1994: 35). The Lacanian *split subject* is continuously engaged in acts of (dis)identification and driven to misrecognize the fact that no identity will ever fully satisfy his or her desire for wholeness. Politics is therefore doomed to remain a fundamentally dissatisfying and agonistic activity.

This Lacanian take on subjectivity carries political implications (Glynos and Stavrakakis 2008; Stavrakakis 1999). Politics can be understood as an organized attempt to obscure or exploit the lack of ontological ground on which social actors attempt to base identities and political imaginaries. Ideology then becomes a category to name the discursive forms and functions that mask our radical separation from the Real and obscure the fact that social reality is grounded on inherently political decisions.

3.2 The articulation of nodal points and empty signifiers in politics

To be meaningful, different signifiers must be articulated in relatively stable discourses. Within such networks some signifiers acquire a more central position than others. Laclau and Mouffe call such signifiers *nodal points*, a translation of Lacan's *points de capiton* (see Laclau and Mouffe 1985: 112).

Nodal points quilt a discourse together and arrest the flow of meaning temporarily. They function as reference points that allow political actors to articulate a set of norms, values, identities, or demands into a relatively coherent discourse. The imaginary unity and coherence of a discourse depends on the extent to which such privileged signifiers structure the relations between concepts, people, movements, within a discourse. Thomas Jacobs draws an analogy between the role of nodal points in a discursive universe and the way gravity structured the physical universe after the Big Bang:

> Because the discursive universe is assumed to be uneven and not perfectly balanced, like the physical universe after the Big Bang, there are denser and less dense regions, regions where the (discursive) elements are located closer to each other and regions where they sit further apart. In the denser areas (discursive) gravity pulls elements closer and closer, until they form recognizable structures around a very dense core: a star in astronomy, a

> nodal point in Discourse Theory. A few elements that were originally situated in the less dense areas of the (discursive) universe, meanwhile, never become integrated in any structure but instead float around undeterminedly in outer space ("the field of discursivity"). When they collide with a (discursive) structure, however, they can completely ravage (dislocate) its internal organization. (Jacobs 2018: 303)

We now have all we need to understand the concept of articulation as defined by Laclau and Mouffe in *Hegemony and Socialist Strategy*:

> The practice of articulation therefore, consists in the construction of nodal points which partially fix meaning; and the partial character of this fixation proceeds from the openness of the social, a result, in its turn, of the constant overflowing of every discourse by the infinitude of the field of discursivity. (Laclau and Mouffe 1985: 113)

Not all discourses share the same nodal points. For instance, the signifier 'solidarity' may be an important nodal point within the discourse of a socialist party but may not occupy such a central place in the discourse of a (neo-)liberal party. Both parties may have their own explicit or implicit definitions of solidarity (e.g. solidarity as state-organised redistribution of wealth vs. solidarity as a voluntary act of charity), but it is the way the signifier 'solidarity' gets articulated with signifiers such as social justice, citizenship, political struggle, and democracy, that makes it a nodal point in the case of the socialist party, to the extent that 'solidarity' allows this party to articulate a relatively coherent project and political identity.

In their pursuit of a radical democratic project, Laclau and Mouffe attempted to imagine how disparate emancipatory projects may be articulated into a radically democratic movement through the 'fixation' of new *points de capiton*. This requires a complex articulation of multiple identities, values, demands, and discourses into a common imaginary for social change. The articulation of multiple identities and discourses requires the use of a common signifier that can act as an umbrella term for collective action. What is needed is a signifier that can cancel out internal differences in pursuit of a common (set of) demand(s) and/or in opposition to a common foe. Laclau (1994) calls such signifiers *empty signifiers*.

Empty signifiers are so over-coded with meaning that they mean everything and nothing at the same time (Torfing 1999: 301). They mean 'everything' because our social and political identities, and sometimes even our sense of self, seem to be dependent on their realization. They propel us to action and political mobilisation. If 'solidarity' becomes a nodal point in the discourse of a socialist political party as well as in the discourses of anti-racists, feminists, and labour unions, it may acquire the status of empty signifier, especially if a lack of 'solidarity' is deemed to threaten the structure. Empty signifiers mean 'nothing' in the sense that they evoke ideals and mythical futures that can never be fully realized. They are not 'empty' in the sense that they *lack* meaning, but in the sense that they attempt to symbolize a constitutive lack. They also mean 'nothing' in the sense that they have to remain vague enough to allow for a multiplicity of identifications (Zienkowski 2017: 54).

Empty signifiers promise meaning while withholding it. They function as objects of desire, urging us with great affect to search for something that is absent or lacking in our identities and societies (Glynos and Howarth 2007: 131). They function as projection screens upon which subject project their aspirations, hopes, and fears. If a political movement demands '(more) solidarity', it presupposes that there is a lack of solidarity that needs to be filled for society to realize itself. Discourse theorists are keen to point out that 'society' itself operates as an empty signifier. Laclau (1990) even wrote about the *impossibility of society*, an idea that can be captured as follows:

> We continuously produce society and act as if it exists as a totality, and we verbalise it as a totality. With words like 'the people' or 'the country' we seek to demarcate a totality by ascribing it an objective content. But the totality remains an imaginary entity.
> (Jørgensen and Philips 2002: 39)

Society — signified with signifiers such as 'social order', 'the nation' or 'the people' — is an impossible object in the sense that it requires a constitutive outside to make sense. Laclau does not deny that countries or other social structures exist, but he insists that their unity is not an objective given. He argues that signifiers such as 'order' or 'unity' operate as signifiers that signify a lack in situations of radical disorder: "various political forces can compete in their efforts to present their particular objectives as those which carry out the filling of that lack". Moreover, "to hegemonize something is to carry out this filling function" (Laclau 1994: 44).

3.3 Logics of equivalence and difference

For Laclau, the presence of empty signifiers is a *conditio sine qua non* for the construction of hegemonic projects. A social actor or discourse is hegemonic to the extent that it manages to present itself as guarantor of emancipation and/or social order for large sections of the population (Laclau 1994: 43). The construction of a hegemonic discourse involves the articulation of chains of equivalence between signifiers, identities, and social demands. There are two basic political logics that account for the way hegemonic projects are constructed: a political *logic of equivalence* and a political *logic of difference*. The logic of equivalence is dominant when a discourse establishes a chain of equivalence in opposition to an antagonistic foe. Logics of equivalence simplify political space by cancelling out differences. They do so "by making reference to an 'us-them' axis: two or more signifiers can be substituted for each other with reference to a common negation or threat". It "entails the construction and privileging of antagonistic relations, which means that the dimension of difference on each side of the frontier is weakened, whether differences are understood as a function of demands or identities" (Glynos and Howarth

2007: 144). For instance, the signifier 'woke' operates as an empty signifier to the extent that it enables the unification of nationalist, conservative, reactionary and/or alt-Right actors in opposition to a seemingly heterogenous alliance of progressive, 'politically correct', '(far-)left', 'gender-crazy', 'globalist', 'snowflake' individuals, groups, and media.

Imagine a situation where various political actors (e.g. socialists, anti-vaxxers, or far-right voters) construct an antagonistic relation between 'the people' and 'the elite', and where this 'elite' is seen as depriving the people from 'democracy' (an empty signifier). The political actor who is able to present himself as representing the demands of those calling for more democracy must establish a chain of equivalence that temporarily cancels out the internal differences (of identities, values, demands) within the coalition. The political logic of difference works in the opposite way, as it complicates the political space for practices of signification and identification. A logic of difference can be observed, for instance, in discourses that promote intersectionality as a prescriptive principle for re-organizing society (see also Jørgensen and Philips 2002: 45). Intersectionality implies that individuals and movements need to focus on multiple intersecting forms of oppression simultaneously. For instance, commenting on progressive activist uses of the term intersectionality, Jane Coaston wrote that "efforts to fight racism would require examining other forms of prejudice (like anti-Semitism, for example); efforts to eliminate gender disparities would require examining how women of color experience gender bias differently from white women (and how non-white men do too, compared to white men)" (Coaston 2019). Within conservative discourses in the US, however, 'intersectionality' operates at the same time as another empty signifier demarcating the contemporary left and right. Within this latter discourse, 'wokeness' and 'intersectionality' operate as almost interchangeable nodal points.

4. New tendencies in poststructuralist discourse theory

Essex-style discourse theory has established itself as an influential approach in the field of critical discourse studies. A second and third generation of scholars continue to advance its agenda in a variety of directions (Glynos et al. 2021; De Cleen et al. 2021). Since the years 2000, scholars have started to examine the role that fantasy, affect, and enjoyment play in our attachment to particular identities, practices, and discourses (Stavrakakis 1999; Glynos and Stavrakakis 2008; Glynos and Howarth 2007; Glynos 2021). Much of this work focuses on the successes and failures of past and present populist projects from across the political spectrum (De Cleen 2019). A great deal of this discourse theoretical work focuses on case studies that involve an operationalization of social scientific and/or discourse analytical methods. Moreover, efforts are being made to develop a more fine-grained understanding of the material dimension of articulatory practices (Carpentier 2017).

4.1 The study of political, social, and fantasmatic logics of critical explanation

Glynos and Howarth gave a powerful new impulse to Essex-style discourse theory with the publication of *Logics of Critical Explanation in Social and Political Theory* (2007). In the years 2000 discourse theory was arguably marked by a methodological deficit. In 2005, Jacob Torfing wrote that "there is an urgent need for critical, explicit, and context-bound discussion of what we do in discourse analysis, why we do it, and what the consequences are" (Torfing 2005: 28). This methodological deficit manifested itself in the fact that much analytic work did not go beyond an illustration of arguments and concepts. Traditional core topics within social and political science had to be addressed. Torfing argued that discourse theory needed to address issues of method and strategy without surrendering to the positivist belief that a set of methodological rules somehow guarantees the truth or reliability of results (Torfing 2005: 25–28). *Logics* was a response to Torfing's call for more explicit methodological reflection and positioned DT "within a wider set of debates in the philosophy of social science" (Glynos et al. 2021: 64). Its authors discussed issues such as data collection, causality, explanation, and understanding in dialogue with epistemological traditions such as (post-)positivism, hermeneutics, and critical realism, carving out a place for a poststructuralist mode of empirical inquiry and retroductive explanation (Glynos and Howarth 2019).

Glynos and Howarth reconceptualized 'articulation' as a methodological principle and elevated the category of 'logic' to the status of "a distinctive unit of explanation" (Glynos et al. 2021: 64). The concept of logic plays a key role in their version of PDT which seeks to "to *redescribe* the ontical (or empirical) level" of phenomena under investigation (Glynos et al. 2021: 64–65). The authors argue that every step in the research process — problematisation, corpus construction, analytical practices, presentation of results — involves rearticulations of signifiers that generate and modify the meanings of social and political phenomena (Howarth 2000: 140–41; Glynos and Howarth 2007: 180–81). At every stage of the research process (e.g. interviewing; transcription; construction of (multi-modal) corpora; analysis; or publication) discourses get re-contextualised and rearticulated. Social scientists (re)articulate their discursively constructed objects of investigation with theoretical concepts in analytical notes, articles, or books. Scientific discourse is subject to the same principles of articulation as any other type of discourse. The meaning(s) of the discursive practices under investigation therefore shift and change throughout the research process. This raises the question how researchers can rearticulate and explain discursive phenomena without disfiguring the research material and the associated interpretive practices beyond recognition.

For Glynos and Howarth, one possible answer lies in the way discourse theorists name and explain the logic(s) that inform social and political phenomena. They distinguish political, social, and fantasmatic logics of explanation. We already discussed the 'political logics' of equivalence and difference initially proposed by Lacau and Mouffe.

These ontological logics account for the way social phenomena can be politicised and depoliticized. In addition, Glynos and Howarth propose a category of 'social logics'.

4.2 Social logics

Social logics structure the interpretive realities of subjects and need to be named and identified by the analysts. It should be noted that logics are no 'objects' to be 'found' in textual material. They need to be constructed and named by an analyst who takes the self-interpretations of subjects into account while doing so (Glynos and Howarth 2008).

Social logics are meant to explain the rules and regularities informing the social practices or regime under investigation. The naming of a logic by the analyst is an act of (re)articulation whereby academic concepts and perspectives get linked to the discourses under investigation (Glynos and Howarth 2007; Glynos et al. 2021). Social logics are meant to shed light on the way actors interpret and shape themselves and their realities in everyday life. Glynos and Howarth wrote that "social logics of competition, for example, might describe the way that social actors interact with, and understand, each other as competitors" (2007: 139–140).

The process of naming a social logic involves a redescription of the discursive phenomena under investigation (Zienkowski 2017: 60–61). This implies that researchers should describe the discourses under investigation but also participate in acts of judgement that open possibilities for epistemological and ontological critique. Redescriptions of social reality with(in) the vocabulary of the logics framework can open up a space for the articulation of counter-logics and critique (Glynos and Howarth 2007: 183–189). Glynos and Howarth emphasize the importance of taking the self-interpretations of subjects seriously and write that discourse theorists need "to pass through the self-interpretations of the social actors involved in the regime and practices under investigation" (2007: 139). The point is not so much to contextualize discursive practices in their correct or original context of enunciation. The discourse theoretical mode of explanation does not consist of a hermeneutics of recovery. Neither does it search for hidden truths via a hermeneutics of suspicion (Howarth 2000: 128–129; Glynos and Howarth 2008). The point is rather to open new possibilities for interpretation and politics.

Glynos and Howarth understand context as yet another outcome of articulatory practices. It nevertheless remains unclear how discourse theorists should "delineate contextual boundaries for interpretation and explanation" (Zienkowski 2017: 62). Judith Butler and Ernesto Laclau wrote that "it is not possible to, strictly speaking, attribute closed boundaries to a context" — a statement with which linguistic pragmaticians and other discourse analysts would agree. For Butler and Laclau however, "contexts are defined by their limits and yet these limits are impossible to fix" (2004: 335). From a pragmatic linguistic point of view, one can object that while context is never given and always the result of interpretive work, it *is* possible to mark provisional contextual boundaries for interpretation in and through discourse. Everyday communicative practices involve constant negotiations of interpretive boundaries. Discourse theorists could find a more fine-grained understanding of contextualization practices in pragmatic and ethnographic approaches to discourse (see Zienkowski 2017: 62, 152–167). They will not simply find a toolbox in linguistic pragmatics but a theoretical framework that can help them to grasp how subjects leave traces of contextual self-interpretations in performative and interactive practices of articulation (Zienkowski 2017: 152–166).

4.3 Fantasmatic logics

Logics was also an important step in the further development of the psychoanalytic aspect of discourse theory. Glynos and Howarth formulated the concept of *fantasmatic logic* as a way "to understand why specific practices and regimes 'grip' subjects" (2007: 145) whereas others do not. The process of identification is an affective experience. Social and political discourse cannot be reduced to a mere chain of signifiers linked to each other according to formal logics of equivalence and difference. Signifiers also acquire value through the way subjects invest them with affect: "If certain signifiers become more central than others and if some signifiers function as nodal points or as empty signifiers in a particular discourse, this is possible because we *feel* some signifiers are more important than others" (Zienkowski 2017: 57).

Glynos proposed *Critical Fantasy Studies* as a sub-domain of poststructuralist discourse theory dedicated to a psychoanalytic exploration of the relation between affect and discourse (see Glynos 2021). Fantasmatic logics inform the way subjects are *gripped* by some ideas, identities, and ideologies while being appalled by others. Some discourses seem to *speak to us* more than others. We consider some statements to be intuitively correct while others seem outlandish or repulsive. Moreover, a focus on fantasy enables researchers to consider "issues linked to *resistance* to change and transformation, just as much as issues linked to our ready *embrace* of change and transformation" (Glynos 2021: 100). The point is that social actors do not 'choose' 'their' discourses in a purely rational way. The logic of fantasy can be characterized as follows:

> First, it has a narrative structure which features, among other things, an ideal and an obstacle for its realisation, and which may take a beautific or horrific form; second, it has an inherently transgressive aspect vis-à-vis officially affirmed ideals; and third, it purports to offer a foundational guarantee of sorts, in the sense that it offers the subject a degree of protection from the anxiety associated with a direct confrontation with the radical contingency of social relations. (Glynos 2008: 287)

Fantasy allows subjects to imagine alternative futures and to transgress sedimented norms that structure understandings of self and society. It "allows us to think about our ideals as if they are achievable and to imagine our identities as objects of desire that can be filled with concrete contents" (Zienkowski 2017: 58). From a psychoanalytic perspective, fantasy is not necessarily opposed to rationality. The point is rather that fantasy structures our relation to social norms, as well as the force with which we pursue them (Glynos 2008: 289). Different modes of attachment to ideological fantasy are possible. The logic of fantasy can help to explain the overinvestment of individuals in particular identities and/or ideological projects.

Subjects in the thrall of ideological fantasy tend to become insensitive to the contingency of their sense of self and society. The problem is not that human beings engage in practices of identification, but that an overinvestment in a particular identity or subject position is usually accompanied by a reductionist and essentialist understanding of self and society. Such a process of phantasmatic (over)identification can be a source of enjoyment for the subject. It is useful to point out that "what binds a community together is often not simply an identification with a common ideal like 'justice' or 'freedom', but also an identification with a common form of *transgression*; and in particular the fantasmatic *enjoyment* derived from this transgression — an enjoyment often supported with reference to a readily available alibi" (Glynos 2021: 102). Glynos illustrates this with reference to the enjoyment that voters take in the transgressions of politicians like George W. Bush, who used his SUV as a symbol of disdain for womanly ecologists, or in Trump's bare faced mega-lies and the way they bamboozle liberal elites (Glynos 2021: 102-3). He adds that "what is important from a psychoanalytic point of view is how such norm transgressions — some more fundamental than others — can provoke fantasmatic enjoyments that create and sustain forms of collective identification which, under certain conditions, can also foster and sustain rather extreme forms of polarization" (Glynos 2021: 103). Fantasy dwells somewhere beyond conscious deliberations and thoughts. It orients us to objects who are constantly out of reach (e.g. 'real democracy', 'freedom', 'being great again'), but also remain central to our understandings of self and other.

Psychoanalytic theory also suggests that through analysis, the 'grip' of fantasmatic narratives can in principle be loosened. Analysis implies that one recognizes a fantasmatic narrative *as* a narrative rather than as an accurate description of the world (Glynos 2021: 106). Subjects may indeed articulate themselves and their political discourse(s) with different degrees of reflexivity and critical awareness (Zienkowski 2017: 59). When an individual self-identifies as a 'white male', he may do so because he believes in his 'natural' or 'God-given' superiority, but he may also articulate an ironic and/or critical relation to this subject position. It is possible for such a person to develop a critical and reflexive form of (self-)awareness regarding his place in society and its discourses about gender and/or whiteness.

4.4 A populist logic across the ideological spectrum

A great deal of work in discourse theory has gone into the study of populism, or more accurately, into the study of the populist logic. In DT populism is not automatically reduced to (far-)right or xenophobic modes of politics, but conceptualised as a formal logic through which distinct ideological elements and discourses can be articulated. De Cleen, Goyvaerts, Carpentier, Glynos, and Stavrakakis summarize the DT concept of populism as follows:

> DT considers the specificity of populism to lie in its *formal* characteristics rather than in its ideological contents. The latter can vary, producing different, even antithetical populisms (left-wing and right-wing, inclusionary and exclusionary). Populist politics claim to put forward popular demands and interests against an 'establishment', seen as undermining and frustrating these demands. Populism constructs a dichotomic representation of social and political space in an attempt to mobilize social sectors that are (and/or feel) marginalized and establish linkages between them. This is how 'the people' emerges as a result of the populist performance. (De Cleen et al. 2021: 15)

Essex-style discourse theorists do not simply analyse and criticise (right-wing forms of) populism, as is often the case in CDA. They frequently apply their framework in studies of left-wing populist projects as well (e.g. Stavrakakis and Katsambekis 2014; García Agustín and Briziarelli 2018). Moreover, the strategy of the Spanish left-wing party Podemos was at least in part inspired by the political philosophy of Laclau and Mouffe (see Cervera-Marzal 2023). De Cleen defines the populist logic in the language of nodal points and antagonisms:

> populism is a political logic centred around the nodal points 'the people' and 'the elite', in which the meaning of 'the people' and 'the elite' is constructed through a down/up antagonism between 'the people' as a large powerless group and 'the elite' as a small and illegitimately powerful group. Populism is a claim to represent 'the people' against a (some) illegitimate 'elite', and constructs its political demands as representing the will of 'the people'. (De Cleen 2019: 29)

Laclau conceptualized populism as a (hegemonic) strategy (2005), conflating 'hegemony' and 'populism' to a significant extent, especially in his later writings. Contemporary discourse theorists prefer to keep these notions analytically separate (De Cleen et al. 2021: 15). Both Laclau (2005) and Mouffe (2018) favoured the development of left-wing populist projects, arguably blurring descriptive and prescriptive understandings of populism as far as left-wing populism is concerned.[1]

---

[1] I refer to the work of Arthur Borriello and Anton Jäger (2021) for an insightful critical discussion of Laclau's approach to populism.

In the Essex approach to discourse the populist logic informs the discursive construction of categories such as 'the people' or 'the elite'. The 'people' is not dealt with as "as an objective socio-economic or socio-cultural category" but as a discursive construct in which disparate identities and demands are articulated together through chains of equivalence in opposition to a constitutive outside (De Cleen 2019: 32). It is also worth noting that discourse theorists have drawn attention to the fact that the signifier 'populism' itself plays a role in the way actors fix the meaning(s) of politics and political actors (De Cleen, Glynos, and Mondon 2021; Goyvaerts 2023).

4.5   Studying the discursive-material knot in DT

While Laclau and Mouffe explicitly affirmed "the material character of every discursive structure" (1985: 108), the relationships and dynamics between the material and discursive dimensions of reality have long been under-theorized in discourse theory. In *The discursive-material knot*, Nico Carpentier (2007) engages with Bruno Latour's Actor-Network theory and Barad's new materialism, taking discourse theory in another promising direction.

Carpentier argues that there is a need "to look at other approaches that have developed more in-depth reflections about the material" (2017: 42). He proposes to consider agency as an effect of heterogeneous entanglements of discursive and material dimensions of reality. He thereby relies on Latour to make the point that material things are actants able to modify states of affairs. Objects are dealt with as mediators or intermediaries implicated in the social through their connection with humans. He also relies on the new materialism of Barad to argue that agency, defined as the capacity to impact the way reality is configured, can be inscribed into and generated by the interaction of objects and technologies, as well as human and non-human actors. Agency is not dealt with as a property of humans but as an emergent phenomenon, it is "a matter of possibilities for reconfiguring entanglements" that can (re)configure the world (Carpentier 2017: 43–45).

Carpentier proposes to conceptualize the relation between the material and the discursive in terms of *invitations* that can originate in the material. The material invites meanings in a way that is reminiscent of texts: "texts do not produce or determine meaning, they 'invite' their readers to accept particular positions […]" (Turner 2005: 127, cited in Carpentier 2017: 45). The invitations that originate from the material "do not fix or determine meanings, but their material characteristics still privilege and facilitate the attribution of particular meanings through invitation" (Carpentier 2017: 42). Carpentier argues that the materiality of objects and technologies might facilitate some discourses while frustrating others:

> Materials like objects and technologies consist of an endless and restless combination of the material and the discursive, where the material invites for particular discourses, and assisting in other discourses (and materials) to be produced. But the material is also always invested with meaning. Hegemonic orders provide contextual frameworks of intelligibility that intervene in these assemblages. (Carpentier 2017: 42–43)

Bodies, media technologies, and other material objects are characterized by a structuring materiality. This materiality structures the social: "It allows and disallows bodies to move, in providing access to some spaces (and places) and impeding access to others" (Carpentier 2017: 69–70). Objects offer affordances that "allow for some actions to be performed, and dissuade the performance of others" (Carpentier 2017: 70). They can exert some form of agency of their own, but the material also offers building blocks for human agency. At the same time, the material always escapes representation and discourse to some extent. The materiality of events (e.g. unexpected terrorist attacks, manifestations of climate change, unknown viruses) can dislocate existing representations and invite the (re)articulation and/or (re)activation of particular discourses (2017: 71). Carpentier argues that through the logics of invitation and dislocation, the material "talks back" to the discursive (2017: 73). Nevertheless, discourses remains relevant as "they structure the social by making it visible and thinkable" and have "affordances that gear us towards specific interpretations and identifications (Carpentier 2017: 74). Discourse theoretical studies working with the concept of the discursive-material knot are still rare but examples include studies of assemblages such as community media in Cyprus (2017, 2019), alternative media in Ukraine (Baysha 2022), Zines in Prague (Hroch and Carpentier 2021), and Massive Open Online Courses (MOOCs) (Zienkowski and Lambotte 2023).

4.6 The methodological pluralism of discourse theoretical analysis

In a recent article that takes stock of the way Essex discourse theory has been put to work, Glynos, Howarth, Love, Roussos, and Vazquez (2021) address a set of methodological critiques levelled at DT. They identify a tension between authors like Hawkins who point out that "there is no single, prescriptive methodological approach for conducting discourse theoretically informed research" (2015: 145), and authors like Zienkowski who seek to develop more "heuristic guidelines ... to articulate concepts and practices with one another in innovative ways" and "to deal with the linguistic and textual data that provide the raw material" for the bulk of discourse theoretical research (Zienkowski 2012: 509). A call for more heuristic guidelines does not imply a devaluation of methodological pluralism though.

A more fundamental tension among discourse theoretical scholars can perhaps be observed between those who treat methodology as a peripheral concern (like Laclau himself), and those who consider a more thorough methodological reflection essential for the further empirical *and* theoretical development of the post-foundational perspective. Contemporary authors in discourse theory recognize that "methodology remains an area where DT could be strengthened" and explicitly welcome "growing methodological rigor of DT" (De Cleen et al. 2021: 8) that results from its dialogue with other approaches in discourse studies and the social sciences. Moreover, they explicitly state that "DT work would benefit from further engagement with more linguistically-inspired forms of discourse analysis" while nevertheless emphasizing that "DT is not and should be considered as a method of (linguistic) discourse analysis in any strict sense: it remains a discursive approach to social and political phenomena with significant theoretical ambitions and these remain central to its project" (De Cleen et al. 2021: 8).

Researchers have articulated the discourse theoretical perspective with methods as varied as active interviewing (Zienkowski 2015), constructivist grounded theory (Zienkowski 2017), audience research (Van Brussel 2018), action research (Roussos 2019), topic modelling (Jacobs and Tschötschel 2019), and survey research (Stavrakakis, Andreadis, and Katsambekis 2017). All these techniques for data construction and analysis offer ways to examine articulatory practices and the logics informing them. In the domain of critical discourse studies, scholars have articulated DT with CDA (Bartlett and Montesano Montessori 2021), textual analysis (e.g. Remling 2018), corpus analysis (Nikisianis et al. 2019), lexicographic discourse analysis (Borriello and Mazzolini 2018), ethnomethodology (D'hondt 2013), and linguistic pragmatics (Zienkowski 2017). This list is far from exhaustive.

Despite the rather positive attitude towards methodological pluralism, the core conceptual framework of discourse theory remains rather stable and rarely integrates concepts and theoretical or methodological insights developed in other strands of discourse studies. There are nevertheless real *theoretical* — not merely *methodological* — contributions to be made. This can be illustrated with reference to the case of linguistic pragmatics. The very principle of articulation presupposes that a combination of theoretical and methodological frameworks implies shifts in meaning. Combining discourse theory with other theoretical and methodological frameworks is never a matter of mere *application* or *operationalization*. When combining two frameworks one should therefore consider how the meaning of each element changes in the process of their articulation.

5. Articulating DT and linguistic pragmatics: The pragmatic dimension of articulation[2]

Laclau and Mouffe would probably dismiss the bulk of linguistic pragmatic concepts of discourse as a form of linguistic reductionism. Their discourse theory was never meant to offer an account of the variable, adaptable, and negotiable forms and functions of discourse. Moreover, key topics of linguistic pragmatics (e.g. presupposition, inference, deixis, or indexicality) hardly received any attention in their work. It is therefore important to point out that linguistic pragmatics offers more than a set of analytic 'tools' for discourse theorists to use or to ignore. The pragmatic perspective offers methodological *and* theoretical insights into the nature and dynamics of articulatory practices. As a case in point, I offer an introduction into the linguistic pragmatic perspective on language use, context, and ideology developed by Jef Verschueren (Verschueren 2011, 1999; Verschueren and Brisard 2009; Verschueren 2004).

Despite differences in vocabulary, style, research objects, methods, disciplinary backgrounds, and despite the different socio-historical contexts and intellectual environments in which linguistic pragmatics and DT developed (Nerlich and Clarke 1994; Zienkowski 2011), *both* approaches are fundamentally poststructuralist in orientation. Scholars in linguistic pragmatics and DT consider language use and/or discourse as open structures whose boundaries cannot be fixed in a final way. Both approaches share a deep suspicion of reified notions of context, and many linguistic pragmaticians consider the self as inherently 'split' or multiple. Moreover, both traditions recognize the role played by the reflexive capacities of subjects in how actors negotiate and fix meaning(s) in language use and other semiotic practices.

5.1 Pragmatics as a poststructuralist approach to language use

Let us start with an admittedly basic observation: language involves the "continuous making of choices, consciously or unconsciously, for language-internal (i.e. structural) and/or language-external reasons" (Verschueren 1999: 55–56). According to Verschueren, these choices are not random but informed by the principles of variability, adaptability, and negotiability. Verschueren describes variability as "the property of language which defines the range of possibilities from which choices can be made" (1999: 59). Language users continuously make choices at the levels of morphology, grammar, discourse strategy, textual structure, or genre, and so on. Every communicative choice introduces expectations and possibilities in contexts that are constantly being negotiated (1999: 59). When scholars of linguistic pragmatics write about phonetic, syntactic, or narrative

---

[2]. A more elaborate account of the combined linguistic pragmatic and discourse theoretical perspective outlined here can be found in Zienkowski (2017).

'structures', they are aware these structures do not exist outside actual language use. Put differently, structures only exist to the extent that they are being fixed in performative practices of articulation.

It is useful to note that the pragmatic notion of variability was explicitly developed in opposition to structuralist concepts of language that can be found in the work of authors such as Saussure or even Chomsky (Gumperz 1982: 24–29). The structures that pragmaticians write about have therefore nothing to do with the closed and centred totalities criticised by poststructuralist thinkers. Instead, Verschueren conceptualizes structures as offering 'structural objects of adaptability'. It is useful to quote him at length:

> Any (combination of) element(s) at any layer or level of linguistic organisation or form at which choices can be made, constitutes a structural object of adaptability or, for short, an element of 'structure'. Thus, languages, codes and styles are objects of adaptability albeit at a high level of structuring. So are all utterance-building ingredients, from sounds, over morphemes, words, clauses, sentences and propositions all the way to supra-sentential units. Also, utterances and utterance clusters (from the exclamation of 'ouch' to a full conversation or an entire novel) fit in here, as well as utterance-building principles such as coherence, relevance, information structuring, foregrounding, backgrounding, and the like. Usually, choices are not isolated, but rather part of an integrated process of choice-making that interrelates phenomena at different structural levels. (Verschueren 2008: 18)

The principle of variability can easily be extended to non-linguistic discursive structures. The concept of the field of discursivity, for instance, can be re-interpreted as offering structural objects of adaptability – linguistic or other – that form the raw material for articulatory practices. Articulation can thus be approached as a multi-layered process that functions at multiple levels simultaneously. For instance, the construction of a concrete political demand or identity in an interview or a pamphlet involves multiple rearticulations of that claim or identity with a whole set of other demands, identities, categories, narratives and so on. Such an articulation implies choices at the levels of phonemes, words, tonality pitch, tempo, grammatical structure, speech acts, argumentation, topic selection, narrative, genre, ideology, and every other imaginable level of structure (see Verschueren 1999: 120–146).

This does not imply that subjects are aware of everything they are doing while communicating. The point is rather that the interpretive logics that structure our understandings of self and politics leave traces in language use and other semiotic systems: "we mark our limited awareness of such logics through linguistic and non-linguistic discursive forms that allow us to guide and influence each other's (self)understandings" (Zienkowski 2017: 93). Glynos and Howarth argue that the naming and identification of logics implies a passage through the self-interpretations of subjects (2008: 157–159; 2007: 157–159). While it is not possible to access anyone's self-interpretation directly – subjectivity being an inherently opaque phenomenon – it is possible to investigate the way subjects mark their awareness of the way language and communication are used in discourse. Subjects routinely leave metadiscursive or metapragmatic traces of reflexive awareness in language use, and these traces can be used as proxies for the investigation of self-interpretations and logics.

The concept of metapragmatic awareness does not offer a not a simple 'add-on' for discourse theorists. As a concept, it comes with a theoretical and methodological framework for understanding and investigating subjectivity and reflexivity. The notion helps us to explain how social actors relate to their own discourse as well as to the discourse(s) of others. Metadiscourse and metapragmatic awareness play a key role in the way social actors negotiate relevant contextual boundaries for interpretation, and in the way actors fix meaning(s) in empirically observable ways. Metapragmatic or meta-discursive awareness is a *condition sine qua non* for political awareness to emerge. Without an awareness of the (implications of) discursive choices that fix the meanings that constitute our social world, social actors cannot even hope to imagine alternative futures. Research on metadiscursive or metapragmatic statements in political discourse sheds light on the construction of affective and fantasmatic relations to the identities, claims and ideologies that constitute their reality (Zienkowski 2015, 2017).

5.2 Negotiability and adaptability as principles of articulation

The second principle that structures the making of linguistic and discursive choices is *negotiability*, defined as "the property of language responsible for the fact that choices are not made mechanically or according to strict rules or fixed form-function relationships, but rather on the basis of highly flexible principles and strategies" (Verschueren 1999: 59). Meaning cannot be found *within* semiotic forms, but it gets fixed through interpretive, interactive, and dialogical processes whereby actors map interpretive functions onto specific forms of discourse. Much political debate revolves around the question what interpretive functions should be attributed to the statements of political actors. It makes a difference whether one functionally interprets the Dutch far-right politician Geert Wilders' call for 'fewer Moroccans' as 'saying things as they are', as 'pure ideology (in the deceptive sense)' or as 'the articulation of a popular demand'. Linguistic choices and their interpretive functions can always be (re)negotiated in texts, discussions, and interactions.

The third principle informing language use and discourse identified by Verschueren is *adaptability*. If language and discourse are characterized by shifting form-function relationships and if choices can be permanently renegotiated, this raises the question how meanings can acquire some degree of stability. The principle of adaptability refers to "the property of language which enables human beings to make negotiable linguistic choices from a variable range of possibilities in such a way as to approach points of satisfaction for communicative needs" (Verschueren 1999: 62). Such points of satisfaction can be reached by approximation only. Social actors use language and other semiotic systems to orient each other's behaviour in attempts to achieve reasonable satisfying outcomes. In the process, they carve a 'context' out of an infinitely complex mental, social, and physical reality (Verschueren 1999, 2004; 2008).

By making communicative choices, social actors indicate to each other which aspects of (con)textual reality they consider to be relevant for practical interpretive purposes. In the process of communication, social actors guide each other's gaze and orient each other other's reflexive or metadiscursive awareness in particular ways. The point is that 'context' can never be grasped in its entirety. Context does not overlap with a 'reality' that is objectively out there. It is rather a precarious outcome of negotiations over symbolic resources, their interpretive functions, and the aspects of (discursive) reality that should be taken into account. This implies that context and common ground are never really 'shared'. Communicative and interpretive choices are made from different social positions. 'Common ground' is therefore largely an imaginary but productive and pragmatic result of articulatory performances (Zienkowski 2017: 163).

While the principles of adaptability and negotiability imply that the meanings of identities, discourses, and narratives cannot be fixed in a definitive sense, social and political institutions reduce the multiplicity of interpretive options by generating normative and hierarchical rankings of preferred modes of interpretation. Critical scholars in the field of linguistic pragmatics are keen to point out that linguistic choices are not made in an ideological vacuum. Communicative and interpretive choices frequently perform ideological functions. These functions include the relative fixation of meaning, the obfuscation of the contingent character of reality, and the affective and fantasmatic functions of discourse, as conceptualized by Essex-style discourse theorists. Linguistic pragmatic authors do not reduce ideology to language use but point out that language use is "(one of) the most visible manifestations of ideology" (Verschueren 2011: 17).

The pragmatically oriented discourse scholar Jan Blommaert proposed to deal with "ideology as part of meaningfulness". This implies that one should study "conscious, planned, creative activity as well as unintentional reproductions of 'determined' meanings." According to Blommaert, ideology "comprises processes at various levels ranging from the individual to the world system, passing through different degrees of awareness, speed, and capacity of development, and capacity to create innovative practices. With respect to hegemony, he remarks that "hegemony may lie not so much in a single, unified set of ideological elements, but in connections between various sets" (Blommaert 2005: 74).

5.3 On the performative dimension of discourse as an articulatory practice

It should be clear by now that linguistic pragmatics has the potential to deepen the discourse theoretical conceptualisation of articulation by drawing attention to its performative dimension. While the bulk of discourse theory considers articulation as a practice of connection, linguistic pragmatics specialises in the study of multimodal and interactive linguistic performances, practiced with different degrees of reflexive awareness. Moreover, discourse theory can inspire pragmatically oriented scholars to look beyond the linguistic functions of discourse and to explore the ways in which language is performatively used to sustain or to challenge ideological fantasies, political subjectivities, and hegemonic projects. A combined perspective involves a rearticulation of the concept of articulation along the following lines.

Articulations of signifiers, identities, narratives, and/or political identities imply linguistic and/or non-linguistic performances that allow for their empirical investigation. The practice of articulation involves the mapping of semiotic forms onto interpretive – including ideological – functions. As two elements get articulated to each other meanings necessarily shift in subtle and less subtle ways. They become 'moments' in a discourse. Social actors rely on semiotic forms and performances to indicate and negotiate the interpretive and political logics that allow for reflexive modes of subjectivity. In the process they (re)produce their subjectivities with varying degrees of political and metadiscursive awareness. Performance should not be thought of in opposition to articulation. The point is rather that an adequate understanding of articulation requires a consideration of its performative dimension.

The logics that inform social reality cannot be observed directly, but they leave textual and material traces that can be picked up by social actors trying to make sense of themselves and their world. When social actors challenge and/or reproduce social, political and/or phantasmatic logics, they do so with varying degrees of reflexivity and explicitness. The principle of articulation is not merely a matter of *connecting* signifiers to each other. The *way in which signifiers are articulated* with each other in communicative *performances* matters too. The performative way in which social actors articulate themselves impacts the way they fix the boundaries of self, other(s), and society (see Zienkowski 2017: 399).

Bibliography

Angermuller, Johannes, Dominique Maingueneau, and Ruth Wodak. 2014a. "An introduction." In *The Discourse Studies Reader*, ed. by Johannes Angermuller, Dominique Maingueneau, and Ruth Wodak, 1–14. Amsterdam: John Benjamins.

Angermuller, Johannes, Dominique Maingueneau, and Ruth Wodak. 2014b. *The Discourse Studies Reader*. Amsterdam: John Benjamins.

Barret, Michèle. 1994. "Ideology, politics, hegemony: From Gramsci to Laclau and Mouffe." In *Mapping Ideology*, ed. by Slavoj Žižek, 235–277. London / New York: Verso.

Bartlett, Tom, and Nicolina Montesano Montessori. 2021. "Towards webs of equivalence and the political nomad in agonistic debate: Contributions from CDA and Scales Theory." *Journal of Language and Politics* 20 (1): 129–144.

Baysha, Olga. 2022. "On the impossibility of discursive-material closures: A case of banned TV channels in Ukraine." *Social Sciences & Humanities Open* 6 (1): 100329.

Blommaert, Jan. 2005. *Discourse*. Cambridge: Cambridge University Press.

Borriello, Arthur, and Anton Jäger. 2021. "The antinomies of Ernesto Laclau: A reassessment." *Journal of Political Ideologies* 26 (3): 298–316.

Borriello, Arthur, and Samuele Mazzolini. 2018. "European populism(s) as a counter-hegemonic discourse? The rise of Podemos and M5S in the wake of the Crisis." In *Imagining the Peoples of Europe: Political Discourses across the Political Spectrum*, ed. by Jan Zienkowski and Ruth Breeze, n.p. Amsterdam: John Benjamins.

Butler, Judith, and Ernesto Laclau. 2004. "Appendix I: The uses of equality." In *Laclau: A Critical Reader*, ed. by Simon Critchley and Oliver Marchart, 329–344. London / New York: Routledge.

Carpentier, Nico. 2017. *The Discursive-Material Knot: Cyprus in Conflict and Community Media Participation*. New York: Peter Lang Publishing.

Carpentier, Nico. 2019. "About dislocations and invitations: deepening the conceptualization of the discursive-material knot." In *Discourse, Culture and Organizaztion: Inquiries into Relational Structures of Power*, ed. by Tomas Marttila, 155–178. Cham: Springer International Publishing.

Carpentier, Nico, and Benjamin De Cleen. 2007. "Bringing discourse theory into media studies: The applicability of discourse theoretical analysis (DTA) for the study of media practices and discourses." *Journal of Language and Politics* 6 (2): 265–293.

Carpentier, Nico, Iliya Tomanić Trivundža, Pille Pruulmann-Vengerfeldt, Sundin Ebba, Tobias Olsson, Richard Kilborn, Hannu Nieminen, and Bart Cammaerts. 2010. "deploying discourse theory: An introduction to discourse theory and discourse-theoretical analysis." In *Media and Communication Studies: Intersectoins and Interventions*, 251–266. Tartu: Tartu University Press.

Cervera-Marzal, Manuel. 2023. "Circulation et usages de l'idée d'hégémonie. De Antonio Gramsci à Pablo Iglesias en passant par Ernesto Laclau et Chantal Mouffe." *Revue du MAUSS* 60 (2): 379–96.

Coaston, Jane. 2019. "The intersectionality wars." *Vox*, 18 May 2019. https://www.vox.com/the-highlight/2019/5/20/18542843/intersectionality-conservatism-law-race-gender-discrimination

Critchley, Simon, and Oliver Marchart. 2004. "Introduction." In *Laclau: A Critical Reader*, ed. by Simon Critchley and Oliver Marchart, 1–13. London: Routledge.

De Cleen, Benjamin. 2019. "The populist political logic and the analysis of the discursive construction of 'the people'and 'the elite'." In *Imagining the Peoples of Europe: Populist Discourses across the Political Spectrum*, ed. by Jan Zienkowski and Ruth Breeze. Amsterdam: John Benjamins Publishing Company.

De Cleen, Benjamin, Jason Glynos, and Aurelien Mondon. 2021. "Populist politics and the politics of 'populism': The radical right in Western Europe." In *Populism in Global Perspective: A Performative and Discursive Approach*, ed. by Pierre Ostiguy, Francisco Panizza, and Benjamin Moffit, 155–177. New York: Routledge.

De Cleen, Benjamin, Jana Goyvaerts, Nico Carpentier, Jason Glynos, and Yannis Stavrakakis. 2021. "Moving discourse theory forward: A five-track proposal for future research." *Journal of Language and Politics* 20 (1): 22–46.

D'hondt, Sigurd. 2013. "Analyzing equivalences in discourse: Are discourse theory and membership categorization analysis compatible?" *Pragmatics. Quarterly Publication of the International Pragmatics Association (IPrA)*, 421–445.

Fairclough, Norman, and Lilie Chouliaraki. 1999. *Discourse in Late Modernity*. Edinburgh: Edinburgh University Press.

Flowerdew, John, and John E. Richardson (eds). 2020. *The Routledge Handbook of Critical Discourse Studies*. New York: Routledge.

Foucault, Michel. 1969. *The Archaeology of Knowledge*. 2007th ed. Routledge Classics. London: Routledge.

García Agustín, Óscar, and Marco Briziarelli. 2018. "Introduction: Wind of change: Podemos, its dreams and its politics." In *Podemos and the New Political Cycle: Left-Wing Populism and Anti-Establishment Politics*, ed. by Oscar García Agustín and Marco Briziarelli, 3–22. Cham: Palgrave Macmillan.

Gee, James Paul. 2015. Discourse, Small d, Big D." In *The International Encyclopedia of Language and Social Interaction*, 1–5.

Glynos, Jason. 2008. "Ideological fantasy at work." *Journal of Political Ideologies* 13 (3): 275–296.

Glynos, Jason. 2021. "Critical fantasy studies." *Journal of Language and Politics* 20 (1): 95–111.

Glynos, Jason, and David Howarth. 2007. *Logics of Critical Explanation in Social and Political Theory*. London: Routledge.

Glynos, Jason, and David Howarth. 2008. "Structure, agency and power in political analysis: Beyond contextualised self-interpretations." *Political Studies Review* 6: 155–169.

Glynos, Jason, and David Howarth. 2019. "The retroductive cycle: The research process in Poststructuralist Discourse Analysis." In *Discourse, Culture and Organizaztion: Inquiries into Relational Structures of Power*, ed. by Tomas Marttila, 105–126. Cham: Springer International Publishing.

Glynos, Jason, David Howarth, Ryan Flitcroft, Craig Love, Konstantinos Roussos, and Jimena Vazquez. 2021. "Logics, discourse theory and methods: Advances, challenges and ways forward." *Journal of Language and Politics* 20 (1): 62–78.

Glynos, Jason, and Yannis Stavrakakis. 2004. "Encounters of the real kind: Sussing out the limits of Laclau's embrace of Lacan." In *Laclau: A Critical Reader*, ed. by Simon Critchley and Oliver Marchart, 201–216. London / New York: Routledge.

Glynos, Jason, and Yannis Stavrakakis. 2008. "Lacan and political subjectivity: Fantasy and enjoyment in psychoanalysis and political theory." *Subjectivity* 24: 256–274.

Goyvaerts, Jana. 2023. "We need to talk about how we talk about populism: The signifier populism and discursive struggles about democracy in the Belgian press." Brussel: Vrije Universiteit Brussel.

Gumperz, John J. 1982. *Discourse Strategies*. Cambridge: Cambridge University Press.

Hawkins, Benjamin. 2015. "Fantasies of subjugation: A discourse theoretical account of British policy on the European Union." *Critical Policy Studies* 9 (2): 139–157.

Howarth, David. 2000. *Discourse*. Buckingham: Open University Press.

Howarth, David. 2005. "Applying discourse theory: The method of articulation." In *Discourse Theory in European Politics: Identity, Policy and Governance*, ed. by David Howarth and Jacob Torfing, 316–349. New York: Palgrave / Macmillan.

Howarth, David, Aletta Norval, and Yannis Stavrakakis. 2000. *Discourse Theory and Political Analysis: Identities, Hegemonies and Social Change*. Manchester: Manchester University Press.

Howarth, David, and Yannis Stavrakakis. 2000. "Introducing discourse theory and political analysis." In *Discourse Theory and Political Analysis: Identities, Hegemonies and Social Change*, ed. by David Howarth, Aletta Norval, and Yannis Stavrakakis, 1–23. Manchester: Manchester University Press.

Hroch, Miloš, and Nico Carpentier. 2021. "Beyond the meaning of zines: a case study of the role of materiality in four Prague-based zine assemblages." *Communication, Culture and Critique* 14 (2): 252–273.

Jacobs, Thomas. 2018. "The dislocated universe of Laclau and Mouffe: An introduction to post-structuralist discourse theory." *Critical Review* 30 (3–4): 294–315.

Jacobs, Thomas, and Robin Tschötschel. 2019. "Topic models meet discourse analysis: A quantitative tool for a qualitative approach." *International Journal of Social Research Methodology* 22 (5): 469–485.

Jørgensen, Marianne, and Louise J. Philips. 2002. *Discourse Analysis as Theory and Method*. London: Sage Publications.

Kortesoja, Matti. 2023. *Power of Articulation: Imagery of Social Structure and Social Change*. Cham: Springer Nature Switzerland.

Lacan, Jacques. 1994. "The mirror-phase as formative of the function of the I." In *Mapping Ideology*, ed. by Slavoj Žižek, 93–99. London / New York: Verso.

Laclau, Ernesto. 1990. "The impossibility of society." In *New Reflections on the Revolution of Our Time*, ed. by Ernesto Laclau, 89–96. London: Verso.

Laclau, Ernesto. 1994. "Why do empty signifiers matter to politics?" In *Emancipation(s)*, ed. by Ernesto Laclau, 36–46. London: Verso.

Laclau, Ernesto. 1996. "Beyond emancipation." In *Emancipations*, 18. London: Verso.

Laclau, Ernesto. 2005. *On Populist Reason*. London: Verso.

Laclau, Ernesto, and Chantal Mouffe. 1985. *Hegemony and Socialist Strategy: Towards a Radical Democratic Politics*. London: Verso.

Laclau, Ernesto, and Lilian Zac. 1994. "Minding the gap: The subject of politics." In *The Making of Political Identities*, ed. by Ernesto Laclau, 11–39. London / New York: Verso.

Marttila, Tomas. 2016. *Post-Foundational Discourse Analysis: From Political Difference to Empirical Research*. Houndmills: Palgrave Macmillan.

Marttila, Tomas (ed). 2019. *Discourse, Culture and Organization: Inquiries into Relational Structures of Power*. Postdisciplinary Studies in Discourse. Cham: Springer International Publishing.

Montesano Montessori, Nicolina. 2011. "The design of a theoretical, methodological, analytical framework to analyse hegemony in discourse." *Critical Discourse Studies* 8 (3): 169–181.

Mouffe, Chantal. 1979. "Hegemony and ideology in Gramsci." In *Gramsci and Marxist Theory*, ed. by Chantal Mouffe, 168–204. London / New York: Routledge.

Mouffe, Chantal. 2018. *For a Left Populism*. London / Brooklyn: Verso.

Nerlich, Brigitte, and David C. Clarke. 1994. "Language, action and context: Linguistic pragmatics in Europe and America (1800–1950)." *Journal of Pragmatics* 22 (5): 439–464.

Nikisianis, Nico, Thomas Siomos, Yannis Stavrakakis, Grigoris Markou, and Titika Dimitroulia. 2019. "Populism versus anti-populism in the Greek press: Post-structuralist discourse theory meets corpus linguistics." In *Discourse, Culture and Organizaztion: Inquiries into Relational Structures of Power*, ed. by Tomas Marttila, 267–296. Cham: Springer International Publishing.

Norval, Aletta. 2015. "Poststructuralist conceptions of ideology." In *The Oxford Handbook of Political Ideologies*, ed. by Michael Freeden, Lyman Tower Sargent, and Marc Stears, 155–174. Oxford: Oxford University Press.

Phelan, Sean, and Lincoln Dahlberg. 2011. "Discourse theory and critical media politics: An introduction." In *Discourse Theory and Critical Media Politics:*, ed. by Lincoln Dahlberg and Sean Phelan, 1–40. Basingstoke: Palgrave Macmillan.

Remling, Elise. 2018. "Logics, assumptions and genre chains: A framework for poststructuralist policy analysis." *Critical Discourse Studies* 15 (1): 1–18.

Robinson, Douglas. 2006. *Introducing Performative Pragmatics*. London / New York: Routledge.

Roussos, Konstantinos. 2019. "Grassroots collective action within and beyond institutional and state solutions: The (re-)politicization of everyday life in crisis-ridden Greece." *Social Movement Studies* 18 (3): 265–283.

Smith, Anna Marie. 1998. *Laclau and Mouffe: The Radical Democratic Imaginary*. London: Routledge.

Stavrakakis, Yannis. 1999. *Lacan and the Political*. London: Routledge.

Stavrakakis, Yannis, Ioannis Andreadis, and Giorgos Katsambekis. 2017. "A new populism index at work: Identifying populist candidates and parties in the contemporary Greek context." *European Politics and Society* 18 (4): 446–464.

Stavrakakis, Yannis, and Giorgos Katsambekis. 2014. "Left-wing populism in the European periphery: The case of SYRIZA." *Journal of Political Ideologies* 19 (2): 119–142.

Torfing, Jacob. 1999. *New Theories of Discourse: Laclau, Mouffe and Žižek*. Oxford: Blackwell.

Torfing, Jacob. 2005. "Discourse theory: Achievements, arguments, and challenges." In *Discourse Theory in European Politics: Identity, Policy and Governance*, ed. by David Howarth and Jacob Torfing, 1–32. New York: Palgrave / Macmillan.

Turner, Graeme. 2005. *British Cultural Studies*. London: Routledge.

Van Brussel, Leen. 2018. "The right to die: A Belgian case study combining reception studies and discourse theory." *Media, Culture & Society* 40 (3): 381–396.

Van Brussel, Leen, Nico Carpentier, and Benjamin De Cleen (eds). 2019. *Communication and Discourse Theory: Collected Works of the Brussels Discourse Theory Group*. Bristol.

Verschueren, Jef. 1999. *Understanding Pragmatics*. 2003rd ed. London: Arnold.

Verschueren, Jef. 2004. "Notes on the role of metapragmatic awareness in language use." In *Metalanguage: Social and Ideological Perspectives*, ed. by Adam Jaworski, Nikolas Coupland, and Dariusz Galasinski, 53–74. Berlin / New York: Mouton de Gruyter.

Verschueren, Jef. 2008. "Context and structure in a theory of pragmatics." *Studies in Pragmatics*, no. 10, 13–23.

Verschueren, Jef. 2011. *Ideology in Language Use: Pragmatic Guidelines for Empirical Research*. Cambridge: Cambridge University Press.

Verschueren, Jef, and Frank Brisard. 2009. "Adaptability." In *Key Notions for Pragmatics*, ed. by Jef Verschueren and Jan-Ola Östman, 28–47. Amsterdam: John Benjamins Publishing Company.

Zienkowski, Jan. 2011. "Discursive pragmatics: A platform for the pragmatic study of discourse." In *Discursive Pragmatics*, ed. by Jan Zienkowski, Jef Verschueren, and Jan-Ola Östman, 296. Amsterdam: John benjamins.

Zienkowski, Jan. 2012. "Overcoming the post-structuralist methodological deficit: Metapragmatic markers and interpretive logics in a critique of the Bologna process." *Pragmatics: Quarterly Publication of the International Pragmatics Association* 22 (3): 501–534.

Zienkowski, Jan. 2015. "Marking a sense of self and politics in interviews on political engagement: interpretive logics and the metapragmatics of identity." *Journal of Language and Politics* 14 (4): 665–688.

Zienkowski, Jan. 2017. *Articulations of Self and Politics in Activist Discourse: A Discourse Analysis of Critical Subjectivities in Minority Debates*. Cham: Palgrave Macmillan.

Zienkowski, Jan. 2019. "Politics and the political in critical discourse studies: State of the art and a call for an intensified focus on the metapolitical dimension of discursive practice." *Critical Discourse Studies* 16 (2): 131–148.

Zienkowski, Jan, and François Lambotte. 2023. "Agency as an emerging phenomenon in the construction of massive open online courses: a discursive–material approach to the techno-pedagogical edX platform and its forums." *Learning, Media and Technology*, August, 1–14.

Revisiting talk in space

The inescapable mobility of social interaction

Elwys De Stefani & Lorenza Mondada
University of Heidelberg | University of Basel

1. Introduction

In the social sciences, the "mobility turn" (Urry 2000) has uncovered numerous aspects of social life that the earlier neglect of mobility had made invisible, or unthinkable, thereby calling for a reconceptualization of culture and society from this perspective. This chapter discusses the way in which similar issues can be raised with regard to social interaction, from the perspective of Ethnomethodology (EM) and Conversation Analysis (CA). It sketches the conceptual consequences of the "mobility turn" for studying social interaction and for revisiting the role of space in talk and interaction (see Haddington et al. 2013). The consequences for EMCA of the neglect of mobile activities by a too exclusive focus on stationary activities are presented (§ 2). The chapter reviews EMCA work on "stationary" and "mobile" interactions (§ 3) and then questions what appears to be a seemingly obvious dichotomy (§ 4). Next, it examines the relevance of space and mobility in social interaction in three classical fields of EMCA, i.e., the analysis of telephone conversations (§ 4.1), the study of mobility mediated by technologies, such as cars (§ 4.2), and the investigation of spatiality in various kinds of interactional spaces (§ 4.3).

2. Background: Towards a mobility turn in EMCA

Debates within the "mobility turn" (Büscher et al. 2011; Cresswell 2006; Urry 2000) have pinpointed a bias towards sedentary culture and values in the social sciences. Sedentary life has been treated and tacitly accepted as a solid standard for studying many facets of social life. Identity, culture, social order, economy, etc. have traditionally been described from the perspective of sedentary groups, whereas phenomena such as nomadism, migration, travel, and displacements have rather been ignored or even made invisible. This holds true for movement in space and change in time in general, also regarding mobilities of people, goods, services, capital, and ideas.

A rise in the number of mobility studies is observable in the EMCA literature from the 2010s onwards (Haddington et al. 2012, 2013; McIlvenny et al. 2009, 2014). These studies furthered the mobility turn (see, e.g., several EMCA contributions to the journal *Mobilities*, launched in 2006: Laurier et al. 2008; McIlvenny 2015; Mondada & Tekin 2024; Pehkonen et al. 2022). They also grounded an autonomous reflection about what changes if social interaction is studied as a phenomenon that is observable "on the move," rather than (just) in stationary settings, with sedentary activities being often privileged by researchers. First, studies of mobile interactions explicitly deal with spatiality: while research on sedentary interactions has often taken space for granted (or ignored it outright), mobility anchors social interaction within spaces and places (Haddington et al. 2013; Hausendorf et al. 2016; McIlvenny et al. 2009). This holds true in relation to the changing spatial coordinates and references generated by navigational activities (De Stefani 2010; Haddington & Keisanen 2009; Mondada 2009a; Psathas 1979), as well as in relation to the changing interactional spaces constituted by the participants' bodies on the move (Mondada 2014a). Second, mobility requires consideration not only of positions but also of specific movements of bodies in space. Hence, mobility generates a renewed interest in embodiment, obliging researchers to contemplate the participants' entire bodies, including their lower parts, in particular in activities such as walking, climbing, running (Mondada 2014a, 2018a; Pehkonen et al. 2022; Simone and Galatolo 2020). As a consequence, the study of multimodality has been refined, and its possible resources have been extended beyond co-speech gestures and gaze to include a multiplicity of embodied resources. These are conceptualized in a way that distinguishes between movements of body parts on the one hand and embodied mobility (i.e., displacement in space) on the other (De Stefani 2013a; Mondada 2018a; in press). Third, mobility invites researchers to consider how stationary distributions of bodies are progressively reached and stabilized, instead of considering them as pre-existing: co-participants are not perpetually involved in stationary interactions such as conversing, dining, meeting, etc. around a table; rather, they progressively reach these configurations, and may alter them or abandon them again (see Broth and Lundström 2013). Fourth, this attention to mobility also prompts an interest in actions or sequences of actions that can be accomplished while being either stationary or mobile: for instance, openings of social interactions are generally preceded by people moving towards each other, converging and negotiating the emergence of a common interactional space and participation framework (D'Antoni et al. 2022; De Stefani and Mondada 2018; Mondada 2009a, 2022); openings of interactions with guests visiting someone at home are preceded by the guests' arrival at the door (Oloff 2010), etc. Likewise, the completion of sequences as well as the closing of the interaction can involve moving away (Broth and Mondada 2013; Deppermann et al. 2010; Goodwin 1987a; Llewellyn and Butler 2011).

By contrast, the analysis of sedentary interactions has often ignored the participants' position in space, usually described as "face-to-face," without precisely specifying (and making sense of) the kind of spatial distribution and orientation of the bodies that constitutes co-presence (De Stefani 2013a). Attention to the spatial organization of the embodied participation framework appears relatively late in the literature (Goodwin 2007). Correspondingly, the relative immobility of participants in stationary activities prompted researchers to mainly focus on resources such as gesture, gaze, and facial expressions, rather than on body posture, body orientation, and body movements. Thus, the privilege of sedentariness over mobility had — and still has — important consequences for the conceptualization of multimodality.

These analytical and conceptual issues crucially depend on the available data and on the methodologies producing them. EMCA's focus on situated action and its temporal-sequential organization led to the development of methodologies able to capture situated temporal details, by means first of audio, then of video-recording devices (Broth et al. 2014; Heath et al. 2010; Mondada 2012a). Although some form of spatialization of sound is perceivable in audio recordings — resulting from the position of the microphones — such perspectivation is not sufficient to finely reconstruct the participants' stationary/mobile position in relation to each other. Because of this, audio data tend to obliterate the attention towards spatiality. By contrast, video recordings enable researchers to see the participants' spatial distributions, and to observe changes in these distributions, but also in the individuals' postures, orientations, etc. The stationary vs. mobile character of the activities studied also has consequences for the choice of technologies and the framing of the video images. For instance, video recordings of stationary activities are often collected with cameras fixed on tripods. This enables researchers to set up the devices and to be absent while the recording happens. By contrast, video recordings of mobile activities are usually collected with mobile cameras oriented towards the action. In the former case, the framing of the images is important (with "including" vs. "excluding" effects concerning the participation framework, especially with regard to the spatial disposition and mobility of more peripheral participants). In the latter case, manipulating a mobile camera affords both a real-time analysis of the unfolding activities, allowing researchers to decide on the spot what to record, and creates challenges and difficulties to be "on time" when following dynamic actions. Thus, whereas EMCA methodology is particularly reliable for filming stationary actions, documenting the relevant details of mobile actions remains a challenge, even with new video technologies (such as 360° cameras, drones, immersive video, etc.; see McIlvenny 2019b).

In addition to issues concerned with the problem of adequately capturing actions on video, stationary vs. mobile actions also raise several challenges for their visual-textual representation in transcripts. A key decision concerns what to transcribe and what to take for granted, to treat as not relevant, or to ignore. The transcription of stationary interactions seems to be more straightforward — although it materializes often in the form of minimal transcripts of talk and co-speech phenomena such as gaze and gestures. By contrast, mobile interactions raise several problems of annotation. A central aspect concerns the representation of mobile actions, their segmentation, their relevant and granular details (e.g., transcribers can hesitate between different, more or less precise annotations, such as "walks" vs. "does 1 step forward" vs. "moves right leg forward"), as well as the problem of continuously tracking the individuals' relevant moves (Mondada 2018b). Textual annotations are analytically useful, because they enable researchers to precisely segment the mobile conduct, to relate their temporality to the global formatting of the ongoing action, and to its projective facets, as well as to represent the coordinated timing of these and other multimodal details. Visual images (screen shots), instead, are more holistic, because they offer a global representation of body configurations, the use of multimodal resources, etc. at a precise moment in time. For researchers interested in the continuous tracking of mobile bodies across space, maps can also be adequate (McIlvenny 2015; Mondada 2022), although video perspectives make it difficult to reconstruct precise cartographic relations, and hence to draw bodies in time/space with the precision necessary for a granular, step-by-step analysis.

In sum, the attention to mobile rather than stationary (in particular, sedentary) activities prompted not only the discovery of new fields of empirical inquiry, but, more significantly, it instigated a change of perspective in the way we look at social life and the dimensions we identify as relevant for the study of its organization. In what follows, we review how EMCA studies have described stationary vs. mobile activities (§ 3). We discuss this apparent dichotomy and show that, beyond its use for describing types of interactions that are characterized by distinct spatialities, it has indeed to be relativized. This allows us to recognize that mobility is not only a set of phenomena but also a viewpoint on events and social interactions. This in turn shows that even so-called stationary settings imply forms of mobility and movement (§ 4).

3. Stationary and mobile activities

"Surprisingly little is known about the way people use space": this is the opening sentence of the psychologist Robert Sommer's (1959) article on personal space. "Using space" entails, of course, both what the anthropologist Edward T. Hall (1966) called "proxemics," in reference to positions and distances between bodies, and what Ray Birdwhistell (1970) called "kinesics," i.e., the movement and displacement of the individuals' bodies. At first sight, stationary and mobile settings of interaction might appear as a perfect dichotomy — the former exemplified by sedentary activities, the latter by activities carried out "on the move." The next sections show that such a dichotomic conceptualization is not supported by analysis and therefore not warranted. Rather, studies on stationary settings of interaction — landline telephone calls, dinner table conversations, etc. — have simply obliterated the observable fact that even in these environments participants do move in space. The examination of mobile interaction, which developed later, allowed EMCA researchers to demonstrate not only the fundamental relevance of spatiality and mobility for interactants, but also to examine how interactants finely coordinate their talk with their movement in space (from the positioning of the bodies to local micro-adjustments). The next sections provide a historical overview of CA research on stationary (§ 3.1) and mobile (§ 3.2) settings of interaction, followed by a further discussion that problematizes this dichotomy (§ 4).

3.1 Stationary activities

The history of CA is importantly bound to the history of the use of audio-visual technologies for recording social life (Broth et al. 2014; Goodwin 1993; Heath et al. 2010; Mondada 2012a). When CA emerged towards the end of the 1960s, audio recordings on tape were the simplest, most accessible, and efficient technology for documenting social interaction. The first recordings of telephone conversations exploited the convergence between the possibilities and limitations of the audio device and the constitutive vocal/verbal resources of the phone call (Schegloff 1967, 1986, 2002). Landline calls are bound to specific places, which produce expectations about who will be reached, their identification and recognition (Schegloff 1979), all of this based on the stability of the location (vs. mobile calls, see infra § 4.1). Even at that time, film and, later, video technologies were also available. However, the size, weight, and arduous maneuvering of early moving image recording devices made capturing mobile activities difficult, thus initially favoring the documentation of sedentary activities.

The first video recordings of naturally occurring interactions made by C. Goodwin and M.H. Goodwin documented ordinary conversations in various stationary settings, such as dinners between friends, family lunches, and backyard picnics (C. Goodwin 1981: 33sv). Meal interactions became a prototypical context for observing language use. Beside enabling researchers to analyze the fundamental order of turn-taking and sequence organization, meal interactions have also been exploited for the study of participation, which is fundamentally achieved through gaze, embodied orientations, and body postures in space. This led to a description of recipient-design, participation frameworks, schisms, by-play, etc. as fundamentally multimodal (C. Goodwin 1981, 1984, 1986; M.H. Goodwin 1997). Although these phenomena do not always imply a conceptualization of space, they are fundamentally related to the positions of participants in the stationary ecology, e.g., around a table (see C. Goodwin 1979 on searching for an adequate recipient across the table; M.H. Goodwin 1997 on phenomena of coalition and by-play around the table, and more generally C. Goodwin 1984, 1986, 1987b on the organization of co-participation in storytelling and other activities). Later, the notion of embodied participation (C. Goodwin 2007) further anchored these issues in the space of social interaction.

Meal conversations are thus an exemplary setting in which a sedentary activity has been fruitfully studied to discover generic structures of social interaction. Other settings characteristic of early CA are institutional contexts (Drew and Heritage 1992), which all revolve around sedentary activities: medical consultations, judiciary settings, police interrogations, meetings, service encounters, etc. While these studies rely on participants who are mostly stationarily distributed in space (standing or sitting), the fact that in the 1990s they were mostly documented with audio recordings made their spatial dimension taken for granted and thus invisible. Later, the growing number of studies based on video recordings of such activities showed the importance of their detailed spatial articulation, including participants' mobility. For example, the analysis of transitions between activities during medical consultations revealed the relevance of the doctor reorienting their body towards different details — be it the patient's body or the medical files (Heath 1986; Modaff 2003; Robinson and Stivers 2001) — which are spatially anchored. Later, workplace studies (Heath and Luff 2000) demonstrated how activities apparently taking place in the same room are actually distributed in fragmented spaces and technologically connected with other places, affording both individual and collaborative actions (Heath and Luff 1992; Heath et al. 1995). Hence, even stationary activities involve dynamic orientations to different locations in a given place, manifested through movements of parts of the body or mobility of the entire body (see infra § 4.3). Moving across space is not absent in these settings and activities: during dinner conversations participants might come and go, e.g., for bringing food (Mondada 2009b: 562), during meetings participants might leave the room (Deppermann et al. 2010), TV news interviews can be closed down by walkouts (Llewellyn and Butler 2011), etc. These moments of mobility in so-called sedentary activities show that these two aspects are not mutually exclusive: rather, mobility is often simply neglected, concealed by the video setup and framing, and ignored by the analytical foci chosen.

3.2 Mobile activities

EMCA developed an early interest in spatiality and mobility as essential dimensions of human life and sociality. For instance, Psathas and Henslin (1967) examined the practical problem of cab drivers, who have to locate the place a passenger wishes to reach. Later research by Psathas (1976, 1986) and Psathas and Kozloff (1976) focused extensively on route descriptions in navigational practices and on the representation of space and mobility in maps (Psathas 1979). In line with early EMCA research, Psathas based his studies on telephone conversations, in particular on sequences of "direction giving" (Psathas 1991).

How individuals actually move in space in an urban space was studied from an EM perspective by Ryave and Schenkein on the basis of "two eight-minute segments of videotape" (1974: 265). The authors identified the practical problem of navigating through space — as a single individual or together with others — which entails methods both for carrying out ("producing" in the authors' terms) navigation and for identifying ("recognizing") others as walking together, constituting what Goffman (1971) called a "vehicular unit" or a "with" (see Mondada 2023). Achieving such togetherness is indeed a practical problem of individuals who have to coordinate each other's movements so as to move in space at the same speed, in the same direction, etc. (De Stefani 2013a). Moreover, they have to coordinate the multiple activities they are engaged in, such as walking and talking (Mondada 2014a). In other words, walking together (Relieu 1999) or running together (Allen-Collinson 2006) are practical achievements of the participants.

Mobile settings of interaction often constitute settings of multiactivity (Mondada 2014b), where movement in space is constitutive of the action carried out, e.g., in the case of guided tours (Best 2012; De Stefani 2010; De Stefani and Mondada 2014, 2017; Mondada 2012b), museum visits (Stukenbrock 2023; vom Lehn 2013; vom Lehn et al. 2001), shopping tours at the supermarket (De Stefani 2011, 2013b, 2023), etc. Such mobility, which involves entire bodies navigating through space, can be distinguished from more reduced movements observable in the continuously readjusted coordination, short-range repositioning of the bodies, and the use of body parts, such as moving arms, hands, head, etc. (De Stefani 2013a: 436; Mondada in press).

EMCA studies have shown, on the one hand, that talk is sensitive to spatial mobility. For instance, there is a reflexive relationship between walking and talking, i.e., the finely tuned coordination between the construction of turns-at-talk, the achievement of conversational sequences, and the participants' mobile actions in space (see Broth and Mondada 2013; De Stefani 2023; Mondada 2017, among others). This also includes how individuals use specific grammatical resources to reorganize the interactants' position in space and their visual orientations (e.g., De Stefani 2021; Mondada 2005). On the other hand, research on pedestrian mobility also demonstrated that, just as with conversation, mobile social behavior is organized sequentially. In other words, individuals orient to initiating and responsive mobile actions. This holds true for what Goffman (1963) called "unfocused" interaction (e.g., when pedestrians pass by each other on a busy street, thereby successfully managing not to bump into each other), as well as in the transition from unfocused to "focused" interaction, for instance, when face-to-face encounters are initiated in public space (D'Antoni et al. 2022; Mondada 2009a). Hence, a fine-tuned coordination of actions — vocal, verbal, embodied, mobile, etc. — can be observed as individuals reflexively intertwine such actions with each other (Mondada 2022). Other forms of social mobility — such as cycling together (McIlvenny 2014), driving together (Haddington 2012; Mondada 2012c), interacting as passengers on a bus (D'hondt 2009) — have also been studied. Interaction in larger vehicles, such as buses, trains, airplane cabins, etc. is characterized by a fairly stationary position of the individuals' bodies relative to each other (unless they change seats, e.g., on a bus), but passengers can witness the changing landscape around them. Airline cockpits constitute yet another setting of interaction, with pilots (captains, first officers) collaboratively and interactively cooperating and engaging with physically distributed parties (air traffic controllers, crew members, etc.) in order to achieve the aircraft's mobility (Melander and Sahlström 2009; Nevile 2004). Airline pilots and car drivers have to orient to various foci of interaction: for instance, car drivers orient to the space outside the car and to the traffic, and the infrastructure of the car (with its multiple windows and mirrors) provides opportunities for doing exactly that. Drivers do so while moving through space in the vehicle, thereby constantly reshaping the mobile ecology in which they partake, while at the same time continuously discovering and adapting to the changing landscape. Furthermore, on occasion, drivers can also engage in talk with passengers in the car (see § 4.2).

The focus on mobile settings of interaction revealed that the participants' orientation to space – through the positioning of their bodies, the adjustment to the local ecologies, etc. – is a fundamental problem that they experience and have to deal with even in settings of stationary interaction.

4. Questioning the dichotomy between stationary and mobile interaction

As touched upon in the previous sections, despite the clear consequences of the neglection of mobility on the conceptualization of social interaction, the distinction between "stationary" vs. "mobile" is not a dichotomic characterization of types of activities or interactions, but rather a perspective privileging some aspects over others – given that even stationary activities comprise movement and mobility and, conversely, mobile situations can have stationary facets. This final section problematizes this dichotomy on the basis of three different, but classical, domains of EMCA – the analysis of telephone conversations (§ 4.1), mobility mediated by vehicles (§ 4.2), and interactional spaces in various types of interaction (§ 4.3) – for which we highlight the role of spatiality and the embeddedness of stationariness and mobility.

4.1 The relevance of space in landline vs. mobile telephone conversations

Landline telephone conversations constitute the early backbone of EMCA research. In his PhD thesis, Harvey Sacks (1966) examined 150 telephone conversations between operators of an emergency psychiatric clinic and suicidal callers (or their acquaintances). One year later, Emanuel A. Schegloff (1967) submitted his PhD thesis based on more than 500 calls to the complaint desk of a US police department. In the first sentence of his thesis, Schegloff explained that his work "may be conceived of as a study in face-to-face interaction" because "actors are together ecologically" (1967: 1) while they interact over the phone. Here, the telephone conversation is conceptualized as a space built by the participants for the duration of the phone call, in which auditory reciprocal access creates a sense of proximity. Moreover, in phone calls, participants may orient to physical space in a variety of ways and for different purposes. They may use spatial reference as a form of "place-self-identification" (e.g., "Smith residence"; Schegloff 1986:123), a practice that is particularly frequent in radio phone-ins (Myers 2006). Interactants may also use "location formulations" (Schegloff 1972) to refer to a place that is relevant for the conversation at hand. Interactants select the appropriate formulation based on an endogenous analysis of the ongoing interaction, in a way that is both recipient-designed and in line with the activity in which they are engaged in. This practice is particularly relevant in emergency calls (Bergmann 1993), in which locating the place of the intervention is a practical problem that callers and call-takers have to tackle together (Mondada 2011) and that has to be dealt with efficiently in order to secure the timely provision of help (Fele 2023).

While in mobile phone conversations these practices are also attested, the facts that mobile phones are "attached" to people's bodies (rather than to their homes, as landline phones) and that information such as the number or name of the caller appears on the screen as the phone rings, are dealt with in specific ways by interactants (Arminen and Leinonen 2006). In particular, in mobile telephony, the task of localizing the caller's and the called person's whereabouts is a critical part of the opening sequence that is sensitive to the participants' individual ongoing activities (Arminen 2006; Kazemi 2020). For instance, one can answer a call on a mobile phone while being at the checkout of a supermarket, while having lunch at a restaurant, or while being in a fitting room, and formulate limited availability for a phone call (Weilenmann 2003). The analysis of ordinary mobile calls has shown, ultimately, that participants strongly orient to location as a critical feature of their interaction and that location formulation is recurrently used to tell the other "what one is doing" (Weilenmann 2003) rather than just "where one is." In this sense, location formulations enable participants to anchor the phone call situationally. Mobile phones hence epitomize the importance of mobility in the life of individuals. As Laurier (2001) has shown, by formulating the place one is calling from, or where one is when answering the call, interactants display their being nomadic members of society.

4.2   The duck/rabbit face of spatiality: The paradoxical space of cars, trains, planes

With regard to spatiality, vehicular units such as cars, buses, trains, airplanes, helicopters can be described as Janus-faced. On the one hand, they are traffic participants who navigate through space and avoid crashes with other traffic participants. On the other hand, they are habitable units (Laurier et al. 2007) in which interaction between the individuals populating them occurs. In this perspective, the inside of cars is a space that can host social life, such as when passengers sitting in the front and back seats talk together (Goodwin and Goodwin 2012; Haddington 2019; Mondada 2012b), but also as they engage in a variety of professional or private activities done in the car (e.g., putting on make-up or reading newspapers; Laurier 2005), as well as in a multitude of actions involving the manipulation of various objects (Nevile 2018). Interactions in cars can also orient to the car's navigation in traffic, e.g., when drivers and passengers discuss which way to go (Haddington 2012; Haddington and Keisanen 2009) or when they try to find a parking space (Laurier 2005). While in-car interaction takes place while sitting in a stable "iron cage" (Urry 2004), participants also organize it in a way that is sensitive to what they witness outside the car and, crucially, to the temporality of the everchanging landscape around them. This is consequential, for instance, for the way in which vocal and gestural deictic reference to the local environment is achieved (De Stefani and Deppermann 2021) and for how sequences of talk are organized, e.g., when a car moves at high speed in a race circuit (Mondada 2018c). A car is, indeed, also an ordinary traffic participant and as such engages in interaction with other "mobile withs" (Jensen 2010) of different kinds – other cars, bikes, pedestrians (Liberman 2013; Merlino and Mondada 2019), users of mobility scooters (McIlvenny 2019a), etc. Specific devices, such as horns (Laurier et al. 2020) and indicators (Broth et al. 2018), are indeed available to drivers to account for the car's traffic behavior and to make it projectable for others.

Driving lessons are one setting of interaction in which the inhabitants of a car – instructor (INS) and learner driver (LDV) – overtly and repeatedly orient to the car's movement in space as a traffic participant (De Stefani and Gazin 2014; Deppermann 2018; Broth et al. 2019). Because of that, driving lessons are a perspicuous setting for examining how in-car participants coordinate their actions with their vehicle in traffic – more specifically, how they adjust the temporality and sequentiality of the in-car interaction with the temporality and sequentiality of their traffic navigation (see also Haddington 2019). The following example provides a case in point. It shows how, during a driving lesson, the instructor articulates a "navigational instruction" (De Stefani and Gazin 2014) and how this instruction entails an attentive monitoring of the environment and an interpretation of the likely behavior of other traffic participants.

Extract 1A. (15sg2BM2; 19:38–20:06)
```
1    INS    $.hh più avan#ti$ (0.3) $scenderemo $verso$ sinistra
            further ahead        we will go down towards the left
     ins    $points ahead---§.......$points left$,,,,,$
     fig               #fig. 1A/B
2           lascia un pochettino il gas,
            release the gas (pedal) a bit
3           +(0.4)
     car    +slowing down-->
4    INS    dunque (.) Uno (0.6) due (0.3) tre, (0.4) freccia.
            so         one       two       three     indicator
5           *(0.6)
     ins    *activates indicator
6    INS    controlla un pelino col freno,#
            check a bit with the brake
     fig                                  #fig.2
7           (0.8)
```

Fig. 1A.   Fig. 1B.

At ll. 01–02, INS asks LDV to turn left "further ahead" while at the same time performing a pointing gesture forward (Figure 1), then to the left. While this instruction is articulated inside the car and LDV is its sole recipient, INS at the same time deictically refers to the surrounding environment, with talk and gesture. That environment is evolving, as the car is moving in space. Next, INS utters a "car control instruction" (l. 04) (De Stefani and Gazin 2014), referring to the "mirror routine" (Björklund 2018), which LDV is expected to perform whenever the car is engaging in a change of direction, and which ends in the activation of the indicator (l. 05). Note that the projected action of "turning left" also requires an adaptation of the car's speed: INS first asks LDV to "release the gas (pedal) a bit" (l. 02) and then to "check a bit with the brake" (l. 06). These instructions are consequential for the behavior of the car as a mobile unit in the traffic, as it is slowing down in a way that is witnessable by other traffic participants.

As the car is approaching the area where it is expected to turn left, another traffic participant becomes visible: a woman walking on the pavement (Figure 2).

Figure 2.

The trajectory of this person and her mobile behavior may be more or less projectable at this point: she could continue to walk on the pavement, she could cross the street that INS and LDV's car is about to engage in, she could halt, etc. At l. 08, INS provides an online analysis of this person's likely behavior:

Extract 1B. (cont.)
```
8    INS    guarda se arriva qualcuno sulle strisce nessuno,
            look if someone's coming on the crossing no one
9           (.)
10   INS    passamano,
            hand over wheel
11          (.)
12   INS    dammi un pochettino di gas,#
            give me a little bit of gas
     fig                             #fig.3
13          +(0.3)
     car    ->+halted at the pedestrian crossing-->
```

INS "sees" the pedestrian as someone who is not "coming on the crossing" (l. 08): This is visible in his *nessuno*/'no one' (l. 08) and in his initiation of the next instruction (l. 10), for which he uses an idiosyncratic expression telling LDV how to manipulate the steering wheel. Moreover, INS asks LDV to speed up (l. 12) manifesting his perception that the car is actually slowing down and eventually coming to a halt before the pedestrian crossing (l. 13). On his part, LDV decides to stop the car, thereby displaying a different interpretation of the pedestrian's mobile behavior in space, namely as displaying that she is going to cross the street (Figure 3). As she does so, she not only orients her gaze to the driver (Figure 3), but also performs a sign of civility (Laurier 2019; Merlino and Mondada 2019), by lifting her right hand as a display of thankfulness (Figure 4; l. 16).

Figure 3.   **Figure 4.**

This fleeting encounter, which takes place between the pedestrian and the driver of the car (rather than between "the pedestrian and the car," or "the pedestrian and the passenger") is consequential also for the interaction that occurs inside the car. At l. 14, LDV discloses to INS that the pedestrian is actually his aunt:

Extract 1C. (cont.)
```
14   LDV    °hh h mia zia°
            my aunt
15   INS    o:cch[ei.
            okay
16   LDV         [°questa è mia zi[a°.#
                 that's my aunt
     fig                          #fig.4
```

```
17   INS                    [metti la prima.
                             go into first (gear)
18          (.)
19   INS    è tua zia lei?
            is she your aunt?
20          (1.1)
21   LDV    (non mi vede) mica,
            she doesn't even (see me)
22          (0.5)#(0.4)+(5.3)
     car            -->+moving forward-->>
     fig         #fig.5
23   INS    e poi mettiamo la seconda.
            and then we go into second (gear)
24          (1.1)
25   INS    bravissimo.
            well done.
```

Whereas LDV announces to INS that he recognizes someone he knows, the pedestrian shows no sign of recognition of the driver (as being her nephew). LDV orients to the absent reciprocal recognition (l. 21). Shortly after, another walking "mobile with" steps onto the crossing and crosses the street (l. 22), namely two boys who recognizably move in space as a single unit. In this case, too, one of the boys orients his gaze towards the driver (Figure 5), thereby identifying LDV as the person responsible for the car's traffic behavior.

Figure 5.

This analysis has shown the complex forms of mobile coordination work carried out by traffic participants. Mobile units engage in different strands of participation: intra-unit participation takes places within the mobile unit (e.g., the car, the couple); inter-unit participation occurs between different traffic participants (e.g., the car as a unit and the two boys as another unit); cross-unit participation occurs across the boundaries of units (e.g., between the driver and one of the boys) (De Stefani and Gazin 2019). Whereas driver and instructor are relatively immobile inside the car, they orient to the changing traffic ecology around them and secure the coordination of car-controlling tasks, changes in speed, and responsible mobile actions in a way that is sensitive to the other traffic participants' projectable behavior in space and time. This can also generate fleeting cross-unit encounters, in which an interactional space is built and dissolved within a fraction of time. While multiple kinds of mobility but also immobility are at stake here, the following section discusses more sustained interactional spaces.

4.3 The dynamics of spatiality: Interactional space

Considering participants' bodies in social interaction grounds an analytical interest in their position, orientation, and changing distribution in space as revealing forms of engagement in the current activity and participation framework. Given that these engagements change continuously, the interactional space is constantly moving, even in stationary activities.

An interest in the spatiality of the interaction characterizes contributions of early precursors of EMCA, such as Erving Goffman, in particular in *Asylums* (1961), *Behavior in Public Places* (1963), and through the notion of "territories of the self" (1971). The territoriality of social encounters is also the focus of Ashcraft and Scheflen's (1976) study, who, on the basis of video-taped encounters, observe that "the unoccupied space in the centre of the group nevertheless becomes a claimed territory. Others outside the circle customarily recognize the territory" (1976: 7). Working with Scheflen, Kendon conceptualized this territory by introducing the notion of *F-formation* (1990: 248–249): body positions and orientations build an arrangement favoring a common focus of attention and the engagement in a joint activity. Later, Goodwin (2000) addressed the mutual relationships between embodied actions and the material environment with the notion of *contextual configuration*. Contextual configurations frame and make visible action as it unfolds and as it is organized by a multiplicity of semiotic resources (2000: 1490). The notion of *interactional space* (Mondada 2009a, 2013) builds on these predecessors: Designed by the local arrangements of the participants' bodies, the interactional space is reflexively shaping and shaped by the ongoing interaction, and thus is constitutively dynamic, adjusting to the organization of the interaction, moment-by-moment, turn-by-turn, and sequence-by-sequence. Beyond the typology of F-formations proposed by Kendon, the interactional space is in constant movement, and transcends the opposition between stationary vs. mobile activities. Even in stationary activities, the participants constantly transform the interactional space, through minimal movements of the bodies reorienting to each other but also, more radically, with mobile bodies stepping back and forth as turns unfold, new sequences are initiated, new actions are recipient-designed and responded to (De Stefani and Mondada 2018; Goodwin and Goodwin 2004; LeBaron and Streeck 1997; Mondada 2009a, 2014a). These dynamic adjustments and transformations of the interactional space show the continuity between stationary and mobile actions.

The interactional space is assembled in the opening of an encounter (Mondada 2009a), it is subsequently transformed during the interaction and dissolved in sequence closings (Broth and Mondada 2013) and at the end of the encounter (Llewellyn and Butler 2011). While openings and closings may involve the participants' mobility as they move in and out of the encounter, the transformations of the interactional space during the encounter may concern other, more minimal, forms of movement. We discuss these diverse forms of movements and mobility in the following shop encounter collected in France, in which a customer enters a bakery, buys bread, then walks away. The opening is achieved between a mobile customer entering the bakery and a stationary seller positioned behind the counter:

Extract 2A. (BAK_STL_2705_39.00_marguerite/CLI21)
```
1      CLI         [bon[jour
                    good morning
2      SEL            [bonjou::r#
                       good morning
       cli         >>walks in->
       cli         >>looks at SEL->
       sel         >>looks at CLI->
       fig                     #fig.6
```

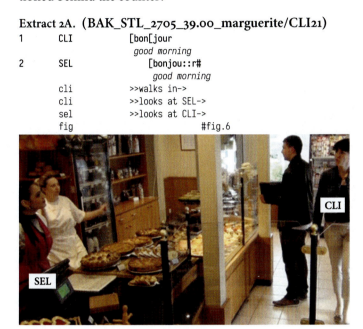

Fig. 6.

The opening of the encounter happens as the customer is still approaching the counter (Figure 6). The customer, walking into the shop, and the seller, stationary behind her counter, mutually gaze at each other and produce a greeting sequence (ll. 01–02). At this point, the interactional space is characterized by the reciprocal orientations and displacement of the participants' bodies. The interactional space is then stabilized when the customer stops at the counter:

Extract 2B. (cont.)
```
3             (0.3) · (0.8) * (0.3)
       cli                 ->*stops and stands->
       cli          ·looks at shelf->
4      CLI    euh j'%vais pren+dre#:::: une: margue±rite,· #
              ehm I will take           a daisy ((= bread name))
       cli           %manipulates purse->
       sel                     +steps to R/shelf->
       sel                              ->±lks shelf->
       cli                                 ->·lks purse->
       fig                  #fig.7         fig.8#
```

```
5          s'il vous plaît
           please
```

Fig. 7.

Fig. 8.
```
6          |  (0.5) +2
   sel     |raises LH->
   sel            ->+stops
7  SEL     a·lors |j'ai  |un euhm (.) un fariné
           PRT    I have a  ehm        a floured
   sel     ->|lowers|
   cli     ->·at SEL/marguerites->
8          multi-†graines ou sésame
           multi-grains   or sesame
   sel           ->†turns to CLI->
9          (0.4)
10 CLI     ømultigraiøt|nes.ø
           multi-grains
   cli     øH/chin upødownø
   sel            ->†turns to shelf/marguerites->
   sel             |RH up->
```

Before stopping, the customer's gaze shifts from the seller to the shelf where the breads are located (Figure 7). This changes the interactional space, adjusted to the next sequence, in which the client looks at the product she is targeting in her next action, a request, while the seller monitors her. The request is formatted with an initial *euh*/'ehm' followed by the verb *prendre*/'take' in the *futur proche* ('near future'), which is audibly stretched. The production of the bread's name (*marguerite*) (l. 04) is thereby delayed. The seller orients to the request in progress by beginning to leave her position at the counter and stepping towards the shelf (Figures 7–8), as she is still uttering the verb, before its argument is produced. She looks at a particular place in the shelf while the customer utters the name of the bread (Figure 8). The seller's steps and bodily orientations reorganize the interactional space as she shifts her attention from the customer to the product. The early mobile response of the seller, stepping and looking towards the bread, displays the projectability of the emergent request. Thus, even in an apparently "stationary" encounter between the seller positioned behind and the customer positioned in front of the counter, we observe gaze and torso movements that reshape the interactional space, as well as a form of micro-mobility of the seller who steps toward the requested item. The response to the request is formatted in a mobile trajectory, in which the entire body of the seller orients to the *marguerite*, as she projects to grasp it. However, this trajectory is suspended (see the left hand moving up, l. 06, and then down, l. 07, while an option is proffered, ll. 07–08). The customer unproblematically picks one of the alternatives (l. 10) and the seller completes the fulfillment of the request by raising her hand (l. 10) and by grasping the bread.

The closure of this expanded sequence (l. 11) is characterized again by a transformation of the interactional space, which projects the next action:

Extract 2C. (cont.)
```
11            (0.4) · (0.5) |  ·  (0.4)  ·   (5.8)   ·(4.0)
   cli          ->·lks at purse·reads price·prep 5€ bill·
   sel                    ->|grasps bread and prep wr pap->
12 SEL    vous aimeriez autre chos[e?
          would you like something else
13 CLI                              [>non *merci.<*
                                     no thanks
   cli                              ->*steps to counter*
14        (0.4)
15 SEL    j'vous remercie.
          I thank you
16        (0.3) | (0.1)
   sel       ->|puts wrapped marguerite on counter->
17 SEL    un euro tren·te-cinq | s'il vous plaît
          one euro thirty-five please
   sel                         ->|
   cli                    ·hands over 5€->
18        (0.2)
19 SEL    [mer·|ci.|
          thanks
20 CLI    [merci
          thanks
   cli    ->·
   sel       |takes 5€|
21        (7.5)
22 SEL    |voilà et pour vous.
          here it is and for you
          |gives change->
23        (0.5)|·(0.2)·
   sel       ->|
   cli       ·takes change·
```

The customer reorients her gaze from the bread to her purse (l. 11) from which she extracts a bill. This projects the action of paying, and the bill (5 euros) displays an estimate of the price. Moreover, while the next sequence is still ongoing – with the seller checking whether the customer wants another product and the customer responding negatively – the customer steps towards the counter. These steps further reconfigure the interactional space, orienting it around the counter and more precisely around the till, where the payment will be made: next, the seller announces the price (l. 17), takes the bill, and gives the change (ll. 17–22).

Finally, the interactional space is dissolved at the completion of the closing sequence:

Extract 2D. (cont.)
```
24  CLI     ·m[erci bien
            thanks a lot
25  SEL     [merci:::
             thanks
    cli     ·puts change in wallet->
26          (1.0)
27  SEL     passez une bonne journ[ée et à bientôt.
            have a nice day        and see you soon
28  CLI                            [à vous aussi
                                    you too
29          au r'voi[r
            good bye
30  SEL             [me:†rci beau|coup.|
                     thank you very much
    sel             †...pivots-->
    sel                      |closes till|
31          (0.3) †(2.0)#(0.3)† (0.5) · (0.3) % # (0.5)·
    sel           †w twd shelf†rearranges breads-->>
    cli                        ->·takes bread-----·
    cli                                    %walks away->>
    fig           #fig.9                   #fig.10
```

Fig. 9.

Fig. 10.

During the sequence of final thanking (ll. 24–25), the customer puts the money in her wallet. This takes some time (until line 31), during which the customer remains immobile in front of the counter. However, during this time, the seller utters a farewell wish (l. 27), which the customer reciprocates (l. 28). The customer utters a final greeting (l. 29), to which the seller responds by thanking her (l. 30). These closing exchanges are articulated while the customer is still manipulating her wallet. The seller closes the till after having arranged the money in it (l. 30) and walks away, turning to the shelf where she begins to rearrange the remaining breads (l. 31; Figure 9). In other words, the seller is the first to dissolve the interactional space by leaving, while the customer is still involved with her wallet. Finally, she leaves too (Figure 10), without any more words being exchanged between the two individuals, as she exits the shop.

In this short transaction of less than one minute, the participants engage in several sequences of action, which shape, and are shaped by, the transformations of the interactional space. These transformations involve embodied resources that show that moving bodies are involved even in a stationary interaction: This concerns movements of the stationary body (gaze shift, gestures, body postures), as well as the mobility of the body (stepping, walking in and out). The notion of interactional space enables these forms of movements to connect in relation to the emergent and progressing sequentiality of the encounter.

5. Conclusion

By offering a review of how stationary vs. mobile interactions have been and currently are discussed in Ethnomethodology and Conversation Analysis (EMCA), this chapter has shown how this field of studies has responded to the "mobility turn" (Urry 2000) and developed an original perspective on mobility in social interaction. In particular, the chapter has scrutinized EMCA studies dealing with stationary and mobile activities, and shown how mobility emerged as an object of study, and which methodological and conceptual issues it enabled to be raised. Research in EMCA has made it possible for us to demonstrate that mobility is not a dimension that pinpoints specific types of settings and activities as "mobile." Mobility is, rather, a perspective from which any setting – stationary as well as mobile – can be examined, namely, as involving different kinds of movement (of body parts) and mobility (in the sense of a displacement in space). Mobility is, in this regard, an inescapable feature of social interaction and, as a consequence, a fundamental analytical dimension that has long been neglected. Paying attention to *mobile moments* in interaction opens up the possibility of considering dynamic phenomena such as the incessant mobilization of multimodal resources, movements within the local material ecology of the interaction, and the dynamic shaping and reshaping of interactional spaces. Furthermore, attending to mobile *moments* entails an accurate examination of the temporal and sequential deployment of mobility, as accomplished by the co-participants. Interactants manage mobility in various ways, in accordance with the specific ecology they inhabit. For instance, the seller and the customer in a shop orient to the counter as the stationary center of their activity, even if they engage in moments of mobility when they take steps within the restricted area of the shop: They arrive at and leave the counter in the opening and the closing of their encounter, and they step away from but also come back to it during the transaction. In this way, mobile moments can inhabit stationary activities. On the other hand, stationary bodies can inhabit mobile activities, such as in cars, trains, and flights. This points at forms of mobility of social life: airline pilots and pedestrians navigate through space not only at different speed, but also by bodily engaging in different ways, by making use of a varying set of multimodal resources and technological means, by engaging in different participation frameworks, etc. Then again, populating the "same" habitable space does not entail the same kind of spatial navigation: in an aircraft, individuals in the cabin and individuals in the cockpit experience mobility in very distinct ways. In fact, mobility is primordially accomplished through action and interaction — and people engage in different actions in the cockpit and in the cabin. Future research might explore such different ways of orienting towards what it is to be moving — both as displacement in space (mobility of the entire body) and as contained body movements (shifting gaze, gesturing, torquing, etc.) and examine their varying temporal and sequential organization.

Funding

This paper resulted from the project *The First Five Words. Multilingual cities in Switzerland and Belgium and the grammar of language choice in public space*, directed by Lorenza Mondada and Elwys De Stefani, funded by the Swiss National Science Foundation/SNSF (project no. 100012L_182296/1) and the Fonds Wetenschappelijk Onderzoek /FWO (project no. G0E1519N), during 2019–2024.

References

Allen-Collinson, Jacquelyn. 2006. "Running-together. Some ethnomethodological considerations." *Ethnographic Studies*, 8: 17–29.
Arminen, Ilkka. 2006. "Social functions of location in mobile telephony." *Personal and Ubiquitous Computing*, 10: 319–323.
Arminen, Illka, and Minna Leinonen. 2006. "Mobile phone call openings: Tailoring answers to personalized summonses." *Discourse Studies*, 8 (3): 339–368.
Ashcraft, Norman, and Albert E. Scheflen. 1976. *People Space: The Making and Breaking of Human Boundaries*. New York: Anchor.
Bergmann, Jörg R. 1993. "Alarmiertes Verstehen: Kommunikation in Feuerwehrnotrufen." In *"Wirklichkeit" im Deutungsprozess: Verstehen und Methoden in den Kultur- und Sozialwissenschaften*, ed. by Thomas Jung and Stefan Müller-Dooh, 283–328. Frankfurt am Main: Suhrkamp.
Best, Katie. 2012. "Making museum tours better: Understanding what a guided tour really is and what a tour guide really does." *Museum Management and Curatorship*, 27 (1): 35–52.
Birdwhistell, Ray L. 1970. *Kinesics and Context*. Philadelphia, PA: University of Pennsylvania Press.
Björklund, Daniel. 2018. "Drilling the mirror routine: From non-situated looking to mobile practice in driver training." *International Journal of Applied Linguistics*, 28 (2): 226–247.

Broth, Mathias, Jakob Cromdal, and Lena Levin. 2018. "Showing where you're going: Instructing the accountable use of the indicator in live traffic." *International Journal of Applied Linguistics*, 28 (2): 248–264.

Broth, Mathias, Jakob Cromdal, and Lena Levin. 2019. "Telling the other's side: Formulating others' mental states in driver training." *Language & Communication*, 65: 7–21.

Broth, Mathias, Eric Laurier, and Lorenza Mondada (eds). 2014. *Studies of Video Practices. Video at Work*. London: Routledge.

Broth, Mathias and Fredrik Lundström. 2013. "A walk on the pier: Establishing relevant places in mobile instruction." In *Interaction and Mobility: Language and the Body in Motion*, ed. by Pentti Haddington, Lorenza Mondada and Maurice Nevile, 99–122. Berlin: De Gruyter.

Broth, Mathias, and Lorenza Mondada. 2013. "Walking away: The embodied achievement of activity closings in mobile interactions." *Journal of Pragmatics*, 47: 41–58.

Büscher, Monika, John Urry, and Katian Witchger (eds). 2011. *Mobile Methods*. London: Routledge.

Cresswell, Timothy. 2006. *On the Move: Mobility in the Modern Western World*. London: Routledge.

D'Antoni, Federica, Thomas Debois, Elwys De Stefani, Philipp Hänggi, Lorenza Mondada, Julia B. Schneerson, and Burak S. Tekin. 2022. "Encounters in public spaces: The establishment of interactional space in face-to-face openings." In *Pragmatics of Space*, ed. by Andreas H. Jucker and Heiko Hausendorf, 281–315. Berlin: De Gruyter Mouton.

Deppermann, Arnulf. 2018. "Instruction practices in German driving lessons: Differential uses of declaratives and imperatives." *International Journal of Applied Linguistics*, 28 (2): 265–282.

Deppermann, Arnulf, Reinhold Schmitt, and Lorenza Mondada. 2010. "Agenda and emergence: Contingent and planned activities in a meeting." *Journal of Pragmatics*, 42 (6): 1700–1718.

De Stefani, Elwys. 2010. "Reference as an interactively and multimodally accomplished practice: Organizing spatial reorientation in guided tours." In *Spoken Communication*, ed. by Massimo Pettorino, Antonella Giannini, Isabella Chiari, and Francesca M. Dovetto, 137–170. Newcastle: Cambridge Scholars Publishing.

De Stefani, Elwys. 2011. "*Ah petta ecco, io prendo questi che mi piacciono.*" *Agire come coppia al supermercato: un approccio conversazionale e multimodale allo studio dei processi decisionali*. Roma: Aracne.

De Stefani, Elwys. 2013a. "Rearranging (in) space: On mobility and its relevance for the study of face-to-face interaction." In *Space in Language and Linguistics: Geographical, Interactional, and Cognitive Perspectives*, ed. by Peter Auer, Martin Hilpert, Anja Stukenbrock and Benedikt Szmrecsanyi, 435–463. Berlin: De Gruyter.

De Stefani, Elwys. 2013b. "The collaborative organization of next actions in a semiotically rich environment: Shopping as a couple." In *Interaction and Mobility: Language and the Body in Motion*, ed. by Pentti Haddington, Lorenza Mondada and Maurice Nevile, 123–151. Berlin: De Gruyter.

De Stefani, Elwys. 2021. "*If*-clauses, their grammatical consequents, and their embodied consequence: Organizing joint attention in guided tours." *Frontiers in Communication*, 6:

De Stefani, Elwys. 2023. "Approaching the counter at the supermarket: Decision-making and the accomplishment of couplehood." In *Encounters at the Counter: The Organization of Shop Interactions*, ed. by Barbara Fox, Lorenza Mondada, and Marja-Leena Sorjonen, 37–72. Cambridge: Cambridge University Press.

De Stefani, Elwys, and Arnulf Deppermann. 2021. "Les gestes de pointage dans un environnement changeant et éphémère: les leçons de conduite." *Langage et Société*, 173: 141–166.

De Stefani, Elwys, and Anne-Danièle Gazin. 2014. "Instructional sequences in driving lessons: Mobile participants and the temporal and sequential organization of actions." *Journal of Pragmatics*, 65: 63–79.

De Stefani, Elwys, and Anne-Danièle Gazin. 2019. "Learning to communicate: Managing multiple strands of participation in driving lessons." *Language and Communication*, 65: 41–57.

De Stefani, Elwys, and Lorenza Mondada. 2014. "Reorganizing mobile formations: When 'guided' participants initiate reorientations in guided tours." *Space and Culture*, 17 (2): 157–175.

De Stefani, Elwys, and Lorenza Mondada. 2017. "Who's the expert? Negotiating competence and authority in guided tours." In *Identity Struggles: Evidence from Workplaces around the World*, ed. by Dorien Van De Mieroop, and Stephanie Schnurr, 95–124. Amsterdam: Benjamins.

De Stefani, Elwys, and Lorenza Mondada. 2018. "Encounters in public space: How acquainted versus unacquainted persons establish social and spatial arrangements." *Research on Language and Social Interaction*, 51 (3): 248–270.

D'hondt, Sigurd. 2009. "Calling the stops in a Dar-es-Salaam minibus: Embodied understandings of place in a drop-off routine." *Journal of Pragmatics*, 41: 1962–1976.

Drew, Paul, and John Heritage (eds). 1992. *Talk at Work: Interaction in Institutional Settings*. Cambridge: Cambridge University Press.

Fele, Giolo. 2023. *Emergency Communication: The Organization of Calls to Emergency Dispatch Centers*. Cham: Palgrave Macmillan.

Goffman, Erving. 1961. *Asylums*. New York: Anchor.

Goffman, Erving. 1963. *Behavior in Public Places*. New York: The Free Press.

Goffman, Erving. 1971. *Relations in Public*. New York: Harper & Row.

Goodwin, Charles. 1979. "The interactive construction of a sentence in natural conversation." In *Everyday Language: Studies in Ethnomethodology*, ed. by George Psathas, 97–121. New York: Irvington Publishers.

Goodwin, Charles. 1981. *Conversational Organization: Interaction between Speakers and Hearers*. New York: Academic Press.

Goodwin, Charles. 1984. "Notes on story structure and the organization of participation." In *Structures of Social Action*, ed. By J. Maxwell Atkinson and John Heritage, 225–246. Cambridge: Cambridge University Press.

Goodwin, Charles. 1986. "Audience diversity, participation and interpretation." *Text*, 6 (3): 283–316.

Goodwin, Charles. 1987a. "Unilateral departure." In *Talk and Social Organisation*, ed. by Graham Button and John R.E. Lee, 206–216. Clevedon: Multilingual Matters.

Goodwin, Charles. 1987b. "Forgetfulness as an interactive resource." *Social Psychology Quarterly*, 50 (2): 115–131.

Goodwin, Charles. 1993. "Recording human interaction in natural settings." *Pragmatics*, 3 (2): 181–209.

Goodwin, Charles. 2000. "Action and embodiment within situated human interaction." *Journal of Pragmatics*, 32 (10): 1489–1522.

Goodwin, Charles. 2007. "Participation, stance and affect in the organization of activities." *Discourse and Society*, 18 (1): 53–73.

Goodwin, Charles, and Marjorie H. Goodwin. 2004. "Participation." In *A Companion to Linguistic Anthropology*, ed. by Alessandro Duranti, 222–244. Oxford: Blackwell.

Goodwin, Marjorie H. 1997. "Byplay: Negotiating evaluation in storytelling." In *Towards a Social Science of Language: Papers in Honor of William Labov*, vol. 2, ed. by Gregory R. Guy, Crawford Faegin, Deborah Schiffrin, and John Baugh, 77–102. Amsterdam: Benjamins.

Goodwin, Marjorie H., and Goodwin, Charles. 2012. "Car talk: Integrating texts, bodies, and changing landscapes." *Semiotica*, 191 (1/4): 257–286.

Haddington, Pentti. 2012. "Movement in action: Initiating social navigation in cars." *Semiotica*, 191 (1/4): 137–167.

Haddington, Pentti. 2019. "Leave-taking as multiactivity: Coordinating conversational closings with driving in cars." *Language & Communication*, 65: 58–78.

Haddington, Pentti, and Tiina Keisanen. 2009. "Location, mobility and the body as resources in selecting a route." *Journal of Pragmatics*, 41 (10): 1938–1961.

Haddington, Pentti, Tiina Keisanen, and Maurice Nevile (eds). 2012. "Meaning in Motion: Interaction in Cars". Special Issue of *Semiotica*, 191 (1/4): 101–333.

Haddington, Pentti, Lorenza Mondada, and Maurice Nevile (eds). 2013. *Interaction and Mobility: Language and the Body in Motion*. Berlin: De Gruyter.

Hall, Edward. T. 1966. *The Hidden Dimension*. New York: Doubleday.

Hausendorf, Heiko, Reinhold Schmitt, and Wolfgang Kesselheim (eds). 2016. *Interaktionsarchitektur, Sozialtopographie und Interaktionsraum*. Tübingen: Narr.

Heath, Christian. 1986. *Body Movement and Speech in Medical Interaction*. Cambridge: Cambridge University Press.

Heath, Christian, Jon Hindmarsh, and Paul Luff. 2010. *Video in Qualitative Research: Analysing Social Interaction in Everyday Life*. London: Sage.

Heath, Christian, Marina Jirotka, Paul Luff, and Jon Hindmarsh. 1995. "Unpacking collaboration: The interactional organisation of trading in a city dealing room." *Computer Supported Cooperative Work*, 3: 147–165.

Heath, Christian, and Paul Luff. 1992. Collaboration and control: Crisis management and multimedia technology in London Underground Line Control Rooms. *Computer Supported Cooperative Work*, 1: 69–94.

Heath, Christian, and Paul Luff. 2000. *Technology in Action*. Cambridge: Cambridge University Press.

Jensen, Ole B. 2010. "Erving Goffman and everyday life mobility." In *The Contemporary Goffman*, ed. by Micheal H. Jacobsen, 333–351. Routledge: Abington.

Kazemi, Ali. 2020. "Fine-tuning locational formulations in mobile phone calls." *Discourse Studies*, 22 (5): 553–570.

Kendon, Adam. 1990. *Conducting Interaction: Patterns of Behavior in Focused Encounters*. Cambridge: Cambridge University Press.

Laurier, Eric. 2001. "Why people say where they are during mobile phone calls." *Environment and Planning D: Society and Space*, 19 (4): 485–504.

Laurier, Eric. 2005. "Searching for a parking space." *Intellectica*, 41–42: 101–115.

Laurier, Eric. 2019. "Civility and mobility: Drivers (and passengers) appreciating the actions of other drivers." *Language & Communication*, 65: 79–91.

Laurier, Eric, Hayden Lorimer, and Barry Brown. 2007. *Habitable Cars: The Organization of Collective Private Travel*. Edinburgh & Swindon: ESRC.

Laurier, Eric, Hayden Lorimer, Barry Brown, Owain Jones, Oskar Juhlin, Allyson Noble, Mark Perry, et al. 2008. "Driving and 'passengering': notes on the ordinary organization of car travel." *Mobilities*, 3 (1): 1–23.

Laurier, Eric, Daniel Muñoz, Rebekah Miller, and Barry Brown. 2020. "A bip, a beeeep, and a beep beep: How horns are sounded in Chennai traffic." *Research on Language and Social Interaction*, 53 (3): 341–356.

LeBaron, Curtis D., and Jürgen Streeck. 1997. "Built space and the interactional framing of experience during a murder interrogation." *Human Studies*, 20: 1–25.

Liberman, Kenneth. 2013. "The local orderliness of crossing Kincaid." In *More Studies in Ethnomethodology*, ed. by Kenneth Liberman, 11–43. New York: State University of New York Press.

Llewellyn, Nick, and Carly W. Butler. 2011. "Walking out on air." *Research on Language and Social Interaction*, 44 (1): 44–64.

McIlvenny, Paul. 2014. "Velomobile formations-in-action: Biking and talking together." *Space and Culture*, 17 (2): 137–156.

McIlvenny, Paul. 2015. "The joy of biking together: Sharing everyday experiences of vélomobility." *Mobilities*, 10 (1): 55–82.

McIlvenny, Paul. 2019a. "How did the mobility scooter cross the road? Coordinating with co-movers and other movers in traffic." *Language & Communication*, 65: 105–130.

McIlvenny, Paul. 2019b. "Inhabiting spatial video and audio data: Towards a scenographic turn in the analysis of social interaction." *Social Interaction: Video-Based Studies of Human Sociality*, 2 (1).

McIlvenny, Paul, Mathias Broth, and Pentti Haddington (eds). 2009. "Communicating place, space and mobility." Special Issue of *Journal of Pragmatics*, 41 (10).

McIlvenny, Paul, Mathias Broth, and Pentti Haddington (eds). 2014. "Mobile formations in interaction." Special Issue of *Space and Culture*, 17 (2).

Melander, Helen, and Fritjof Sahlström. 2009. "Learning to fly: The progressive development of situation awareness." *Scandinavian Journal of Educational Research*, 53 (2): 151–166.

Merlino, Sara, and Lorenza Mondada. 2019. "Crossing the street: How pedestrians interact with cars." *Language & Communication*, 65: 131–147.

Modaff, Daniel P. 2003. "Body movement in the transition from opening to task in doctor-patient interviews." In *Studies in Language and Social Interaction*, ed. by Phillip J. Glenn, Curtis D. LeBaron, and Jenny Mandelbaum, 411–422. Mahwah: Erlbaum.

Mondada, Lorenza. 2005. "La constitution de l'origo déictique comme travail interactionnel des participants: une approche praxéologique de la spatialité." *Intellectica*, 41–42 (2–3): 75–100.

Mondada, Lorenza. 2009a. "Emergent focused interactions in public places: A systematic analysis of the multimodal achievement of a common interactional space." *Journal of Pragmatics*, 41: 1977–1997.

Mondada, Lorenza. 2009b. "The methodical organization of talking and eating: Assessments in dinner conversations." *Food Quality and Preference*, 20: 558–571.

Mondada, Lorenza. 2011. "Géographies mobiles et divergentes: l'établissement interactionnel des lieux d'intervention dans des appels au secours." *Revue d'anthropologie des connaissances*, 5 (2): 390–436.

Mondada, Lorenza. 2012a. "The conversation analytic approach to data collection." In *The Handbook of Conversation Analysis*, ed. by Jack Sidnell and Tanya Stivers, 32–56. London: Wiley-Blackwell.

Mondada, Lorenza. 2012b. "Descriptions en mouvement: l'organisation systématique du déplacement dans une visite guidée." In *Les visites guidées: Discours, interaction, multimodalité*, ed. by Jean-Paul Dufet, 154–206. Trento: Università degli Studi di Trento.

Mondada, Lorenza. 2012c. Talking and driving: Multiactivity in the car. *Semiotica*, 191 (1/4): 223–256.

Mondada, Lorenza. 2013. "Interactional space and the study of embodied talk-in-interaction." In *Space in Language and Linguistics: Geographical, Interactional and Cognitive Perspectives*, ed. by Peter Auer, Martin Hilpert, Anja Stukenbrock, and Benedikt Szmrecsanyi, 247–275. Berlin: De Gruyter.

Mondada, Lorenza. 2014a. Bodies in action: Multimodal analysis of walking and talking. *Language and Dialogue*, 4 (3): 357–403.

Mondada, Lorenza. 2014b. "The temporal orders of multiactivity: Operating and demonstrating in the surgical theatre." In *Multiactivity in Social Interaction: Beyond Multitasking*, ed. by Pentti Haddington, Tiina Keisanen, Lorenza Mondada, and Maurice Nevile, 33–75. Amsterdam: Benjamins.

Mondada, Lorenza. 2017. "Walking and talking together: Questions/answers and mobile participation in guided visits." *Social Science Information*, 56 (2): 220–253.

Mondada, Lorenza. 2018a. "Questions on the move: The ecology and temporality of question-answer sequences in mobility settings." In *Time in Embodied Interaction*, ed. by Arnulf Deppermann, and Jürgen Streeck, 161–202. Amsterdam: Benjamins.

Mondada, Lorenza. 2018b. "Multiple temporalities of language and body in interaction: Challenges for transcribing multimodality." *Research on Language and Social Interaction*, 51 (1): 85–106.

Mondada, Lorenza. 2018c. "Driving instruction at high speed on a race circuit: Issues in action formation and sequence organization." *International Journal of Applied Linguistics*, 28 (2): 304–325.

Mondada, Lorenza. 2022. "Adjusting step-by-step trajectories in public space: The micro-sequentiality of approaching and refusing to be approached." *Gesprächsforschung – Online-Zeitschrift zur verbalen Interaktion*, 23: 36–65.

Mondada, Lorenza. 2023. "Mobile body arrangements in public space: Revisiting 'withs' as local accomplishments." In *New Perspectives on Goffman in Language and Interaction: Body, Participation and the Self*, ed. by Lorenza Mondada and Anssi Peräkylä, 241–275. New York: Routledge.

Mondada, Lorenza. in press. "Moving bodies." In *Research Handbook on Social Interaction*, ed. by Melisa Stevanovic. Cheltenham: Edward Elgar Publishing.

Mondada, Lorenza, and Burak S. Tekin. 2024. "The intelligibility of mobile trajectories: Navigating in public space and coordinating walking bodies." *Mobilities*.

Myers, Greg. 2006. "'Where are you from?': Identifying place." *Journal of Sociolinguistics*, 10 (3): 320–343.

Nevile, Maurice. 2004. *Beyond the Black Box: Talk-in-Interaction in the Airline Cockpit*. Aldershot: Ashgate.

Nevile, Maurice. 2018. "Configuring materiality, mobility, and multiactivity: Interactions with objects in cars." *Social Interaction. Video-Based Studies of Human Sociality*, 1 (1).

Oloff, Florence. 2010. "Ankommen und Hinzukommen: Zur Struktur der Ankunft von Gästen." In *Situationseröffnungen: Zur multimodalen Herstellung fokussierter Interaktion*, ed. by Lorenza Mondada and Reinhold Schmitt, 171–228. Tübingen: Narr.

Pehkonen, Samu, Thomas A. Smith, and Robin J. Smith. 2022. "Maps, mobility, and perspective: Remarks on map use in producing an orienteering course." *Mobilities*, 17 (1): 152–178.

Psathas, George. 1976. "Mobility, orientation, and navigation: Conceptual and theoretical considerations." *New Outlook for the Blind*, 70 (9): 385–391.

Psathas, George. 1979. "Organizational features of direction maps." In *Everyday Language: Studies in Ethnomethodology*, ed. by George Psathas, 203–226. New York/London: Irvington.

Psathas, George. 1986. "Some sequential structures in direction-giving." *Human Studies*, 9 (2–3): 231–246.

Psathas, George. 1991. "The structure of direction-giving in interaction." In *Talk and Social Structure: Studies in Ethnomethodology and Conversation Analysis*, ed. by Deirdre Boden and Don H. Zimmerman, 195–216. Berkeley: University of California Press.

Psathas, George, and James M. Henslin. 1967. "Dispatched orders and the cab driver: A study of locating activities." *Social Problems*, 14 (4): 424–443.

Psathas, George, and Martin Kozloff. 1976. "The structure of directions." *Semiotica*, 17 (2): 111–130.

Relieu, Marc. 1999. "Parler en marchant. Pour une écologie dynamique des échanges de paroles." *Langage et Société*, 89: 37–67.

Robinson, Jeffrey D. and Tanya Stivers. 2001. "Achieving activity transitions in primary-care encounters: From history taking to physical examination." *Human Communication Research*, 27 (2): 253–298.

Ryave, A. Lincoln, and James N. Schenkein. 1974. "Notes on the art of walking." In *Ethnomethodology*, ed. by Roy Turner, 265–274. Middlesex: Penguin.

Sacks, Harvey. 1966. The Search for Help: No One to Turn to. PhD thesis, Berkeley: University of California.

Schegloff, Emanuel A. 1967. The First Five Seconds: The Order of Conversational Opening. PhD thesis, Berkeley: University of California.

Schegloff, Emanuel A. 1972. "Notes on a conversational practice: Formulating place." In *Studies in Social Interaction*, ed. by David Sudnow, 75–119. New York: The Free Press.

Schegloff, Emanuel A. 1979. "Identification and recognition in telephone conversations openings." In *Everyday Language: Studies in Ethnomethodology*, ed. by George Psathas, 111–152. New York: Irvington Publishers.

Schegloff, Emanuel A. 1986. "The routine as achievement." *Human Studies*, 9: 111–151.

Schegloff, Emanuel A. 2002. "Beginnings in the telephone." In *Perpetual Contact: Mobile Communication, Private Talk, Public Performance*, ed. by James E. Katz and Mark A. Aakhus, 284–300. Cambridge: Cambridge University Press.

Simone, Monica, and Renata Galatolo. 2020. "Climbing as a pair: Instructions and instructed body movements in indoor climbing with visually impaired athletes." *Journal of Pragmatics*, 155: 286–302.

Sommer, Robert. 1959. "Studies in personal space." *Sociometry*, 22 (3): 247–260.

Stukenbrock, Anja. 2023. "Temporality and the cooperative infrastructure of human communication: Noticings to delay and to accelerate onward movement in mobile interaction." *Language & Communication*, 92: 33–54.

Urry, John. 2000. *Sociology beyond Societies: Mobilities for the Twenty-First Century*. London: Routledge.

Urry, John. 2004. "The 'system' of automobility." *Theory, Culture & Society*, 21 (4/5): 25–39.

vom Lehn, Dirk. 2013. "Withdrawing from exhibits: The interactional organization of museum visits." In *Interaction and Mobility: Language and the Body in Motion*, ed. by Pentti Haddington, Lorenza Mondada, and Maurice Nevile, 65–90. Berlin: De Gruyter.

vom Lehn, Dirk, Christian Heath, and Jon Hindmarsh. 2001. "Exhibiting interaction: Conduct and collaboration in museums and galleries." *Symbolic Interaction*, 24 (2): 189–216.

Weilenmann, Alexandra. 2003. "'I can't talk now, I'm in a fitting room': Formulating availability and location in mobile-phone conversations." *Environment & Planning A: Economy and Space*, 35 (9): 1589–1605.

Cumulative index

This index refers to the whole of the *Handbook of Pragmatics*, its **Manual** as well as the 26 installments (the present one included), and it lists:

i. all labels used as entry headings in some part of the Handbook, with an indication of the part in which the entry is to be found, and with cross-references to other relevant entries;
ii. labels for traditions, methods, and topics for which separate entries have not (yet) been provided, indicating the entry-labels under which information can be found and the part of the Handbook where this is to be found.

The following abbreviations are used:

(MT) the Traditions section of the Manual
(MM) the Methods section of the Manual
(MN) the Notational Systems section of the Manual
(H)   the thematic main body of the loose-leaf Handbook or (from the 21st installment onwards) of the specific annual installment (marked as H21, H22, etc.)
(T)   the Traditions update/addenda of the printed Handbook (further specified for the bound volumes as T21, T22, etc.)
(M)   the Methods update/addenda of the printed Handbook (further specified for the bound volumes as M21, M22, etc.)
(N)   the Notational Systems update/addenda of the printed Handbook (further specified for the bound volumes as N21, N22, etc.)

References in the index may take the following forms:

"**Label (section reference)** (abbreviated as above)" — for labels which occur only as headings of an autonomous article

"**Label (section reference)**; label(s)" — for labels which occur as article headings and for which it is relevant to refer to other articles as well

"**Label** label(s)" — for labels which do not (yet) occur as article headings, but which stand for topics dealt with under the label(s) indicated

"**Label** → label(s)" — for labels that are considered, for the time being and for the purposes of the Handbook, as (near)equivalents of the label(s) following the arrow; a further search must start from the label(s) following the arrow

A

Abduction see Grounded theory (M); Language change (H)
Abuse see Obscenity, slurs, and taboo (H24)
Academic concept see Vygotsky (H)
Academic language see Applied linguistics (MT); Postcolonial pragmatics (T)
Acceptability see Generative semantics (MT)
Accessibility see Anaphora (H)
Accommodation see Contact (H); Presupposition (H)
Accommodation theory (MT); Adaptability (H); Age and language use (H); Bilingualism and multilingualism (H); Context and contextualization (H); Social psychology (MT)
Accounting see Collaboration in dialogues (H); Social psychology (MT)
Acoustics see Sound symbolism (H)
Action see Action theory (MT); Agency and language (H); Austin (H); Bühler (H); Cognitive psychology (MT); Ethnomethodology (MT); Intentionality (H); Nexus analysis (T); Perception and language (H); Philosophy of action (MT); Speech act theory (MT)
Action theory (MT); Agency and language (H); Grounded theory (M); Philosophy of action (MT)
Activation see Relational ritual (H)
Activity see Action theory (MT)
Activity types and pragmatic acts (H26); Pragmemes (H22)
Adaptability (H); Activity types and pragmatic acts (H26); Evolutionary pragmatics (T); Methods in language-attitudes research (M); (The) pragmatic perspective (M)
Adjacency pair see Prosody (H); Sequence (H)
Adjective see Experimental pragmatics (M)
Adjunct control see Control phenomena (H)
Adolescent see Youth language (H25)
Adorno, T. see Critical theory (MT)

Affect see Appraisal (H); Complaining (H25); Computational pragmatics (T); Emotion display (H); Emotions (H21); Emphasis (H); Interpreter-mediated interaction (H); Laughter (H); Overlap (H); Stance (H21); Text and discourse linguistics (T); Think-aloud protocols (M)
Affiliation/disaffiliation → see Affect
Affirmation see Negation (H)
Affordance see Pragmatics of script (H22); Social media research (T)
Age and language use (H); 'Other' representation (H); Swearing (H25); Youth language (H25)
Ageism see Age and language use (H)
Agency and language (H); Action theory (MT); Case and semantic roles (H); Computational pragmatics (T); Intentionality (H); Metapragmatics (MT); Motivation and language (H)
Agreement see Social media research (T); Therapeutic conversation (H)
Aisatsu (H)
Aktionsart see Tense and aspect (H)
Alignment see Nigerian hospital setting discourse (H24); Pragmatics of script (H22); Stance (H21)
Allegory see Conceptual integration (H)
Allopract see Activity types and pragmatic acts (H26)
Ambiguity see Indeterminacy and negotiation (H); Mental spaces (H); Obscenity, slurs, and taboo (H24); Polysemy (H); Sound symbolism (H); Truthfulness (H)
Amerindian languages see Anthropological linguistics (MT); Boas (H)
Analysis see Analytical philosophy (MT)
Analytical philosophy (MT); Austin (H); Conversational implicature (H); Hermeneutics (M); Philosophy of language (MT); Speech act theory (MT); Truth-conditional semantics (MT); Wittgenstein (H)
Anaphora (H); Grounding (H); Indexicals and demonstratives (H); Lexically triggered veridicality inferences (H22); Tense and aspect (H)
Anderson, Benedict (H21)
Animal communication see Adaptability (H); Communication (H); Primate communication (H)
Annotation see Corpus analysis (MM); Corpus pragmatics (M)
Antecedent see Anaphora (H)
Anthropological linguistics (MT); Anderson (H21); Bilingualism and multilingualism (H); Chronotope (H25); Cognitive anthropology (MT); Componential analysis (MT); Context and contextualization (H); Ethnography of speaking (MT); Fieldwork (MM); Gesture research (T); Gumperz (H); Hermeneutics (M); Hymes (H26); Indexicality (); Intercultural communication (H); Language ideologies (H); Malinowski (H); Metalinguistic awareness (H); Metapragmatics (MT); Nexus analysis (T); Phatic communion (H); (The) pragmatic perspective (M); Pragmatics of script (H22); Sapir (H); Sociolinguistics (MT); Ta'ārof (H22); Taxonomy (MM); Transience (H22); Truthfulness (H); Whorf (H)
Anthropology see Hymes (H26)
Anti-language see Jargon (H)
Apel, K. O. see Universal and transcendental pragmatics (MT)
Aphasia see Adaptability (H); Cerebral representation of language; Clinical pragmatics (T); Jakobson (H21); Neurolinguistics (MT)
Apology see Corpus pragmatics (M); Mediated performatives (H)
Appeal → see Functions of language

Applied linguistics (MT); Forensic linguistics (T); Intercultural communication (H); Language policy, language planning and standardization (H); Sociolinguistics (MT)
Appraisal (H); Emphasis (H); Halliday (H26); Heteroglossia (H26)
Appreciation see Appraisal (H); Ọmọlúàbí (H)
Appropriateness see Creativity in language use (H); Workplace interaction (H25)
Approval and disapproval see Ta'ārof (H22)
Arbitrariness see Adaptability (H); Iconicity (H); Sound symbolism (H); Structuralism (MT)
Archive see Postcolonial pragmatics (T)
Archiving see Working with language data (M25)
Areal linguistics see Contact linguistics (MT); Language change (H)
Argument structure (H23); Dependency
Argumentation see Argumentation in discourse and grammar (H); Argumentation theory (MT); Rhetoric (MT)
Argumentation in discourse and grammar (H); Argumentation theory (MT)
Argumentation theory (MT); Argumentation in discourse and grammar (H); Rhetoric (MT)
Articulation see Humboldt (H); Sound symbolism (H)
Artificial intelligence (MT); Cognitive psychology (MT); Cognitive science (MT); Communication (H); Computational linguistics (MT); Connectionism (MT); Context and contextualization (H); Frame analysis (M); Frame semantics (T); Speech act theory (MT)
Artificial life see Language acquisition (H)
Ascription see Functional discourse grammar (T)
Aspect see Event representation (H22);

Markedness (H); Tense and aspect (H)
Assertion see Austin (H); Speech act theory (MT)
Assimilation see Language rights (H)
Asymmetric interaction see Applied linguistics (MT); Communicative success vs. failure (H); Computer-mediated communication (H); Conversation types (H); Frame analysis (M); Mass media (H); Nigerian hospital setting discourse (H24)
Attention and language (H)
Attitude see Appraisal (H); Dialectology (MT); Methods in language-attitudes research (M); Pluricentric languages (H23); Social psychology (MT); Stance (H21)
Attribution theory see Social psychology (MT)
Audience → see Hearer
Audience design → see Recipient design
Audience effect see Primate communication (H)
Augmentative see Morphopragmatics (H)
Austin, J. L. (H); Analytical philosophy (MT); Communicative success vs. failure (H); Contextualism (T); Grice (H); Speech act theory (MT)
Authenticity (H); Identity (H24); Reported speech (H)
Authier-Revuz, J. see Énonciation (H)
Authority (H); Evidentiality (H22); Honorifics (H)
Authorship see Experimental pragmatics (M); Forensic linguistics (T)
Autism (H); Clinical pragmatics (T); Conceptual integration (H)
Auto-ethnography see Postcolonial pragmatics (T)
Automata theory see Computational linguistics (MT)
Automated communication see Globalization (H25)
Automaticity see Think-aloud protocols (M)

Autonomous vs. non-autonomous syntax (MT); Chomskyan linguistics (MT); Functionalism vs. formalism (MT); Structuralism (MT)
Autonomy see Legitimation Code Theory (T25)
Avoidance see Obscenity, slurs, and taboo (H24); Wakimae (H26)
Awareness see Metalinguistic awareness (H); Orthography and cognition (H22)
Axiology see Morris (H)

B
Baby talk → see Motherese
Back channel cue see Listener response (H)
Background information see Cognitive science (MT); Collaboration in dialogues (H); Common ground (H); Communication (H); Context and contextualization (H); Text and discourse linguistics (T)
Backgrounding see Argument structure (H23); Grounding (H)
Bakhtin, M.M. (H); Chronotope (H25); Collaboration in dialogues (H); Crossing (H26); Dialogical analysis (MM); Genre (H); Heteroglossia (H26); Ideology (H); Intertextuality (H); Polyphony (H); Reported speech (H)
Bally, C. see Énonciation (H)
Basilect see Creole linguistics (MT)
Bateson, G. (H); Communication (H)
Behaviorism (MT); Cognitive psychology (MT); Grice (H); Morris (H); Objectivism vs. subjectivism (MT)
Benveniste, E. (H); Énonciation (H)
Bernstein, B. see Applied linguistics (MT); Communicative success vs. failure (H); Legitimation Code Theory (T25)
Bilingual interactive activation (BIA) see The multilingual lexicon (H)
Bilingualism and multilingualism (H); Accommodation theory (MT); Anderson (H21); Anthropological linguistics (MT); Borrowing (H);

Code-switching (H); Code-switching and translanguaging (H22); Contact (H); Contact linguistics (MT); Developmental psychology (MT); Ervin-Tripp, S. (H24); Intercultural communication (H); Language contact (H); Language dominance and minorization (H); Language maintenance and shift (H21); Language policy, language planning and standardization (H); The multilingual lexicon (H); Pragmatics of script (H22); Social psychology (MT); Sociolinguistics (MT); Transience (H22); Translanguaging pedagogy (T)
Binding see Anaphora (H)
Biodiversity see Language ecology (H)
Biology see Morris (H)
Biosemiotics see Communication (H)
Blended data see Social media research (T)
Blog see Social media research (T)
Boas, F. (H); Anthropological linguistics (MT); Culture (H); Fieldwork (MM); Sapir (H); Typology (MT); Whorf (H)
Body see Ta'ārof (H22); Tactile sign languages (H21)
Bootstrapping see Language acquisition (H)
Borrowing (H); Contact (H); Interjections (H); Language contact (H)
Bourdieu, P. (H); Anderson (H21); Ideology (H); Legitimation Code Theory (T25); Power and the role of language (H25); Social institutions (H)
Brain see Clinical pragmatics (T); Developmental dyslexia (H); Emotions (H21); Neurolinguistics (MT); Neuropragmatics (T)
Brain imaging → see Cerebral representation of language; Cognitive science (MT); Language acquisition (H); Neurolinguistics (MT); Neuropragmatics (T); Perception and language (H); Psycholinguistics (MT)

Bureaucratic language see Applied linguistics (MT)
Business communication see Communication (H)
Bühler, K. (H); Language psychology (T); Phatic communion (H)

C

Caretaker discourse see Age and language use (H)
Carnap, R. see Analytical philosophy (MT); Intensional logic (MT)
Carnival(esque) see Bakhtin (H); Intertextuality (H)
Cartesian philosophy see Chomskyan linguistics (MT)
Case and semantic roles (H); Agency and language (H); Case grammar (MT); Cognitive grammar (MT); Cognitive linguistics (MT); Dependency and valency grammar (MT); Functional grammar (MT); Role and reference grammar (MT)
Case grammar (MT); Case and semantic roles (H); Construction grammar (MT); Dependency and valency grammar (MT); Frame semantics (T); Functional grammar (MT); Role and reference grammar (MT)
Caste and language (H23)
Catastrophe theory (MT)
Categorial imperative see Truthfulness (H)
Categorization (H); Adaptability (H); Cognitive grammar (MT); Cognitive linguistics (MT); Language dominance and minorization (H); Membership categorization analysis (T); Polysemy (H)
Causality (H)
Census see Caste and language (H23)
Centering theory see Tense and aspect (H)
Cerebral division of labour in verbal communication (H)
Cerebral representation of language see Cerebral division of labour in verbal communication (H); Neurolinguistics (MT)

Channel (H); Computer-mediated communication (H); Conversation types (H); Literacy (H); Mass media (H); Non-verbal communication (H); Politeness (H); Social media research (T); Text and discourse linguistics (T)
Chaos theory see Catastrophe theory (MT)
Chat see Computer-mediated communication (H)
Child language see Ellipsis (H); Ervin-Tripp, S. (H24); Language acquisition (H)
'CHILDES' see Language acquisition (H)
Choice-making see Adaptability (H)
Chomskyan linguistics (MT); Autonomous vs. non-autonomous syntax (MT); Interpretive semantics (MT); Language acquisition (H); Mentalism (MT)
Chronometric studies see Psycholinguistics (MT)
Chronotope (H25); Bakhtin (H)
Chunking see Linear Unit Grammar (T)
Cicourel, A. V. see Cognitive sociology (MT)
Citation see Working with language data (M25)
Class see Social class and language (H)
Classification1 see Typology (MT)
Classification2 see Taxonomy (MM)
Classroom interaction see Applied linguistics (MT); Communicative success vs. failure (H); Language learning in immersion and CLIL classrooms (H)
Clause structure see Attention and language (H); Control phenomena (H); Role and reference grammar (MT)
Clinical pragmatics (T); Cerebral representation of language; Nigerian hospital setting discourse (H24); Perception and language (H)
Co-ordination see Cognitive psychology (MT); Ellipsis (H)
Code see Code-switching (H); Code-switching and translanguaging (H22); Metalinguistic awareness (H);

Pragmatics of script (H22); Register (H); Semiotics (MT)
Code-autonomy see Code-switching and translanguaging (H22)
Code-switching (H); Bilingualism and multilingualism (H); Borrowing (H); Code-switching and translanguaging (H22); Contact linguistics (MT); Crossing (H26); Heteroglossia (H26); Language contact (H); Language learning in immersion and CLIL classrooms (H); Language maintenance and shift (H21); Pragmatics of script (H22)
Code-switching and translanguaging (H22); Crossing (H26); Heteroglossia (H26)
Codemixing see Code-switching (H); Crossing (H26)
Coding see Bateson (H); Evidentiality (H22)
Cognate see The multilingual lexicon (H)
Cognition see Adaptability (H); Caste and language (H23); Language acquisition (H); Orthography and cognition (H22)
Cognitive anthropology (MT); Anthropological linguistics (MT)
Cognitive grammar (MT); Case and semantic roles (H); Cognitive linguistics (MT); Metaphor (H)
Cognitive linguistics (MT); Attention and language (H); Case and semantic roles (H); Cognitive grammar (MT); Cognitive science (MT); Directive (H26); Embodiment (H); Emotions (H21); Event representation (H22); Gesture research (T); Hermeneutics (M); Humor (H23); Language psychology (T); Mental spaces (H); (The) pragmatic perspective (M)
Cognitive pragmatics see Clinical pragmatics (T); Philosophy of mind (MT)
Cognitive psychology (MT); Artificial intelligence (MT); Behaviorism (MT); Clinical pragmatics (T); Cognitive science (MT); Comprehension vs. production (H); Connectionism (MT); Developmental psychology (MT); Experimentation (MM); Frame semantics (T); Gesture research (T); Intentionality (H); Perception and language (H); Psycholinguistics (MT)
Cognitive science (MT); Artificial intelligence (MT); Cognitive linguistics (MT); Cognitive psychology (MT); Connectionism (MT); Context and contextualization (H); Experimentation (MM); Grice (H); Mentalism (MT); Perception and language (H); Philosophy of mind (MT)
Cognitive semantics see Cognitive science (MT); Componential analysis (MT); Conceptual semantics (T); Frame semantics (T); Lexical semantics (T)
Cognitive sociology (MT); Emphasis (H); Ethnomethodology (MT); Sociolinguistics (MT); Symbolic interactionism (MT); Text and discourse linguistics (T)
Cohesion and coherence (H); Communicative success vs. failure (H); Computational pragmatics (T); Ellipsis (H); Frame analysis (M); Systemic functional grammar (MT); Tense and aspect (H); Text and discourse linguistics (T)
Collaboration in dialogues (H); Common ground (H); Conversational implicature (H); Conversational logic (MT); Listener response (H)
Colligation see Collocation and colligation (H); Metaphor (H)
Collocation and colligation (H)
Colonization see Caste and language (H23); Language dominance and minorization (H)
Color terms see Anthropological linguistics (MT); Lexical semantics (T); Perception and language (H)
Commodification see Ideology (H)
Common ground (H); Cognitive science (MT); Collaboration in dialogues (H); Communication (H); Context and contextualization (H); Lexically triggered veridicality inferences (H22); Text and discourse linguistics (T)
Common sense see Ethnomethodology (MT)
Communication (H); Common ground (H)
Communication disorders → see Language disorders
Communication failure see Applied linguistics (MT)
Communicational dialectology see Dialectology (MT)
Communicative competence see Ethnography of speaking (MT); Gumperz (H); Hymes (H26); Linguistic explanation (MM); Motivation (H)
Communicative dynamism (H); Functional sentence perspective (H); Ọmọlúàbí (H); Word order (H)
Communicative effect see Interlanguage pragmatics (T)
Communicative style (H); Cultural scripts (H); Ervin-Tripp, S. (H24); Non-verbal communication (H); Register (H)
Communicative success vs. failure (H)
Community see Pragmatics of script (H22)
Community of practice see Social class and language (H); Workplace interaction (H25)
Comparative method see Contrastive analysis (MM)
Competence vs. performance → see Cerebral representation of language; Chomskyan linguistics (MT)
Complaining (H25)
Complement control see Control phenomena (H)
Complexity see Workplace interaction (H25); Youth language (H25)
Compliment see Corpus pragmatics (M)
Componential analysis (MT); Anthropological linguistics (MT); Cultural scripts (H); Generative semantics (MT); Lexical field

analysis (MT); Lexical semantics (T); Structuralism (MT)
Comprehension vs. production (H); Cohesion and coherence (H); Communication (H); Irony (H); Mediated performatives (H); Psycholinguistics (MT); Speech act theory (MT); Text comprehension (H)
Compression see Conceptual integration (H)
Computational linguistics (MT); Artificial intelligence (MT); Lexical functional grammar (MT); Text and discourse linguistics (T)
Computational pragmatics (T)
Computer communication see Artificial intelligence (MT); Computational pragmatics (T); Computer-mediated communication (H)
Computer corpora see Notation Systems in Spoken Language Corpora (N)
Computer modeling see Cognitive science (MT)
Computer programming see Artificial intelligence (MT)
Computer-mediated communication (H); Chronotope (H25); Complaining (H25); Computational pragmatics (T); Literacy (H); Social media research (T)
Conceptual blending see Conceptual integration (H); Metaphor (H)
Conceptual dependency theory see Artificial intelligence (MT)
Conceptual integration (H)
Conceptual metaphor theory see Metaphor (H)
Conceptual semantics (T); Interpretive semantics (MT)
Conceptual vs. linguistic representation see Cognitive anthropology (MT); Cognitive psychology (MT); Event representation (H22)
Conceptualization see Cognitive grammar (MT); Cognitive linguistics (MT); Event representation (H22)
Condition of satisfaction see Intentionality (H)
Conditional see Lexically triggered veridicality inferences (H22)
Conflict talk see Applied linguistics (MT)
Connectionism (MT); Artificial intelligence (MT); Cognitive psychology (MT); Cognitive science (MT); Language acquisition (H); Psycholinguistics (MT)
Connectivity see Cohesion and coherence (H)
Connotation → see Cerebral representation of language; Obscenity, slurs, and taboo (H24)
Consciousness and language (H); Attention and language (H); Folk pragmatics (T); Metapragmatics (MT); Participation (H); Perception and language (H)
Considerateness → see Tact
Consistency-checking device see Manipulation (H)
Construction grammar (MT); Case grammar (MT); Emergent grammar (T); Frame semantics (T); Word order (H)
Constructional analysis (T); Collocation and colligation (H); Construction grammar (MT); Constructional analysis (T)
Constructionism see Applied linguistics (MT); Argumentation theory (MT); Cognitive anthropology (MT); Critical Linguistics and Critical Discourse Analysis (MT); Developmental psychology (MT); Intercultural communication (H); Narrative (H); Social institutions (H)
Constructivism → see Constructionism
Contact (H); Bilingualism and multilingualism (H); Bilingualism and multilingualism (H); Contact linguistics (MT); Creole linguistics (MT); Creoles and creolization (H); Crossing (H26); Language change (H); Language contact (H); Language maintenance and shift (H21)
Contact linguistics (MT); Bilingualism and multilingualism (H); Contact (H); Creole linguistics (MT); Creoles and creolization (H); Dialectology (MT); Intercultural communication (H); Interjections (H); Language policy, language planning and standardization (H); Sociolinguistics (MT); Speech community (H); Typology (MT); Variational pragmatics (T)
Context and contextualization (H); Accommodation theory (MT); Activity types and pragmatic acts (H26); Aisatsu (H); Anthropological linguistics (MT); Argument structure (H23); Artificial intelligence (MT); Bateson (H); Cerebral representation of language; Cognitive science (MT); Cohesion and coherence (H); Common ground (H); Communication (H); Communicative style (H); Computational pragmatics (T); Contextualism (T); Conversation analysis (MT); Conversation types (H); Conversational implicature (H); Conversational logic (MT); Crossing (H26); Dialogical analysis (MM); Discourse markers (H); Ellipsis (H); Emphasis (H); Énonciation (H); Ervin-Tripp, S. (H24); Ethnography of speaking (MT); Ethnomethodology (MT); Evolutionary pragmatics (T); Experimental pragmatics (M); Firthian linguistics (MT); Frame analysis (M); Generative semantics (MT); Goffman (H); Gumperz (H); Halliday (H26); Hymes (H26); Impoliteness (H); Indexicals and demonstratives (H); Integrational linguistics (T); Intensional logic (MT); Interactional sociolinguistics (MT); Intercultural communication (H); Intertextuality (H); Language psychology (T); Laughter (H); Literary pragmatics (MT); Metalinguistic awareness (H);

Model-theoretic semantics (MT); Motivation and language (H); Narrative (H); Notation in formal semantics (MN); Politeness (H); Polysemy (H); Presupposition (H); Prosody (H); Rhetoric (MT); Social media research (T); Stance (H21); Style and styling (H21); Symbolic interactionism (MT); Tactile sign languages (H21); Text comprehension (H); Truthfulness (H); Workplace interaction (H25)
Context change see Context and contextualization (H)
Context modelling see Formal pragmatics (MT)
Context-of-situation see Context and contextualization (H); Firthian linguistics (MT); Malinowski (H); Register (H); Systemic functional grammar (MT)
Context-sensitive vs. context-free grammar see Computational linguistics (MT); Functional sentence perspective (H)
Context-sensitiveness see Context and contextualization (H)
Contextualism (T); Context and contextualization (H)
Contextualization
 cue see Gumperz (H); Style and styling (H21)
Continuity see Historical politeness (T)
Continuity
 hypothesis see Language acquisition (H)
Contrast see Functional discourse grammar (T)
Contrastive analysis (MM); Developmental psychology (MT); Error analysis (MM); Historical politeness (T); Intercultural communication (H); Interlanguage pragmatics (T); Language change (H); Pragmatic markers (H)
Contrastive pragmatics (T); Contrastive pragmatics (T); Ethnography of speaking (MT); Intercultural communication (H); Interlanguage pragmatics (T); Mianzi / lian (H21); Translation studies (T); Typology (MT); Variational pragmatics (T)
Control see Public discourse (H); Social institutions (H)
Control phenomena (H)
Conventional
 implicature see Grice (H); Implicitness (H); Truth-conditional pragmatics (T)
Conventionalism see Lexically triggered veridicality inferences (H22)
Conventionality see Adaptability (H); Conventions of language (H); Gesture research (T); Metaphor (H); Nigerian hospital setting discourse (H24); Primate communication (H); Speech act theory (MT); Wakimae (H26)
Conventions of language (H); Austin (H); Conversational implicature (H); Conversational logic (MT); Grice (H); Speech act
Convergence see Accommodation theory (MT); Contact (H)
Conversation see Collaboration in dialogues (H); Conversation analysis (MT); Gesture research (T); Humor (H23); Indeterminacy and negotiation (H); Institutional interaction (H23); Mass media (H); Narrative (H)
Conversation analysis (MT); Age and language use (H); Communication (H); Communicative success vs. failure (H); Computational pragmatics (T); Context and contextualization (H); Conversation types (H); Conversational storytelling (H24); Discourse markers (H); Embodied interaction (H23); Emphasis (H); Ethnography of speaking (MT); Ethnomethodology (MT); Forensic linguistics (T); Goffman (H); Gumperz (H); Hermeneutics (M); Humor (H23); Institutional interaction (H23); Interactional linguistics (T); Interactional sociolinguistics (MT); Intertextuality (H); Language psychology (T); Laughter (H); Linear Unit Grammar (T); Listener response (H); Mass media (H); Membership categorization analysis (T); Notation Systems in Spoken Language Corpora (N); Overlap (H); (The) pragmatic perspective (M); Prosody (H); Repair (H); Sacks (H); Sequence (H); Social psychology (MT); Text and discourse linguistics (T); Therapeutic conversation (H); Transcription systems for spoken discourse (MN); Workplace interaction (H25)
Conversation types (H)
Conversational implicature (H); Analytical philosophy (MT); Clinical pragmatics (T); Context and contextualization (H); Conversational logic (MT); Ellipsis (H); Experimental pragmatics (M); Grice (H); Implicature and language change (H); Implicitness (H); Interlanguage pragmatics (T); Language and the law (H); Politeness (H); Relevance theory (MT); Speech act theory (MT); Truth-conditional pragmatics (T); Truthfulness (H)
Conversational logic (MT); Context and contextualization (H); Conversational implicature (H); Generative semantics (MT); Grice (H); Philosophy of language (MT); Relevance theory (MT); Speech act theory (MT)
Conversational move → see Move
Conversational storytelling (H24); Conversation analysis (MT); Life stories (H); Narrative (H)
Conversationalism see Lexically triggered veridicality inferences (H22)
Cooperative
 principle see Computational pragmatics (T); Conversational implicature (H); Conversational logic (MT); Creativity in language use (H); Grice (H); Humor (H23); Implicature and language change (H); Implicitness (H); Irony (H); Politeness (H); Silence (H); Truthfulness (H); Universals (H23)

Copenhagen
  circle see Structuralism (MT)
Coreference see Anaphora (H)
Corpus analysis (MM); Collocation and colligation (H); Corpus pragmatics (M); Language acquisition (H); Leech (H); Postcolonial pragmatics (T); Pragmatic markers (H); Psycholinguistics (MT); Statistics (MM); Structuralism (MT); Text and discourse linguistics (T); Translation studies (T); Variational pragmatics (T)
Corpus pragmatics (M); Corpus analysis (MM)
Correlational sociolinguistics (T); Dialectology (MT); Methods in language-attitudes research (M); Pluricentric languages (H23); Sociolinguistics (MT); Statistics (MM)
Coseriu see Structuralism (MT)
Cosmology see Legitimation Code Theory (T25)
Courtroom
  conversation see Forensic linguistics (T); Interpreter-mediated interaction (H); Language and the law (H)
Creativity in language use (H); Authenticity (H); Bühler (H); Code-switching and translanguaging (H22); Cognitive science (MT); Euphemism (H24); Humboldt (H); Language acquisition (H); Think-aloud protocols (M)
Creature construction see Grice (H)
Creole linguistics (MT); Contact (H); Contact linguistics (MT); Creoles and creolization (H); Historical linguistics (MT); Sociolinguistics (MT)
Creoles and creolization (H); Contact (H); Contact linguistics (MT); Creole linguistics (MT); Historical linguistics (MT); Intercultural communication (H); Language contact (H); Sociolinguistics (MT)
Critical Linguistics and Critical Discourse Analysis (MT); Emphasis (H); General semantics (MT); Ideology (H); Intercultural communication (H); Intertextuality (H); Language ideologies (H); Manipulation (H); Marxist linguistics (MT); Mass media (H); Nexus analysis (T); Polyphony (H); Postcolonial pragmatics (T); Text and discourse linguistics (T); Text linguistics (MT); Truthfulness (H)
Critical theory (MT); Intercultural communication (H); Universal and transcendental pragmatics (MT)
Cross-cultural
  communication see Intercultural communication (H)
Cross-cultural
  pragmatics see Directive (H26); Listener response (H); Overlap (H); Text and discourse linguistics (T); Wakimae (H26)
Cross-cultural
  psychology see Cognitive anthropology (MT); Developmental psychology (MT)
Cross-sectional
  method see Developmental psychology (MT)
Crossing (H26); Code-switching and translanguaging (H22); Heteroglossia (H26); Style and styling (H21)
Crying see Emotion display (H)
Culioli, A. see Énonciation (H)
Cultural
  anthropology see Anthropological linguistics (MT); Cognitive anthropology (MT)
Cultural model see Cognitive science (MT)
Cultural scripts (H); Communicative style (H); Componential analysis (MT); Culture (H)
Cultural studies see Ethnography of speaking (MT); Literary pragmatics (MT); Translation studies (T)
Culture (H); Anthropological linguistics (MT); Behaviorism (MT); Boas (H); Context and contextualization (H); Contrastive analysis (MM); Cultural scripts (H); Default interpretations (H); Ethnography (MM); Evolutionary pragmatics (T); Fieldwork (MM); Gumperz (H); Humboldt (H); Ideology (H); Intercultural communication (H); Interjections (H); Mentalism (MT); Mianzi / liàn (H21); Morphopragmatics (T); Objectivism vs. subjectivism (MT); Ọmọlúàbí (H); Politeness (H); Repair (H); Sapir (H); Semiotics (MT); Sociolinguistics (MT); Style and styling (H21); Whorf (H)
Curse see Impoliteness (H)
Cynicism see Irony (H)

D
Data collection/coding/
  analysis see Working with language data (M25)
Davidson, D. see Analytical philosophy (MT)
Deception see Truthfulness (H)
Decolonizing see Postcolonial pragmatics (T)
Deconstruction (MM); Literary pragmatics (MT)
Deduction see Grounded theory (M)
Default interpretations (H)
Default semantics see Default interpretations (H)
Deference see Ọmọlúàbí (H); Ta'ārof (H22)
Definite
  articles see Definiteness (H)
Definite description see Game-theoretical semantics (MT); Reference and descriptions (H)
Definiteness (H)
Degree see Communicative dynamism (H)
Deixis (H); Bühler (H); Context and contextualization (H); Énonciation (H); Honorifics (H); Mental spaces (H); Non-verbal communication (H); Peirce (H); Politeness (H); Universals (H23)
Deletion see Ellipsis (H)
Dementia see Clinical pragmatics (T)
Demonstrative see Indexicals and demonstratives (H)

Denotation → see Cerebral representation of language; Polysemy (H)
Deontic logic (MT); Epistemic logic (MT); Logical semantics (MT); Modal logic (MT); Modality (H)
Dependency see Argument structure (H23); Dependency and valency grammar (MT); Frame semantics (T); Polysemy (H); Predicates and predication (H); Role and reference grammar (MT)
Dependency and valency grammar (MT); Case and semantic roles (H); Case grammar (MT); Role and reference grammar (MT)
Depiction see Gesture research (T)
Derogatory language see Feminism and language (H24); Obscenity, slurs, and taboo (H24)
Derrida, J. see Deconstruction (MM)
Detention hearing → see Police interrogation
Deutero-learning see Bateson (H)
Developmental dyslexia (H); Clinical pragmatics (T); Developmental psychology (MT); Language acquisition (H); Literacy (H); Pragmatic acquisition (H); Psycholinguistics (MT)
Developmental pragmatics see Developmental psychology (MT); Ervin-Tripp, S. (H24); Language acquisition (H); Second language acquisition
Developmental psychology (MT); Bilingualism and multilingualism (H); Cognitive psychology (MT); Ervin-Tripp, S. (H24); Psycholinguistics (MT); Vygotsky (H)
Dewey, J. see Morris (H); Pragmatism (MT)
Diachrony see Language change (H)
Diacritic see Phonetic notation systems (N)
Dialect (H); Anderson (H21); Argument structure (H23); Dialectology (MT); Dialectology and geolinguistic dynamics (T); Folk pragmatics (T); Heteroglossia (H26); Integrational linguistics (T)
Dialect formation see Dialectology and geolinguistic dynamics (T)
Dialect geography see Dialectology (MT)
Dialect leveling/loss see Dialectology and geolinguistic dynamics (T)
Dialectology (MT); Contact linguistics (MT); Correlational sociolinguistics (T); Dialect (H); Dialectology and geolinguistic dynamics (T); Historical linguistics (MT); Reconstruction (MM); Sociolinguistics (MT); Youth language (H25)
Dialectology and geolinguistic dynamics (T)
Dialog modeling see Artificial intelligence (MT); Computational pragmatics (T)
Dialog system see Artificial intelligence (MT); Computational pragmatics (T)
Dialogical analysis (MM); Collaboration in dialogues (H); Context and contextualization (H); Foucault (H); Humboldt (H); Interactional linguistics (T); Peirce (H)
Dialogism see Appraisal (H); Heteroglossia (H26); Intertextuality (H); Stance (H21)
Dialogue see Bakhtin (H); Collaboration in dialogues (H); Interpreter-mediated interaction (H); Polyphony (H)
Diaphor see Metaphor (H)
Digital world see Chronotope (H25); Complaining (H25); Computer-mediated communication (H); Youth language (H25)
Digitization see Working with language data (M25)
Diglossia see Language contact (H)
Dik, S. see Functional grammar (MT)
Diminutive see Morphopragmatics (T)
Direct vs. indirect speech see Reported speech (H)
Directive (H26); Ervin-Tripp, S. (H24); Speech act; Speech act theory (MT)
Discourse see Argumentation in discourse and grammar (H); Bakhtin (H); Cognitive sociology (MT); Critical Linguistics and Critical Discourse Analysis (MT); Discourse markers (H); Ethnography (MM); Foucault (H); Grounding (H); Intertextuality (H); Language psychology (T); Mental spaces (H); Narrative (H); Neuropragmatics (T); Nexus analysis (T); Polyphony (H); Public discourse (H); Social institutions (H); Systemic functional grammar (MT); Text and discourse linguistics (T); Text structure (H)
Discourse act see Functional discourse grammar (T)
Discourse analysis see Channel (H); Cognitive sociology (MT); Common ground (H); Conversation analysis (MT); Corpus analysis (MM); Creole linguistics (MT); Critical Linguistics and Critical Discourse Analysis (MT); Geneva school (MT); Grounding (H); Historical pragmatics (T); Ideology (H); Mass media (H); Multimodality (H); Nigerian hospital setting discourse (H24); Prague school (MT); Rhetoric (MT); Social psychology (MT); Structuralism (MT); Stylistics (MT); Text and discourse linguistics (T); Text linguistics (MT); Truthfulness (H)
Discourse attuning see Accommodation theory (MT)
Discourse completion test see Intercultural communication (H)
Discourse focus see Anaphora (H)
Discourse genre see Genre (H)
Discourse linking see Discourse representation theory (MT)
Discourse markers (H); Historical pragmatics (T); Interjections (H); Polyphony (H); Pragmatic markers (H); Pragmatic particles (H)
Discourse mode see Register (H)

Discourse representation theory (MT); Default interpretations (H); Game-theoretical semantics (MT); Logical semantics (MT); Montague and categorial grammar (MT); Situation semantics (MT); Tense and aspect (H)
Discourse sociolinguistics see Critical Linguistics and Critical Discourse Analysis (MT)
Discourse topic see Consciousness and language (H)
Discursive ethics see Universal and transcendental pragmatics (MT)
Discursive formation see Foucault (H)
Discursive order see Foucault (H)
Discursive psychology see Authority (H); Language psychology (T); Motivation (H)
Discursive relation see Legitimation Code Theory (T25)
Dismissal see Impoliteness (H)
Displacement see Adaptability (H)
Distinctive feature see Jakobson (H21)
Divergence see Accommodation theory (MT)
Diversity see Anderson (H21); Language maintenance and shift (H21); Superdiversity (H21)
Doctor-patient interaction → see Medical interaction
Document design see Applied linguistics (MT)
Donnellan, K. see Reference and descriptions (H)
Double bind see Bateson (H)
Double object construction see Argument structure (H23)
Drift see Language change (H)
Ducrot, O. see Argumentation theory (MT); Énonciation (H); Polyphony (H)
Dummett, M. see Analytical philosophy (MT)
Durkheim, Emile see Sociology of language (T)
Dyadic interaction see Conversation types (H); Statistics (MM)

Dynamic semantic functions see Communicative dynamism (H)
Dynamic semantics see Presupposition (H)
Dyslexia see Orthography and cognition (H22)
Dysphasia see Cerebral division of labour in verbal communication (H)
Dysphemism see Obscenity, slurs, and taboo (H24)

E
E-mail communication see Computer-mediated communication (H)
Ebonics see 'Other' representation (H)
Education see Applied linguistics (MT); Code-switching and translanguaging (H22); Ideology (H); Language learning in immersion and CLIL classrooms (H); Language rights (H); Linguistic landscape studies (T); Literacy (H); Translanguaging pedagogy (T)
Effectiveness see Communicative success vs. failure (H); Swearing (H25)
Egocentric speech see Vygotsky (H)
Elicitation (MM); Fieldwork (MM); Interview (MM); Methods in language-attitudes research (M)
Elite multilingualism ()
Ellipsis (H); Argument structure (H23)
Emancipation see Feminism and language (H24); Postcolonial pragmatics (T)
Emancipatory pragmatics see Postcolonial pragmatics (T)
Embedding see Frame analysis (M)
Embodied interaction (H23)
Embodiment (H); Embodied interaction (H23); Gesture research (T); Humor (H23); Pragmatics of script (H22)
Emergence see Adaptability (H)
Emergent grammar (T)
Emotion display (H); Laughter (H); Silence (H)
Emotions (H21); Appraisal (H); Emotion display (H); Impoliteness (H); Obscenity,

slurs, and taboo (H24); Swearing (H25)
Emphasis (H)
Encoding see Orthography and cognition (H22)
Endangered languages see Language ecology (H)
Engagement see Appraisal (H); Evidentiality (H22); Nexus analysis (T)
Engels, Friedrich see Ideology (H)
English (as a global language) see Linguistic landscape studies (T); Postcolonial pragmatics (T)
Énonciation (H); Benveniste (H)
Enregisterment see Crossing (H26)
Entailment see Implicitness (H); Lexically triggered veridicality inferences (H22)
Entrenchment see Conceptual integration (H)
Enunciation see Benveniste (H); Polyphony (H)
Environment see Context and contextualization (H); Gesture research (T); Tactile sign languages (H21)
Epiphor see Metaphor (H)
Epistemic authority see Conversational storytelling (H24); Evidentiality (H22)
Epistemic dynamics see Epistemic logic (MT)
Epistemic logic (MT); Deontic logic (MT); Logical semantics (MT); Modal logic (MT); Modality (H); Possible worlds semantics (MT)
Epistemic relation see Legitimation Code Theory (T25)
Epistemology (MT); Austin (H); Foucault (H); Objectivism vs. subjectivism (MT); Ontology (MT); Perception and language (H)
Epistemology of testimony (T)
Erklären vs. Verstehen see Grounded theory (M)
Error analysis (MM); Contrastive analysis (MM)
Ervin-Tripp, S. (H24); Developmental psychology (MT);

Language acquisition (H);
Sociolinguistics (MT)
Ethnicity see Crossing (H26);
Culture (H); Humor (H23);
Intercultural communication (H);
Language dominance and
minorization (H); Language
policy, language planning and
standardization (H)
Ethnographic
semantics see Anthropological
linguistics (MT); Taxonomy (MM)
Ethnography (MM);
Anderson (H21); Anthropological
linguistics (MT); Bourdieu (H);
Developmental psychology (MT);
Ethnography of speaking (MT);
Fieldwork (MM); Hymes (H26);
Linguistic landscape studies (T);
Social media research (T)
Ethnography of
communication see Ethnography
of speaking (MT); Hymes (H26)
Ethnography of speaking (MT);
Anthropological linguistics (MT);
Context and
contextualization (H);
Conversation analysis (MT);
Ervin-Tripp, S. (H24);
Gumperz (H); Hymes (H26);
Interactional
sociolinguistics (MT);
Intercultural communication (H);
Nexus analysis (T); Phatic
communion (H); Style and
styling (H21)
Ethnomethodology (MT);
Cognitive sociology (MT);
Context and
contextualization (H);
Conversation analysis (MT);
Humor (H23); Interactional
sociolinguistics (MT); Language
psychology (T); Membership
categorization analysis (T);
Phenomenology (MT); (The)
pragmatic perspective (M);
Sacks (H); Social
psychology (MT); Symbolic
interactionism (MT)
Ethnopoetics see Hymes (H26)
Ethnoscience see Anthropological
linguistics (MT)
Ethogenics see Social
psychology (MT)

Euphemism (H24);
Morphopragmatics (T);
Obscenity, slurs, and taboo (H24)
Evaluation see Appraisal (H);
Chronotope (H25); Emphasis (H);
Stance (H21)
Evaluation task see Methods in
language-attitudes research (M)
Event representation (H22)
Event types see Event
representation (H22)
Event-related
potential see Cognitive
science (MT); Language
acquisition (H)
Evidence see Evidentiality (H22)
Evidentiality (H22); Appraisal (H);
Authority (H); Modality (H);
Stance (H21)
Evolution
(theory) see Adaptability (H);
Evolutionary pragmatics (T)
Evolutionary pragmatics (T)
Executive function see Clinical
pragmatics (T)
Exemplar
model see Psycholinguistics (MT)
Expectation see Frame analysis (M);
Mediated performatives (H)
Experimental pragmatics (M);
Experimentation (MM)
Experimentation (MM); Cognitive
psychology (MT); Cognitive
science (MT);
Ethnomethodology (MT);
Experimental pragmatics (M);
Methods in language-attitudes
research (M); Orthography and
cognition (H22);
Psycholinguistics (MT); Sound
symbolism (H); Statistics (MM);
Think-aloud protocols (M);
Variational pragmatics (T)
Expertise see Cognitive
sociology (MT); Forensic
linguistics (T)
Explaining vs. understanding →
see Erklären vs. Verstehen
Explanation see Linguistic
explanation (MM)
Explicature see Implicitness (H);
Truth-conditional pragmatics (T)
Expression → see Functions of
language
Extension → see Intension vs.
extension

F
Face see Directive (H26);
Goffman (H); Impoliteness (H);
Mianzi / lian (H21);
Politeness (H); Silence (H);
Ta'ārof (H22); Wakimae (H26)
Face-to-face
interaction see Accommodation
theory (MT); Cognitive
sociology (MT); Computer-
mediated communication (H);
Conversation analysis (MT);
Intercultural communication (H);
Prosody (H)
Facebook see Social media
research (T)
Factivity see Lexically triggered
veridicality inferences (H22)
False friends see The multilingual
lexicon (H)
Familiarity see Information
structure (H)
Feedback see Adaptability (H);
Tactile sign languages (H21)
Feeling(s) see Appraisal (H)
Felicity condition see Speech act
theory (MT)
Feminism and language (H24)
Ferguson, C. see Register (H)
Field see Register (H)
Fieldwork (MM); Anthropological
linguistics (MT); Boas (H);
Elicitation (MM);
Ethnography (MM); Ethnography
of speaking (MT);
Interview (MM); Malinowski (H)
Figure vs.
ground see Grounding (H)
Figures of speech (H); Cultural
scripts (H); Emphasis (H)
File change
semantics see Computational
linguistics (MT); Discourse
representation theory (MT)
Fillmore, C. J. see Case
grammar (MT); Frame
semantics (T)
Firth, J. R. (H); Firthian
linguistics (MT); Halliday (H26);
Register (H); Systemic functional
grammar (MT)
Firthian linguistics (MT); Context
and contextualization (H);
Firth (H); Phatic
communion (H); Systemic
functional grammar (MT)

Flexibility see Primate communication (H)
Focalisation see Tense and aspect (H)
Focalizer see Functional sentence perspective (H)
Focus → see Topic vs. focus
Focus domain see Argument structure (H23)
Focus structure see Role and reference grammar (MT)
Folk
 classification see Anthropological linguistics (MT); Cognitive anthropology (MT); Language ideologies (H); Metalinguistic awareness (H); Taxonomy (MM)
Folk linguistics see Socio-onomastics (T)
Folk pragmatics (T); Methods in language-attitudes research (M)
Folk psychology see Philosophy of mind (MT)
Footing see Frame analysis (M); Goffman (H); Participation (H)
Foregrounding see Grounding (H)
Foreigner talk see Intercultural communication (H); Register (H)
Forensic linguistics (T); Applied linguistics (MT)
Form vs. function see Corpus pragmatics (M); Sapir (H)
Form-function mapping → see Form vs. function
Formal
 dialectics see Argumentation theory (MT)
Formal linguistics see Linguistic explanation (MM)
Formal pragmatics (MT); Analytical philosophy (MT); Logical semantics (MT); Montague and categorial grammar (MT)
Formality see Conversation types (H); Register (H)
Formulaic language (H26) (); Routine formula
Formulation see Rhetoric (MT)
Foucault, M. (H); Critical theory (MT); Ideology (H); Jargon (H); Power and the role of language (H25)
Frame (analysis) (M); Artificial intelligence (MT); Bateson (H); Cognitive science (MT); Emphasis (H); Frame semantics (T); Gesture research (T); Goffman (H);

Humor (H23); Mental spaces (H); Metalinguistic awareness (H); Non-verbal communication (H); (The) pragmatic perspective (M)
Frame semantics (T); Collocation and colligation (H); Context and contextualization (H); Dependency and valency grammar (MT); Event representation (H22); Lexical field analysis (MT); Lexical semantics (T)
Frankfurt school → see Adorno; Habermas
Frege, G. see Analytical philosophy (MT); Intensional logic (MT); Reference and descriptions (H); Semantics vs. pragmatics (T); Speech act theory (MT)
Fremdverstehen see Grounded theory (M)
Frequency see Markedness (H); Statistics (MM); Swearing (H25)
Functional discourse grammar (T)
Functional
 explanation see Linguistic explanation (MM)
Functional grammar (MT); Case and semantic roles (H); Case grammar (MT); Mathesius (H); Prague school (MT); Predicates and predication (H); Systemic functional grammar (MT); Word order (H)
Functional sentence
 perspective (H); Communicative dynamism (H); Mathesius (H); Prague school (MT); Word order (H)
Functionalism vs. formalism (MT); Autonomous vs. non-autonomous syntax (MT); Cognitive science (MT); Communicative dynamism (H); Emergent grammar (T); Linguistic explanation (MM); Mathesius (H); (The) pragmatic perspective (M); Translation studies (T)
Functions of
 language see Bühler (H); Emotion display (H); Evolutionary pragmatics (T); Functional discourse grammar (T); Functionalism vs. formalism (MT); Historical

politeness (T); Impoliteness (H); Jakobson (H21); Participation (H); Prague school (MT); Relational ritual (H); Silence (H); Systemic functional grammar (MT)
Fund see Predicates and predication (H)
Fuzziness → see Vagueness
Fuzzy set
 theory see Categorization (H); Lexical semantics (T)

G

Game-theoretical semantics (MT); Discourse representation theory (MT); Logical semantics (MT); Model-theoretic semantics (MT)
Gapping see Ellipsis (H)
Garfinkel,
 H. see Ethnomethodology (MT)
GDPR see Working with language data (M25)
Gender (H); Authority (H); Caste and language (H23); Computer-mediated communication (H); Critical Linguistics and Critical Discourse Analysis (MT); Feminism and language (H24); Humor (H23); Identity (H24); Interjections (H); Laughter (H); Listener response (H); Overlap (H); Silence (H); Swearing (H25); Workplace interaction (H25)
General rhetoric see Rhetoric (MT)
General semantics (MT); Critical Linguistics and Critical Discourse Analysis (MT)
Generalized
 catastrophe see Catastrophe theory (MT)
Generalized phrase structure grammar see Computational linguistics (MT); Construction grammar (MT); Interpretive semantics (MT)
Generative semantics (MT); Componential analysis (MT); Conceptual semantics (T); Conversational logic (MT); Interpretive semantics (MT); (The) pragmatic perspective (M)
Generative(-transformational) linguistics see Attention and language (H); Chomskyan

linguistics (MT); Cognitive linguistics (MT); Computational linguistics (MT); Creativity in language use (H); Historical linguistics (MT); Interpretive semantics (MT); Language acquisition (H); Language change (H); Lexical semantics (T)
Genetic linguistics see Historical linguistics (MT); Language change (H); Reconstruction (MM)
Geneva school (MT); Structuralism (MT); Text and discourse linguistics (T)
Genre (H); Bakhtin (H); Channel (H); Conversation types (H); Conversational logic (MT); Narrative (H); Tense and aspect (H); Text and discourse linguistics (T); Text type (H)
Geographical origin see Laughter (H)
Geolinguistics see Contact linguistics (MT); Dialectology and geolinguistic dynamics (T); Linguistic landscape studies (T)
Gestalt psychology see Behaviorism (MT); Cognitive psychology (MT); Metaphor (H)
Gesticulation see Gesture research (T)
Gesture see Communication (H); Gesture research (T); Non-verbal communication (H); Primate communication (H); Prosody (H)
Gesture research (T); Non-verbal communication (H)
Given vs. new see Argument structure (H23); Argumentation in discourse and grammar (H); Computational pragmatics (T); Definiteness (H); Functional sentence perspective (H); Information structure (H); Word order (H)
Globalization (H25); Code-switching and translanguaging (H22); Dialectology and geolinguistic dynamics (T); Language dominance and minorization (H); Power and the role of language (H25); Translanguaging pedagogy (T); Youth language (H25)
Glossematics see Semiotics (MT); Structuralism (MT)
Glottochronology see Historical linguistics (MT)
Goffman, E. (H); Conversation analysis (MT); Frame analysis (M); Participation (H); Politeness (H); Public discourse (H); Reported speech (H); Symbolic interactionism (MT)
Government and binding theory see Chomskyan linguistics (MT); Construction grammar (MT); Interpretive semantics (MT)
Gradience see Categorization (H)
Grammar see Argumentation in discourse and grammar (H); Leech (H); Nigerian hospital setting discourse (H24)
Grammatical constraints see Code-switching (H)
Grammatical metaphor see Metaphor (H)
Grammatical relations see Agency and language (H); Polysemy (H); Role and reference grammar (MT)
Grammatical status see Grammaticalization and pragmatics (T)
Grammaticalization see Constructional analysis (T); Emergent grammar (T); Implicature and language change (H); Language change (H); Metaphor (H); Modality (H); Negation (H); Pragmatic markers (H); Predicates and predication (H)
Grammaticalization and pragmatics (T)
Grammatization see Emergent grammar (T)
Gramsci, A. see Hegemony (H23); Marxist linguistics (MT)
Greeting see Ọmọlúàbí (H); Taʼārof (H22)
Grice, H. P. (H); Analytical philosophy (MT); Clinical pragmatics (T); Conversational implicature (H); Conversational logic (MT); Default interpretations (H); Humor (H23); Semantics vs. pragmatics (T); Silence (H); Speech act theory (MT); Truth-conditional pragmatics (T); Truthfulness (H); Universals (H23)
Grounded theory (M)
Grounding (H); Anaphora (H); Computational pragmatics (T); Text and discourse linguistics (T)
Guillaume, G. see Énonciation (H)
Gumperz, J. J. (H); Anthropological linguistics (MT); Communicative success vs. failure (H); Culture (H); Ethnography of speaking (MT); Interactional sociolinguistics (MT); Intercultural communication (H); Prosody (H); Register (H)

H

Habermas, J. see Critical theory (MT); Ideology (H); Public discourse (H); Universal and transcendental pragmatics (MT)
Habitus see Anderson (H21); Bourdieu (H); Communication (H); Lifestyle (H)
Half-truth see Truthfulness (H)
Halliday, M. A. K. (H26); Critical Linguistics and Critical Discourse Analysis (MT); Firthian linguistics (MT); Genre (H); Jargon (H); Phatic communion (H); Register (H); Social semiotics (T); Systemic functional grammar (MT)
Harold Garfinkel and pragmatics (H); Conversation analysis (MT); Ethnomethodology (MT); Metapragmatics (MT); Sacks (H)
Head-driven phrase structure grammar see Computational linguistics (MT); Construction grammar (MT); Formal pragmatics (MT); Interpretive semantics (MT)
Hearer see Appraisal (H); Mass media (H)
Hegemony (H23); Ideology (H); Intertextuality (H); Language ecology (H); Metalinguistic awareness (H); Postcolonial pragmatics (T)

Hemisphere dominance see Neurolinguistics (MT)
Heritage language see Language maintenance and shift (H21)
Hermeneutics (M); Analytical philosophy (MT); Anthropological linguistics (MT); Cognitive linguistics (MT); Cohesion and coherence (H); Conversation analysis (MT); Language psychology (T); Literary pragmatics (MT); Structuralism (MT); Truthfulness (H); Universal and transcendental pragmatics (MT)
Heterogeneity see Language dominance and minorization (H)
Heteroglossia (H26); Appraisal (H); Bakhtin (H); Dialogism; Ideology (H); Intertextuality (H); Polyphony (H)
Heterosemy see Polysemy (H)
Hierarchy see Nigerian hospital setting discourse (H24); Power and the role of language (H25)
Historical linguistics (MT); Borrowing (H); Creole linguistics (MT); Creoles and creolization (H); Dialectology (MT); Historical pragmatics (T); Language change (H); Reconstruction (MM); de Saussure (H); Typology (MT)
Historical politeness (T)
Historical pragmatics (T); Historical linguistics (MT); Interjections (H); Mass media (H); Text and discourse linguistics (T)
Historical sociolinguistics (T); Correlational sociolinguistics (T); Dialectology and geolinguistic dynamics (T); Historical linguistics (MT); Historical pragmatics (T); Interactional sociolinguistics (MT); Language change (H); Sociolinguistics (MT)
History see Critical Linguistics and Critical Discourse Analysis (MT); Dialectology (MT); Hegemony (H23)
Homogeneity see Anderson (H21); Metalinguistic awareness (H)
Homogenisation see 'Other' representation (H)
Homonymy see Indeterminacy and negotiation (H); Obscenity, slurs, and taboo (H24); Polysemy (H)
Honorifics (H); Politeness (H); Terms of address (H); Universals (H23); Wakimae (H26)
Humboldt, W. von (H)
Humor (H23); Computer-mediated communication (H); Emotion display (H); Ervin-Tripp, S. (H24); Irony (H); Laughter (H); 'Other' representation (H); Truthfulness (H)
Hybridity see Genre (H); Intensional logic (MT); Intertextuality (H); 'Other' representation (H); Presupposition (H)
Hymes, D. (H26); Anthropological linguistics (MT); Culture (H); Ethnography of speaking (MT)
Hyperlink see Social media research (T)
Hyponymy see Polysemy (H)

I
I-principle see Anaphora (H); Semantics vs. pragmatics (T)
Iconicity (H); Jakobson (H21); Language change (H); Sound symbolism (H)
Identifiability see Definiteness (H)
Identity (H24); Age and language use (H); Anderson (H21); Chronotope (H25); Dialectology and geolinguistic dynamics (T); Feminism and language (H24); Gumperz (H); Ideology (H); Language maintenance and shift (H21); Laughter (H); Life stories (H); Membership categorization analysis (T); Motivation and language (H); Pluricentric languages (H23); Postcolonial pragmatics (T); Pragmatics of script (H22); Social class and language (H); Social media research (T); Superdiversity (H21); Swearing (H25); Teasing (H25); Translanguaging pedagogy (T); Variational pragmatics (T); Youth language (H25)
Ideology (H); Critical Linguistics and Critical Discourse Analysis (MT); Culture (H); Hegemony (H23); Honorifics (H); Manipulation (H); Marxist linguistics (MT); Mass media (H); Nigerian hospital setting discourse (H24); Postcolonial pragmatics (T); Public discourse (H); Social psychology (MT); Social semiotics (T); Workplace interaction (H25)
Idiolect see Forensic linguistics (T); Integrational linguistics (T)
Idéologues see Humboldt (H)
Illiteracy see Literacy (H)
Illocution see Directive (H26); Functional discourse grammar (T); Functional discourse grammar (T); Functional discourse grammar (T); Functional grammar (MT); Indeterminacy and negotiation (H); Intentionality (H); Modality (H); Non-verbal communication (H); Speech act theory (MT)
Illocutionary force see Speech act theory (MT)
Illocutionary force-indicating device see Corpus pragmatics (M); Speech act theory (MT)
Imagined community see Anderson (H21)
Immersion see Language learning in immersion and CLIL classrooms (H)
Implication see Lexically triggered veridicality inferences (H22)
Implicature → see Conventional implicature; Conversational implicature (H); Implicature and language change (H)
Implicature and language change (H); Conventional implicature; Conversational implicature (H)
Implicitness (H); Argument structure (H23); Cerebral representation of language; Discourse markers (H); Emphasis (H); Lexically triggered veridicality inferences (H22); Methods in language-attitudes research (M); Truth-conditional pragmatics (T)
Implicitness see Implicitness (H)
Impoliteness (H); Euphemism (H24); Historical

politeness (T); Obscenity, slurs, and taboo (H24); Politeness (H); Swearing (H25); Teasing (H25); Wakimae (H26)
Incongruity resolution see Humor (H23)
Indeterminacy and negotiation (H); Ellipsis (H); Integrational linguistics (T); Truthfulness (H)
Indexicalism see Contextualism (T)
Indexicality (); Anthropological linguistics (MT); Ethnomethodology (MT); Gesture research (T); Jakobson (H21); Language change (H); Language psychology (T); Metalinguistic awareness (H); Prosody (H); Stance (H21); Truth-conditional semantics (MT)
Indexicals and demonstratives (H); Anaphora (H); Context and contextualization (H)
Indifference see Postcolonial pragmatics (T)
Indirect speech act see Activity types and pragmatic acts (H26)
Indirectness (); Complaining (H25); Conversational logic (MT); Discourse representation theory (MT); Leech (H)
Individualism see Sociology of language (T)
Individuality see Intentionality (H)
Induction see Grounded theory (M)
Industrialization see Sociology of language (T); Workplace interaction (H25)
Inequality see Power and the role of language (H25)
(In)felicity see Communicative success vs. failure (H)
Inferencing → see Cerebral representation of language; Clinical pragmatics (T); Cognitive psychology (MT); Cognitive sociology (MT); Computational pragmatics (T); Conceptual semantics (T); Default interpretations (H); Discourse representation theory (MT); Ellipsis (H); Emphasis (H); Evidentiality (H22); Experimental pragmatics (M); Figures of speech (H); Grice (H);

Gumperz (H); Implicature and language change (H); Irony (H); Language psychology (T); Lexically triggered veridicality inferences (H22); Prosody (H); Speech act theory (MT)
Informal logic see Argumentation theory (MT)
Information processing see Attention and language (H); Cognitive psychology (MT); Cognitive science (MT); Comprehension vs. production (H); Evidentiality (H22); Text comprehension (H)
Information source see Evidentiality (H22)
Information structure (H); Argument structure (H23); Argumentation in discourse and grammar (H); Computational pragmatics (T); Discourse markers (H); Emphasis (H); Narrative (H); Signed language pragmatics (T); Tense and aspect (H); Text and discourse linguistics (T); Text structure (H); Word order (H)
Informativeness see Definiteness (H); Humor (H23); Information structure (H); Presupposition (H)
Informing see Mediated performatives (H)
Innateness see Language acquisition (H)
Inner speech see Vygotsky (H)
Instagram see Social media research (T)
Institutional interaction (H23); Social institutions (H)
Institutional role see Laughter (H)
Institutional setting see Complaining (H25); Nigerian hospital setting discourse (H24); Social institutions (H)
Instructional science see Applied linguistics (MT)
Instrumentality see Evolutionary pragmatics (T)
Insult see Impoliteness (H); Obscenity, slurs, and taboo (H24)
Integration see Language rights (H)
Integrational linguistics (T); Pragmatics of script (H22)
Integrity see Truthfulness (H)

Intension vs. extension see Intensional logic (MT); Notation in formal semantics (MN)
Intensional logic (MT); Logical semantics (MT)
Intensional semantics see Analytical philosophy (MT)
Intention see Artificial intelligence (MT); Computational pragmatics (T); Directive (H26); Grice (H); Intentionality (H); Irony (H); Mediated performatives (H); Neuropragmatics (T); Philosophy of action (MT); Philosophy of mind (MT); Primate communication (H); Speech act theory (MT); Truthfulness (H)
Intentionality (H); Agency and language (H); Communication (H); Impoliteness (H); Philosophy of mind (MT)
Interaction-organization theory see Metaphor (H)
Interactional analysis see Multimodality (H)
Interactional linguistics (T); Emergent grammar (T); Linear Unit Grammar (T)
Interactional relation see Legitimation Code Theory (T25)
Interactional sense-making → see Meaning construction
Interactional sociolinguistics (MT); Code-switching (H); Communicative style (H); Context and contextualization (H); Conversation analysis (MT); Ethnography of speaking (MT); Ethnomethodology (MT); Gumperz (H); Intercultural communication (H); Metapragmatics (MT); Mianzi / lian (H21); Nexus analysis (T); (The) pragmatic perspective (M); Sociolinguistics (MT); Workplace interaction (H25)
Interactive failure → see Communication failure
Interactive-activation model see Psycholinguistics (MT)

Interactivity see Computer-mediated communication (H); Conversational storytelling (H24); Deixis (H); Functional discourse grammar (T); Psycholinguistics (MT); Reported speech (H)
Intercultural communication (H); Aisatsu (H); Anthropological linguistics (MT); Applied linguistics (MT); Bilingualism and multilingualism (H); Code-switching (H); Communication (H); Communicative success vs. failure (H); Contact linguistics (MT); Context and contextualization (H); Contrastive analysis (MM); Creoles and creolization (H); Critical Linguistics and Critical Discourse Analysis (MT); Critical theory (MT); Crossing (H26); Culture (H); Ethnography of speaking (MT); Gumperz (H); Interactional sociolinguistics (MT); Interlanguage pragmatics (T); Language and the law (H); Language policy, language planning and standardization (H); Non-verbal communication (H); Text and discourse linguistics (T); Truthfulness (H)
Intercultural politeness research →
Interference see Contact linguistics (MT); Language contact (H); Psycholinguistics (MT)
Interjections (H)
Interlanguage pragmatics (T); Contrastive analysis (MM); Conversational implicature (H); Intercultural communication (H); Politeness (H)
Internalization see Foucault (H)
Internet see Chronotope (H25); Computer-mediated communication (H); Social media research (T)
Interpersonal relation see Complaining (H25); Intentionality (H); Mianzi / lian (H21); Swearing (H25)
Interpreter-mediated interaction (H)

Interpretive processes → see Inferencing
Interpretive semantics (MT); Chomskyan linguistics (MT); Conceptual semantics (T); Generative semantics (MT)
Interpretive sociolinguistics see Interactional sociolinguistics (MT)
Interrogative see Lexically triggered veridicality inferences (H22)
Interruption see Overlap (H)
Intersubjectivity see Appraisal (H); Bourdieu (H); Bühler (H); Collaboration in dialogues (H); Communication (H); Language psychology (T); Peirce (H)
Intertextuality (H); Bakhtin (H); Computer-mediated communication (H); Heteroglossia (H26); Polyphony (H)
Interview (MM); Elicitation (MM); Fieldwork (MM); Methods in language-attitudes research (M)
Intervision (M26) ()
Intimacy see Laughter (H)
Intonation see Communicative dynamism (H); Information structure (H); Markedness (H); Prosody (H)
Intonation unit see Consciousness and language (H)
Intuition and introspection (MM); Cognitive science (MT)
Involvement → see Affect
Irony (H); Experimental pragmatics (M); Frame analysis (M); Humor (H23); Polyphony (H)
Isomorphism see Iconicity (H)
Isotopy see Humor (H23)

J
Jakobson, R. (H21); Emotions (H21); Hymes (H26); Participation (H); Phatic communion (H); Prague school (MT); Structuralism (MT)
James, W. see Morris (H); Pragmatism (MT)
Jargon (H); Nigerian hospital setting discourse (H24)
Joke see Humor (H23); Irony (H)
Journalism see Mass media (H); Mediated performatives (H)
Judgement see Appraisal (H)

Jury instruction see Forensic linguistics (T)

K
Kilivila see Malinowski (H)
Kinesics see Non-verbal communication (H)
Knowledge see Artificial intelligence (MT); Austin (H); Authority (H); Epistemology of testimony (T); Foucault (H); Power and the role of language (H25)
Knowledge representation see Artificial intelligence (MT); Cognitive psychology (MT); Cognitive science (MT); Connectionism (MT)
Koineization see Dialectology and geolinguistic dynamics (T)
Kripke, S. see Reference and descriptions (H)
Kristeva, J. see Intertextuality (H)

L
L2 → see Second language acquisition
Labov, W. see Correlational sociolinguistics (T); Creole linguistics (MT); Sociolinguistics (MT)
Language acquisition (H); Developmental psychology (MT); Discourse markers (H); Ervin-Tripp, S. (H24); Interjections (H); Irony (H); Jakobson (H21); Literacy (H); Metalinguistic awareness (H); Morphopragmatics (T); Pragmatic particles (H); Psycholinguistics (MT); Repair (H); Text and discourse linguistics (T); Text structure (H); Vygotsky (H)
Language acquisition device see Language acquisition (H)
Language and the law (H)
Language and thought see Boas (H); Consciousness and language (H); Developmental psychology (MT); Embodiment (H); Humboldt (H); Perception and language (H); Sapir (H); Vygotsky (H); Whorf (H)

Language attitudes → see Attitude; Methods in language-attitudes research (M); Pluricentric languages (H23)
Language change (H); Borrowing (H); Contact linguistics (MT); Correlational sociolinguistics (T); Creativity in language use (H); Creoles and creolization (H); Dialectology (MT); Dialectology and geolinguistic dynamics (T); Genre (H); Historical linguistics (MT); Historical politeness (T); Historical pragmatics (T); Implicature and language change (H); Language maintenance and shift (H21); Morphopragmatics (T); Obscenity, slurs, and taboo (H24); Polysemy (H); Pragmatic markers (H); de Saussure (H); Structuralism (MT); Superdiversity (H21); Text and discourse linguistics (T); Text structure (H); Youth language (H25)
Language choice see Bilingualism and multilingualism (H); Ervin-Tripp, S. (H24); Intercultural communication (H); Language policy, language planning and standardization (H)
Language comprehension see Comprehension vs. production (H)
Language conflict see Identity (H24); Language contact (H); Language dominance and minorization (H)
Language contact (H); Borrowing (H); Contact (H); Language change (H); Literacy (H)
Language death see Language contact (H); Language ecology (H); Language rights (H)
Language disorders → see Cerebral representation of language; Clinical pragmatics (T); Neurolinguistics (MT)
Language dominance and minorization (H); Language ecology (H); Pluricentric languages (H23)
Language ecology (H)

Language for special purposes (LSP) see Applied linguistics (MT); Genre (H)
Language game see Game-theoretical semantics (MT); Wittgenstein (H)
Language generation and interpretation → see Natural language generation and interpretation
Language ideologies (H); Bilingualism and multilingualism (H); Bourdieu (H); Feminism and language (H24); Identity (H24); Ideology (H); Language dominance and minorization (H); Literacy (H); Metalinguistic awareness (H); Wakimae (H26)
Language impairment → see Cerebral representation of language; Clinical pragmatics (T); Neurolinguistics (MT); Perception and language (H)
Language learning in immersion and CLIL classrooms (H)
Language maintenance and shift (H21); Contact (H); Interjections (H); Language ecology (H); Language policy, language planning and standardization (H); Translanguaging pedagogy (T)
Language pathology → see Cerebral representation of language; Clinical pragmatics (T); Language acquisition (H); Perception and language (H)
Language planning see Language policy, language planning and standardization (H)
Language policy, language planning and standardization (H); Applied linguistics (MT); Authority (H); Bilingualism and multilingualism (H); Contact linguistics (MT); Feminism and language (H24); Intercultural communication (H); Language ideologies (H); Language maintenance and shift (H21); Linguistic landscape studies (T); Literacy (H); Sociolinguistics (MT)
Language processing → see Natural language processing
Language psychology (T)

Language rights (H)
Language shift see Language maintenance and shift (H21)
Language teaching see Applied linguistics (MT); Code-switching and translanguaging (H22); Error analysis (MM); Ideology (H); Interlanguage pragmatics (T); Language learning in immersion and CLIL classrooms (H); Motivation and language (H); Orthography and cognition (H22); Pragmatic particles (H); Register (H); Translanguaging pedagogy (T)
Language technology see Artificial intelligence (MT)
Language universals see Universals (H23)
Language variation see Dialect (H); Dialectology (MT); Variational pragmatics (T)
Languaging see Code-switching and translanguaging (H22); Translanguaging pedagogy (T)
Langue vs. parole see de Saussure (H); Structuralism (MT)
Lateralization see Neurolinguistics (MT)
Laughable see Laughter (H)
Laughter (H); Emotion display (H)
Learnability see Language acquisition (H)
Least-effort hypothesis see Semantics vs. pragmatics (T)
Lect see Dialect (H)
Leech, G. (H)
Left vs. right hemisphere → see Cerebral representation of language; Clinical pragmatics (T); Neurolinguistics (MT)
Legal aspects of research see Working with language data (M25)
Legal language see Applied linguistics (MT); Authority (H); Forensic linguistics (T); Language and the law (H); Sequence (H); Silence (H)
Legal settings see Forensic linguistics (T)
Legitimation see Foucault (H)
Legitimation Code Theory (T25)
Lesion syndrome see Neurolinguistics (MT)
Lexical bundle/cluster/string see Collocation and colligation (H)

Lexical decomposition see Componential analysis (MT)
Lexical field analysis (MT); Componential analysis (MT); Lexical semantics (T); Structuralism (MT)
Lexical functional grammar (MT); Computational linguistics (MT)
Lexical primitive → see Semantic primitive
Lexical semantics (T); Componential analysis (MT); Frame semantics (T); Lexical field analysis (MT); Markedness (H); Metonymy (H); Polysemy (H); Vygotsky (H)
Lexicalist hypothesis see Interpretive semantics (MT)
Lexically triggered veridicality inferences (H22)
Lexicase see Case grammar (MT)
Lexico-grammar see Metaphor (H)
Lexicography see Discourse markers (H); Frame semantics (T); Pragmatic particles (H)
Lexicology see Caste and language (H23)
Lexicometry see Critical Linguistics and Critical Discourse Analysis (MT)
Lexicon see Collocation and colligation (H); Comprehension vs. production (H); Default interpretations (H); Discourse representation theory (MT); Euphemism (H24); Feminism and language (H24); Interactional linguistics (T); Language acquisition (H); Lexically triggered veridicality inferences (H22); The multilingual lexicon (H); Obscenity, slurs, and taboo (H24); Predicates and predication (H); Word (H)
Lexicostatistics see Historical linguistics (MT)
Life stories (H); Conversational storytelling (H24); Narrative (H)
Lifestyle (H)
Linear modification see Communicative dynamism (H)
Linear Unit Grammar (T)

Linearization see Word order (H)
Lingua franca see Pragmatics of script (H22)
Linguicide see Language ecology (H); Language rights (H)
Linguistic action verb → see Metapragmatic term
Linguistic activism see Feminism and language (H24)
Linguistic anthropology see Hymes (H26)
Linguistic atlas see Dialectology (MT)
Linguistic determinism see Manipulation (H); Perception and language (H)
Linguistic diversity see Heteroglossia (H26); Language ecology (H)
Linguistic dominance see Language ecology (H); Language rights (H)
Linguistic engineering see Artificial intelligence (MT)
Linguistic explanation (MM); Functionalism vs. formalism (MT)
Linguistic genocide → see Linguicide
Linguistic hierarchy see Language dominance and minorization (H)
Linguistic human rights see Language dominance and minorization (H); Language ecology (H); Language rights (H)
Linguistic imperialism see Language ecology (H)
Linguistic landscape studies (T)
Linguistic relativity (principle) see Anthropological linguistics (MT); Boas (H); Cognitive anthropology (MT); Culture (H); Lexical semantics (T); Manipulation (H); 'Other' representation (H); Perception and language (H); Sapir (H); Speech act theory (MT); Taxonomy (MM); Whorf (H)
Linguistic repertoire see Gumperz (H)
Linguistic turn see Analytical philosophy (MT)
Linking see Conceptual semantics (T)
Listener response (H); Conversational storytelling (H24)

Literacy (H); Anderson (H21); Applied linguistics (MT); Channel (H); Computer-mediated communication (H); Identity (H24); Language acquisition (H); Language ideologies (H); Language policy, language planning and standardization (H); Metalinguistic awareness (H); Multilingualism; Orthography and cognition (H22); Social media research (T)
Literary criticism see Figures of speech (H)
Literary pragmatics (MT); Bakhtin (H); Caste and language (H23); Context and contextualization (H); Creativity in language use (H); Deconstruction (MM); Figures of speech (H); Hermeneutics (M); Narrative (H); Rhetoric (MT); Structuralism (MT); Stylistics (MT)
Localization problem see Neurolinguistics (MT)
Location see Contact linguistics (MT)
Logic see Generative semantics (MT); Grice (H); Modality (H); Semiotics (MT); Truth-conditional pragmatics (T); Wittgenstein (H)
Logic-based formalism see Artificial intelligence (MT)
Logical analysis (MM)
Logical atomism see Analytical philosophy (MT)
Logical empiricism/Logical positivism see Analytical philosophy (MT); Grice (H); Morris (H)
Logical notation see Notation in formal semantics (MN)
Logical semantics (MT); Deontic logic (MT); Discourse representation theory (MT); Epistemic logic (MT); Formal pragmatics (MT); Game-theoretical semantics (MT); Intensional logic (MT); Modal logic (MT); Model-theoretic semantics (MT); Montague and categorial grammar (MT); Ontology (MT); Possible worlds

semantics (MT); Situation semantics (MT); Truth-conditional semantics (MT)
Logical typing of communication see Bateson (H); Communication (H)
Longitudinal method see Developmental psychology (MT)
Loudness see Prosody (H)
Lying see Truthfulness (H)

M
M-principle see Anaphora (H); Semantics vs. pragmatics (T)
Machine translation see Translation studies (T)
Macro-sociolinguistics see Sociolinguistics (MT)
Malinowski, B. K. (H); Anthropological linguistics (MT); Culture (H); Firthian linguistics (MT); Participation (H); Phatic communion (H)
Manipulation (H); Truthfulness (H)
Mapping see Cognitive science (MT)
Markedness (H); Emphasis (H); Language change (H); Negation (H)
Marrism see Marxist linguistics (MT)
Marx, Karl see Bourdieu (H); Ideology (H); Sociology of language (T)
Marxist linguistics (MT); Critical Linguistics and Critical Discourse Analysis (MT); Halliday (H26)
Mass media (H); Argumentation in discourse and grammar (H); Channel (H); Communication (H); Conversation analysis (MT); Critical Linguistics and Critical Discourse Analysis (MT); Ideology (H); Manipulation (H); Membership categorization analysis (T); Public discourse (H); Silence (H); Text and discourse linguistics (T)
Matched guise see Methods in language-attitudes research (M)
Materialism see Cognitive science (MT)
Mathematical linguistics see Communication (H)

Mathesius, V. (H); Prague school (MT)
Maxims of conversation → see Cooperative principle
Mead, G. H. see Morris (H); Symbolic interactionism (MT)
Mead, M. see Culture (H)
Meaning see Analytical philosophy (MT); Austin (H); Cohesion and coherence (H); Deixis (H); Emotions (H21); Firth (H); Grice (H); Integrational linguistics (T); Linear Unit Grammar (T); Model-theoretic semantics (MT); Phatic communion (H); Semiotics (MT); Situation semantics (MT); Sound symbolism (H); Truth-conditional pragmatics (T); Wittgenstein (H)
Meaning construction see Cognitive science (MT); Cognitive sociology (MT); Critical Linguistics and Critical Discourse Analysis (MT); Grounded theory (M)
Meaning definition see Predicates and predication (H)
Meaning postulate see Lexical semantics (T)
Meaning potential see Social class and language (H)
Media see Mass media (H)
Media panic see Youth language (H25)
Mediated communication see Globalization (H25); Youth language (H25)
Mediated performatives (H)
Medical interaction see Institutional interaction (H23); Interpreter-mediated interaction (H); Nigerian hospital setting discourse (H24); Therapeutic conversation (H)
Medical language see Applied linguistics (MT); Authority (H)
Medium see Channel (H); Computer-mediated communication (H); Mass media (H); Mediated performatives (H); Multimodality (H); Social media research (T)

Medvedev, P. N. see Bakhtin (H)
Membership categorization see Age and language use (H); Conversational storytelling (H24); Membership categorization analysis (T); Sacks (H)
Membership categorization analysis (T)
Memory see Attention and language (H); Consciousness and language (H); Perception and language (H)
Mental map see Methods in language-attitudes research (M)
Mental spaces (H); Conceptual integration (H)
Mental states see Experimental pragmatics (M); Language psychology (T)
Mentalism (MT); Chomskyan linguistics (MT); Cognitive science (MT); Objectivism vs. subjectivism (MT); Philosophy of mind (MT)
Mesolect see Creole linguistics (MT)
Metacommunication see Bateson (H); Gesture research (T)
Metadata see Working with language data (M25)
Metalanguage see Corpus pragmatics (M); Feminism and language (H24); Feminism and language (H24); Impoliteness (H); Methods in language-attitudes research (M); Reported speech (H)
Metalinguistic awareness (H); Adaptability (H); Collaboration in dialogues (H); Computer-mediated communication (H); Consciousness and language (H); Evolutionary pragmatics (T); Folk pragmatics (T); Language acquisition (H); Language ideologies (H); Literacy (H); Metapragmatics (MT)
Metalinguistic negation see Negation (H)
Metalinguistics see Bakhtin (H)
Metaphor (H); Cerebral representation of language; Cognitive linguistics (MT); Embodiment (H); Emphasis (H); Euphemism (H24); Experimental pragmatics (M); Figures of speech (H); Gesture research (T); Iconicity (H); Implicature and

language change (H); Language
change (H); Metonymy (H);
Polysemy (H); Silence (H);
Truthfulness (H)
Metaphysics see Grice (H)
**Metapragmatic
term** see Metapragmatics (MT)
Metapragmatics (MT); Agency and
language (H); Aisatsu (H);
Anthropological linguistics (MT);
Cerebral representation of
language; Folk pragmatics (T);
Halliday (H26); Humor (H23);
Interactional
sociolinguistics (MT); Language
ideologies (H); Metalinguistic
awareness (H); Teasing (H25);
Wakimae (H26)
**Methods in language-attitudes
research (M)**
Metonymy (H); Euphemism (H24);
Figures of speech (H);
Implicature and language
change (H); Lexical
semantics (T); Metaphor (H);
Polysemy (H); Speech act
Metrolingualism see Heteroglossia (H26);
Transience (H22)
Mey, J. see Activity types and
pragmatic acts (H26)
Mianzi / lian (H21)
**Micro-
sociolinguistics** see Sociolinguistics (MT)
Micro-sociology see Social
psychology (MT)
Mind-body problem see Philosophy
of mind (MT)
Minority see Language dominance
and minorization (H); Language
ecology (H); Language rights (H);
Linguistic landscape studies (T);
'Other' representation (H)
Misunderstanding see Communicative
success vs. failure (H);
Truthfulness (H)
Mitigation see Laughter (H)
Mixed languages see Language
contact (H)
Mixed methods see Social media
research (T)
Mobility see Globalization (H25);
Mobility of social interaction ();
Transience (H22)
Mobility of social interaction ();
Conversation analysis (MT)

Modal logic (MT); Deontic
logic (MT); Epistemic logic (MT);
Logical semantics (MT)
Modal particle see Pragmatic
particles (H)
Modality (H); Appraisal (H);
Authority (H); Énonciation (H);
Event representation (H22);
Evidentiality (H22); Implicature
and language change (H);
Lexically triggered veridicality
inferences (H22); Modal
logic (MT); Signed language
pragmatics (T)
Mode see Firth (H);
Multimodality (H); Social
semiotics (T)
Model-theoretic semantics (MT);
Game-theoretical
semantics (MT); Logical
semantics (MT); Montague and
categorial grammar (MT);
Notation in formal
semantics (MN); Possible worlds
semantics (MT); Situation
semantics (MT)
Modeling see Regression
analysis (M)
Modularity → see Cerebral
representation of language;
Clinical pragmatics (T);
Cognitive psychology (MT);
Cognitive science (MT);
Conceptual semantics (T);
Irony (H); Language
acquisition (H);
Psycholinguistics (MT)
Monolingualism see Language
dominance and minorization (H)
Monologizing see Interpreter-
mediated interaction (H)
Monologue see Think-aloud
protocols (M)
Monosemy see Polysemy (H)
**Montague and categorial
grammar (MT)**; Discourse
representation theory (MT);
Formal pragmatics (MT);
Intensional logic (MT); Logical
semantics (MT); Model-theoretic
semantics (MT)
Moore, G. E. see Analytical
philosophy (MT)
Morpheme see Orthography and
cognition (H22)
Morphology see Deixis (H);
Discourse markers (H);

Euphemism (H24);
Jakobson (H21); Language
change (H);
Morphopragmatics (T); Word (H)
Morphopragmatics (T)
Morris, C. (H)
Motherese see Register (H)
Motivation (H)
Motivation and language (H)
Move see Predicates and
predication (H); Therapeutic
conversation (H)
MTA see Tense and aspect (H)
Multi-party talk see Collaboration
in dialogues (H); Conversation
types (H)
Multiculturalism see Culture (H)
Multifunctionality see Pragmatic
markers (H)
Multilingual lexicon (The) (H)
Multilingualism see Bilingualism
and multilingualism (H); Code-
switching (H); Code-switching
and translanguaging (H22);
Creativity in language use (H);
Language contact (H); Language
ecology (H); Linguistic landscape
studies (T); Literacy (H); The
multilingual lexicon (H); Power
and the role of language (H25);
Translanguaging pedagogy (T)
Multimodality (H); Computational
pragmatics (T); Computer-
mediated communication (H);
Embodied interaction (H23);
Embodiment (H); Emphasis (H);
Genre (H); Historical
politeness (T); Metaphor (H);
Social semiotics (T); Translation
studies (T)
Multiscriptality see Pragmatics of
script (H22)
Multisensoriality see Embodied
interaction (H23)
Multivoicedness see Heteroglossia (H26)
Mutual knowledge see Common
ground (H)

N
Name see Linguistic landscape
studies (T); Reference and
descriptions (H); Socio-
onomastics (T)
Narrative (H); Appraisal (H);
Collaboration in dialogues (H);
Conversational storytelling (H24);
Emotion display (H); Ervin-

Tripp, S. (H24); Grounded theory (M); Grounding (H); Metalinguistic awareness (H); Reported speech (H); Sequence (H); Text and discourse linguistics (T); Text type (H)
Narratology see Semiotics (MT); Text and discourse linguistics (T)
Nationalism see Anderson (H21); Identity (H24); Language dominance and minorization (H)
Native-nonnative interaction see Discourse markers (H); Intercultural communication (H)
Nativism see Authenticity (H); Language acquisition (H)
Natural history of discourse see Metalinguistic awareness (H)
Natural language generation and interpretation → see Natural language processing
Natural language processing see Artificial intelligence (MT); Borrowing (H); Cognitive psychology (MT); Computational linguistics (MT); Connectionism (MT); The multilingual lexicon (H); Psycholinguistics (MT)
Natural logic see Argumentation theory (MT)
Natural semantic metalanguage see Componential analysis (MT)
Naturalness see Authenticity (H); Language change (H)
Nature vs. nurture see Cognitive science (MT)
Negation (H); Indeterminacy and negotiation (H); Lexically triggered veridicality inferences (H22); Modality (H); Polyphony (H); Truthfulness (H)
Negotiation see Activity types and pragmatic acts (H26); Adaptability (H); Applied linguistics (MT); Indeterminacy and negotiation (H); Prosody (H); Truthfulness (H)
Neo-Gricean pragmatics see Anaphora (H); Grice (H); Implicature and language change (H); Semantics vs. pragmatics (T)

Neo-Kaplanean semantics see Semantics vs. pragmatics (T)
Neogrammarians see Historical linguistics (MT); Lexical field analysis (MT); Prague school (MT); Reconstruction (MM); de Saussure (H)
Neoliberalism see Ideology (H)
Network (social) see Computer-mediated communication (H); Language change (H); Social media research (T)
Neuroimaging → see Brain imaging
Neurolinguistic programming see General semantics (MT)
Neurolinguistics (MT); Adaptability (H); Bilingualism and multilingualism (H); Cerebral representation of language; Clinical pragmatics (T); Emotions (H21); Language acquisition (H); Perception and language (H)
Neurophysiology see Connectionism (MT); Irony (H); Neurolinguistics (MT); Neuropragmatics (T)
Neuropragmatics (T); Clinical pragmatics (T)
Neuropsychology see Cognitive science (MT); Perception and language (H)
New Left see Bourdieu (H)
New rhetoric see Argumentation theory (MT); Genre (H); Rhetoric (MT)
News interview see Mass media (H)
Newspaper see Mass media (H)
Nexus analysis (T); Bourdieu (H)
Nigerian hospital setting discourse (H24); Clinical pragmatics (T); Institutional interaction (H23); Social institutions; Therapeutic conversation (H)
Nils Erik Enkvist (H26) ()
Nominalization see Predicates and predication (H)
Non-literal meaning see Neuropragmatics (T); Swearing (H25)
Non-modular grammar see Construction grammar (MT)
Non-seriousness see Laughter (H)

Non-verbal communication (H); Channel (H); Cultural scripts (H); Frame analysis (M); Gesture research (T)
Normality see Ethnomethodology (MT)
Norms see Creativity in language use (H); Ethnomethodology (MT); Methods in language-attitudes research (M); Power and the role of language (H25); Workplace interaction (H25)
Notation in formal semantics (MN)
Notation Systems in Spoken Language Corpora (N); Transcription systems for spoken discourse (MN)
Noun phrase see Situation semantics (MT)
Novelty see Creativity in language use (H)

O

Object language see Metalinguistic awareness (H)
Objectivism vs. subjectivism (MT); Behaviorism (MT); Epistemology (MT); Foucault (H); Mentalism (MT)
Obscenity, slurs, and taboo (H24); Euphemism (H24); Swearing (H25)
Observation see Cognitive science (MT); Culture (H); Fieldwork (MM); Regression analysis (M)
Offence see Obscenity, slurs, and taboo (H24); Swearing (H25)
Ọmọlúàbí (H)
Online communication see Chronotope (H25); Complaining (H25); Computer-mediated communication (H); Youth language (H25)
Onomastics see Socio-onomastics (T)
Ontic relation see Legitimation Code Theory (T25)
Ontology (MT); Epistemology (MT); Logical semantics (MT)
Opacity see Mental spaces (H)
Open science see Working with language data (M25)
Operationism see Behaviorism (MT)
Optimality theory see Default interpretations (H)

Orality see Channel (H)
Orders (of discourse) see Critical Linguistics and Critical Discourse Analysis (MT); Ideology (H); Workplace interaction (H25)
Ordinary language philosophy see Analytical philosophy (MT); Conversational logic (MT); Grice (H); Indeterminacy and negotiation (H); Metalinguistic awareness (H); Metapragmatics (MT); (The) pragmatic perspective (M); Pragmatism (MT); Speech act theory (MT); Wittgenstein (H)
Organizational setting see Social institutions (H)
Organon model see Bühler (H)
Orientalism see Postcolonial pragmatics (T)
Origins of language see Cognitive anthropology (MT); Evolutionary pragmatics (T); Humboldt (H)
Orthography see Developmental dyslexia (H); Orthography and cognition (H22); Pragmatics of script (H22)
Orthography and cognition (H22); Pragmatics of script (H22)
'Other' representation (H); Age and language use (H)
Other(ing) see Authority (H); Crossing (H26); Mianzi / lian (H21); 'Other' representation (H)
Other-repair see Repair (H)
Othering see 'Other' representation (H)
Overhearer → see Audience
Overlap (H)

P
Paralanguage → see Cerebral representation of language; Non-verbal communication (H)
Paraphrase semantics see Componential analysis (MT)
Parole → see Langue vs. parole
Parsing see Computational linguistics (MT)
Participant observation → see Observation
Participation (H); Frame analysis (M); Goffman (H)

Participation framework see Participation (H)
Pêcheux, M. see Marxist linguistics (MT)
Peirce, C. S. (H); Iconicity (H); Morris (H); Pragmatism (MT); Semiotics (MT); Sign (H)
Pejorative see Morphopragmatics (T); 'Other' representation (H)
Perception and language (H); Austin (H); Embodiment (H); Iconicity (H); Language acquisition (H)
Perceptron see Connectionism (MT); Psycholinguistics (MT)
Performance see Computer-mediated communication (H)
Performativity see Austin (H); Benveniste (H); Mediated performatives (H); Metalinguistic awareness (H); Speech act theory (MT)
Perlocution see Intentionality (H); Speech act theory (MT)
Persian see Ta'ārof (H22)
Persistence see Obscenity, slurs, and taboo (H24)
Person reference see Wakimae (H26)
Personality see Sapir (H)
Perspectives on language and cognition (H)
Persuasion see Manipulation (H)
Phatic communion (H); Anthropological linguistics (MT); Ethnography of speaking (MT); Evolutionary pragmatics (T); Firthian linguistics (MT); Malinowski (H); Participation (H)
Phenomenology (MT); Austin (H); Embodiment (H); Ethnomethodology (MT); Semiotics (MT)
Philosophy of action (MT); Action theory (MT); Austin (H)
Philosophy of language (MT); Analytical philosophy (MT); Austin (H); Conversational logic (MT); Emotions (H21); Humboldt (H); (The) pragmatic perspective (M); Speech act theory (MT); Wittgenstein (H)
Philosophy of mind (MT); Cognitive science (MT); Grice (H); Mentalism (MT)

Phoneme see Orthography and cognition (H22)
Phonetic notation systems (N)
Phonetics see Boas (H); Discourse markers (H); de Saussure (H)
Phonology see Developmental dyslexia (H); Euphemism (H24); Jakobson (H21); Structuralism (MT)
Phrase-structure grammar see Chomskyan linguistics (MT); Computational linguistics (MT)
Physical symbol system see Artificial intelligence (MT); Cognitive psychology (MT); Cognitive science (MT)
Picture-theory of meaning see Wittgenstein (H)
Pidgins and pidginization see Contact (H); Contact linguistics (MT); Creole linguistics (MT); Creoles and creolization (H); Intercultural communication (H)
Pitch see Prosody (H)
Plagiarism → see Authorship
Planning see Computational pragmatics (T)
Pluricentric languages (H23)
Poetic language see Figures of speech (H); Grounding (H)
Poetics see Bakhtin (H)
Point of view see Grounding (H)
Polarity see Negation (H)
Police interrogation see Applied linguistics (MT); Forensic linguistics (T); Interpreter-mediated interaction (H)
Politeness (H); Aisatsu (H); Conversational implicature (H); Conversational logic (MT); Directive (H26); Goffman (H); Historical politeness (T); Historical pragmatics (T); Honorifics (H); Implicitness (H); Impoliteness (H); Interlanguage pragmatics (T); Leech (H); Mianzi / lian (H21); Morphopragmatics (T); Obscenity, slurs, and taboo (H24); Silence (H); Social media research (T); Swearing (H25); Ta'ārof (H22); Teasing (H25); Terms of address (H);

Truthfulness (H); Universals (H23); Wakimae (H26)
Political correctness see Euphemism (H24); 'Other' representation (H)
Political language see Authority (H)
Political linguistics see Critical Linguistics and Critical Discourse Analysis (MT)
Polylanguaging see Transience (H22)
Polylingualism see Heteroglossia (H26)
Polyphony (H); Appraisal (H); Bakhtin (H); Collaboration in dialogues (H); Dialogical analysis (MM); Heteroglossia (H26)
Polysemy (H); Implicature and language change (H); Indeterminacy and negotiation (H)
Polysystemic analysis see Firth (H)
Positioning see Evidentiality (H22); Social media research (T); Stance (H21)
Positivism see Sociology of language (T)
Possible worlds semantics (MT); Epistemic logic (MT); Logical semantics (MT); Model-theoretic semantics (MT); Truth-conditional semantics (MT)
Postcolonial pragmatics (T); Caste and language (H23); Critical Linguistics and Critical Discourse Analysis (MT); Hegemony (H23); Ideology (H)
Postcolonial studies see Caste and language (H23); Postcolonial pragmatics (T)
Postcolonialism →
Posthumanist pragmatics ()
Postmodernism see Postcolonial pragmatics (T)
Poststructuralism see Critical Linguistics and Critical Discourse Analysis (MT); Deconstruction (MM); Poststructuralist discourse theory ()
Poststructuralist discourse theory (); Poststructuralism
Posture see Non-verbal communication (H); Ta'ārof (H22)
Power and the role of language (H25); Authority (H); Cognitive sociology (MT); Critical Linguistics and Critical

Discourse Analysis (MT); Foucault (H); Gumperz (H); Honorifics (H); Ideology (H); Manipulation (H); Metalinguistic awareness (H); Nigerian hospital setting discourse (H24); Politeness (H); Postcolonial pragmatics (T); Silence (H); Social institutions (H)
Pract see Activity types and pragmatic acts (H26)
Practice (theory) see Agency and language (H); Nexus analysis (T); Social class and language (H)
Pragma-dialectics see Argumentation theory (MT)
Pragmalinguistics see Leech (H)
Pragmastylistics see Stylistics (MT)
Pragmatic acquisition (H); Cognitive psychology (MT); Developmental dyslexia (H); Developmental psychology (MT); Experimental pragmatics (M); Experimentation (MM); Language acquisition (H); Psycholinguistics (MT)
Pragmatic enrichment see Truth-conditional pragmatics (T)
Pragmatic explanation see Linguistic explanation (MM)
Pragmatic function see Functional grammar (MT)
Pragmatic impairment see Clinical pragmatics (T)
Pragmatic intrusion see Semantics vs. pragmatics (T)
Pragmatic markers (H); Discourse markers (H); Pragmatic particles (H)
Pragmatic norm see Interlanguage pragmatics (T)
Pragmatic particles (H); Discourse markers (H); Interjections (H)
Pragmatic perspective (The) (M)
Pragmatic scale → see Scalarity
Pragmatic transfer see Interlanguage pragmatics (T)
Pragmaticalization see Pragmatic markers (H)
Pragmaticism see Evolutionary pragmatics (T); Morris (H); Objectivism vs. subjectivism (MT); Pragmatism (MT)

Pragmatics → see Cognitive pragmatics; Corpus pragmatics (M); Experimental pragmatics (M); Folk pragmatics (T); Formal pragmatics (MT); Historical pragmatics (T); Interlanguage pragmatics (T); Literary pragmatics (MT); Metapragmatics (MT); Neo-Gricean pragmatics; Neuropragmatics (T); Postcolonial pragmatics (T); (The) pragmatic perspective (M); Pragmatics of script (H22); Semantics vs. pragmatics (T); Truth-conditional pragmatics (T); Variational pragmatics (T)
Pragmatics of script (H22)
Pragmatism (MT); Morris (H); Peirce (H); Semiotics (MT)
Pragmemes (H22); Activity types and pragmatic acts (H26)
Prague school (MT); Communicative dynamism (H); Functional grammar (MT); Functional sentence perspective (H); Halliday (H26); Markedness (H); Mathesius (H); Structuralism (MT); Text and discourse linguistics (T); Text linguistics (MT); Word order (H)
Pre-request see Directive (H26)
Precisification principle see Indeterminacy and negotiation (H)
Predicate logic see Artificial intelligence (MT); Notation in formal semantics (MN)
Predicates and predication (H); Event representation (H22); Lexically triggered veridicality inferences (H22)
Preference organization see Complaining (H25); Repair (H); Sequence (H)
Prejudice see 'Other' representation (H)
Prestige see Language dominance and minorization (H)
Presumptive meaning see Default interpretations (H)
Presupposition (H); Argumentation in discourse and grammar (H); Context and contextualization (H); Discourse representation theory (MT);

Formal pragmatics (**MT**);
Implicitness (**H**); Mental
spaces (**H**); Truthfulness (**H**)
Primate communication (**H**)
Priming see Psycholinguistics (**MT**)
Print see Channel (**H**)
**Private
 language** see Wittgenstein (**H**)
**Probabilistic
 technique** see Statistics (**MM**)
Problematization see Foucault (**H**)
Problematology see Argumentation
 theory (**MT**); Rhetoric (**MT**)
Procedural semantics see Cognitive
 psychology (**MT**)
Processing see Comprehension vs.
 production (**H**); Inferencing;
 Information processing;
 Production; Text
 comprehension (**H**)
Production see Conceptual
 semantics (**T**);
 Psycholinguistics (**MT**)
Productivity see Creativity in
 language use (**H**)
**Projection
 problem** see Presupposition (**H**)
Pronoun see Anaphora (**H**); Creole
 linguistics (**MT**); Humboldt (**H**);
 Negation (**H**); Ta'ārof (**H22**)
Proper name → see Name
Property theory see Intensional
 logic (**MT**)
**Propositional
 attitude** see Discourse
 representation theory (**MT**);
 Intensional logic (**MT**)
**Propositional
 semantics** see Evolutionary
 pragmatics (**T**)
Prosody (**H**); Cerebral
 representation of language;
 Emphasis (**H**); Firth (**H**);
 Gumperz (**H**); Information
 structure (**H**); Interactional
 linguistics (**T**); Language
 acquisition (**H**)
Proto-grammar see Iconicity (**H**)
**Prototype
 (theory)** see Categorization (**H**);
 Cognitive linguistics (**MT**);
 Dependency and valency
 grammar (**MT**); Language
 acquisition (**H**); Lexical
 semantics (**T**); Polysemy (**H**);
 Taxonomy (**MM**)
Proxemics see Non-verbal
 communication (**H**)

Psychiatry see Bateson (**H**);
 Therapeutic conversation (**H**)
Psycholinguistics (**MT**);
 Bilingualism and
 multilingualism (**H**);
 Borrowing (**H**); Bühler (**H**);
 Cognitive psychology (**MT**);
 Comprehension vs.
 production (**H**);
 Connectionism (**MT**);
 Developmental psychology (**MT**);
 Ervin-Tripp, S. (**H24**);
 Experimental pragmatics (**M**);
 Experimentation (**MM**); Gesture
 research (**T**); Language
 psychology (**T**); The multilingual
 lexicon (**H**); Non-verbal
 communication (**H**); Perception
 and language (**H**); (The)
 pragmatic perspective (**M**); Text
 comprehension (**H**); Translation
 studies (**T**); Vygotsky (**H**)
**Psychological
 anthropology** see Cognitive
 anthropology (**MT**)
Psychosemantics see Philosophy of
 mind (**MT**)
Psychotherapy → see Psychiatry
Public discourse (**H**); Goffman (**H**);
 Mediated performatives (**H**);
 Social institutions (**H**)
Putnam, H. see Analytical
 philosophy (**MT**)

Q

Q-principle see Anaphora (**H**);
 Semantics vs. pragmatics (**T**)
Qualitative methods see Grounded
 theory (**T**)
Quantifier see Model-theoretic
 semantics (**MT**); Notation in
 formal semantics (**MN**)
Quantitative method see Regression
 analysis (**M**); Statistics (**MM**)
**Question
 answering** see Computational
 pragmatics (**T**); Tactile sign
 languages (**H21**)
Question word see Repair (**H**)
Questionnaire see Interview (**MM**)
Quine, W.v.O. see Reported
 speech (**H**)
Quotation see Analytical
 philosophy (**MT**);
 Evidentiality (**H22**)

R

Race see Caste and language (**H23**)
Racism see Ideology (**H**); Obscenity,
 slurs, and taboo (**H24**); 'Other'
 representation (**H**)
**Radical
 argumentativism** see Argumentation
 theory (**MT**)
Radical pragmatics see Grice (**H**)
Radio see Mass media (**H**)
Rampton, B. see Crossing (**H26**)
Ranking task see Methods in
 language-attitudes research (**M**)
Rationality see Default
 interpretations (**H**);
 Emotions (**H21**);
 Ethnomethodology (**MT**);
 Foucault (**H**); Grice (**H**);
 Ideology (**H**)
Reading analysis see Critical
 Linguistics and Critical Discourse
 Analysis (**MT**); Text
 comprehension (**H**)
Recall see Collaboration in
 dialogues (**H**)
Reception theory see Literary
 pragmatics (**MT**)
Recipient design see Collaboration
 in dialogues (**H**); Communicative
 style (**H**)
Reconstruction (**MM**);
 Dialectology (**MT**); Historical
 linguistics (**MT**); Language
 change (**H**)
Recording see Working with
 language data (**M25**)
Recoverability see Ellipsis (**H**)
Reference see Anaphora (**H**);
 Definiteness (**H**); Experimental
 pragmatics (**M**); Functional
 discourse grammar (**T**);
 Functional grammar (**MT**);
 Information structure (**H**);
 Mental spaces (**H**); Metalinguistic
 awareness (**H**); Model-theoretic
 semantics (**MT**); Polysemy (**H**);
 Pragmemes (**H22**); Predicates and
 predication (**H**); Reference and
 descriptions (**H**);
 Tagmemics (**MT**);
 Universals (**H23**)
Reference and descriptions (**H**)
**Referential
 choice** see Definiteness (**H**)
Referring → see Reference;
 Reference and descriptions (**H**)

Reflection see Communicative success vs. failure (H); Humboldt (H)
Reflexive see Anaphora (H)
Reflexivity see Adaptability (H); Ethnomethodology (MT); Foucault (H); Metalinguistic awareness (H); 'Other' representation (H); Style and styling (H21)
Reflexology see Behaviorism (MT)
Refusal see Ta'ārof (H22)
Register (H); Applied linguistics (MT); Channel (H); Context and contextualization (H); Correlational sociolinguistics (T); Error analysis (MM); Firthian linguistics (MT); Frame analysis (M); Gumperz (H); Halliday (H26); Honorifics (H); Intercultural communication (H); Regression analysis (M); Rhetoric (MT); Sociolinguistics (MT); Stylistics (MT); Systemic functional grammar (MT)
Regression analysis (M); Statistics (MM)
Regularity see Relational ritual (H)
Reinforcement see Emphasis (H)
Relational grammar see Lexical functional grammar (MT)
Relational ritual (H)
Relevance see Computational pragmatics (T); Conversation analysis (MT); Conversational logic (MT); Irony (H); Relevance theory (MT)
Relevance theory (MT); Anaphora (H); Clinical pragmatics (T); Communication (H); Conversational implicature (H); Conversational logic (MT); Emotions (H21); Experimental pragmatics (M); Humor (H23); Manipulation (H); Semantics vs. pragmatics (T); Tense and aspect (H); Truth-conditional pragmatics (T); Truth-conditional semantics (MT); Truthfulness (H)
Religion see Authority (H); Caste and language (H23)
Repair (H); Communicative success vs. failure (H); Conversation analysis (MT); Conversational

storytelling (H24); Prosody (H); Sequence (H)
Repertoire → see Linguistic repertoire
Repetition see Emergent grammar (T)
Reported speech (H); Énonciation (H); Evidentiality (H22); Intertextuality (H)
Representation see Adaptability (H); Conceptual semantics (T); Event representation (H22); Evolutionary pragmatics (T); Foucault (H); Iconicity (H); Indeterminacy and negotiation (H); Intentionality (H); Metalinguistic awareness (H); 'Other' representation (H); Psycholinguistics (MT); Social psychology (MT); Truthfulness (H); Wittgenstein (H)
Request see Directive (H26)
Requests see Directive (H26)
Research ethics see Working with language data (M25)
Resistance see Power and the role of language (H25); Therapeutic conversation (H)
Resource see Multimodality (H)
Respect → see Deference
Response see Complaining (H25); Conversational storytelling (H24); Listener response (H); Obscenity, slurs, and taboo (H24); Ọmọlúàbí (H); Teasing (H25)
Response cry see Emotion display (H); Goffman (H)
Responsibility see Austin (H); Membership categorization analysis (T)
Responsiveness see Social media research (T)
Rheme → see Theme vs. rheme
Rhetoric (MT); Argumentation theory (MT); Figures of speech (H); Functional discourse grammar (T); Genre (H); Gesture research (T); Literary pragmatics (MT); Manipulation (H); Metalinguistic awareness (H); Narrative (H); Social psychology (MT); Stylistics (MT); Text and discourse linguistics (T)

Rhetorical relations see Discourse representation theory (MT)
Rhetorical structure theory see Artificial intelligence (MT); Computational pragmatics (T); Text and discourse linguistics (T)
Ritual see Goffman (H); Relational ritual (H)
Role and reference grammar (MT); Case and semantic roles (H); Case grammar (MT); Dependency and valency grammar (MT)
Role vs. value see Mental spaces (H)
Rossi-Landi, F. see Morris (H)
Routine (formula) see Aisatsu (H); Impoliteness (H); Ọmọlúàbí (H); Relational ritual (H); Swearing (H25)
Routinization see Emergent grammar (T); Nigerian hospital setting discourse (H24)
Rule see Ethnomethodology (MT); Psycholinguistics (MT); Speech act theory (MT); Wittgenstein (H)
Rule-based formalism see Artificial intelligence (MT)
Russell, B. see Analytical philosophy (MT); Definiteness (H); Reference and descriptions (H)
Russian formalism see Deconstruction (MM); Literary pragmatics (MT); Prague school (MT); Semiotics (MT); Stylistics (MT); Text and discourse linguistics (T)

S
Sacks, H. (H); Conversation analysis (MT)
Sales encounter see Institutional interaction (H23)
Salience see Anaphora (H); Emphasis (H); Experimental pragmatics (M); Grounding (H); Irony (H); Word order (H)
Sameness see Youth language (H25)
Sampling → see Data collection
Sapir, E. (H); Anthropological linguistics (MT); Boas (H); Culture (H); Whorf (H)
Sapir-Whorf hypothesis → see Linguistic relativity principle
Sarcasm see Irony (H)

Saturation see Truth-conditional pragmatics (T)
Saussure, F. de (H); Geneva school (MT); Participation (H); Sign (H); Structuralism (MT)
Scalarity see Conceptual integration (H); Experimental pragmatics (M); Implicitness (H); Negation (H)
Scale see Chronotope (H25)
Scale and category grammar see Systemic functional grammar (MT)
Scaling see Pragmatics of script (H22)
Scenario see Frame semantics (T); Lexical semantics (T)
Scene see Frame semantics (T); Lexical semantics (T)
Scene-and-frame semantics see Frame semantics (T)
Schema see Cognitive science (MT); Frame analysis (M)
Schizophrenia see Clinical pragmatics (T)
Schooling see Aisatsu (H); Language acquisition (H)
Scientific language see Analytical philosophy (MT); Applied linguistics (MT); Text comprehension (H)
Script1 see Orthography and cognition (H22); Pragmatics of script (H22)
Script2 see Cognitive science (MT); Frame analysis (M); Frame semantics (T); Humor (H23)
Searle, J. R. see Analytical philosophy (MT); Contextualism (T); Intentionality (H); Reference and descriptions (H); Speech act theory (MT)
Second language acquisition see Applied linguistics (MT); Contact linguistics (MT); Conversational storytelling (H24); Ervin-Tripp, S. (H24); Intercultural communication (H); Interlanguage pragmatics (T); Language learning in immersion and CLIL classrooms (H); Motivation (H); The multilingual lexicon (H); Silence (H); Text comprehension (H)

Securitization see Power and the role of language (H25)
Selection restrictions see Predicates and predication (H)
Self see Authenticity (H); Authority (H); Goffman (H); Laughter (H); Life stories (H); Mianzi / lian (H21)
Self-discipline see Power and the role of language (H25)
Self-repair see Repair (H)
Self-report see Methods in language-attitudes research (M)
Semantic density see Legitimation Code Theory (T25)
Semantic differential see Social psychology (MT)
Semantic field analysis see Lexical field analysis (MT)
Semantic gravity see Legitimation Code Theory (T25)
Semantic minimalism see Contextualism (T)
Semantic network see Artificial intelligence (MT)
Semantic primitive see Componential analysis (MT); Cultural scripts (H)
Semantic structure see Role and reference grammar (MT)
Semantics vs. pragmatics (T); Anaphora (H); Cerebral representation of language; Discourse representation theory (MT); Emotions (H21); Generative semantics (MT); Grice (H); Implicitness (H); Indeterminacy and negotiation (H); Leech (H); Metalinguistic awareness (H); Metaphor (H); Montague and categorial grammar (MT); Reference and descriptions (H); Semiotics (MT); Structuralism (MT); Truth-conditional pragmatics (T)
Semiology see Integrational linguistics (T); de Saussure (H); Semiotics (MT)
Semiophysics see Catastrophe theory (MT)
Semiotic resource see Social semiotics (T)
Semiotics (MT); Bakhtin (H); Benveniste (H); Iconicity (H); Morris (H); Peirce (H); (The) pragmatic perspective (M);

Pragmatism (MT); Sign (H); Social semiotics (T); Speech community (H)
Sense see Analytical philosophy (MT); Polysemy (H)
Sensorimotor dysfunction see Clinical pragmatics (T)
Sensuous theory →
Sentence fragment see Ellipsis (H)
Sentence grammar → see Cerebral representation of language
Sentence linearity see Communicative dynamism (H)
Sentence processing see The multilingual lexicon (H)
Sentence type see Markedness (H)
Sequence (H); Chronotope (H25); Conversation analysis (MT); Embodied interaction (H23); Grounding (H); Language and the law (H); Notation Systems in Spoken Language Corpora (N); Prosody (H); Relational ritual (H); Repair (H); Stance (H21); Therapeutic conversation (H)
Sequencing see Sequence (H)
Sequentiality see Iconicity (H)
Sexism see Feminism and language (H24); Obscenity, slurs, and taboo (H24)
Sexual orientation see Silence (H)
Shared knowledge see Common ground (H)
Shibboleth see Anderson (H21)
Sign (H); Evolutionary pragmatics (T); Iconicity (H); Integrational linguistics (T); Morris (H); de Saussure (H); Semiotics (MT); Signed language pragmatics (T); Social semiotics (T); Speech community (H)
Sign language(s) see Language ecology (H); Non-verbal communication (H); Tactile sign languages (H21)
Signed language pragmatics (T)
Silence (H)
Silencing see 'Other' representation (H); Silence (H)
Simile see Metaphor (H)
Simmel, Georg see Sociology of language (T)

Sincerity see Authenticity (H); Truthfulness (H)
Singular term see Indexicals and demonstratives (H)
Situated action theory see Cognitive science (MT)
Situation semantics (MT); Communication (H); Discourse representation theory (MT); Logical semantics (MT); Model-theoretic semantics (MT)
Slang see Jargon (H)
Sluicing see Ellipsis (H)
Slur see Obscenity, slurs, and taboo (H24)
Smith, Adam see Sociology of language (T)
Social anthropology see Anthropological linguistics (MT); Cognitive anthropology (MT)
Social class and language (H); Caste and language (H23)
Social cognition see Bühler (H); Language psychology (T); Social psychology (MT); Style and styling (H21)
Social difference/inequality see Power and the role of language (H25)
Social distancing see 'Other' representation (H)
Social dynamics see Obscenity, slurs, and taboo (H24)
Social institutions (H); Applied linguistics (MT); Authority (H); Cognitive sociology (MT); Communication (H); Conversation types (H); Forensic linguistics (T); Frame analysis (M); Institutional interaction (H23); Intercultural communication (H); Narrative (H); Nigerian hospital setting discourse (H24); Politeness (H); Public discourse (H); Therapeutic conversation (H)
Social media research (T)
Social organization see Aisatsu (H); Authority (H); Cognitive sociology (MT)
Social psychology (MT); Accommodation theory (MT); Bilingualism and multilingualism (H); Conversation analysis (MT); Ethnomethodology (MT); Language psychology (T); Methods in language-attitudes research (M); Motivation (H); Nexus analysis (T); Overlap (H); Symbolic interactionism (MT); Terms of address (H)
Social relation see Legitimation Code Theory (T25)
Social relationship → see Social organization
Social science see Grounded theory (M)
Social semiotics (T); Appraisal (H); Critical Linguistics and Critical Discourse Analysis (MT); Critical theory (MT); Linguistic landscape studies (T); Literary pragmatics (MT); Multimodality (H); Semiotics (MT); Sign (H)
Socialization see Aisatsu (H); Developmental psychology (MT); Vygotsky (H)
Socio-onomastics (T)
Sociolect see Dialect (H); Heteroglossia (H26)
Sociolinguistics (MT); Anthropological linguistics (MT); Applied linguistics (MT); Bilingualism and multilingualism (H); Code-switching (H); Code-switching and translanguaging (H22); Cognitive sociology (MT); Contact linguistics (MT); Correlational sociolinguistics (T); Creole linguistics (MT); Creoles and creolization (H); Dialectology (MT); Ervin-Tripp, S. (H24); Gumperz (H); Hymes (H26); Interactional sociolinguistics (MT); Language contact (H); Language dominance and minorization (H); Language maintenance and shift (H21); Language policy, language planning and standardization (H); Lifestyle (H); Linguistic landscape studies (T); Metalinguistic awareness (H); Methods in language-attitudes research (M); Pragmatic markers (H); (The) pragmatic perspective (M); Social class and language (H); Social media research (T); Speech community (H); Superdiversity (H21); Transience (H22); Translanguaging pedagogy (T)
Sociology see Bourdieu (H); Cognitive sociology (MT); Goffman (H); Gumperz (H); Sociology of language (T)
Sociology of language (T); Dialectology (MT); Methods in language-attitudes research (M); Sociolinguistics (MT)
Sociopragmatics see Leech (H)
Sociosemiotics see Social semiotics (T)
Sonority see Language change (H)
Sound symbolism (H); Iconicity (H)
Space see Mobility of social interaction ()
Speaker vs. listener see Comprehension vs. production (H); Dialogical analysis (MM); Manipulation (H); Participation (H); Terms of address (H); Truthfulness (H)
Speaker's meaning see Evidentiality (H22); Speech act theory (MT)
Speaking vs. writing see Applied linguistics (MT); Channel (H); Communicative style (H); Computer-mediated communication (H); Integrational linguistics (T); Language acquisition (H); Notation Systems in Spoken Language Corpora (N); Pragmatics of script (H22); Register (H); de Saussure (H); Text and discourse linguistics (T)
Specialization see Legitimation Code Theory (T25)
Speech accommodation see Accommodation theory (MT); Social psychology (MT)
Speech act see Adaptability (H); Adaptability (H); Argumentation theory (MT); Austin (H); Cerebral representation of language; Conventions of language (H); Directive (H26); Formal pragmatics (MT); Grice (H); Historical pragmatics (T); Intercultural

communication (H); Interlanguage pragmatics (T); Mediated performatives (H); Metonymy (H); Modality (H); Morphopragmatics (T); Neuropragmatics (T); Non-verbal communication (H); Politeness (H); Pragmatic particles (H); Speech act theory (MT); Truth-conditional pragmatics (T); Universals (H23); Workplace interaction (H25)

Speech act classification see Speech act theory (MT)

Speech act theory (MT); Analytical philosophy (MT); Artificial intelligence (MT); Austin (H); Benveniste (H); Clinical pragmatics (T); Conversational implicature (H); Conversational logic (MT); Directive (H26); Indeterminacy and negotiation (H); Intentionality (H); Language and the law (H); Philosophy of language (MT); (The) pragmatic perspective (M); Truthfulness (H)

Speech circuit see Participation (H)

Speech community (H); Anderson (H21); Computer-mediated communication (H); Gumperz (H); Superdiversity (H21)

Speech event see Directive (H26); Pragmatic particles (H)

Speech genre see Bakhtin (H); Metalinguistic awareness (H)

Spelling see Language acquisition (H); Orthography and cognition (H22); Pragmatics of script (H22); Psycholinguistics (MT); Social media research (T)

Spoken discourse → see Speaking vs. writing

Spoken language corpora see Notation Systems in Spoken Language Corpora (N)

Sprachbund ('linguistic area') see Contact linguistics (MT); Language change (H); Language contact (H); Sociolinguistics (MT)

Stance (H21); Appraisal (H); Emotion display (H); Evidentiality (H22)

Standard language see Dialectology and geolinguistic dynamics (T)

Standardization see Anderson (H21); Authority (H); Integrational linguistics (T); Language dominance and minorization (H); Language policy, language planning and standardization (H); Literacy (H)

State of Affairs see Predicates and predication (H)

State-space search see Artificial intelligence (MT)

Statistics (MM); Computational linguistics (MT); Corpus analysis (MM); Correlational sociolinguistics (T); Experimentation (MM); Regression analysis (M)

Stereotype see 'Other' representation (H)

Stigmatization see Caste and language (H23)

Story(-telling) see Conversational storytelling (H24); Narrative (H)

Strategy see Impoliteness (H); Nigerian hospital setting discourse (H24); Ta'ārof (H22)

Strawson, P. F. see Analytical philosophy (MT); Definiteness (H); Reference and descriptions (H)

Stress see Information structure (H); Prosody (H)

Stripping see Ellipsis (H)

Structuralism (MT); Autonomous vs. non-autonomous syntax (MT); Benveniste (H); Bourdieu (H); Componential analysis (MT); Corpus analysis (MM); Geneva school (MT); Hermeneutics (M); Language change (H); Lexical field analysis (MT); Lexical semantics (T); Prague school (MT); de Saussure (H); Semiotics (MT); Sign (H); Text and discourse linguistics (T)

Style see Communicative style (H); Creole linguistics (MT); Ellipsis (H); Ervin-Tripp, S. (H24); Figures of speech (H); Register (H)

Style and styling (H21); Crossing (H26)

Stylistic stratification see Social class and language (H)

Stylistics (MT); Communicative style (H); Emphasis (H); Figures of speech (H); Literary pragmatics (MT); Mathesius (H); Rhetoric (MT); Text and discourse linguistics (T); Text linguistics (MT)

Subject see Communicative dynamism (H)

Subjective relation see Legitimation Code Theory (T25)

Subjectivity see Benveniste (H); Énonciation (H); Foucault (H); Implicature and language change (H); Signed language pragmatics (T)

Substitution see Anaphora (H)

Superdiversity (H21); Code-switching and translanguaging (H22); Transience (H22); Translanguaging pedagogy (T)

Surveillance see Power and the role of language (H25)

Swearing (H25)

Syllable structure see Prosody (H)

Symbol see Jakobson (H21)

Symbolic behavior see Evolutionary pragmatics (T); Ta'ārof (H22)

Symbolic capital see Bourdieu (H); Social institutions (H)

Symbolic interactionism (MT); Bourdieu (H); Cognitive sociology (MT); Context and contextualization (H); Ethnomethodology (MT); Goffman (H); Social psychology (MT)

Symbolic vs. subsymbolic architecture see Cognitive science (MT)

Symbolism see Morris (H)

Symbolization see Bühler (H); Cognitive grammar (MT)

Symmetry see Language change (H)

Synchrony see Iconicity (H); Non-verbal communication (H); Structuralism (MT)

Synergetics see Catastrophe theory (MT)

Synesthesia see Metaphor (H)

Syntax see Anaphora (H); Comprehension vs. production (H); Discourse markers (H); Ellipsis (H); Ervin-Tripp, S. (H24); Grice (H); Interactional linguistics (T);

Language acquisition (H); Language change (H); Polysemy (H)
Systemic functional grammar (MT); Appraisal (H); Emphasis (H); Firth (H); Firthian linguistics (MT); Functional grammar (MT); Genre (H); Halliday (H26); Heteroglossia (H26); Metaphor (H); Multimodality (H)
systemic functional linguistics see Systemic functional grammar (MT)

T
Taboo see Obscenity, slurs, and taboo (H24); Swearing (H25)
Tact see Leech (H); Ọmọlúàbí (H); Politeness (H)
Tactile sign languages (H21)
Tagging see Corpus analysis (MM)
Tagmemics (MT)
Taxonomy (MM)
Ta'ārof (H22)
Teasing (H25)
Technology see Power and the role of language (H25)
Telephone conversation see Emotion display (H)
Television see Argumentation in discourse and grammar (H); Channel (H); Mass media (H)
Temporal reference see Narrative (H)
Tenor see Register (H)
Tense see Event representation (H22); Modality (H); Regression analysis (M); Tense and aspect (H)
Tense and aspect (H); Event representation (H22)
Tense logic see Modal logic (MT)
Terms of address (H); Honorifics (H)
Territoriality see Language rights (H)
Testimony see Epistemology of testimony (T); Interpreter-mediated interaction (H)
Testing see Text comprehension (H)
Text see Boas (H); Culture (H); Systemic functional grammar (MT)

Text analysis see Computational linguistics (MT); Text type (H)
Text and discourse linguistics (T); Common ground (H); Text linguistics (MT)
Text comprehension (H)
Text linguistics (MT); Critical Linguistics and Critical Discourse Analysis (MT); Prague school (MT); Stylistics (MT); Text and discourse linguistics (T); Translation studies (T)
Text structure (H); Narrative (H)
Text type (H); Genre (H); Pragmatic particles (H); Text and discourse linguistics (T); Think-aloud protocols (M)
Theme vs. rheme see Communicative dynamism (H); Functional grammar (MT); Word order (H)
Theory and theorizing see Firth (H); Grounded theory (M)
Theory of mind see Adaptability (H); Clinical pragmatics (T); Communication (H)
Therapeutic conversation (H)
Think-aloud protocols (M)
Thirdness see Morris (H)
Threat see Impoliteness (H)
Timing problem see Neurolinguistics (MT); Neuropragmatics (T)
Topic management see Laughter (H)
Topic vs. focus see Anaphora (H); Argumentation in discourse and grammar (H); Functional discourse grammar (T); Functional grammar (MT); Functional sentence perspective (H)
Topic-comment structure see Computational pragmatics (T); Information structure (H); Signed language pragmatics (T); Word order (H)
Topicality see Argument structure (H23); Signed language pragmatics (T)
Toponym see Socio-onomastics (T)
Trajectory see Sequence (H)
Transcription see Grounded theory (M); Laughter (H); Phonetic notation systems (N)

Transcription systems for spoken discourse (MN); Conversation analysis (MT); Notation Systems in Spoken Language Corpora (N)
Transformational grammar → see Generative(-transformational) linguistics
Transience (H22)
Transitivity see Event representation (H22); Grounding (H)
Translanguaging see Code-switching and translanguaging (H22); Crossing (H26); Heteroglossia (H26); Transience (H22); Translanguaging pedagogy (T)
Translanguaging pedagogy (T)
Translation see Interpreter-mediated interaction (H); Postcolonial pragmatics (T); Pragmatic particles (H); Think-aloud protocols (M); Translation studies (T)
Translation studies (T); Pragmatic markers (H)
Traumatic brain injury see Clinical pragmatics (T)
Triangulation see Grounded theory (M)
Troubles talk see Complaining (H25); Emotion display (H); Laughter (H)
Trust see Adaptability (H)
Truth see Austin (H); Euphemism (H24); Euphemism (H24); Grice (H); Ideology (H); Model-theoretic semantics (MT); Speech act theory (MT); Truthfulness (H)
Truth-conditional pragmatics (T); Default interpretations (H)
Truth-conditional semantics (MT); Analytical philosophy (MT); Logical semantics (MT); Possible worlds semantics (MT); Relevance theory (MT)
Truthfulness (H); Lexically triggered veridicality inferences (H22); Manipulation (H); Ọmọlúàbí (H)
Turing machine see Computational linguistics (MT)
Turn(-taking) see Conversation analysis (MT); Embodied

interaction (H23); Frame analysis (M); Intertextuality (H); Language and the law (H); Prosody (H); Silence (H); Tactile sign languages (H21)

Twitter see Social media research (T)

Typology (MT); Boas (H); Contact linguistics (MT); Deixis (H); Historical linguistics (MT); Language acquisition (H); Language change (H); Language contact (H); Negation (H); Sound symbolism (H); Universals (H23); Word order (H)

U

UN language system see Language ecology (H)

Underspecification → see Vagueness

Understanding see Comprehension vs. production (H)

Unidirectionality see Language change (H)

Universal and transcendental pragmatics (MT); Critical theory (MT); Hermeneutics (M); Truthfulness (H)

Universal grammar see Language acquisition (H); Language change (H)

Universals (H23); Conversational logic (MT); Dialectology (MT); Humboldt (H); Jakobson (H21); Language acquisition (H); Sound symbolism (H); Speech act theory (MT); Typology (MT); Word order (H)

User modeling see Artificial intelligence (MT); Computational pragmatics (T)

Utterance see Predicates and predication (H); Speech act theory (MT)

V

Vagueness see Indeterminacy and negotiation (H); Polysemy (H); Tense and aspect (H); Truthfulness (H)

Valency → see Dependency

Variability → see Variation

Variable rule see Correlational sociolinguistics (T)

Variable, dependent/response vs independent/

predicting see Regression analysis (M)

Variable-rule analysis see Statistics (MM)

Variation see Adaptability (H); Argument structure (H23); Bilingualism and multilingualism (H); Communicative style (H); Context and contextualization (H); Correlational sociolinguistics (T); Creole linguistics (MT); Creoles and creolization (H); Dialectology (MT); Hegemony (H23); Honorifics (H); Humor (H23); Language acquisition (H); Language change (H); Language dominance and minorization (H); Language policy, language planning and standardization (H); Methods in language-attitudes research (M); Pluricentric languages (H23); Polysemy (H); Register (H); Regression analysis (M); Sociolinguistics (MT); Variational pragmatics (T)

Variational pragmatics (T); Contact linguistics (MT); Language change (H); Pluricentric languages (H23)

Variationist sociolinguistics see Correlational sociolinguistics (T); Youth language (H25)

Verb see Communicative dynamism (H); Ta'ārof (H22)

Verba dicendi see Reported speech (H)

Verbal guise see Methods in language-attitudes research (M)

Veridicality see Lexically triggered veridicality inferences (H22)

Vernacular see Anderson (H21); Authenticity (H); Dialect (H)

Versioning see Working with language data (M25)

Verstehen → see Erklären vs. Verstehen

Vitality see Motivation (H)

Vocabulary see Borrowing (H); Language acquisition (H)

Voice see Polyphony (H)

Vološinov, V. N. see Bakhtin (H); Deconstruction (MM); Intertextuality (H); Marxist

linguistics (MT); Reported speech (H)

Vygotsky, L. (H)

W

Wakimae (H26)

Web 2.0 see Social media research (T)

Weber, Max see Sociology of language (T)

WhatsApp see Social media research (T)

Whitewashing see Euphemism (H24)

Whorf, B. L. (H); Anthropological linguistics (MT); Boas (H); Culture (H); Iconicity (H); Sapir (H)

Whorfianism → see Linguistic relativity principle

Wittgenstein, L. (H); Analytical philosophy (MT); Austin (H); Contextualism (T); (The) pragmatic perspective (M); Speech act theory (MT)

Word (H)

Word order (H); Negation (H); Typology (MT)

Word recognition see The multilingual lexicon (H); Orthography and cognition (H22); Psycholinguistics (MT)

Word root see Orthography and cognition (H22)

Word-search see Gesture research (T)

Working with language data (M25); Conversation analysis (MT); Developmental psychology (MT); Grounded theory (M); Historical pragmatics (T); Linguistic landscape studies (T); Statistics (MM); Tactile sign languages (H21); Terms of address (H); Typology (MT)

Workplace interaction (H25); Aisatsu (H); Applied linguistics (MT)

Writing system see Identity (H24); Orthography and cognition (H22); Pragmatics of script (H22)

Written discourse → see Speaking vs. writing

X

X-bar syntax see Chomskyan linguistics (MT); Computational linguistics (MT); Role and reference grammar (MT)

Y

Youth language (H25); Crossing (H26)
Youtube see Social media research (T)